PETER R. SENICH

THE ONE-ROUND WAR

USMC Scout-Snipers in Vietnam

Paladin Press • Boulder, Colorado

Also by Peter R. Senich:

The Complete Book of U.S. Sniping

The German Assault Rifle: 1935–1945

The German Sniper: 1914–1945

The Long-Range War: Sniping in Vietnam

U.S. Marine Corps Scout-Sniper: Korea and Vietnam

The One-Round War:
USMC Scout-Snipers in Vietnam
by Peter R. Senich

Copyright 1996 by Peter R. Senich

ISBN 0-87364-867-6

Printed in the United States of America

Published by Paladin Press, a division of
Paladin Enterprises, Inc., P.O. Box 1307,
Boulder, Colorado 80306, USA.
(303) 443-7250

Direct inquiries and/or orders to the above address.

PALADIN, PALADIN PRESS, and the "horse head" design
are trademarks belonging to Paladin Enterprises and
registered in United States Patent and Trademark Office.

Front cover photo: David Douglas Duncan
Back cover photo: U.S. Marines Corps
Front flap photo: Remington Arms Co.
Back flap photo: U.S. Marine Corps
End sheet photo: U.S. Marine Corps

CONTENTS

CONTENTS

"Ships, men, and weapons change, but tradition, which can neither be bought nor sold, nor created, is a solid rock amidst shifting sands."

—Sir Bruce Fraser

PREFACE

From World War II to the present day, the term Scout-Sniper in the U.S. Marine Corps has defined a highly trained combat specialist whose primary function is to eliminate enemy personnel with precision rifle fire.

Even though the words used to describe scouts and snipers, or simply "scout-snipers," as they came to be known in the Corps, have changed since the war with Japan, the definition set forth in the early *USMC Manual of Occupational Specialties* (June 1945) is as relevant today as it was at the height of the island campaign in the South Pacific:

SCOUT-SNIPER

An especially trained RIFLEMAN (SSN745) who engages in scouting and patrolling activities to obtain information concerning strength, disposition, and probable intentions of enemy forces; disrupts enemy communications; destroys enemy personnel by rifle fire. May perform supervisory duties involving the control, coordination, and tactical employment of other SCOUT-SNIPERS. Must possess all the qualifications of SSN745 (Rifleman). Must be particularly skilled in employing the principles of camouflage to conceal himself. Must know how to move over various kinds of terrain without being detected. Must be skilled in the use of the rifle, with and without telescope sight. Must know techniques of searching terrain for signs of enemy activity. Must be able to read maps, make sketches, and use compass and field glass.

Marine snipers had clearly demonstrated their value during World War II and the conflict in Korea. Yet, except for a small but dedicated group of Marine officers and men who made every effort to maintain some semblance of Scout-Sniper training in the years following the Korean War, on an overall basis, the Marine Corps sniping program was all but nonexistent until the initial stages of the war in Vietnam. Then the need for trained snipers and sniping equipment became a matter of necessity rather than an opinion.

The decision to reestablish a formal sniping program came as the Marine Corps was expanding its role in South Vietnam in early 1965.

Though many of the basic principles formulated during earlier conflicts would serve as the foundation for training snipers during early action in Vietnam, it was necessary to devise new tactics to deal with the enemy the Marine Corps was now facing.

As part of the overall effort to field snipers and satisfactory sniping equipment, in addition to evaluating rifles and telescopic sights for combat use, the Marine Corps set about to determine the best course of action for training Scout-Snipers in Vietnam and the United States.

It is interesting to note that amidst the flurry of preparations necessary to sustain the anticipated level of Marine Corps combat operations in Southeast Asia (SEA), various official documents, including many concerning sniper training and equipment, were stamped "Urgent SEA."

Though months would pass before a sniper program was operating effectively, the Scout-Sniper had clearly regained a place in the U.S. Marine Corps.

This second book in the sniping in Vietnam series deals primarily with the Marine Corps sniper program, the circumstances behind the training and employment of sniper personnel, the equipment sent to Vietnam for sniper use, and the transition from the Vietnam-era M700 sniping rifle to the M40A1, the contemporary Marine Corps Scout-Sniper rifle.

This work is the culmination of an information-gathering process that began as the war in Vietnam was in full swing during the late 1960s. The material herein was obtained from official correspondence, reports, ordnance documents, intelligence sources, and the recollections of the military and civilian personnel who were involved with the Army and Marine Corps sniping programs during this era.

In the interest of factuality, with few exceptions, the material for this book was not drawn from secondary sources. Regardless of the original intent, secondary sources—books about books—are not accurate because they tend to replicate errors made by the writer they quote. With this in mind, I consulted an unprecedented number of veteran Marine snipers, armorers, ordnance personnel, and former rifle team members in the quest for accuracy. As the Marines who supported this project will attest, every effort was made to arrive at the truth and "get the facts straight." Moreover, unlike other offerings of the day, this work makes no attempt to aggrandize or demean any individual associated with the Marine Corps sniper program both past and present. Nor does it contain any questionable or subjective material that would tend to detract from the dignity and respect this unique military endeavor richly deserves.

Though rarely acknowledged, the Army and Marine Corps sniping programs were among the most successful operations of the Vietnam War. And while there was no way of knowing exactly how many of the enemy were rendered KIA by American marksmen armed with telescopic sighted rifles, the overall U.S. sniping effort in Southeast Asia proved to be an extremely effective means of countering the tactics and activities of the Viet Cong and the North Vietnamese Army.

If you were a part of the Vietnam-era Army or Marine Corps sniper program, a hearty "well done" is long overdue and definitely in order.

—Peter R. Senich

ACKNOWLEDGMENTS

Having obtained much of the material in this book from the officers and men who were part of the sniping effort in Vietnam, I want to extend a special note of appreciation to them for granting me access to their personal archives, for sharing their experiences, and for having the foresight to retain pertinent documents and miscellaneous hardware relating to the Army and Marine Corps sniping programs that otherwise would have been lost or destroyed. In addition, my eternal gratitude to the persons and organizations who provided me with information, photographs, and access to their collections. For this help I wish to thank:

Dean H. Whitaker
Robert A. Russell
Thomas F. Shannon
Donald G. Barker
William R. Melton
Ludwig P. Gogol
Frank W. Hackley
James L. O'Neill
William H. Woodin

Carl J. Decker
Edward J. Land Jr.
Charles W. Karwan
Gary Allain
Eloise N. Land
William D. Abbott
Frank de Haas
Scott A. Duff
Robert J. Faught
Mark K. Edmondson
Robert L. Goller
Bob Bell
George E. Hijar
Danny J. Crawford
Daniel E. Kihs
Neil W. Goddard
Lawrence A. Reynolds
K.L. Smith-Christmas
Kenneth Kogan
Don L. Smith
David Douglas Duncan
John G. Griffiths
Russell E. Martin
William K. Hayden
Fred Martin
William M. Douglas
Donald G. Thomas
Edward J. Wages
J.C. Cuddy
R. James Bender
Herb Rosenbaum
Keith W. Nolan
James R. Bowen
Walter R. Walsh
John P. Wallace
Dennis L. Caudle
John Vaninetti
Jim Shults
William J. Zaro
Thomas F. Swearengen
Richard H. Thomas
Robert I. Landies
Walt Sides
John L. Plaster
Jack Rodgers
Ted L. Hollabaugh
Gordon A. Russell
Kenneth D. Fryer
Charles B. Mawhinney

Bruce Nelson
William D. Harris
Max Crace
Joseph T. Ward
Maxwell G. Atchisson
Rita Ward
Nobel L. Beck
Wayne P. Gagner
James E. McCollum
William W. Wiseman
Bill Grube
William E. Thomas
Rich Urich
Mrs. William S. Brophy
Donald Urtz
Elliott R. Laine Jr.
Steven L. Walsh
Irl Otte
James A. Leatherwood
William S. Brophy III
Albert W. Hauser
Francis B. Conway
John W. Johnson
Michael R. Lau
Robert W. Fisch
Sam A. Miller
Paul M. Senich
John W. Scott
Carlos N. Hathcock
Bill Mangels
Allan D. Cors
Michael P. Hayes
Allen C. Boothby Jr.
Blair M. Gluba
Mick Nance
Gil Parsons
Craig Roberts
Ronald D. Feekes
Elroy Sanford
Keith R. Pagel
Willis L. Powell
Leonard J. Wilson
William E. Donovan
Archie Mayer
Walt Ewen

American Rifleman magazine
Library of Congress
West Point Museum

Leatherneck magazine
U.S. Patent Office
Guns & Ammo magazine
Springfield Armory NHS
Excalibur Enterprises
Marine Corps Gazette
Redfield, Inc.
Marine Corps Air-Ground Museum
Marine Corps Historical Center
Remington Arms Co., Inc.
Parsons Riflescope Service
National Archives and Records Administration
DBI Books, Inc.
MAC Sales, Inc.
Woodin Laboratory

Although these individuals and organizations deserve proper credit for helping me locate and piece together the vast amount of information this project required, any error in putting this material in its final form properly rests with me.

This book is intended as an instrument of historical reference for the sole purpose of describing and illustrating the activities and equipment of the U.S. Army and Marine Corps sniper during the Vietnam War.

—Peter R. Senich

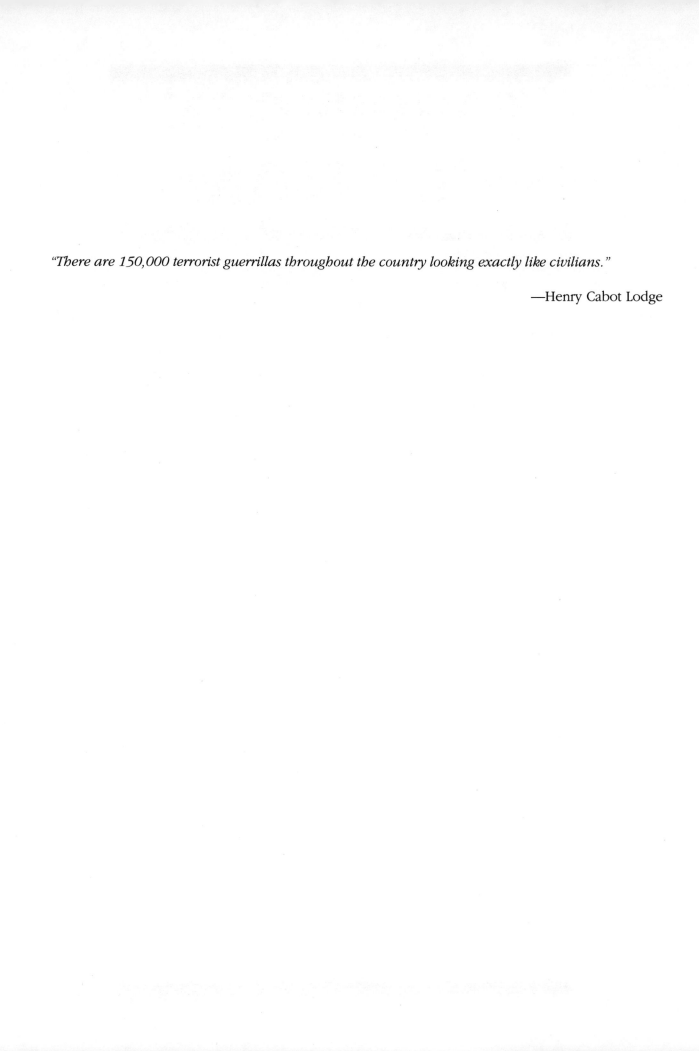

"There are 150,000 terrorist guerrillas throughout the country looking exactly like civilians."

—Henry Cabot Lodge

CHAPTER 1

SNIPING IN VIETNAM

The Beginning

When the armed forces of the United States were finally committed to full-scale combat operations in the Republic of Vietnam (RVN) in 1965, the Army and Marine Corps found themselves confronted by a unique problem. The Communist insurgents, or Viet Cong (VC), were moving about freely in the areas surrounding the American positions, almost at will.

In the process of harassing U.S. military personnel in and around the bases and airfields, the VC were quick to realize they were relatively safe from small-arms fire, especially at long range.

Even though the 7.62mm (.308 caliber) M14 service rifle then in use was entirely capable of delivering accurate medium- and long-range fire in the hands of a competent rifleman, according to a Marine Corps spokesman, "M14 rifles with conventional sights were found inadequate for precise long-range shooting." As the range increased, the chances of hitting the enemy with conventional rifle sights decreased proportionately.

As a result, the Viet Cong were not the least bit intimidated by ordinary rifle fire. Individuals and small groups of enemy personnel were frequently observed in full view of the American positions directing mortar and rocket fire or simply going about their business with virtual impunity. As one Marine sergeant recalled, "The sight of those damn VC standing out there like that was almost too much for some of our people."

Although "calling for" mortar and artillery fire in return did work to some extent, neither measure could be carried out without providing some advance warning. Consequently, as soon as the firing started, the Viet Cong simply disappeared from view. In any case, the chances of "taking out" one or two of the enemy under the circumstances were less than satisfactory, and the entire process proved to be an exercise in futility more often than not.

To many of the "seasoned veterans" in the Army and Marine Corps, the solution was obvious: employ skilled riflemen capable of engaging enemy personnel at various ranges with consistent results in and around the enclaves. There was no other choice; trained snipers armed with telescopic-sighted rifles were the only answer.

In spite of the fact that the Army and the Marine Corps chose to field vastly different weapon systems for their snipers, the nucleus of both sniper programs comprised a resolute group of accomplished riflemen and competitive marksmen. Many of these men had been actively involved with their respective rifle teams and marksmanship training units (MTUs) prior to the war in South Vietnam, and they were "professionals" in every sense of the word.

Though considerable time and effort would be spent training and equipping snipers for combat before the results clearly justified the course of action, when the first Marine marksman, a Third Marine Division sniper, brought down an unsuspecting enemy soldier with his telescopic-sighted rifle in 1965 as part of an emerging sniper program, the everyday life of the Communist forces operating in Southeast Asia became infinitely less secure.

NOTE: S.Sgt. Donald G. Barker, a member of the original 3d MarDiv sniper cadre, was credited with the "first USMC sniper kill" in Vietnam. Barker's rifle was a Model 70 Winchester.

In retrospect, despite only limited use of telescope-equipped rifles during the period Marine Corps historians define as "the advisory and combat assistance era" (1954–1965), the decision to establish a sniper program came as the Marine Corps was expanding its role in South Vietnam in early 1965. Acting on recommendations from the field, Headquarters, United States Marine Corps (HQMC) arrived at the conclusion that snipers would be an essential part of ground combat operations in the days ahead.

NOTE: The first U.S. ground combat forces to deploy to Vietnam, the Ninth Marine Expeditionary Brigade (MEB), landed at Da Nang on 8 March 1965. The Ninth MEB was deactivated shortly afterward and replaced by the newly formed III Marine Amphibious Force (III MAF) in early May. At this point, seven of the nine infantry battalions of the Third Marine Division, and most of the Twelfth Marines, the artillery regiment of the division, were committed in Vietnam. By mid-1965, the combat arm of III MAF was made up almost entirely of the Third Marine Division. The Seventh Marines, a First Marine Division (1st MarDiv) regiment, arrived in August 1965. The First and Second Battalions of the First Marines were deployed in South Vietnam by the end of the year.

So far as the sniper program was concerned, Third Marine Division organizational activities were actually part of an overall plan to train and field snipers for combat in South Vietnam.

As Vietnam-era Marine Corps documents relate:

> As an interim expedient, Commanding General, 3d Marine Division has
> established a training program under the supervision of the Division Sniper Project
> Officer and is utilizing to the maximum those personnel and facilities available locally.

Drawing from the lessons learned during World War II and the conflict in Korea when Scout-Snipers were trained and employed successfully, experienced marksmen were given the task of establishing a sniper school in Vietnam.

As events transpired, the U.S. Marine Corps, Third Marine Division (III MAF) was credited with establishing the first sniper program in the Republic of Vietnam.

In addition to Capt. Robert A. Russell, the officer assigned to form the unit (Division Sniper Project Officer), the original sniper-instructor staff comprised M.Sgt. George H. Hurt, the senior NCO at the sniping school, Gy.Sgt. Marvin C. Lange, S.Sgt. Donald G. Barker, Sgt. James R. Bowen, and Sgt. Robert L. Goller.

The personnel selected by Captain Russell were rated among the best shooters in the Marine Corps. The men were all competitive marksmen with an impressive list of match shooting accomplishments to their credit.

Commenting on the collective skill of the original 3d MarDiv sniper cadre years later, Major Russell was quick to point out:

> The men were arguably among the ten best shooters in the entire nation at the time. Very rarely does anyone have a group as talented as this. I was truly blessed with those Marines.

NOTE: In addition to those named, members of the early staff included Gy.Sgt. Harold B. O'Connor (replaced by Lange) and S.Sgt. Mel Dunham (replaced by Goller). As the war expanded and the need for Marine snipers increased, personnel from the original 3d MarDiv program went on to serve the Marine Corps as sniper instructors in Vietnam and the United States.

Although various contemporary publications cite the USMC sniper program as having started during "mid-1965" or "early fall" 1965, according to a "basic order of events" furnished by Maj. Robert A. Russell, USMC (Ret.), events transpired as follows:

NOTE: The commanding officer of the 3d MarDiv sniper program Capt. R.A. Russell was promoted to the rank of major in early 1966. The seasoned combat veteran was serving in his third war with the Marine Corps. As Russell listed the events:

> My group was activated in September 1965. The sniper cadre trained as a unit (September–November 1965) attaching ourselves to fire teams, platoons, companies, recon and battalion size operations. The objective was to determine the best methods of employing snipers in general, and to develop a concept of sniper operations. We combined what we gleaned from these employments with what we already knew—advanced marksmanship—and came up with a syllabus for training snipers. From November 1965 into 1966 and the months that followed, we trained snipers, formulated new techniques, and gathered more data.

NOTE: According to USMC personnel then active, the "first" sniper class graduated in November 1965. The original group was reportedly made up of "12 men from different units."

Given the circumstances and the nature of the USMC sniping effort in RVN, very little official documentation appears to have been generated at the time. Though years after the fact, a small amount of information concerning early sniping activity was presented in *U.S. Marines in Vietnam: The Landing and the Buildup 1965*, the second volume in a series of chronological histories published by the History and Museums Division, Headquarters, U.S. Marine Corps (written by Jack Shulimson and Charles M. Johnson, USMC, June 1978):

> 14 Oct—The CG, I Corps approved extension of the Chu Lai TAOR. A USMC sniper team was formed in the Hue-Phu Bai TAOR. The team used Winchester Model 70 rifles with 8-Unertl telescopic sights [8-power] and killed two Viet Cong

at a range of more than 700 yards in the first exercise of the new tactic. Later, M1D rifles with telescopic sights were utilized.

23 Nov—By this date there were approximately 20 scout-sniper teams of four men each positioned throughout the III MAF area. On 23 November a team at Phu Bai killed two VC and wounded one at a range of 1000 meters.

III MAF developed and modified techniques and tactics for the employment of small Marine units. The Marines experimented with specially trained and equipped sniper teams. Fifty of the best marksmen were selected from each of the regiments. These troops were divided into four-man teams and equipped with Winchester Model 70 rifles and telescopic sights. After training, the teams rejoined their regiments. During November and December, 20–30 teams operated in the Marine TAORs daily.

Official recommendations and proposals pertaining to "Scout-Sniper Requirements" began moving back and forth between Vietnam and the United States concurrent with 3d MarDiv sniping activity.

In response to various messages and memorandums generated by the Commandant of the Marine Corps (CMC), Fleet Marine Force Pacific (FMFPac), III Marine Amphibious Force, and Headquarters Staff, a memorandum from the Assistant Chief of Staff, G-3, to the Chief of Staff, Headquarters, Marine Corps (Subject: Scout-Sniper Requirements, 27 November 1965) recommended changing the Tables of Organization (T/O) to accommodate "Scout-Sniper Platoons" in the infantry structure and projected long-term Marine Corps requirements for Scout-Sniper personnel training and equipment.

NOTE: The original memorandum in this series (Subject: Scout-Sniper Training) was dated 17 September 1965. A number of documents pertaining to "sniping" were generated by the Marine Corps during the latter part of 1965.

Various armed forces and civilian periodicals published accounts of early Marine Corps sniping activity. In addition to providing one of the earliest, if not the first of these (*Marine Corps Gazette,* December 1965), Marine correspondent Gy.Sgt. Jack Childs went on to chronicle Third Marine Division sniping activity in *SEA TIGER, Marine Corps Gazette, Leatherneck* magazine, and *American Rifleman.* His article "Sniping in Vietnam," which appeared in the June 1966 issue of *American Rifleman,* stated in part:

> After a shipment of Winchesters and scopes arrived, the captain and his instructors pooled their considerable knowledge and put together a training syllabus. The snipers themselves would be picked from some 40,000 Marines on duty in Vietnam.
>
> [**NOTE:** The first Model 70 rifles fielded for the 3d MarDiv sniper program were .30-caliber (.30-06) Winchester target rifles with heavy barrels and marksman stocks.]
>
> However, although the captain and his 5 men were qualified marksmanship instructors, they had never done any sniping. So following a snapping in period with the Winchester rifle and scope, the instructors went after Viet Cong.
>
> From their home base at Da Nang, they traveled 55 miles south to sand and scrub-covered slopes of Chu Lai. Then, 45 miles north of Da Nang to the plains and mountains surrounding the Hue-Phu Bai Marine area.
>
> For endless hours the 6 men trained themselves in the art of sniping. Working in pairs to afford a 360-degree range of view, they stalked the Viet Cong. Under the cover of darkness the teams would move into a pre-arranged position

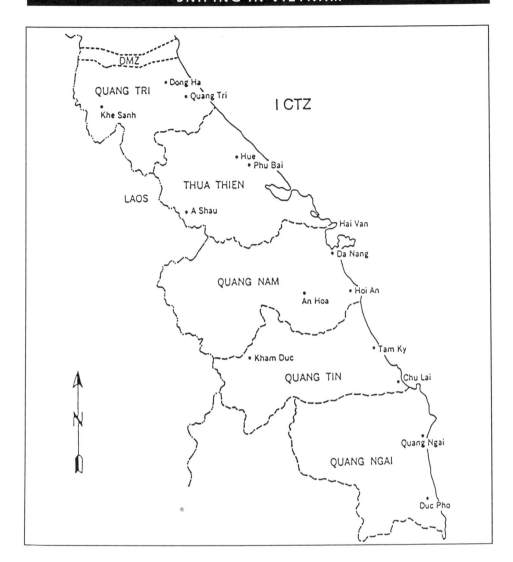

The I Corps Tactical Zone (I CTZ), the northernmost of the four Vietnamese corps areas included five provinces: Quang Tri, Thua Thien, Quang Nam, Quang Tin, and Quang Ngai. The demilitarized zone (DMZ) separated North and South Vietnam at the seventeenth parallel. The I CTZ was the principal area of responsibility for the Marine Corps during the war in Vietnam. (U.S. Marine Corps.)

where there had been previous sightings of Viet Cong movements. They found mental discipline of utmost importance.

Two men, by themselves, armed only with bolt-action rifles, sat in Viet Cong territory. Any movement would disclose their position. They spoke, when necessary, in a whisper. They did not smoke. Sometimes they waited as long as 13 hours without a sighting. It was frustrating, but they learned. . . .

When the sniper-instructors felt fully qualified to start teaching and could speak from experience, they requested volunteers from each Marine infantry unit in the Republic of Vietnam. To qualify for the school, a Marine had to be a proven combat veteran, an expert rifleman (shooting a minimum score of 220x250 the last time he had fired for record), and hand-picked by his commanding officer.

Capt. Russell and his team located a small Army of the Republic of Vietnam (ARVN) rifle range a few miles southwest of Da Nang. Arrangements were made with the ARVN for the student snipers to use a portion of the range 3 days a week. The existing targets were only 300 yards from the firing line—no challenge.

Four-hundred yards from the firing line a mass of hills was covered with head-high elephant grass and thick thorn-covered shrubbery. A bulldozer and operator from a nearby shore party battalion cleared target sites from 400 to 1000 yards from the firing line. The targets, which were 8" cans, came from Marine mess halls [depending on the source of information, "water cans," "mess-hall containers," and "155mm propellant canisters" were used as targets].

The 3-day training period decided on by the sniper-instructors was a dawn-to-dusk ordeal of schooling and shooting. On the first day, after the rifles and scopes were issued, the future snipers were welcomed aboard and their mission was explained. Then, in rapid-fire succession, they were taught safety precautions, nomenclature of the Winchester, telescopic sight and adjustment, sling adjustment and positions, trigger control, aiming and range determination, effects of weather, care and cleaning of the weapon and scope, sniper log, use of binoculars, and the technique of observation.

On the second day the instruction included prone and sitting snapping-in, demonstrations of sniper firing by the instructors, a review and critique of all the aforementioned subjects, and then individual snapping-in.

The third day was devoted entirely to rifle practice as each man became accustomed to his individual weapon. He would keep the same rifle as long as he was "in-country." . . .

U.S. Marine Corps Headquarters in Washington, D.C., has kept a watchful eye on the progress of the sniper school. The results produced by the snipers in combat are worthwhile. Presently under consideration by the Marine Corps is a Military Occupational Specialty (MOS) number to be assigned to Marines who qualify as snipers [Marines qualified as Scout-Snipers were eventually assigned MOS number 8541]. Furthermore, each Marine infantry regiment in Vietnam will have its own sniper platoon of 39 enlisted men and one officer [35 enlisted men and one officer in final form]. The first platoon graduated from the school March 19, 1966. [The "first platoon" cited by Childs is believed to have been the Fourth Marines Sniper Platoon. With proper regards to the date noted, from all indications, the original Fourth Marines Sniper Platoon, a 39-man unit, received its actual training somewhat later.]

The activation of Sniper Platoons was summarized by the Marine Corps as follows:

As a result of experience gained by III MAF forces in the Republic of Vietnam, and on recommendation of the Commanding General, Fleet Marine Force, Pacific and subsequent approval of the Commandant of the Marine Corps, CMC ltr A03H22-jew of 29 December 1965 approves the organization and formation of Sniper Platoons within each Regiment's Headquarters Company and the Headquarters and Service Company, Reconnaissance Battalion.

The mission of the Sniper Platoon is to support the infantry battalion and/or Reconnaissance Battalion in conjunction with other supporting arms by:
a. Locating and destroying the enemy by precision fire.
b. Destroying or neutralizing enemy personnel that oppose the approach of friendly personnel to an objective area.
c. Deny the enemy movement in the TAOR.

Although CMC "approval" for the organization and formation of Sniper Platoons came in December 1965, measures to form entire Sniper Platoons were limited by the availability of qualified personnel, instructors, and suitable sniping equipment.

NOTE: A "33-man contingent from Third Marines" received sniper training at the ARVN range near Da Nang in December 1965. According to personnel then involved, the unit was referred to by their Marine instructors as a "Sniper Platoon." Without the benefit of official documentation, however, at this juncture it is not entirely clear if Third Marines or Fourth Marines fielded "the first Sniper Platoon" in the U.S. Marine Corps.

Even though the Third Marine Division sniper school took shape at Da Nang, the syllabus and the program were later expanded with the members of the sniper-instructor team serving as a mobile unit moving from one Marine enclave to another helping to establish schools for training snipers.

While the exact number of Marine snipers operating in South Vietnam during late 1965 and the early months of 1966 may never be known, in the interest of avoiding any possible confusion in this matter and the chapters to follow, it is important to point out that details concerning specific dates, the units and personnel involved, and the methods of training and employing USMC snipers in South Vietnam often conflict.

With proper regards to the recollections of the personnel who were "there," the correspondents who gave their impressions of the program in the civilian and military periodicals and the historical information generated by the Marine Corps at this juncture, a concise chronological order of events has not taken shape.

In any case, it will suffice to say that by the end of 1965, Marine snipers trained by Captain Russell and the original 3d MarDiv sniper-instructor team were actively engaged in the III MAF area of operations in South Vietnam exacting their toll on the Viet Cong.

NOTE: According to information published in the December 1965 issue of *American Rifleman:*

> The 3rd Marine Division in Vietnam, according to reports, is utilizing snipers to keep the enemy outside effective range of Marine infantrymen. A total of 92 marksmen are being employed, with 20 attached to each of the division's 4 regiments and 12 with the division's reconnaissance unit. They use bolt-action rifles which are equipped with telescopes.

In view of the efforts and accomplishments of the early Marine Corps sniping program, it is important to draw attention to the fact that III Marine Amphibious Force had mounted effective sniping operations in Vietnam more than two years before the U.S. Army had a comparative program in place.

• • •

"When 1965 ended, there were 38,000 Marines in South Vietnam."

—U.S. Marine Corps

Marine sniper-instructor team "on patrol south of Marble Mountain" (1965). A 20-power observation telescope (M49) was fitted to a modified M14 rifle stock for spotting purposes. According to an original team member, "The scope was taped toward the rear of the stock and turned so when you put it to your shoulder it was almost like sighting in with your rifle scope. We used it to find targets and then, by using reference points, to find the target with an 8-power Unertl. The scope was carried at sling arms and was favored over binoculars." Capt. Robert A. Russell is shown with the observation scope. (Barker Collection.)

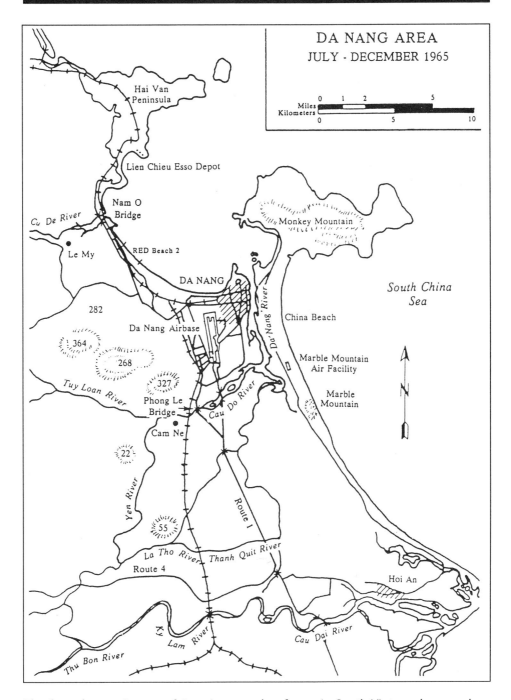

DA NANG AREA
JULY - DECEMBER 1965

The formal commitment of American combat forces in South Vietnam began when elements of the Ninth Marine Expeditionary Brigade (MEB) came ashore at Red Beach 2 near Da Nang on 8 March 1965. The Ninth MEB mission was to defend the Da Nang Airbase. This was the first U.S. ground combat unit to land in RVN. The Third Marine Division and, later, the First Marine Division were based at Hill 327 just west of the Da Nang Airbase. A number of Marine snipers were trained in the shadow of Hill 327 during the course of the war. The "Hill 55" mentioned in conjunction with 1st MarDiv sniping activity in South Vietnam is also shown on this map. (U.S. Marine Corps.)

Capt. Robert A. Russell, the Officer in Charge (OIC) of the Third Marine Division sniper program, with Marine sniper candidates following a training exercise. The gathering of Model 70 Winchester rifles with Unertl telescopic sights was enough to "raise the pulse rate" of any Winchester aficionado. An unknown quantity of USMC Model 70 target rifles was also furnished to the First Marine Division when its sniper program, led by Capt. Edward J. (Jim) Land Jr., shifted into high gear during the latter part of 1966. Securing adequate sniping equipment proved no less of a problem for the First Marine Division than it had for its counterparts. The M1 Garand in sniper trim and the Model 70, in both target and sporter form, served 1st MarDiv during early going as well. (U.S. Marine Corps.)

The Marine Corps used a limited number of 3X-9X variable-power rifle scopes manufactured in Japan (the scopes were trademarked "MARINE"; the brand name and Marine Corps use were coincidental in this case) with the Model 70 for early USMC sniping activity beginning in 1965. While hardly an optimum rifle sight, its ranging capability (variable power adjustment) was seen as a "desirable feature" in a field scope. The Japanese hunting sights were purchased on Okinawa as a supplemental measure. The Marine sniper (Donald G. Barker) maintains his vigil following a patrol near Marble Mountain. The Model 70 has a heavy barrel and target stock. According to Marine Corps documents, "The first Model 70 rifles fielded for the 3rd Marine Division sniper program (12) were Winchester target rifles with heavy barrel and target stock." The rifle was known as a "factory heavy" to many of the Marines. A Distinguished Marksman and Pistol Shot, Don Barker was officially credited with the "1st kill with a sniper rifle in RVN." (U.S. Marine Corps.)

South Vietnamese Army (ARVN) rifle range near Da Nang circa late 1965. The "Hoa-Cam training area," as it was known to countless Marines, served as a principal sniper training facility for both the Third Marine Division and the First Marine Division during the Vietnam War. The impact area is at the far right; the sheds (center) were used for training sessions and are located behind the firing lines. The ARVN installation was near Hill 327. Said one veteran instructor, "We trained a lot of good Marines to be snipers at this place." Even though the site was fairly close to Da Nang, a major U.S. base in Vietnam, a great deal of combat activity took place in the areas surrounding the Hoa-Cam range during the course of the war. (U.S. Marine Corps.)

Senior NCO, M.Sgt. George H. Hurt, USMC, shown sighting an 8-power Unertl scope at Da Nang, late 1965. In an effort to provide the best training possible, the sniper-instructor team spent many days traveling with units on patrol around Chu Lai, Da Nang, Qui Nhon, and Hue-Phu Bai. The men trained themselves to be effective snipers under diverse conditions and circumstances. The information obtained was included in the sniper school's training syllabus. The dovetail base at the front of the barrel served as a mounting point for target-type front sights. (U.S. Marine Corps.)

Sniper-instructor and students at the Third Marine Division sniper school at Da Nang. The shipping cartons (cardboard containers) for the Model 70 rifles are clearly visible. According to Marine Corps personnel, the Unertl sights sent to Vietnam with the rifles were packed in cartons last inspected and marked "August 1946." The III Marine Amphibious Force (III MAF) field photo is dated 23 January 1966. At this juncture, adequate sniping equipment was still in short supply. The instructor (standing) is Sgt. Robert L. Goller. (U.S. Marine Corps.)

Marine snipers during an early training session. The rigors of a dawn-to-dusk program demanded a great deal of the men. The strain is obvious in this case. The rifles are Model 70 Winchesters. (U.S. Marine Corps.)

Da Nang, Vietnam (3 November 1965). Captain Russell checks one of the weapons his men will use against the Viet Cong. Said Russell, "We feel that we have the best qualified men in the division going to school here. All Marines selected as snipers must be expert riflemen or have been a team shooter. All are combat veterans and volunteers. The snipers make life uneasy for the Viet Cong around the three main Marine enclaves at Da Nang, Chu Lai, and Hue-Phu Bai." (U.S. Marine Corps.)

Third Marine Division sniper during a training exercise in the jungle. Though barely visible, the marksman is scanning the area with binoculars. His Model 70 Winchester is equipped with one of the early-issue 3X-9X variable-power Japanese rifle scopes. The jungle proved to be a relatively safe haven for snipers who mastered the art of cover and concealment. (U.S. Marine Corps.)

Third Marine Division sniper-instructor Gy.Sgt. Marvin C. Lange is shown with a Model 70 target rifle used for early sniping in RVN. The telescope is a Unertl model. (Barker Collection.)

Marine sniper candidates on the firing line during early training activity in Vietnam. The center rifleman has an M1D with an M84 telescope; the others are sighting Unertl-equipped Model 70 Winchesters. The Marines used 155mm propellant canisters to define the firing areas. With a wide, white band as an aiming point, the same canisters were partially buried at 100-yard intervals out to 1,000 yards. According to personnel then involved, the Marine Corps ranges at Da Nang, Chu Lai, and Phu Bai "were set up using this system." (U.S. Marine Corps.)

Gy.Sgt. Marvin C. Lange (left), Sgt. James R. Bowen, and M.Sgt. George H. Hurt (right), following a day of sniper training near the Marine enclave at Phu Bai. The men were members of the original 3d MarDiv sniper-instructor team in RVN. (Barker Collection.)

A Marine officer (Captain Russell) with a student sniper during a "sighting and adjustment exercise" on the firing line at Da Nang. (U.S. Marine Corps.)

An alternate view of Sergeant Hurt with the USMC Model 70/Unertl system. The .30-caliber (.30-06) Winchester extended the Marine Corps "kill radius" to 1,000 yards during early action in South Vietnam. A heavy-barrel Winchester target rifle and Unertl telescopic sight were capable of producing a level of performance beyond the ability of the average sniper. (U.S. Marine Corps.)

A sniper candidate with a Model 70 rifle and Unertl sight with much of the finish worn from the tube. As worn as the finish (bluing) was on many of the rifles and telescopes sent to Vietnam, the moisture and humidity made equipment care a major concern from this standpoint alone. The illustration also provides a close view of the 155mm propellant canisters. (U.S. Marine Corps.)

Captain Russell and sniper trainees during a briefing on match ammunition. The men were familiarized with the performance characteristics of .30-caliber match ammunition as part of their training. Although special and/or "hand-loaded" cartridges had seen limited field use in past conflicts, the Marine Corps, in an unprecedented move, was the first branch of the armed forces to issue match-grade rifle ammunition for combat purposes. (U.S. Marine Corps.)

Even though elaborate camouflage measures were rarely used in Vietnam, Marine marksmen were taught to make effective use of cover and concealment while plying their trade. The proper use of "natural camouflage" provided an effective means of avoiding detection by the enemy. The sniper is sighting a Unertl telescope, the rifle is a Model 70 Winchester. (U.S. Marine Corps.)

Marine combat personnel (Ninth Marines) during operation Harvest Moon (December 1965). The photograph shows the Unertl scope in the forward, or recoil, position; the weapon has just been fired, and the sniper appears to be reaching for another cartridge. The men are burdened by the weight of their field gear and equipment. Note the 66mm M72 HEAT rocket launchers (LAW). The rice paddy is typical of those encountered in South Vietnam. (U.S. Marine Corps.)

Vietnam-era USMC combat photo: "A Marine sniper from 'G Company,' 2nd Battalion, 9th Marines (3d MarDiv) takes aim at Hill 251 during Operation Harvest Moon." The rifle is a Winchester Model 70 with an 8-power Unertl telescopic sight, the principal Marine Corps sniping issue during early combat activity in South Vietnam. During the course of U.S. military involvement in Southeast Asia, several hundred major and thousands of smaller combat "operations" were conducted by American and Allied ground forces. The operations named in the various photo captions were a part of these. (U.S. Marine Corps.)

CHAPTER 2

"GOOD MORNING GENTLEMEN"

When Maj. Robert A. Russell returned to the United States in 1966, efforts to share his experiences in South Vietnam included a number of lectures intended to point out the advantages of employing trained snipers in Southeast Asia.

During the course of this activity, the officer responsible for establishing the Marine Corps sniper program in Vietnam spoke to various groups, including the U.S. Army Infantry School, the American Ordnance Association, and the U.S. Army Combat Developments Command. The lecture, complete with a slide presentation, provided a firsthand account of the Vietnam-era Marine Corps sniper program during its formative stages.

In the interest of providing the best possible insight on the origins of the USMC program, the following highlights from the address given by Major Russell during early 1967 are presented:

> Good morning gentlemen, my name is Russell. I'm from the Ground Combat Division of the Marine Corps Landing Force Development Center at Quantico, Virginia. Although my primary duty is in infantry equipment, I've been temporarily assigned to the Educational Center

for the past few months writing several field manuals on field firing techniques and the employment of the sniper rifle. . . .

The Marine Corps sniper program, as we knew it in the early stages, started back in May 1965. At that time, "Charlie," as he was known, roamed the battlefield almost at will. As a result, we lost a number of men from small-arms fire.

The Viet Cong would maneuver through the tall grass and the rice paddies until he was within the effective range of the weapon he was armed with, fire a shot or two, and then disappear. We eventually determined that the Viet Cong would simply "melt" into the countryside by hiding the rifle and playing the role of a pacified farmer.

When the Marine patrol sent out to find the sniper would arrive, the "farmer" would point in one direction or another. It took us some time to catch on to this.

In due course, Colonel Garretson, the Regimental Commander of the 9th Marines [Col. Frank E. Garretson], recognized the need for snipers. A Marine who, by the aid of a telescopic sight, could observe the battlefield, deliver accurate rifle fire, and "see" far better than the average rifleman. These qualifications defined the term "sniper" as we employed him in Vietnam early on.

The gears were set in motion and an urgent call went out throughout the Marine Corps for rifles and telescopic sights. The Corps also started looking for someone to take charge of the program; the name "Russell" was submitted and accepted by General Walt [Maj. Gen. Lewis W. Walt, Commanding General III MAF, and 3d Marine Division].

I recall being called into division headquarters at Da Nang thinking I'd be given a rather eloquent briefing, elaborate guidelines and, if I was real lucky, my own Jeep. My expectations were short-lived, however. My briefing was quickly summarized by Colonel Wyckoff, the G-3 [Col. Don P. Wyckoff, 3d Marine Division G-3]: "You're Russell, huh, fine, start a sniper school. Let me know when you're ready to go." And that concluded the interview.

With all due respect for Colonel Wyckoff, those were busy days for the man who controlled all operations of a Marine division in combat and amenities were neither important or necessary. I learned later, however, that I had carte blanche authority to select whomever I wanted as instructors. In this respect, I couldn't have been more fortunate. There happened to be five of the finest Distinguished Marksmen in the Marine Corps serving in various infantry outfits throughout the division. I knew them well, knew their capabilities, and I knew at that point, "we were in business."

After assembling my instructor staff, we started developing a syllabus. It became apparent that we were "long" on marksmanship, so to speak, and "short" on knowing the best techniques of employing snipers. Which, of course, would be the most important aspect of our training program. Consequently, the next two or three months were spent inserting ourselves into the operations of every size combat unit there was in an effort to learn the best ways of employing snipers. We were looking for answers, and the Viet Cong . . .

Our initial success occurred near the Marine enclave at Phu Bai. Reconnaissance platoons operating in the area would frequently catch sight of Viet Cong observers on the crest of a ridgeline near the southern edge of the base. However, since the terrain separating the recon people and the VC was nothing but 750 meters of rice paddy, the distance made small-arms fire impractical and there was no cover from which they could get a close shot at "Charlie."

The recon patrol would take an artillery observer along and call for artillery fire on an almost routine basis. The Viet Cong would wait for the first round to "splash," and, knowing they had sufficient time to move before a correction was made, would simply stroll over the ridgeline and take cover.

This was obviously a job for a man armed with a rifle that could reach out and zap someone with the first shot.

On this particular morning, "Charlie" got his first taste of the business end of a Model 70 Winchester. We worked our way to within 750 meters of the hill under cover of darkness, concealed our positions, and waited for daylight. The sun came up, and sure enough, there were two VC observers standing on the ridgeline.

I didn't want to take a chance on losing either one of them, so I had all of my people open fire at the same time. They had apparently all aimed at the VC on the left, however, since he fell first. In the process of dragging his comrade from the crest, the men had reloaded and fired again bringing the second man down. Within seconds, both of the Viet Cong observers had been taken care of. All in all, it was a successful encounter. . . .

By this time, we had sufficient background to prepare our lesson plans, finalize our syllabus, and choose a training facility, a South Vietnamese Army rifle range near Da Nang.

Later on we selected training sites at Phu Bai and Chu Lai as well. We found it best to take the schools to the regiments rather than having them come to us.

We sent out a message requesting volunteers who were classified as expert riflemen, were recommended by their respective commanding officers as being "combat wise," and possessed a hunting or competitive shooting background.

In order to get these men into the field as quickly as possible, the initial emphasis, I might add, was on quantity, not quality. Classes graduated in just three days and were considered adequate to provide fundamentals and familiarize the men with the rifles and the sights, but little more.

To begin with, most of the three days was devoted to marksmanship with an hour or two on the technique of employment. There were a lot of sore shoulders, but we turned out some fair snipers.

We instructed men from each of the infantry regiments, which gave us a sniper capability throughout all three of the Marine enclaves [Da Nang, Phu Bai, and Chu Lai].

It wasn't long before we had issued all of the rifles and were able to sit back temporarily and await the results. As each sniper would complete the school and return to his unit, we handed him a number of questionnaires. He was required to fill out a questionnaire each time he was employed, and return it to me. The questionnaire contained questions such as, location and type of employment, number of enemy observed, did you fire, if so, at what range, what portion of the body was exposed, was the target stationary or moving, and so forth. The purpose, of course, was to obtain information useful to the program.

Before long, based on 100 kills, we found that "Charlie" was moving when he was fired on more than 62 percent of the time. The average kill was made at a range of 557 meters [609 yards], the vast majority of kills were made with the first shot, the longest kill was 1100 meters [1202 yards].

By analyzing information such as this, we were able to make appropriate changes to our lesson plans. For example, we placed more emphasis on engaging moving targets and, by determining the average range for kills, we changed the recommended zero setting the men would maintain on their rifles to 600 meters [656 yards]. . . .

Gentlemen, at this point you are probably wondering if our program was truly effective. I can answer that question in several ways; however, please permit me to draw a comparison.

By February 1966, when some 84 of our snipers had accounted for over 100 enemy kills, we had entire 200-man rifle companies in the division that had not accounted for that many Viet Cong. This comparison is not entirely fair, however, since the rifle companies were performing many other tasks the snipers were not. Nevertheless, on an across-the-board basis, in terms of actual kills, snipers were doing their share and then some.

There is one other point I would like to make, and that is, on any given day throughout the division, there were probably a maximum of 15 snipers operating at one time. Rifle companies were running short of personnel in those days and they had other jobs for the snipers to perform as well.

Frankly, had all 84 men been operating at the same time, day in and day out, the results would have been considerably better. I might add that the incident rate of VC infiltrating in-close to our positions and shooting at short ranges dropped off tremendously. Contemporaries have told me that in cases where they had previously observed "Charlie" move openly from one point to another, he now utilized more cover and concealment and took the long way home. So, in many respects, the sniper program was really paying off.

During the early stages of the program, our snipers were employed along with patrols, as members of a blocking force and as part of daylight ambushes. When employed in direct support of patrols, snipers were invaluable in detecting, and eliminating, enemy snipers who would fire harassing shots at a passing patrol and then flee. It didn't take a patrol leader long to realize that an 8-power telescope [Unertl 8-power telescopic sight] enabled a sniper to see much better than any man he had in his patrol. Not only could the sniper see better, he could also deliver accurate fire at twice the range of the M14 and, by virtue of his "glass eye," get in an hour or more shooting time each day. I would say that patrolling was the most prevalent means of sniper employment in the early stages of the program.

Snipers are also used in support of the blocking force in search and clear, or destroy operations. A maneuvering group will sweep through a village in search of the enemy. The blocking force is positioned tactically to kill or capture Viet Cong fleeing from the rear or sides of the village. Frequently, open terrain prohibits the blocking force from getting close to the village without being seen. Here, the long range and accuracy capability of the sniper is a welcome asset to the blocking force commander.

On daylight ambushes, sniper teams, under cover of darkness, move to preselected areas in which there is a likelihood of encountering "Charlie," assume a position, and wait for sunup. If they get a shot, they have the option of remaining in position or returning to their unit. If they don't fire, they remain in position throughout the day and return after dark. Needless to say, this requires the utmost patience and a truly dedicated individual. Snipers are also placed out about 300 meters in front of friendly positions with the mission of observing and shooting any Viet Cong that might appear.

These, then, are the basic methods of employing snipers during the initial stages of the program. Their employment is limited only by the imagination of the commander to which they are attached.

In early 1966 we received notification that a sniper platoon had been authorized for each Infantry Regiment and for the Reconnaissance Battalion of the Marine Division. The platoons were considered Table of Organization and would constitute a new platoon in the Regimental Headquarters Company.

The organization of each platoon was broken down in the following manner. The platoon is led by a lieutenant. He has a gunnery sergeant as his number one assistant. The maintenance problems of the platoon are handled by a sergeant, MOS 2112 which is an RTE, or Rifle Team Equipment Armorer. Three 11-man sniper squads, each squad consisting of a squad leader and five 2-man sniper teams, complete the 1 officer and 35 enlisted organization. There are 3 infantry battalions in a Marine regiment. So theoretically, one sniper squad supports an infantry battalion. If, however, one battalion is going on a large operation, all three sniper squads may be attached for the period of the operation. At the present time, a sniper squad is generally attached to one of the three battalions for a period of a week or so, then returns to their platoon for training, rest, rezeroing of rifles and the like. A rotation system has been established in each regiment to insure that a battalion has a sniper capability at all times. The reconnaissance battalion T/O is similar in all respects, however, the sniper squads are smaller to better conform to the reconnaissance battalion's organization. I might add here that the basic operating unit of the sniper platoon is the two-man sniper team. Snipers always operate in pairs.

[**NOTE:** As a matter of reader interest, Sniper Organization in the Fleet Marine Forces circa 1969 was defined by the Marine Corps as follows:

INFANTRY REGIMENT SNIPER PLATOON

The sniper platoon, infantry regiment, is comprised of a platoon commander, platoon sergeant, rifle team equipment (RTE) repairman, and three sniper squads. Each squad consists of a squad leader and five two-man sniper teams; total: one officer and 35 enlisted. The platoon is under the command and administrative control of the regimental headquarters company and the operational control of the regimental commander.

RECONNAISSANCE BATTALION SNIPER PLATOON

The sniper platoon, reconnaissance battalion, is comprised of a platoon commander, platoon sergeant, RTE repairman, and four squads. Each squad consists of a squad leader and three two-man sniper teams; total: one officer and 30 enlisted. The platoon is under the command and administrative control of the battalion Headquarters and Service company and the operational control of the battalion commander.]

I would like to mention the employment of snipers once again very briefly. Since the sniper platoons have been formed, snipers are being used more extensively, and in a far more sophisticated manner. For example, helicopters are inserting sniper teams in remote areas, allowing them to "hunt" for several days and then picking them up again at a predetermined time and location. A very effective technique, and from a purely psychological point of view, has created a few new problems for Ho Chi Minh's political advisors. Getting "zapped" in your own backyard does create a serious morale problem. . . .

There are a few today in the Marine Corps who, for various reasons, have failed to acknowledge the sniper as a formidable means of waging war and contend that only volume of fire is the answer. I disagree, of course! I have seen what firepower will do, and I have also witnessed what snipers can accomplish. I recognize, as do the vast majority of my contemporaries, the need for both methods of delivering fire, depending upon the situation. It must be remembered, however, that there is no other weapon in the inventory that is as accurate, mobile, and versatile as the sniper rifle.

Given his experience in Vietnam, Major Russell was tasked with developing a sniper training manu-

The officer responsible for establishing the Third Marine Division sniper program in South Vietnam, Capt. Robert A. Russell, is shown conducting one of the early classes. A Soviet Mosin-Nagant M91/30 sniper rifle, the type used by the VC and the NVA, is leaning against the makeshift podium. (U.S. Marine Corps.)

al while he was assigned to the Educational Center (Marine Corps Schools, Publications Branch) at Quantico. As Russell relates:

> I labored nearly eight months on the initial draft. During that time I was fortunate to have the help of George Hurt and some of the other men that had been with my original group in Vietnam. They were serving with the MTU at Quantico and rendered invaluable assistance and technical support. Data on the psychological aspects of sniping came from Captain Sam Mullins, USN, who was Chief of the Psychiatric Department at Bethesda.

NOTE: The initial draft of Marine Corps field manual *FMFM 1-3B, SNIPING* (October 1967) served as the foundation for the Vietnam-era USMC sniper training manual. An interim draft edition followed in December

1968. In final form, Marine Corps *FMFM 1-3B, SNIPING* was published under date of 5 August 1969. The 264-page manual was the first USMC publication intended specifically for sniper training and employment.

A little-known aspect of Marine Corps efforts to recruit sniper candidates from III Marine Amphibious Force during the early months of the war included the unprecedented use of a specially prepared tape recording. The official USMC presentation was intended to increase the number of volunteers by drawing from the personnel already serving in Vietnam.

The unique recording stated the purpose and objectives of the program and offered the viewpoints of Major Russell, members of the sniper instructor staff, and graduate Marine snipers as well.

NOTE: The personnel named and or interviewed on this tape included Major Russell, M.Sgt. George Hurt, Gy.Sgt. Harold O'Connor, S.Sgt. James Feathers, Cpl. Donald Edmundson, Cpl. Ronald Koster, and Pfc. Russ Barrett.

Reflecting on his involvement and the early Marine Corps sniper program during the preparation of this book, Major Russell added the following postscript:

> If I were asked to come up with a word which best characterized the entire sniper effort, it would have to be, "informal." There were never any parameters, time frame, or special instructions other than my initial verbal command to start a sniper program.
>
> In retrospect, I am confident that someone, somewhere had a vision, but I never saw any official directives or correspondence concerning the program. My only contact was with the Division G-3. Our relationship was very casual. I kept him informed of what progress we were making, but I was not required to submit formal reports, etc. Consequently, every aspect of our effort was handled internally, in great haste, and informally. A typical Marine Corps "field expedient" approach.
>
> As it turned out, this proved beneficial. The program moved forward rapidly and was not bogged down in red tape. Under the circumstances, nothing of historical value was generated or retained, for that matter. My priority was getting the program off the ground and functional, and that we did, at the expense of history! [According to veteran 3d MarDiv sniper-instructor James R. Bowen, records and information pertaining to the personnel, weapons, and the program were kept in a small wooden box that traveled with the instructor team. Unfortunately, there is no way of knowing what became of the contents of this box.]
>
> I feel compelled to add there was a significant amount of resistance to the sniper effort, just as there is in competitive shooting throughout the Corps. It manifested itself in various ways. At the onset of the program we endeavored to answer the question as to how snipers would be best utilized by attaching ourselves to different size units in order to develop a concept of employment. Some commanders just didn't want to be "bothered" with us, but fortunately, most did. After the sniper platoon was authorized, commanders didn't know what to do with them.
>
> Graduates of our sniper school would contact me after returning to their units and request that I intervene because they were not being used properly or not at all.
>
> Looking back, however, I can understand the reasons for some of the problems we experienced. There was no sniping manual or precedent. Commanders really didn't have any knowledge on the potential of a sniper or how to employ them effectively.

A full complement of Marine sniper trainees and instructors during one of the many practice firing sessions. By all accounts, early emphasis was placed on marksmanship and the art of sniping. The scouting aspect (Scout-Sniper) came into focus as the training syllabus was refined and expanded. In addition to the Model 70 Winchesters with Unertl telescopes, there are at least three M84-equipped M1D sniper rifles on the firing line as well. (Barker Collection.)

Maj. Gen. Lewis W. Walt, Commanding General, III MAF and Third Marine Division, speaks to Marines from the Second Battalion, Seventh Marines (BLT 2/7) at the Qui Nhon enclave 175 miles south of Da Nang (July 1965). The regimental headquarters of the Seventh Marines came ashore at Chu Lai on 14 August 1965. (U.S. Marine Corps.)

Third Marine Division sniper candidates taking their turn on the firing line. The photo provides a good comparison between the Model 70 with target barrel and target/marksman stock and the target barrel version with the modified standard stock ("sporter stock"). Note the spent cartridges and empty boxes of .30-caliber match ammunition (M72) in the foreground. Although M70 rifles with target stocks pictured in various field photos dating from this era give the impression this weapon type was fielded in quantity, most of the Model 70 rifles employed by Marine snipers during the early months of the war made use of the modified standard stocks with an enlarged barrel channel (to accommodate the medium-heavy target barrel). (U.S. Marine Corps.)

S.Sgt. Walt Sides, the platoon sergeant for the first Fourth Marines Sniper Platoon, is shown with a Model 70 Winchester target rifle (heavy barrel and marksman stock) mounting one of the commercial 3X-9X variable-power Japanese rifle scopes. A competitive marksman with the Marine Corps, Sergeant Sides had been sought out by members of the original 3d MarDiv sniper-instructor team soon after his arrival in Vietnam. In addition to training Marines for sniper duty, the sergeant was also actively involved with sniping operations. Efforts to formulate effective sniping tactics for his unit included 47 days in the bush on one occasion. Of all the information provided by Sides, the one point stressed repeatedly was that their sniper personnel "were never allowed to work alone." The sniper team concept was emphasized, with two- and six-man teams employed most often. As Sides was quick to point out, "If I had ever put a sniper out there by himself, they would have relieved me of my command." The photograph was made in the spring of 1966 near Phu Bai. (Sides Collection.)

Sergeant Sides (far left) pictured with members of the original Fourth Marines Sniper Platoon. The unit was equipped with Model 70 Winchester rifles mounting 8-power Unertl scopes, and M1Ds with the 2.2-power M84 sight. According to Sides, many of the boxes used to ship sniping equipment to the unit contained notes from stateside USMC ordnance personnel with comments such as "shoot one for us," "this weapon zeroed for Viet Cong," and words of that nature. The sunglasses worn by the men were issued to counteract the effects of the sun. By all accounts, the original "39-man" Fourth Marines sniper platoon received its training during May–June 1966. (Sides Collection.)

The firing line of the 1,000-yard range employed by the Fourth Marines sniper platoon at an ARVN training center near Phu Bai. The personnel are (from left to right): S.Sgt. Walt Sides, an Army officer, the ARVN base commander, and Gy.Sgt. Lawrence N. Dubia, the Fourth Marines Sniper Platoon commander. In addition to his responsibilities as the platoon commander, Gunnery Sergeant Dubia maintained the rifles and telescopic sights fielded by the unit. The sergeant was killed in action during his second tour of duty in RVN. (Sides Collection.)

L.Cpls. Leonard J. Wilson (left) and Jerome F. Witt, while attached to a reconnaissance patrol ("B" Company, Third Recon Battalion) working the mouth of the A Shau Valley west of Hue-Phu Bai, discovered an armed Viet Cong force moving down an open road. As Wilson recalls, "We spotted several people on a road approximately 600 meters behind us. The sun was in their faces, and we had a clear view of the entire column as they came around a bend. We counted 24 people all clad in black outfits. Jerry and I quickly decided that we would try to get as many as possible. The recon squad would be our rear security, and their corporal would spot for us. Jerry took the left and I started on the right. The firing lasted less than 20 minutes. We killed 10 and wounded 11." The Viet Cong force had been taken completely by surprise. Some of them stood on the road trying to locate the sound of the firing. Others scattered in different directions, with some actually running toward the Marine marksmen. When it was over, "Viet Cong bodies were strewn along the road for 300 yards." The Marine snipers, both members of the original Fourth Marines sniper platoon, were armed with Model 70 Winchester rifles mounting Unertl telescopes. The action took place on 6 September 1966, at which point in time the entire area literally belonged to the Communist guerrillas. (Wilson Collection.)

Marine marksman with a Unertl-equipped Model 70 Winchester, the mainstay of the III MAF sniper program during 1965 and 1966. Even though combat use of the Model 70 is usually attributed to the Marine Corps, the Winchester rifle, in one form or another, was also employed by Army personnel for sniping in Vietnam. (U.S. Marine Corps.)

Marine sniper/observer team during early combat activity in South Vietnam. Even though the concept of employing two-man sniper teams originated before the war in Southeast Asia, the practice reached a state of near perfection in Vietnam. According to Marine Corps training doctrine, "The two-man sniper team is the basic operational element of the sniper platoon." Although Marine snipers were trained to operate in teams of two, there were situations where the specialists were known to work by themselves. The situation at hand usually determined the course of action in this regard. (U.S. Marine Corps.)

A Viet Cong cari-
cature used as a
target by the South
Vietnamese Army in
its marksmanship
training program
(1965). (U.S. Marine
Corps.)

Marine Corps sniper instructor explaining the various components of the M72 .30-
caliber match cartridge to sniper candidates, Vietnam circa 1966. (U.S. Marine Corps.)

L.Cpl. Richard L. Morrison and Pvt. Charles Harris ("B" Company, First Battalion, Third Marines) were credited with killing 18 Viet Cong during Operation Orange, April 1966. The Marine snipers are equipped with M70 Winchester rifles mounting Unertl telescopes. (U.S. Marine Corps.)

A plaque presented to Maj. Robert A. Russell by the Sniper Platoon, Third Marines, when he left Vietnam. (Peter R. Senich.)

Marine snipers proved their worth in Vietnam by denying free movement to "Old Charlie" in his own backyard during the early stages of the war. As time passed, enemy combat personnel learned to avoid situations where they might expect to encounter Marine sniping activity. In areas where snipers were employed effectively, the threat of an unseen marksman forced the VC and NVA to change their patterns of movement and operations. (U.S. Marine Corps.)

RIFLES FOR SNIPING

The Early Issue

The principal sniper rifles employed by the Marine Corps during the early months of the war in South Vietnam were the .30-caliber (.30-06) Model 70 Winchester and the .30-caliber M1D, a sniping version of the battle-proven M1 Garand rifle.

The semiautomatic M1D rifles, mounting 2.2-power M84 telescopic sights, were reportedly fielded in standard (as issued) and "armorer-prepared" (glass-bedded and accurized) form as well.

Although M1 sniping rifles (M1C and M1D) had proven more than satisfactory in Korea, combat sniping reports indicated the maximum effective range as 600 yards, with rather consistent results between 400 to 600 yards. However, in deference to the M1, limitations of telescopic sights and ammunition used with this system did little to increase the chance of long-range hits. While adequate at short to medium ranges, the issue telescopes' (2.5-power M81 and M82 and some 2.2-power M84 scopes) resolving power made long-range target definition extremely difficult.

At this juncture, special match-grade ammunition was not available or even considered for sniping purposes. USMC snipers drew regular .30-caliber ball ammunition that showed up fairly well at shorter ranges but was not reliable at 500 and 600 yards. When obtainable, .30-caliber armor-piercing ammunition was employed since its heavier bullet provided increased stability over longer ranges.

The Marine Corps had made a commitment to a semiautomatic sniper rifle as early as 1945 when Marine Corps Equipment Board (MCEB) Test Report, Project No. 395, Rifle (Sniper's) M1C, 11 August 1945 "authorized" the M1C rifle for Marine Corps use. This course of action was reaffirmed as a result of MCEB testing at Quantico, Virginia, in 1951 (Study of Sniper Rifles, Telescopes, and Mounts, Project No. 757, 31 August 1951), which culminated in the formal adoption of the Marine Corps version of the M1C (MC 1952). Ironically, however, aside from some combat use of M1 sniping rifles during the Korean War, and to a lesser extent, in Southeast Asia, the field use of sniper rifles based on the M1 Garand (M1C-M1D) did not reach practical proportions in the Marine Corps. The M1 rifles were eventually superseded by the M14.

NOTE: Contrary to the definition of obsolete (that is, no longer in use), the M1C and M1D remained as quasi-official sniping arms of the Army and Marine Corps through the mid-1960s, when combat requirements in Southeast Asia necessitated the upgrading of sniper equipment. Even though the M1 sniping rifle has been long removed from "Standard Type" classification, a substantial number of these rifles remained in National Guard armories across the United States and in ordnance base depots throughout the world. In addition to their protracted military use for special applications by indigenous forces in low-intensity conflicts, the venerable .30-caliber sniping rifles (M1D) were drawn from base depots in Europe to supplement the long-range sniping capability of American combat forces in the Kuwait Theater of Operations (KTO) during the Persian Gulf War in 1991. Although M1 sniping rifles would have undoubtedly remained in reserve following the Persian Gulf War, in keeping with the policies of the present administration, a considerable number of original M1 sniping rifles have been destroyed.

When U.S. combat forces began operations in Southeast Asia in 1965, rather than base their sniping issue on the 7.62mm (.308-caliber) M14 rifle, which was the successor to the M1 Garand and the standard Army and Marine Corps service rifle at the time, the Marine Corps decided to return to a bolt-action rifle for sniper use.

Interestingly, even though the M14 would serve as the principal USMC infantry arm for more than two years after the initial landings at Da Nang in early 1965, there is no evidence to indicate that the Marine Corps gave even passing consideration to the M14 rifle for use in a sniping capacity. The era of the semiautomatic sniping rifle had officially ended in the U.S. Marine Corps.

NOTE: As personnel close to the early USMC sniper program have indicated, there simply "wasn't enough time" to develop a satisfactory sniping rifle from scratch. Even though the M14 was not specifically mentioned in this context, judging from the intent of the Marine Corps documents that preceded the actual selection process in late 1965, the USMC sniping issue was going to be a bolt-action rifle, and only the specific manufacturer was left to be determined.

The Army, on the other hand, chose to base its sniper issue on the highly refined version of the M14 ultimately referenced as the XM21. In addition to the XM21, however, both standard and match-grade M14s mounting the M84 telescopic sight remained in service as well.

By the time the last American combat forces left Southeast Asia, at least three types of telescopic-sighted M14 rifles saw duty in the hands of U.S. military personnel. These were the standard M14 rifles with commercial scopes, improvised mounts, and, in some cases, M84 sights in the receiver mounting bracket developed by Army Weapons Command (AWC); the basic match-grade M14 rifles prepared by AWC at Rock Island Arsenal (RIA) with the M84 telescope in the aforementioned mounting; and finally, the XM21 system with the Adjustable Ranging Telescope (ART).

It is interesting to note that during the height of U.S. combat involvement in Southeast Asia, the principal news magazines ran an occasional wire-service photo-illustration of a Marine Corps rifleman armed with an M14 mounting a commercial rifle scope. Although Marine Corps use of the M14 in a sniping capacity is rarely mentioned, a number of "field expedient" M14 sniper rifles were employed by enterprising Marine marksmen during the war in Vietnam.

Despite limited use of telescope-equipped M14 rifles, standard M14s were employed by USMC Scout-Sniper teams for security and "open-sighted sniping" on a routine basis. Among the various forms of employment used, Marine snipers were known to establish an arbitrary range at which the second member of the team would "take over" and engage the enemy with semiautomatic or automatic fire in defense of their position. In addition to providing team security, Marine snipers using the M14 with standard sights as well as the Starlight Scope neutralized any number of VC and NVA personnel. The "fourteens," as the rifles were also known, were often fitted with bipods and, in some cases, were glass-bedded and accurized to enhance their performance. Judging from the comments of various Marine snipers, the versatile weapon made the difference between "staying behind" and "making it back" on more than one occasion.

So far as overall M14 performance was concerned, M.Sgt. Donald G. Barker, USMC (Ret.), an accomplished marksman and member of the original 3d MarDiv sniper-instructor team, made the following comments:

> In my opinion, a standard M14 in good condition is considered as a sniper rifle out to 1,000 yards in the hands of an expert marksman. The target is a little harder to find but, when you do, all of the elements are there.

Barker's viewpoint was shared by many Marines with combat experience in Vietnam. There was nothing wrong with the range capability of an M14; the difference was the rifleman. An M14 could shoot just as well without a telescopic sight as it did with one.

A particularly interesting means of altering "Charlie's" work habits in the areas surrounding the Marine enclaves during early combat included the use of "sniper-teams" armed with conventional M14 rifles. Even though this practice was limited, Marine riflemen acting as snipers were employed under diverse conditions and circumstances for the express purpose of harassing the Viet Cong.

In one case, Lt. Col. William R. Melton, USMC (Ret.), while serving with the Ninth Marines (3d MarDiv) as a squad leader in 1965, was tasked with forming a "two-man sniper team" to deal with the Viet Cong in the areas adjacent to his unit's command post. According to Melton, the "team" comprised himself and another "expert marksman" (Pfc. A.W. Kinney). Their equipment included a field radio, binoculars, and an M79 grenade launcher, and both were armed with standard M14 rifles. Measures such as this were indicative of the efforts by small units to field snipers as best they could, despite only marginal success.

Though the M14 was eventually replaced by the 5.56mm (.223-caliber) M16 assault rifle for general field use, a considerable number of M14s remained in Marine Corps service during the course of the war. It was not uncommon to see Marine combat personnel armed with an equal mix of M14 and M16 rifles. For many Marines, if an option existed, the M14 was their choice.

In any case, however, the adoption of the M16 rifle was noted by the Marine Corps as follows:

> The decision to equip Marine forces in the Western Pacific with the M16 had been made in March 1966. . . . The rifle was procured in quantity from the Army and issued to maneuver units in March and April 1967, in time for the heavy fighting at Khe Sanh.

Despite some field use of the M16 mounting the 3-power Colt/Realist scope by Marine riflemen and recon personnel, telescopic-sighted M16 rifles were rarely employed by Marines trained as snipers. The range limitations of the 5.56mm assault rifle limited its value as a sniping arm.

Although USMC snipers were known to experiment with M16s mounting telescopes of one kind or another, except for the occasional use of M16s by sniper teams for security purposes, the 5.56mm rifle was not viewed as part of Marine Corps sniping operations in Vietnam.

NOTE: As uncomplicated as it was to mount a rifle scope on the M16, a surprising variety of telescopic sights were to see combat with this weapon system in Southeast Asia.

Describing the early Marine Corps sniping issue in detail, the October 1966 issue of *Guns & Ammo,* in an article entitled "The Snipers of Da Nang," stated in part:

Two types of rifles are presently being employed by the Marine sniper platoon; they are the Model 70 Winchester (.30-06) and the M1D (.30 caliber).

The Unertl 8X sniperscope and the 3X9 "Marine Scope" (manufactured in Japan) are used on the Model 70 Winchester rifles. The M1D is equipped with the M84 scope, designed especially for the rifle.

All Model 70 Winchester rifles are equipped with target barrels; however, some have sporter stocks while others have target stocks. The sporter stocks are favored most because they are lighter and easy to carry. The M1D rifle is equipped with a standard military stock.

All rifles presently in use by the sniper platoon have been glass-bedded by a Marine Rifle Team Equipment (RTE) Armorer since arriving in Vietnam. The rifles have also been accurized by an RTE armorer.

The rifles presently in use by the sniper teams were once maintained by the Marksmanship Training Unit at Marine Corps Schools, Quantico, Va., and have been used in rifle matches, including the National Matches at Camp Perry.

Ammunition used by the snipers for both target and actual work is the standard match Lake City load. It is not hand-loaded.

NOTE: In their effort to publicize and place information directly into the "media pipeline," military personnel wrote articles for the express purpose of drawing both public and official attention to the success of one operation or another in Vietnam. On different occasions, magazine articles dealing with early Marine Corps sniping activity appeared in stateside periodicals without a byline or under a pseudonym. In this case, the article appearing in the October 1966 issue of *Guns & Ammo* was written by a Marine correspondent.

Even though the Marine Corps eventually replaced the Winchester Model 70 and the M1D with the 7.62mm Remington M700 (M40) bolt-action sniper rifle (adopted 7 April 1966), the Model 70 and M1D remained in service in Vietnam for an extended period.

Adding to our perspective in this matter, Donald G. Barker provided the following insight on the early USMC sniping equipment fielded in Vietnam:

> We started out with approximately 12 target Model 70s that had heavy barrels and were glass-bedded. We also received 40 or more sporter stock Model 70s [heavy barrel, modified sporter stock] that were not glass-bedded but, after talking with the FLSG small arms repair section [Force Logistic Support Group] these were also glass-bedded and test fired at the training area we worked out of near Da Nang. . . . All of the rifles which we started the program with were run through the FLSG small arms shop at Da Nang and were fine-tuned prior to issue . . .
>
> The M1D was also gone over by the shop.

According to Vietnam-era Marine Corps information:

> The III MAF Force Logistic Support Group (FLSG), commanded by Colonel Mauro J. Padalino, was built around the nucleus of the 3d Service Battalion from the 3d Marine Division and reinforced by support elements from the 3d Force Service Regiment on Okinawa. Colonel Padalino, a veteran supply officer, maintained his headquarters at Da Nang while two force logistic support units, FLSU-1 and -2, serviced Chu Lai and Phu Bai. The Force Logistic Support Group engaged in a wide variety of tactical support and combat support activities.

In view of his vast experience with the Model 70 Winchester and the Remington M700 sniper rifle, when asked, "Which weapon would you prefer in combat," Barker replied:

At the time I would have chosen the Model 70 Winchester, as I was more familiar with it and the 8-power Unertl. It was the same type of rifle I had shot for years, and I also liked the .30-caliber cartridge. I think I would still prefer the Model 70 as my weapon. However, I do feel that the M700 and the M70 are equal to each other. I never had the Redfield Accu-Range scope on a Model 70, but that 8-power Unertl was a class act in my book.

Taking the choice of one rifle over the other one step further in this case, Maj. Robert A. Russell responded to the same question as follows:

I strongly suspect I would have selected the Model 70, if for no other reason than it was a time-tested and proven rifle with a level of performance that exceeded the capabilities of the average sniper. Don Barker, for example, could get consistent hits at 1,000 yards or more with a heavy barrel M70 and a 8X Unertl, but the average sniper could not. There was no arguing with results like that.

Expanding on his views of the Vietnam-era sniping issue, and the Remington M700 in particular, Barker added this postscript:

I never had an opportunity to carry one in Vietnam when I was there in 1968 and 1969. If I had I felt it would be taking advantage of the enemy. With the rifle and scope taking care of everything, it was back to basics and if you missed a shot, you must have been asleep.

NOTE: In addition to serving with the 3d MarDiv sniper cadre, Barker was also directly involved in establishing the USMC Scout-Sniper School at Camp Pendleton, California (January 1967), as the first M700 sniper rifles were being shipped to the Marine Corps.

As a matter of historical interest, in response to an early 1966 request from the Assistant Chief of Staff for Force Development, Headquarters, Department of the Army, for information concerning Marine Corps sniping activity in RVN, correspondence from Headquarters, USMC (28 January 1966), in addition to advising the U.S. Army on "Scout-Snipers in Current Operations," made specific note of the sniper equipment then in use by III Marine Amphibious Force, Third Marine Division:

The bulk of the sniper weapons are pre-1964 Model 70 Winchesters with target-weight barrels and sporter-weight stocks. These are equipped with Unertl 8-power telescopes in target-type mounts. Also on hand in the 3d Marine Division are 12 pre-1964 Model 70 rifles of the National Match pattern equipped with variable-power (3-9X) commercial telescopes and M1D rifles procured from the Army. All of these weapons utilize the U.S. cartridge caliber .30.

It is important to note the "12" 3d MarDiv Model 70 target rifles were originally fitted with the 3X-9X variable-power commercial rifle scopes trademarked "MARINE." The Japanese sights were purchased on Okinawa. The Model 70s with target scopes and sporter stocks made use of the Unertl ("USMC-SNIPER") 8-power telescopic sights dating from World War II, and the M1Ds mounted 2.2-power M84 telescopes. According to USMC procurement documents, a small quantity of M84 telescopes were also purchased from the U.S. Army for Marine sniper use in RVN.

• • •

"As 1966 ended, there were 67,729 Marines in South Vietnam."

—U.S. Marine Corps

An early Vietnam War photo (31 July 1965) with caption that reads: "Cpl. Ronald S. Newman of 3rd Battalion, 4th Marines, conceals himself in the tall grass during an attack by the Viet Cong. His unit is involved in a sweep of the Hue-Phu Bai district." The men are equipped with M14 rifles, the mainstay of Marine Corps combat personnel during early going in South Vietnam. Even though the rifle was considered outdated officially, the 7.62mm M14 remained the weapon of choice for many Marines long after the 5.56mm M16 rifle was adopted. It was not uncommon to see an equal mix of M14 and M16 rifles during Marine combat operations throughout the war. (U.S. Marine Corps.)

Lt. Col. William R. Melton, USMC (Ret.), while serving as a sergeant with First Battalion, Ninth Marines (3d MarDiv), was tasked with forming a "two-man sniper team" for the express purpose of dealing with the Viet Cong in the areas surrounding his unit's command post. Standard M14s were employed for "open-sighted sniping" early on. Sergeant Melton (center) and the second member of the ad hoc sniper team, Pfc. Allen W. Kinney (right center), are pictured with Marines from Delta Company during Operation Golden Fleece, October 1965. (U.S. Marine Corps.)

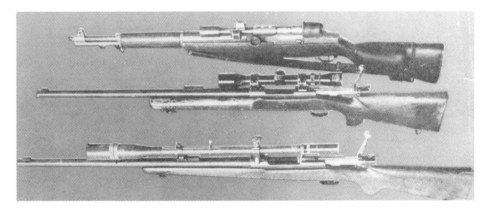

The nucleus of the Marine Corps sniping issue during early combat in South Vietnam: the M1D rifle and 2.2-power M84 scope (top); Model 70 Winchester with target stock, heavy barrel, and 3X-9X variable-power commercial scope; and Model 70 Winchester with "sporter stock," heavy barrel, and 8-power Unertl telescopic sight. Although most of the equipment was considered "well-used" when it was sent to Vietnam, many of the same weapons were still in service when USMC combat forces began redeploying to the United States. Marginal photographic quality aside, this is the only known photo showing the three weapon types in a single group. The unique photograph was taken in South Vietnam. (U.S. Marine Corps.)

Marine sniper (3d MarDiv) with heavy barrel Model 70 mounting the 8-power Unertl telescope (Operation Virginia, 1966). According to the original caption, L.Cpl. Dalton Gunderson was "checking the area for Viet Cong snipers." In this case, the Unertl telescope mount is positioned at the back of the front base (6-inch mount spacing). The front mount was normally set at the forward "notch" (7.2-inch spacing). The alternate setting provided slightly different adjustment values. (U.S. Marine Corps.)

A Third Marine Division sniper in Vietnam, January 1966 (Operation Double Eagle). M1Ds were pressed into service during early combat in RVN and in many cases were accurized and glass-bedded by USMC armorers to improve performance. The .30-caliber semiautomatic sniping rifles were also employed by the First Marine Division during the early stages of its sniping program. According to the original caption, the sniper was attached to E Company, Second Battalion, Fourth Marines. (U.S. Marine Corps.)

Model 70 target rifle mounting a 3X-9X variable-power rifle sight made in Japan (trademarked "MARINE"). The rifle shown was one of the first Winchester rifles sent to Vietnam for 3d MarDiv sniper use. The size of the target barrel (medium-heavy) and the heavy marksman stock is readily apparent in this view. (U.S. Marine Corps.)

A part of the supplemental sniping equipment sent to Vietnam for Third Marine Division use—an M1D sniper rifle with M84 telescopic sight on the firing range at Da Nang. Although leather cheek pads were furnished, flash hiders were "not available." The semiautomatic M1 sniping rifles fired the same .30-caliber match ammunition (M72) used with the Model 70 Winchester. (U.S. Marine Corps.)

Model 70 Winchester mounting an 8-power Unertl telescopic sight. The weapon is typical of those fielded for Marine sniper use in Southeast Asia (medium-heavy barrel, modified standard stock). The rifle and scope were part of the supplemental sniping equipment sent to RVN beginning in late 1965. (U.S. Marine Corps.)

Model 70 Winchester with 3X-9X variable-power telescopic sight. Mounting hardware for the Japanese hunting sights was obtained from the Force Logistic Support Group (FLSG). At least two types of scope rings were used with this sighting system. The Fourth Marines sniper L.Cpl. Leonard J. Wilson was taking part in Operation Prairie in late 1966. (U.S. Marine Corps.)

Sgt. Howard J. Greene, the NCO in charge (NCOIC) of the First Battalion, Ninth Marines sniper team (3d MarDiv) checks his weapon while preparing for Operation Prairie II at Cam Lo (Quang Tri Province), 28 February 1967. The M14 is equipped with a variable-power commercial telescope in an improvised mounting. The standard M14 rear sight has been removed. (U.S. Marine Corps.)

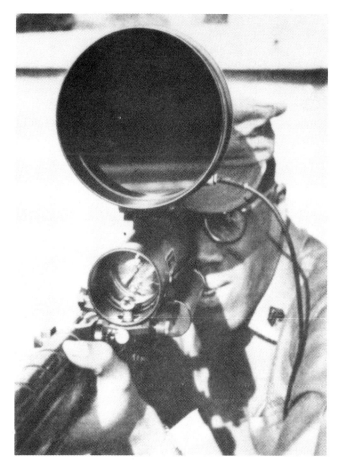

Marine Corps rifleman with an Infrared Weapon Sight and M14 rifle. The principal use of the AN/PAS-4 by the Marine Corps came during early combat activity in Vietnam when infrared sights were employed by "automatic riflemen" armed with bipod-equipped M14 rifles. In some cases, the obsolete infrared equipment was used to acclimate Scout-Sniper candidates to night vision equipment in RVN and the United States. (U.S. Marine Corps.)

The AN/PAS-4 Infrared Weapon Sight produced by Varo, Inc. (9903) and Polan Industries (P-155), as used by ARVN, U.S. Army, and Marine Corps personnel in Vietnam. Utilized primarily with the M14 rifle, the sight could be adapted to the M16 with a special mount. Though later replaced by Starlight Scopes for combat purposes, infrared weapon sights saw continued use in a training capacity. The telescope assembly was 13 inches long; the telescope and light source were approximately 14 inches high. The entire system weighed slightly over 12 pounds. The Infrared Weapon Sight and supporting equipment were issued with a carrying case. (Excalibur Enterprises.)

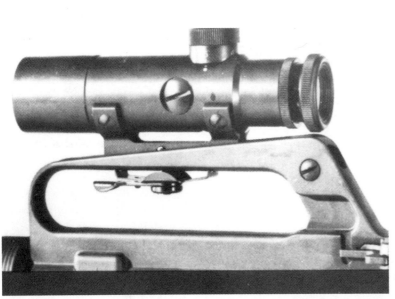

A 1965 catalog illustration for the Colt AR15 Sporter Scope. The 3-power rifle scope was specifically designed for the AR15 (M16) by Realist, Inc., of Menomonee Falls, Wisconsin, as a "private label brand" for Colt Industries. Though referenced as a "sporter scope," the compact sight was also pictured in sales literature for the Colt 5.56mm "Military Weapon Systems." The Colt/Realist model saw widespread use by U.S. combat personnel during the Vietnam War. For the sake of clarification, the 5.56mm rifle started out in Southeast Asia as the AR15, progressed in form as the M16, XM16E1, and finally, the Colt assault rifle became the M16A1. The weapon replaced the M14 as the standard infantry rifle for both the Army and the Marine Corps. (Thomas Collection.)

Marine Sgt. H.J. Greene (First Battalion, Ninth Marines) following Operation Prarie II near the DMZ. Even though M14 rifles were not a viable part of the Marine Corps sniper program, Marine snipers and riflemen occasionally employed telescope-equipped M14s. More than one RTE armorer recall mounting rifle scopes on the M14 rifle in Vietnam. (U.S. Marine Corps.)

Vietnam-era U.S. Army Special Forces trooper is shown with an M84-equipped .30-caliber (.30-06) M1903A4 sniper rifle. In advance of full-scale U.S. involvement in RVN, many of the American military advisors tasked with "enhancing the combat capabilities" of the "friendly forces" in Southeast Asia were known to include telescopic-sighted rifles among the wide range of small arms categorized as "personal defense weapons." Commercial sporting rifles; "well-traveled" M1903A4, M1C, and M1D sniper rifles mounting both World War II and contemporary rifle scopes; and various examples of foreign military sniping hardware were all represented during the "early days" in South Vietnam. This period was referenced by the Marine Corps as "The Advisory and Combat Assistance Era." According to USMC historical documents, "There were some 700 Marines involved with advisory and combat support activities in RVN at the end of 1964." (R. James Bender.)

Model 1903A4 sniper rifle with the 2.2-power M84 telescope. The versatility of the Redfield Junior telescope mounting allowed for the use of contemporary rifle scopes as well as the M84 sights. While hardly "issue equipment," a variety of fixed-power and variable-power commercial telescopic sights (1-inch tube) were reportedly fitted to the M1903A3 and M1903A4 rifles for use in South Vietnam. With many American advisors—and, eventually, the special mission groups—operating "off the books" with respect to their equipment and activities in particular, the "special small arms" fielded in RVN, especially during the combat advisory era and the early months of full-scale U.S. military involvement, were, in many cases, a simple matter of "whatever it takes." The rifles and telescopic sights employed for sniping purposes were no exception in this regard. The M84 telescope is positioned on the receiver as it is shown in the Vietnam-era Army technical manual for the M1903A4 sniper rifle. (Peter R. Senich.)

Remington M1903A4 sniper rifle with the telescope removed. The mount (bridge-type base) was simply a commercial system adapted to military use. In contemporary form, the Redfield-designed "rotary dovetail" telescope mounting was also employed with the Remington M700/M40 USMC Scout-Sniper rifle fielded during the Vietnam War. (West Point Collection.)

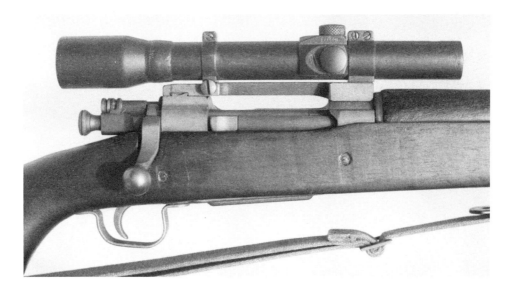

Model 1903A4 rifle and telescope sold as surplus (surplus disposal) at the U.S. Navy base at Lakehurst, New Jersey. The 2.75-power Unertl Falcon telescope dates from the 1960s. The scope was painted (dark gray) at some point in its military service. Even though there is nothing to connect this rifle with Vietnam, the weapon is representative of the ad hoc sniping equipment fielded during early U.S. military involvement in Southeast Asia. As a matter of interest, personnel tasked with flying "unmarked aircraft" in and out of SEA (1962–1965) recall seeing "large quantities of 03A4s with mounts, but no scopes or rings." The weapons were among the military hardware furnished to the Republic of South Vietnam as part of the overall "military advice and assistance plan" practiced by the United States. (Wayne P. Gagner.)

CHAPTER 4

A PROGRAM TAKES HOLD

As the Marine Corps sniping effort grew in size and strength, First Marine Division Scout-Snipers were making life as complicated as they could for the Communist forces operating in the areas southwest of Da Nang.

Although snipers were reportedly operating with the First Marine Division almost from the day it landed in Vietnam, it remained for a formal sniping program to yield the results Maj. Gen. Herman Nickerson Jr. envisioned when he assumed command of the division in 1966.

NOTE: According to Marine Corps information, the introduction of the First Marine Division to RVN took place in the following order: The Seventh Marines, a First Marine Division regiment, arrived in RVN (Chu Lai) in August 1965. The First and Second Battalions of the First Marines were deployed in South Vietnam by the end of the same year. The First Marine Division deployed to the Western Pacific (Okinawa) from Camp Pendleton in August 1965. In March 1966, the division command post was moved to Chu Lai. (Chu Lai was located approximately 55 miles south of Da Nang on the coast.) The zone of action assigned to the First Marine Division at that time encompassed the southern two provinces of I Corps (I CTZ), Quang Tin and Quang Ngai. In October 1966, lst MarDiv shifted its headquarters north from Chu Lai, moving into the command post vacated by Third Marine Division on the reverse slope of Hill 327, approximately 2 miles west of Da Nang (the 3d MarDiv CP was moved 42 miles north to Phu Bai, outside of Hue). In the course of its combat involvement in Vietnam, the First Marine Division controlled the First, Fifth, and Seventh Marine Regiments, as well as the Twenty-sixth and Twenty-seventh Marine Regiments attached from the Fifth Marine Division. First Marine Division headquarters remained at Da Nang until the division redeployed from Vietnam.

The task of organizing a First Marine Division sniper program was assigned to Capt. Edward J. "Jim" Land Jr., an accomplished marksman and member of several championship Marine Corps shooting teams. Captain Land had actively campaigned for an ongoing sniper training and equipment program in the Marine Corps long before the conflict in Vietnam escalated in 1965.

While serving with the First Battalion, Fourth Marines (Rein.), First Marine Brigade in Hawaii during the early 1960s, First Lieutenant Land was directly involved with a successful "Scout-Sniper School" run by Chief Warrant Officer (CWO) Arthur F. Terry. The innovative sniper school, a Hawaii Marine Rifle and Pistol Team operation, was the only training program of its type in the Army or Marine Corps at the time.

NOTE: Sniper candidates attending the school received training in "advanced marksmanship, field-craft, and sniping techniques." The M1C and the Model 70 Winchester were used for training purposes; the M70 was used at ranges out to 1,000 yards.

As a matter of interest, Marine Marksman Carlos N. Hathcock received his initial sniper training at the Scout-Sniper School in Hawaii.

When a Marine Corps-wide sniper program became a necessity rather than an opinion in 1965, Land, a captain with the Marksmanship Training Unit at Quantico, Virginia, was called on to assist with the initial plans to train and equip Marine snipers in South Vietnam.

Apart from the distinct lack of sniping equipment, a significant problem in itself, there was no cohesive doctrine or field manuals for training snipers in the Marine Corps. Consequently, as part of the overall effort to "get a program started," reference material dating as far back as World War I was brought forth once again. By all accounts, "every training aid imaginable" was reviewed to see if it could be adapted for use in Vietnam.

Although many of the precepts established during World War I, the Pacific War, and Korea would serve for training Marine Corps snipers in Vietnam, it was necessary to devise tactics consistent with the area of operations and the enemy the Marines were now facing. If ever the term "trial and error" was applicable, it certainly described the job of the officers and men of III MAF tasked with fielding snipers during those hectic early days in South Vietnam in 1965 and 1966.

The initial phases of the Marine Corps sniping program in RVN were documented in an earlier chapter. In this case, the origins of the First Marine Division Scout-Sniper program can be traced to a chance meeting between Captain Land and Major General Nickerson.

The meeting was described by Charles Henderson in his work *Marine Sniper* (Stein and Day 1986):

> In August of 1966, Maj. Gen. Herman Nickerson was on his way to Chu Lai, Vietnam, to assume command of the 1st Marine Division, and he stopped for staging at Camp Butler, Okinawa, where Land commanded the ordnance company [Land went to Okinawa from the MTU in February 1966]. . . .
> Nickerson encountered Land by coincidence at a command briefing. "Captain!" the general said, "What are you doing here?"
> "I'm Ordnance Company's Commander."
> "Ordnance! You're no ordnance officer—you're a shooter. You did all that

work selling and developing the sniper program. Why aren't you over in Vietnam, killing the Viet Cong?"

"Sir, I'm afraid I don't have an answer for you," Land replied.

"I have a proposal for you, Captain Land. You get your gear together and report to me in Chu Lai. You have thirty days to be effecting sniper casualties on the enemy in Vietnam."

The groundwork for the First Marine Division sniper program had been laid on Okinawa. The events leading to the actual formation of the Scout-Sniper program in RVN, as detailed by Maj. E.J. Land Jr., USMC (Ret.) for this book, were as follows:

I flew into the air base at Da Nang [early October 1966] on my way to 1st Marine Division Headquarters. When I arrived I was told to report to the Division Chief of Staff for further instructions. I made my way up the winding road to "The Bunker," as the Division Headquarters was known, and reported to the Chief of Staff. The colonel informed me that General Nickerson wanted to see me and he told me to come back the next morning.

The next day I was standing outside Division Headquarters waiting to see the General. I went in and reported, he looked up and began, "Land, you briefed me on a sniper's capabilities at the National Championships last year when I was at Camp Perry. Well, I want snipers operating in this division and I want them killing Viet Cong. I don't care how you do it—if you've got to go out and kill them yourself." He asked if I had any questions, I told him "No Sir!" and he replied, "Then get started." I gave him an appropriate "Aye, Aye Sir!", did an about face and walked out of his office.

Even though I was relieved, it didn't take long for me to realize that starting a program like this would be a difficult proposition under the circumstances. There were no people available and no sniping equipment, but I knew exactly what had to be done. I had pushed for a sniping program in the Marine Corps before Vietnam and this was an opportunity to put what many of us had been advocating into practice, in a combat environment no less. I couldn't wait to get started!

Before I left the States I had put together a list of every Distinguished Rifle and Pistol shooter who was serving with the Marine Corps in Vietnam. I was fortunate enough to locate MSgt Don Reinke to begin with and the sergeant became the cornerstone of the organization.

We located an oversized CON-X box [a large reusable box intended for "containerized shipping"] which we used for storage and a makeshift office. MSgt Reinke soon had everything shipshape and also much of the equipment we needed to get started. Several other shooters were brought into the fold, and it was quickly decided that before we could train the regimental snipers with any credibility we would have to do the job ourselves first.

[**NOTE:** The nucleus of the original First Marine Division Scout-Sniper instructor team was made up of the following:

M.Sgt. Donald L. Reinke
Gy.Sgt. James D. Wilson
S.Sgt. Charles A. Roberts
Sgt. Carlos N. Hathcock

Although all of the men were accomplished marksmen, only Hathcock had received prior sniper training.]

Working with the division Recon troops and analyzing the G-3 situation reports, we decided that Hill 55 looked like an excellent place to go hunting.

[**NOTE:** Hill 55 was a strategically located elevation approximately 7 miles south of the Da Nang air base. The numbers indicated the height of the hill in meters. In this case, 55 meters or 180 feet. A considerable amount of lst MarDiv sniping activity took place on or near Hill 55 during the Vietnam War.]

We met with unit commanders, debriefed patrols, and soon identified a pattern for a VC sniper unit that was making life miserable for the Marines on that hill.

Operating under the assumption that it takes one to catch one or, it takes a sniper to effectively neutralize another sniper, we started hunting down the Viet Cong snipers one at a time. In approximately three weeks the incoming sniper fire had been reduced from 30 or more rounds each day to where it was rare to take even a single round of VC sniper fire on any given day.

Building on that experience, we started sending teams out with patrols for drop-off operations, utilizing sniper teams in long-range blocking forces and insertions by helicopter deep into "Indian Country" [a generic term used by Marine Corps combat personnel to define and/or describe the areas or regions with high levels of Viet Cong activity]. While this was going on we prepared a training syllabus and worked on the lesson plans for our sniper school.

[**NOTE:** Although specific dates remain unconfirmed, by all accounts (Marine Corps historical information and the recollections of personnel then involved), the earliest lst MarDiv sniping activity by Captain Land and his "hand-picked" sniper-instructor team took place during October 1966. Plans for sniper training were finalized in late October. The "first" sniper school was held in November 1966. Initial training consisted of 5 days of classes with at least as much time spent in the field for on-the-job training" (OJT). Early lst MarDiv sniping activity took place at Hill 55; sniper training was conducted at the Hoa-Cam range opposite Hill 327 near Da Nang.]

I prepared a Division Order establishing the criteria for selecting personnel and spoke with many of the commanding officers trying to motivate them to send us good field Marines with excellent marksmanship backgrounds to train as snipers.

The firing range we used for sniper training was located in an unsecured area so it was necessary to sweep the road to the range every morning and also, to sweep the firing line before we started our daily training. That effort paid off because on one morning we found two grenades had been set up with trip wires directly on the firing line. There weren't many things you took for granted in Vietnam.

We didn't have targets that could be raised and lowered for scoring purposes. The range was laid-out using artillery powder canisters [155mm propellant canisters] as range markers at 100-yard intervals. When they were struck by a round they gave a resounding ring and it was easy to tell that a hit had been made. Also, their subdued color [olive drab] made the canisters difficult to see and they provided some realism to the range by making it seem more like a battlefield than a training area.

For firing training we would start off at 50 yards using C-ration boxes with small black bulls-eyes applied with grease pencils. The boxes were used for zeroing the rifles but the primary purpose was to have the sniper work to shoot a group. The boxes were then moved out to 100 yards. We established a standard that was 1 inch at 100 yards or a minute of angle. When the sniper was able to group consistently, we would move out to a known distance of 400 yards shooting at the powder canisters to ensure that we were properly sighted in.

When we were certain the rifle was sighted-in at 400 yards, we worked the shooter with an observer as a team. The observer selected the target, provided the information to the shooter and the shooter engaged the target.

In the beginning, the sniper equipment we employed were Model 70 Winchesters with Unertl telescopes and both M1C and M1D rifles. Most of the equipment were M1 sniping rifles, however. The M1C made use of the 4-power Stith-Kollmorgen telescopic sight and the M1D was equipped with the M84 military scope.

[**NOTE:** Of all the ad hoc sniping equipment fielded by the Marine Corps early on, this is the first time combat use of the USMC Stith-Kollmorgen telescope in RVN has been acknowledged. According to Major Land, the M1 sniper rifles were obtained "in country," and the Winchester ("target") rifles came from the United States. In keeping with Marine Corps practice in RVN, match-grade ammunition was used for training and combat purposes.]

The rifles were in rough shape and we took them to the 3d Force small arms maintenance shop to have them reworked.

[**NOTE:** The III MAF Force Logistic Support Group in RVN was built around the Third Service Battalion (3d MarDiv) and elements of the Third Force Service Regiment from Okinawa. The FLSG maintained headquarters at Da Nang, while two force logistic support units serviced Chu Lai and Phu Bai. When the First Marine Division joined III MAF in 1966, it brought along the First Force Service Regiment, and the FLSG was expanded into the Force Logistic Command or FLC.]

Fortunately, there was an armorer at the shop who had been with the rifle team and knew exactly what it took to accurize a rifle. I can't recall his full name; but we called him "Little Johnson."

As it turned out the timing couldn't have been better as the sergeant was going on R&R to Okinawa and he brought back some bedding material and the tools he needed to accurize the rifles properly.

Considering the condition of the equipment and the limited resources, SSgt Johnson was able to make a significant improvement to the accuracy of the rifles. Once the equipment was up to standards and the training completed, we took to the field with the students for some on-the-job training.

The students were usually employed with two teams of two men each and one of our instructors as the NCOIC or Team Leader. The biggest difficulty we faced was that none of the officers we were working with had any training, background or experience in employing a sniper team.

For example, on one occasion a company commander ordered one of our sniper teams to move approximately 100 yards in front of the unit's position, instructing them to climb trees so they could observe and shoot much better.

Fortunately, we had an instructor with the unit who was able to reason with the company commander, otherwise the sniper team would have been facing certain death.

Under the circumstances, much of my time was spent talking to the commanding officers and unit leaders trying to educate them in the capabilities, proper employment and care of the sniper. With the proper use of snipers as genuine a concern as it was, we always felt more comfortable when we were detached and operating on our own. It was standard practice to regularly admonish the teams to "watch out for the grunts—they'll get you killed."

Perhaps the greatest problem we had with the unit leaders was their lack of understanding of what a sniper was capable of. Their training had focused on concentrated fire and fire superiority and while the majority of the Marine combat units were reasonably effective at 150 to 200 yards, it was difficult for them to comprehend that an individual rifleman could place a single shot on target at 700 yards on a regular basis and also possess the capability of making a kill at 1000 yards. In many respects, the concept was alien to them.

It took time for all of this to come together, of course, but, the results were certainly what we expected. There were a number of people who made the program work. The men I was fortunate to have with me were tough and extremely resourceful. They were also some of the best marksmen in the Marine Corps. Without the support and enthusiasm of General Nickerson, however, it is doubtful that the 1st Marine Division sniping program would have been as successful as it was in Vietnam.

Major Land, the Marine officer responsible for establishing the Vietnam-era First Marine Division sniper program, is internationally recognized as an authority on firearms and advanced marksmanship training. In addition to his involvement with 1st MarDiv sniper operations in South Vietnam, Land served as the commanding officer of the Marine Security Guards at the U.S. Embassy in Saigon, and the marksmanship coordinator for the Corps.

A *Miami News* photo of Capt. E.J. Land Jr., taken in December 1965 while Land was competing in South Florida with the Marine Corps Pistol Team. In a matter of months, the Marine officer would find himself in Vietnam organizing a sniper program for the First Marine Division. (Pat Canova.)

Right: 2nd Lt. Dale Luedlke (1st MarDiv) with a Winchester rifle used to shoot a Viet Cong at a distance of "1200 yards with his first shot" (27 June 1966). The Model 70 is a regular "sporting" or "hunting" rifle with a standard barrel. There is no telescopic sight. The .30-caliber (.30-06) rifle is a good example of the sniping equipment pressed into service by the Marine Crops during early combat in Vietnam. (U.S. Marine Corps.)

Left: One of the few known combat photos depicting early First Marine Division sniping activity. A Marine marksman makes use of an M84-equipped M1D sniper rifle at Hill 55 south of Da Nang. A considerable amount of sniping activity took place on or near Hill 55 during the formative stages of the 1st MarDiv sniper program in late 1966. Although Model 70 Winchesters were used early on, "the majority" of the 1st MarDiv sniper rifles were .30-caliber M1C and M1D rifles obtained in South Vietnam. (Edward J. Land Jr.)

A typical M1D sniper rifle with the M84 telescopic sight. The 2.2-power telescope was designed and developed for use with the M1 rifle during World War II. The overall length with rubber eyepiece and extended sunshade was 13.188 inches, with a tube diameter of .870 inch. While hardly a state-of-the-art weapon system when the conflict in Vietnam escalated, an accurized M1D firing match-grade ammunition was more than equal to the task in Southeast Asia. Although limitations of the issue telescope did little to enhance the long-range capability of the M1D, there were Marine snipers who expressed a preference for the .30-caliber semiautomatic sniper rifle during early action. (Peter R. Senich.)

Winchester Model 70 (serial no. 48218) with a USMC contract 8-power Unertl telescopic sight (no. 2282). A Winchester "Standard Rifle" in original form, the weapon had its "sporter barrel" replaced with a 24-inch medium-heavy target barrel during the course of Marine Corps service. The barrel channel (stock) was enlarged to accommodate the thicker barrel. According to Winchester records, rifle no. 48218 was manufactured in 1941. (Cors Collection.)

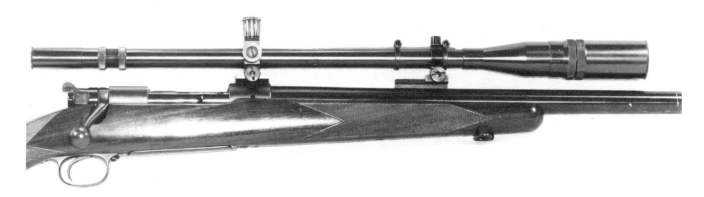

Close-up view, USMC Model 70 (no. 48218) with Unertl contract scope. Although medium-heavy target barrels supplied by Winchester (24-inch length) and commercial suppliers (26-inch length) were reportedly used to rebarrel some of the World War II Marine Corps Model 70s during the 1950s, in this case, the target barrel was made by Winchester and bears a 1952 date of manufacture. Many of the same rifles were shipped out as supplemental sniping equipment during early Marine Corps involvement in Southeast Asia. (Cors Collection.)

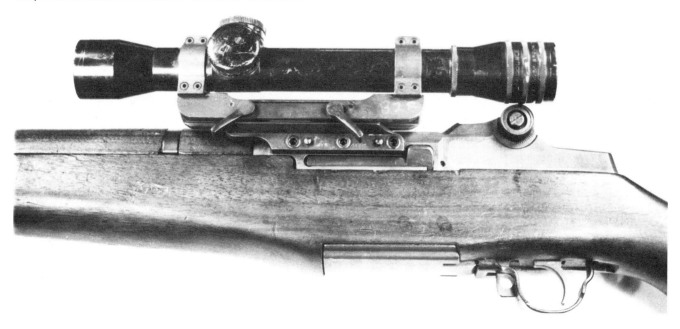

An M1C sniper rifle with a USMC Stith-Kollmorgen Model 4XD telescope. The 4-power scope was slightly over 11 inches long with a main tube diameter of approximately 1 inch. The unusually large elevation and windage knobs (1 1/8-inch diameter) were designed to meet Marine Corps specifications. Kollmorgen 4XD rifle scopes were manufactured for the Marine Corps on a contract basis following the Korean War. The telescope saw limited combat use with the M1C during the early stages of the First Marine Division sniper program in Vietnam. (Peter R. Senich.)

Vietnam-era M72 (.30-caliber) match cartridge. According to veteran Army and Marine corps snipers, the availability of match-grade rifle ammunition "was never a problem" in Vietnam. The experienced riflemen often referred to the special cartridges as "Camp Perry ammunition." (Peter R. Senich.)

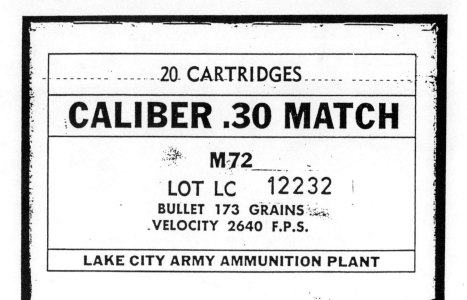

Typical M72 match ammunition issued to Marine Corps snipers in Vietnam. In this case, the cartridges were manufactured at the Lake City Army Ammunition Plant in 1966. The .30-caliber M72 cartridge was used with the Winchester Model 70 and the M1 Garand sniping rifles. The front (top) and the back of the 20-cartridge cardboard box are shown. (Lau Collection.)

A unique sequence photo showing Captain Land (right), the officer in charge of the 1st MarDiv sniping program, demonstrating a Unertl-equipped Browning machine gun to photographers and reporters at a sandbagged bunker on Hill 55—a "media event" that nearly cost Land his life when he inadvertently exposed himself to Viet Cong sniper fire during his briefing. Note the cross-section of the telescope mounting base. According to Land, the steel base was made by an RTE armorer ("Little Johnson") who had also rendered support to the early First Marine Division sniping effort. (Edward J. Land Jr.)

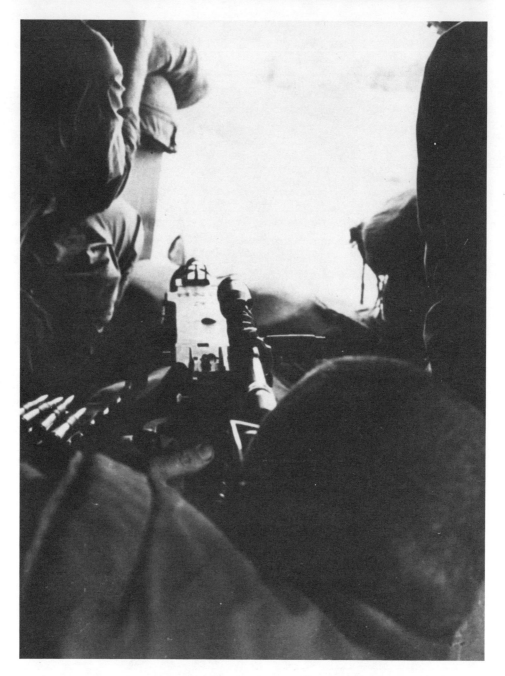

First Marine Division sniper personnel with the telescopic-sighted machine gun attempting to seek out and eliminate the VC sniper who came "damn close" to killing Captain Land while he was briefing reporters on Hill 55. The event is detailed in Charles Henderson's book, *Marine Sniper*. This is the first time the photographs taken during the memorable occasion have been published. (Edward J. Land Jr.)

A post-Vietnam photograph of Winchester Model 70 serial no. 47262 taken at the Marksmanship Training Unit (MTU) at Quantico, Virginia. Note the receiver bracket mounted on the left side of the receiver bridge and the screw-mounted front sight base. Mounting blocks for target sights were dovetailed or attached by screws as shown. The target telescope is a Unertl commercial model. The classic Marine Corps Winchester is detailed in another chapter. (Faught Collection.)

A Marine Corps M1D in combat trim complete with M84 telescope, leather cheek pad, flash hider, and sling. According to Vietnam-era documents, a small quantity of M1D rifles and M84 telescopes were obtained from the U.S. Army (Army Weapons Command) for Marine sniper use in RVN in 1965. Records also indicate that small lots of M1D rifles were procured from the Army as late as 1968. The photograph was taken after the war in Vietnam. (Faught Collection.)

Left: Even though this Marine Corps photograph has been published many times, no serious work on sniping in Vietnam would be complete without an appropriate illustration of Gy.Sgt. Carlos N. Hathcock. The photo was taken on 26 August 1965, the day Hathcock won the 1,000-yard National High-Power Rifle Championship, the Wimbledon Cup, at Camp Perry, Ohio. The original caption reads as follows: "Wimbledon Winner—Corporal Carlos N. Hathcock (left) is congratulated by Major General Richard G. Weede at the trophy presentation immediately following the Wimbledon Cup Match shoot-off. Hathcock out-shot some 2000 other shooters to capture the coveted trophy. General Weede, who is the assistant Chief of Staff, G-3, HQMC, was at Camp Perry to observe the shooting and was a spectator when Corporal Hathcock won the match." Said Hathcock in the book *Marine Sniper* (Stein and Day 1986): "The day that I won the Wimbledon Cup was special. It was the biggest day of my life as far as shooting goes." The win at Camp Perry came the day after Hathcock went Distinguished. One of the foremost soldiers of the Vietnam War, Hathcock has been featured in numerous publications in recent years, wherein his marksmanship accomplishments, his 93 confirmed kills as a Marine sniper, and his extraordinary heroism during his second tour of duty have been thoroughly documented. As part of the Foreword in *Marine Sniper*, Major Land had this to say about Hathcock: "To be a nationally recognized shooting champion takes a special kind of individual. To be effective on the battlefield as a sniper requires even more extraordinary qualities. Gunnery Sergeant Carlos Hathcock is one of those rare individuals who has carved a niche in Marine Corps history by being both." (U.S. Marine Corps.)

The Carlos N. Hathcock benefit drawing rifle (1995), a contemporary M700 Remington reconfigured to Marine Corps specifications. The unique rifle possesses the principal characteristics of a Vietnam-era M700/M40 USMC sniper rifle, including an original issue 3X-9X variable-power "green scope" rebuilt by the Redfield firm. In addition, the stock features a German silver inlay, a "White Feather," to signify the small feather Hathcock wore in his bush hat while plying his trade as a Marine sniper in Vietnam. Also pictured is a copy of *Marine Sniper*, an account of Hathcock's combat activities in South Vietnam. Even though it would be difficult to get the man largely responsible for the project to admit to it, the idea for the rifle, to help defray the mounting medical expenses for the Marine warrior, originated with Archie Mayer, a retired Marine gunnery sergeant, competitive shooter, and close friend of Hathcock. With the crossroads of the Marine shooting fraternity in the Quantico area centered at a local institution known as the Triangle Reloading Bench (TRB), the owner-operator, Mayer, was in a position to enlist the "best hands" in the shooting business to bring this unique rifle and the concept of a benefit drawing to the point of reality. Even though the drawing will have taken place by the time this book is published, it was important to focus attention on the comradeship that exists between Marine Corps veterans. (George E. Hijar.)

"There's never a bond, old friend, like this — We have drunk from the same canteen!"

—Charles Graham Halpine

CHAPTER 5

THE MODEL 70 WINCHESTER

The Winchester Model 70 bolt-action rifle, while never officially adopted for field use, was employed by Army, Navy, Air Force, and Marine Corps marksmen for one combat application or another during World War II, Korea, and again in Southeast Asia.

From the time of its introduction some five years prior to World War II, the Model 70 in its various forms was considered to be one of the finest commercial rifles (if not the finest) then available for hunting and competitive match shooting. As such, the Model 70 was highly regarded by many in the military who considered this rifle both extremely efficient and readily adaptable for specialized use.

NOTE: According to Winchester authority Dean H. Whitaker in *The Model 70 Winchester: 1937–1964* (Taylor Publishing Co. 1978), a standard reference work on the "pre-64" Model 70:

> Developed and first marketed during the lean depression years of the 1930s, the rifle became an instant success for a variety of reasons. First, the Model 70 was, in reality, a modified and improved version of an earlier bolt-

action rifle, the Model 54. This rifle had been marketed by Winchester some years earlier in an attempt to meet the growing demand for a quality bolt-action repeater. Secondly, the new rifle was a quality firearm, well-designed and well-made. Thirdly, the rifle was, from the beginning, an accurate one. This popularized it immediately with target shooters and varmint hunters. In addition, the rifle was offered in a great variety of styles and calibers, thus assuring a wide spectrum of market appeal. Also contributing to its popularity was the fact that the new rifle was a Winchester, with the company name and mystique that is so closely interwoven with the fabric of American history.

Even though the Marine Corps had seriously considered adopting the Model 70 for sniper use in 1941 on the basis of recommendations set forth in *Equipment for the American Sniper*, an official report by Capt. George O. Van Orden and Chief Marine Gunner Calvin A. Lloyd, it ultimately decided against the Winchester rifle in 1942.

Nevertheless, according to firsthand accounts, a fair number of unauthorized telescope-equipped "personal and Marine Corps property" Model 70s brought the reality of war to Japanese combat personnel during the early stages of World War II in the South Pacific.

In the years following the war, Winchester continued development of its Model 70 with extremely heavy barrels to meet the requirements of long-range target shooting. The Model 70 came in three target weights of about 9 1/2, 10 1/2, and 13 pounds, and after having first been designated the National Match and Target Grade, the rifles were later redesignated Standard and Heavy Weight, with the 28-inch-barrel Bull Gun rounding out the trio. All three rifles were correctly stocked for telescopic sights and metallic sights as well (special receiver and target front sights).

NOTE: Though fitted with the target or marksman stock, the rifle referenced as the "Standard" target model made use of a barrel similar in weight and configuration to the Model 70 "sporter" or "hunting" rifle.

There is little to be said about the quality and desirability of the Model 70 rifles, which were just about the only over-the-counter factory arms made for target shooting after the war. There just were not enough "big bore" competition shooters to induce other manufacturers to enter into the market. As a result, Model 70 target rifles gained considerable favor among military rifle teams for match shooting.

Apart from the occasional use of telescope-equipped Model 70s by a variety of U.S. military personnel during the Korean War, the most notable combat application of the Winchester rifle predating its field use in Southeast Asia came early in 1952 at the hands of the late Lt. Col. William S. Brophy, USAR (Ret.)

NOTE: In addition to Army and Marine Corps combat use best described as "limited," "Model 70s with telescopes" were used during naval operations in Korea, recall veteran navy personnel. By all accounts, the rifles were directed against individuals and small groups of enemy personnel near the shoreline.

While attached to IX Corps Ordnance as a captain, Bill Brophy visited several field units for the purpose of discussing the tactical employment of snipers and the equipment necessary for effective sniping.

Using a Winchester target rifle furnished at his own expense (.30-06 Model 70 Bull Gun with 28-inch barrel, mounting a 10-power, 2-inch objective Unertl target telescope), Captain Brophy and individuals trained to handle this equipment were responsible for several enemy casualties at 1,000-plus yards. Despite general consensus that equipment of this type could be maintained under combat conditions in the hands of trained marksmen, the official viewpoint regarding sniper weapons of special configuration (other than standard issue) remained one of particular disdain, due to the difficulty in field supply and replacement of nonstandard parts. Consequently, despite Captain Brophy's efforts in this case, bolt-action target-grade rifles saw only limited sniper use in Korea.

Interestingly, in a segment of the extensive *Study of Sniper Rifles, Telescopes and Mounts* (Project

No. 757, 31 August 1951) conducted by the Marine Corps Equipment Board at Quantico, Virginia, the Winchester Model 70 was reconsidered for sniper use but rejected for essentially the same reasons that were cited in 1942. According to the 1951 study:

> There is no Marine Corps requirement for a special rifle for use by snipers in the Marine Corps. It is undesirable to inject another rifle into the supply system, and if another rifle is injected into the supply system, it is necessary to inject non-standard ammunition for this rifle into the supply system in-order to exploit fully any gain in accuracy. The U.S. Rifle, Caliber .30, M1C is sufficiently accurate for use by snipers in the Marine Corps.

Despite its rejection, the review board held the Winchester in high regard:

> Investigation of the better grades of commercial rifles indicates that the Model 70 Winchester is the most accurate American made rifle, Caliber .30 on the market.

NOTE: Even though the Marine Corps was reluctant to "inject non-standard ammunition" into the supply system in 1951, the field use of match-grade rifle ammunition became an integral part of the USMC sniper program during the Vietnam War. Judging from the comments of Marine Corps personnel then involved, there were no supply problems associated with combat use of match ammunition. In fact, some of the men questioned on this point indicated that the availability of match ammunition was always the "least of their concerns" while engaged as snipers.

When events in South Vietnam called for direct U.S. military intervention, The Model 70 Winchester, though previously rejected as a sniper rifle, wound up as the quasi-official sniping arm of the Marine Corps.

Starting out as the sole specialized Marine sniper armament, the first Model 70s pressed into service in Vietnam (12 rifles), from the Third Marine Division Rifle Team, were originally used in rifle matches including the National Matches at Camp Perry, Ohio (Winchester Model 70 target rifles ["factory heavies"] with heavy barrels and marksman stocks).

As a matter of interest, when asked if the sniper cadre had any knowledge of where the original Model 70 sniping rifles came from, Major Russell replied:

> We didn't know the origin of the first batch of rifles we received in Vietnam. We were simply told one day that they could be picked up at the III MAF armory.

When these turned out to be too few, additional Model 70 rifles fitted with target barrels and either modified standard stocks (enlarged barrel channel) or factory target/marksman stocks were shipped to South Vietnam as well.

Both 3X-9X variable-power "MARINE" scopes (so marked) of Japanese manufacture, and World War II-era Unertl "USMC-SNIPER" 8-power telescopic sights saw early use with the .30-caliber Winchester rifles.

In addition to the two batches of Model 70s, a small quantity of M1D service rifles mounting the 2.2-power M84 telescopic sight were also sent to Vietnam as supplemental equipment.

A firsthand account of the efforts to furnish 3d MarDiv with sniper equipment is provided by Maj. William K. ("Kam") Hayden, USMC (Ret.):

> I was officer-in-charge of the Marksmanship Training Unit at Quantico when Winchester made major changes to their Model 70 rifle in 1964. The service teams were still permitted to shoot the match rifle (bolt-action) in competition from 200 to 600 yards, and we used Model 70 rifles for that purpose.
> We were concerned about a supply of spares for the Model 70s we had on-

hand, and I was very pleased to discover a quantity of about 85–90 .30-caliber Model 70 Winchester rifles listed in the Defense Department listing of excess property.

Items appearing on the list are excess where they are but may be usable elsewhere and are procurable by the organizations of the Department of Defense for the cost of shipping.

We ordered the rifles from their location at MCSC [Marine Corps Supply Center], Albany, Georgia, thinking they were recreational equipment and probably in poor condition. When the rifles arrived we were elated to find they were "sniper pattern" rifles. The rifles, with medium-heavy target weight barrels and sporter stocks, had been used by Marine shooters in national competition in the early 1950s. At that time the NRA had placed a weight limit on the NRA Match Rifle which precluded use of both a target barrel and a target/marksman stock. The weight limit remained in effect until 1957.

The rifles were in excellent condition, and one, I recall, had a tag with the name of SSgt Don L. Smith, USMC, the 1953 National High Power Match Rifle Champion, hanging from the trigger guard. The Model 70s were virtually identical to the rifle recommended by George O. Van Orden and Calvin A. Lloyd in their World War II study of sniper equipment for the Marine Corps. The rifles went into storage and were still there when I was transferred to HQMC for assignment to the Marksmanship Branch of G-3 (AO3M).

When a division deployed, one of the routine preparations was to ask HQMC for disposition instructions for RTE (Rifle Team Equipment). When Third Marine Division was preparing to ship out to Vietnam, the division ordnance officer, William W. McMillan, sent a message requesting such instructions to CMC (AO3M). I was serving in the Marksmanship Branch at the time as assistant to Branch Head, Col. William Barber. We replied to the routine portion of the message with instructions to ship the RTE to MCSC, Barstow, California. In this case, however, McMillan's message contained an additional request; Commanding General 3d MarDiv requested retention of the Model 70 target rifles (heavy target barrels and target/marksman stocks), as his intention was to form a sniper unit in RVN. I got in touch with Bill McMillan for more detail before drafting a response; 3d MarDiv planned to purchase 3X-9X variable-power sporting scopes for their target rifles. When I described the Model 70s still in storage at Quantico to McMillan and asked if his general would like those also, his response was very enthusiastic.

While the MTU at Quantico (RTE shop) was preparing the additional Model 70 rifles for shipment to 3d MarDiv, we called upon our supply system to search their inventories for the Unertl 8-power target-type "SNIPER" marked scopes that had been originally procured for the World War II M1903 Marine sniper rifle. The scopes were located [MCSC, Albany, Georgia] and shipped along with the rifles.

NOTE: Although many match shooters simply referred to a target barrel as a "heavy barrel," for the sake of clarification, the typical .30-06 Winchester target barrel was 24 inches in length with a muzzle diameter of .790 inch (nominal) and was often referenced as a "medium-heavy" barrel. The Bull Gun barrel, otherwise defined by Winchester as *the* heavy barrel, was 28 inches long with a muzzle diameter of .840 inch (nominal). Both barrels were "straight-shanked," and some, but not all, were counterbored at the muzzle. Although some USMC Model 70 team rifles had been fitted with 26-inch barrels, there is no way of knowing if any of these were sent to Vietnam for sniper use. Except for the Model 70 hunting or sporting rifles ("Standard Rifle") that reportedly saw duty in RVN, so far as it is known, the bulk of the Marine Corps Model 70s fielded in Southeast Asia made use of the 24-inch target barrel. As a matter of interest, the 24-inch Model 70 Standard Rifle barrel had a .600-inch muzzle diameter (nominal).

While the Marine Corps used the Model 70 to greatest advantage during this period, the Winchester rifle was also employed by Army personnel for sniping in Vietnam. Though it is rarely noted, Army field use of the "Model 70 Winchester" in a sniping capacity is referenced in various ordnance documents dating from the war in Vietnam. However, whether such use was part of the ad hoc sniping equipment fielded by U.S. combat personnel and units during this hectic era or "official issue" if only on a battalion or regimental level, the extent of this activity has not been clearly defined.

An example of Army use of this weapon was noted by CWO4 Thomas F. Shannon, U.S. Army (Ret.), a combat veteran of Korea with two tours of duty in RVN. As Shannon relates:

> From what I could tell the 1st Division began using M70 rifles in the spring of 1966 along with a unique method of inserting sniper personnel into VC-held areas [the 1st Infantry Division deployed to Vietnam in stages from July through October 1965; the Winchester rifles were sent to RVN "from the States"]. One of a line of helicopter gunships, without skipping a beat or losing its place, would close with the ground at an appropriate place, the snipers would jump, and the chopper was on its way with no one the wiser. Of course, the Viet Cong never knew they had an Army sniper team in their backyard.

Even though match-conditioned M14 rifles emerged as the principal Army sniper issue, so far as can be determined, some of the earliest Army sniping activity in RVN was carried out with telescope-sighted Model 70 Winchester rifles.

As one Army officer, a combat veteran of Vietnam with rifle team experience, summarized the matter, "The Marine Corps didn't have any lock on the Model 70 in Southeast Asia."

NOTE: The U.S. Army had procured Model 70 rifles during World War II and continued this practice after the war. Model 70 rifles in .30-06 and magnum calibers were as well received by the Army as they were by the Marine Corps. In one form or another, the Winchester rifles were fielded for various reasons, including rifle team competition. The Model 70 rifles were categorized as "Commercial Rifles" and were referenced in Department of the Army manuals through the years. Of further interest in this case, 30/338 Magnum team rifles would serve as "comparison items" during Vietnam-era "Rifleman and Sniper Capability Testing" conducted by the United States Army Marksmanship Training Unit (USAMTU) based at Ft. Benning, Georgia. The Model 70 Winchester was certainly no stranger to the Army.

While the Model 70 Winchester would serve as the Marine Corps' principal sniping rifle during 1965 and 1966, in an effort to address the obvious need for suitable sniper equipment, the sweeping Headquarters Staff (HQMC) memorandum from 27 November 1965 (the blueprint for the Vietnam-era Marine Corps sniping program), in addition to making recommendations affecting Scout-Sniper training and personnel, outlined the following "issue requirements" for Marine Corps sniping rifles and telescopes:

> The total requirement for the entire Marine Corps, including the active forces, schools, mobilization structure, 20 division months supply block, and attrition factors is approximately 550 rifles complete with telescope, equipment and repair parts.
> The following items have been shipped to the 1st and 3d Marine Divisions:
>
> 20 M1D caliber .30 sniper's rifles (3d MarDiv)
> 53 Model 70 Winchester rifles, caliber .30-06 (3d MarDiv)
> 59 8X Unertl telescopic sights (3d MarDiv)
> 20 M1D caliber .30 sniper's rifles (1st MarDiv) . . .

New procurement will be necessary in order to meet the total requirement of approximately 550 weapons.

NOTE: So far as can be determined, the "20 M1D" sniper rifles were procured from the U.S. Army

(U.S. Army Weapons Command, Rock Island, IL), the "53 Model 70 Winchester rifles" came from the USMC Weapons Training Battalion (Marksmanship Training Unit) Quantico, Virginia (the "12 rifles" cited earlier were 3d MarDiv team rifles), and the "59 8X Unertl telescopic sights" were drawn from the Marine Corps Supply Center at Albany, Georgia. Even though elements of the First Marine Division had deployed to RVN beginning in August 1965, it is not known if the "20 M1D" rifles mentioned were sent directly to Vietnam or to the division then based on Okinawa. Although evidence suggests these were also "purchased" from Army Weapons Command, in this case, the origin of the lst MarDiv sniper rifles remains obscure at present.

As the memorandum continues:

> It is the opinion of the staff if new procurement is provided, it should concentrate on the merits of either the Winchester Model 70 or the Remington Model 40X rifles. In either case the new weapon will be procured in 7.62mm caliber. The procurement of telescopic sights will have to be determined based on Marine Corps tactical requirements and the availability of commercial stocks or manufacturing schedules which are compatible to our needs.
>
> It is estimated that the time required to determine the appropriate weapon/telescope combination for use by the scout-sniper teams is approximately 60 days. Candidate weapons to be utilized are the M70 Winchester and Remington 40X rifles chambered for 7.62mm ammunition and equipped with various types of telescopic sights. Upon selection of the appropriate weapon/telescope combination, procurement action would be initiated. . . .
>
> Although there are sufficient Model 70 Winchester rifles available to meet the training requirements, there are no telescopic sights. Consequently, it is recommended that training not commence until rifles with scopes become available. Priority for new procurement should be to RVN units and then the Scout-Sniper Course. Simultaneous issue to both areas would be preferable.

Drawing in part from the "Action Recommended," the memo concluded as follows:

> The Assistant Chief of Staff, G-3 direct MTU Quantico, under the sponsorship of Marksmanship Branch, to conduct tests to determine which of the two proposed weapons best meet Marine Corps requirements on an expedited basis. Such test would include the selection of an appropriate telescopic sight.

Following approval by the chief of staff (4 December 1965), Weapons Training Battalion (WTB), Quantico, Virginia, was tasked with finding a satisfactory sniper rifle and telescopic sight for Marine Corps use in Vietnam.

Interestingly, in addition to calling for "weekly progress reports" in a handwritten notation to "G-3" (assistant chief of staff), as a part of the approval process in this case, the chief of staff emphasized that the project be completed "with all possible speed."

There was no mistaking the urgency of the matter: "Scout-Sniper Requirements" had become a priority to the U.S. Marine Corps.

Winchester Model 70 (G7044C) selected by Van Orden and Lloyd as the optimum rifle for Marine Corps sniper use in 1941. As the weapon was then described, "A military-target type, bolt action, 5-shot magazine, chambered for the standard military cartridge (.30-06). It weighs 10 1/2 pounds and is fitted with a medium-weight barrel 24 inches in length, with an accuracy life in excess of 3,000 rounds. It is mounted in a 'four-position' sporting-type stock having a high comb especially suited for telescopic sighting, a broad fore-end, a fully developed pistol grip, and is fitted with a sling swivel adjustable for position. Its bolt handle is so designed that the bolt may be actuated with the telescopic sight in its firing position." The rifle was also fitted with a Lyman No. 77 detachable front sight with interchangeable inserts, Lyman No. 48WH rear sight graduated in quarter minutes of angle, and standard telescopic sight bases. (U.S. Marine Corps.)

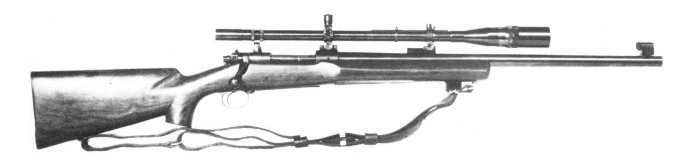

Winchester Model 70 (G7044C) with the Unertl 8-power Sniper Scope as tested by the Marine Corps beginning in late 1940. The Model 70/Unertl combination was considered suitable for sniping at any range up to at least 1,000 yards. Though highly regarded, the rifle and telescope were not adopted by the Marine Corps at the time. (U.S. Marine Corps.)

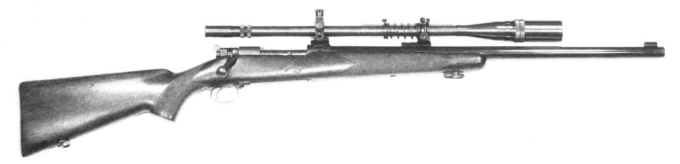

Winchester Model 70 (serial no. 47262), manufactured in 1941 with a commercial Unertl 8-power 1 1/4-inch objective "Combination Target Scope." A Marine Corps modification, the rifle was rebarreled for match shooting purposes in the years following World War II. In this form (24-inch medium-heavy target barrel, .790-inch muzzle diameter), the rifle was similar to the Winchester (G7044C) Model 70 variation recommended for USMC sniper use by Van Orden and Lloyd in 1941. Rifle no. 47262 is part of the Marine Corps small-arms collection. (Peter R. Senich.)

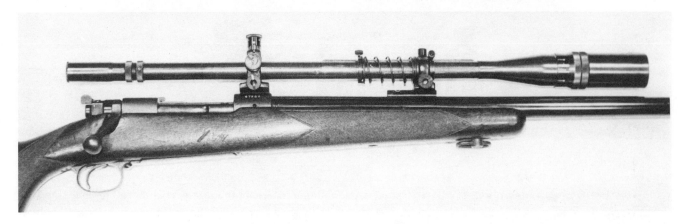

A close-up view of the USMC Model 70 Winchester (no. 47262) and Unertl telescopic sight with standard 1/4-minute click target mount, clamp ring, recoil spring, and dust caps in place on both ends of the scope. The Unertl Combination Target Scope was essentially the same as the USMC contract sight fielded with the M1903A1 sniper rifle. When introduced, the commercial model was available in 8, 10, 12, and 14 power. According to early Unertl sales literature, the "Combination Target Scope" was so-named because the "1 1/4-inch clear aperture objective" enabled the shooter to use the sight for shooting and spotting targets as well, "thus eliminating the need for a separate spotting scope." (Peter R. Senich.)

USMC Model 70 (no. 47262). The double-micrometer "split-frame" rear mounting is typical of those furnished with commercial target scopes. A three-point suspension mount, the steel micrometer screws were milled, hardened, and lapped in their own bearings to ensure accuracy; all steel parts and mounting screws were hardened accordingly. The dovetail was designed to fit all standard target bases. Although World War II-era Model 70 rifles in the 40,000-50,000 serial number range have been categorized by some as "USMC serial block Model 70s," from all indications, the U.S. Army procured a considerable number of .30-06 Model 70 rifles from this same serial number range. Even though Winchester Model 70 rifles intended primarily for competition purposes were added to the small-arms inventories of both services after the Pacific War, in one form or another, the World War II-era Model 70 rifles continued to serve the Army and Marine Corps for many years. (Peter R. Senich.)

Marine Corps Model 70 (no. 47262) front mount and recoil spring assembly ("telescope recoil absorber"), which brought the scope back into position after firing. Offered as an accessory item, the Unertl recoil absorber was designed to fit any 3/4-inch tube and was often used with other target scopes as well. The recoil spring was not furnished with the USMC "Unertl 8-power Sniper" sights. The 1/8-inch "Pope-rib" (top) is clearly visible. The front mount also provided a three-point suspension for the telescope tube. (Peter R. Senich.)

Winchester Model 70 "Target Rifle," serial no. 47835, manufactured in 1941. The .30-caliber (.30-06) Marine Corps target rifle has a 24-inch medium-heavy barrel (.790-inch muzzle diameter) and the heavy "Target/Marksman" stock. The receiver is marked "U.S. Property" on the left side. According to personnel serving in Vietnam, "some" (but not all) of the Model 70 rifles fielded for sniper use bore the "U.S. Property" marking on the left side of the receiver ring (electric pencil). In this form, rifle no. 47835 is essentially the same as the first Model 70 rifles fielded for the Third Marine Division sniper program (12 rifles) in 1965. The rifle is part of the Marine Corps small-arms collection. (Hijar-Gluba-Griffiths.)

A close-up view of the Marine Corps Model 70 target rifle (no. 47835). The .30-caliber Model 70 Standard and Target Rifle receivers were the same for the most part; the size of the target stock forend is readily apparent in this view. As a matter of interest, although Model 70 standard rifles were rebarreled using the medium-heavy target barrel and standard stock with an enlarged barrel channel, from all indications the factory target rifles were also "restocked" using modified standard stocks during the course of Marine Corps service. In this case, however, the target barrel date will correspond with the rifle serial number and the year of manufacture (according to Winchester "experts," the last two digits of the year in which the barrel was made "were almost always stamped on the underside of the barrel" near the recoil lug until sometime during 1956). The vast majority of the rebarreled Model 70 standard rifles made use of "new Winchester barrels." The barrel dates do not correspond with the year the rifle was manufactured. Insofar as Winchester made no distinction between the serial numbering on an early Model 70 Standard or Target Rifle, there is no way of telling one from the other without examining the rifles. From all indications, the majority of the heavy - barrel Winchester rifles fielded in RVN for Marine sniper use were rebarreled Model 70 Standard Rifles. (Hijar-Gluba-Griffiths.)

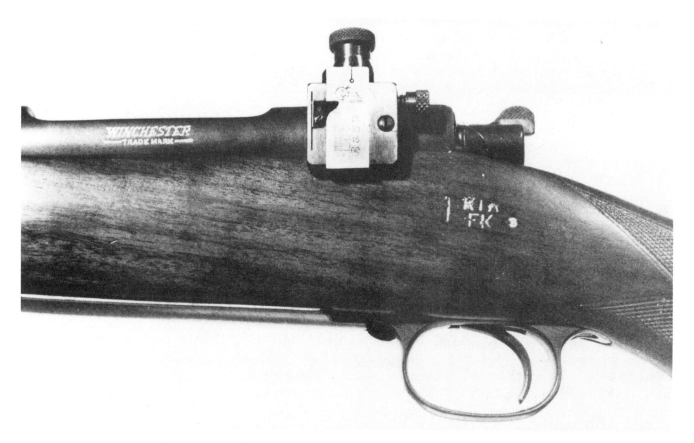

A prime example of a World War II manufacture (1942) "Army" Model 70 Winchester, serial no. 51734, with Lyman receiver sight and Rock Island Arsenal markings (RIA-FK3). (Dean H. Whitaker.)

An early 1950s .30-caliber (.30-06) Model 70 Winchester Rifle. Referenced by many as a "sporting" or "hunting" rifle, the Winchester M70 "Standard Rifle" was furnished with a hand-checkered, walnut pistol-grip stock (straight-comb), hinged steel floorplate, clip-feeding slot, 5-round box magazine, sling swivels, leaf sights, front sight hood, and a steel trigger guard, magazine follower, and butt plate. The 24-inch standard barrel had a .600-inch muzzle diameter (nominal). In this form, the Model 70 was 44 5/8 inches in length with the 24-inch barrel and weighed 7 3/4 pounds without a sling. The most common Model 70s, apart from the early target variations, .30-06 M70 Standard Rifles had been procured by the Marine Corps as a matter of course before and during World War II. Various USMC armorers recall prewar Model 70 rifles with serial numbers going back to original Winchester production (production began in late 1936; the Model 70 was introduced in 1937). Despite some unofficial combat duty as sniper equipment in the Pacific theater, the USMC Model 70 rifles were not procured with sniper use in mind. Winchester experts have advanced the theory that many of the World War II-era Model 70 rifles were originally procured by the Marine Corps for target shooting and hunting purposes by base personnel at the larger USMC installations. The rifles are believed to have been allocated to "Base Special Services" or simply "Special Services" to be checked out for recreational purposes. In some cases, the rifles were marked to indicate this use.

As a matter of interest, in addition to heavy-barrel rifles with sporter and target stocks, a limited number of Model 70 Standard Rifles fitted with hunting or target scopes were also fielded for Marine sniper use in Vietnam. For the most part, however, the Model 70 rifles employed in Southeast Asia in conjunction with the Marine Corps sniper program were rebarreled versions (medium-heavy barrel) of the .30-06 Standard Rifle procured during World War II. (U.S. Marine Corps.)

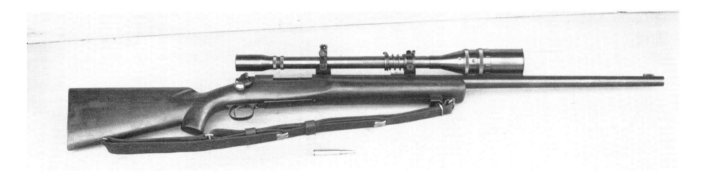

Winchester target rifle used by Capt. William S. Brophy, USA, for 1,000-yard sniping in Korea (1952). The .30-caliber Model 70 "Bull Gun" was fitted with a Unertl 10-power, 2-inch objective target telescope. The 28-inch barrel (.840-inch muzzle diameter) was often referenced as the "extra-heavy" barrel. The target, or marksman stock, was furnished with most of the Winchester "Bull Guns." (Brophy Collection.)

Captain Brophy with Winchester target rifle circa 1952. (Brophy Collection.)

A U.S. Army "Rifle, Cal. .30, Winchester, Model 70 Special Match Grade" target rifle (serial no. 409748) manufactured in 1957. According to Lt. Col. F.B. Conway, USA (Ret.), "The rifle was glass-bedded and fitted with Redfield International target sights when it came from Rock Island Arsenal." The medium-heavy barrel is 24 inches long (.790 inch muzzle diameter); the checkered "standard stock" has an enlarged barrel channel. (Conway Collection.)

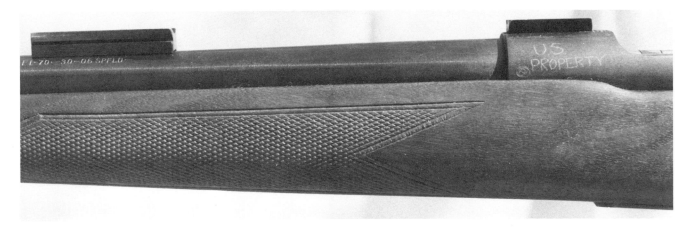

A left view of the Army Model 70 target rifle (no. 409748). Note the telescope mounting blocks, barrel markings, Winchester proof marks, and "U.S. Property" applied to the receiver (electric pencil). Except for minor details, the rifle is essentially the same as the Model 70s fielded for Marine sniper use in RVN. (Conway Collection.)

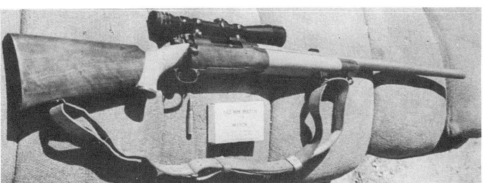

Above: Vietnam-era Winchester 7.62mm (.308) heavy-barrel target rifle mounting a Redfield 3X-9X variable-power commercial sight. The rifle was used by Air Force (USAF) Combat Security Police (CSP) to protect air bases against enemy infiltrators. Note the box of 7.62mm (M118) match ammunition below the rifle. (U.S. Air Force.)

Left: Examples of Redfield micrometer receiver sights (metallic sights) intended for match shooting purposes: the early and late Olympic (top), International with 1/8-minute and 1/4-minute adjustments (center), and the Palma. The sight attached to the left side of the receiver bridge. An appropriate front target sight was mounted on the barrel. (Conway Collection.)

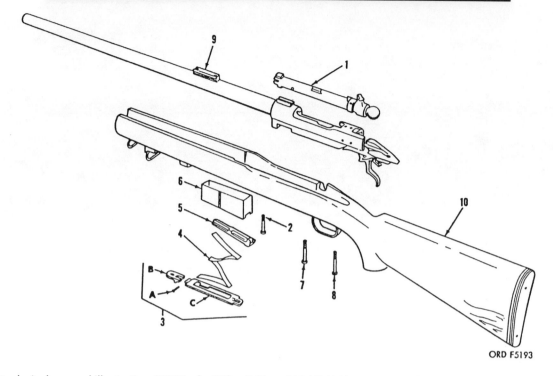

ORD F5193

An Army technical manual illustration (1963) of a "Rifle, Caliber .300 H& H Magnum" Model 70 Winchester Bull Gun (28-inch barrel). (U.S. Army.)

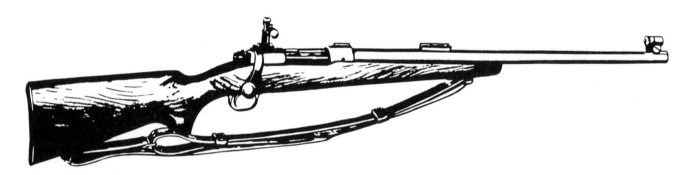

An Army illustration of a "Rifle, Cal. .30, Winchester Model 70 Special Match Grade," circa 1964. The heavy-barrel target rifle is fitted with a receiver sight and a target front sight. The Winchester target rifles fielded by the Army were intended primarily for competition purposes. The Model 70s were categorized as "commercial rifles" by the Department of the Army. (U.S. Army.)

CHAPTER 6

TARGET RIFLE

The Range or Combat

When it came to actual field use of the Model 70 Winchester in Vietnam, in spite of the fact that the USMC sniper-instructors tasked with training snipers were thoroughly familiar with the Model 70 in both standard and target configuration, the typical Marine sniper candidate possessed little knowledge of a Winchester rifle—especially a match or team rifle mounting a target telescope.

A heavy-barrel target rifle with a 24-inch telescopic sight made an "impressive package" to all but the most experienced riflemen. While some Marines reportedly viewed the Model 70 as "awfully damned heavy," most were keenly aware of the capabilities of an armorer-prepared Winchester target rifle and simply made the most of it.

NOTE: By all accounts, the appearance of the heavy barrel, the target scope, and the marksman stock on some of the rifles gave the impression of an extremely heavy weapon, when in fact, the Model 70 with the Unertl telescope and the M1D with the M84 sight were approximately the same weight (12 pounds ±). By comparison, the "firing weight" of a standard M14 rifle (fully loaded with sling) was listed at 10.32 pounds.

Comparative rifle weight and opinions notwithstanding, as a sniper rifle in the hands of a competent Marine marksman, the Model 70 was responsible for some truly phenomenal long-range shooting in Vietnam.

Even though telescopic-sighted Model 70s had found their way to combat zones in previous armed conflicts, this was the first time any of the U.S. armed services had fielded target rifles in the manner in which the Marine Corps was using the Winchester Model 70 in South Vietnam. Nevertheless, despite a long and storied association with "the Corps," the Model 70, as stated earlier, was not officially adopted for combat use.

Along with the heavy-barrel rifles fitted with modified standard or the target/marksman stocks, an unknown quantity of .30-caliber Model 70 Standard Rifles (otherwise known as "sporter" or "hunting" rifles) were subsequently procured in small batches from "commercial sources" for Marine sniper use in Southeast Asia. In addition, USMC property Model 70 "recreational rifles" (Base Special Services) were also sent to Vietnam in an effort to bolster the Marine Corps sniping effort until the Remington M700 sniper rifles were available for combat use.

NOTE: In one case, "10 sporter grade" Model 70 Winchester USMC recreational rifles were fitted with Pachmayr mounts and 3X-9X variable-power Bushnell rifle scopes by Sam A. Miller of Miller Gun Works located on Naha Air Force Base, Naha, Okinawa. (Miller, under contract to the government, provided gunsmithing services to military personnel. The Bushnell sights were made by a Japanese optical company.) The Winchester rifles were sent to Vietnam (mid-1966) for Marine Corps sniper use. According to Miller, "Some of the rifles were very worn, but I understand they were making kills at 1,000 yards with this equipment."

With sniper rifles in relatively short supply, the availability of suitable equipment had a direct bearing on the number of Marine snipers trained and fielded during 1966 in particular. Although official measures to field an entirely new sniping system based on the Remington M700 rifle were well under way by mid-1966, the new sniping equipment would not reach Vietnam in any appreciable quantity until early 1967.

As equal to the task of long-range firing as the Model 70 was, in fact, use of this system at shorter ranges presented an unusual problem for many of the Marine marksmen. The sighting limitations characteristic of a target scope (limited field of view) made it difficult to track and fire on moving targets at relatively close ranges.

NOTE: The term "field of view" was defined by the Marine Corps as follows:

> The field of view is the diameter or width of the picture seen through a scope, and is usually expressed in feet at 100 yards. At 200 yards this field would be twice the field stated at 100, and at 300 yards, three times, etc. Generally, the higher the power of the rifle scope, the smaller the field.

According to USMC technical information, the field of view for the "Unertl 8-power Sniper" sight employed with the Model 70 was listed as "11 feet at 100 yards." By comparison, a typical fixed-power hunting or field scope, as they were often referenced, could easily provide a field of view two or more times greater than a typical target scope.

For the sake of clarification, when a target telescope was used for match shooting as intended, the field of view was relatively unimportant since the primary purpose of the telescope was to view a stationary target. However, when a target sight was employed as a field scope for sniping purposes, in attempting to track targets moving to the right or the left, the closer the range, the more difficult it was to keep the target in view.

While hardly an insurmountable problem, a limited field of view had served as a principal reason the target scope was considered "unacceptable" for combat purposes where extremely diverse shooting conditions were normally encountered.

Alluding to this problem, veteran First Marine Division sniper Craig Roberts made an interesting comparison between the Unertl-equipped Model 70 Winchester and a standard M14 rifle in *The Walking Dead*, by Roberts and Charles W. Sasser (Simon & Schuster 1989):

> The Winchesters were good with long fields of fire. Otherwise, at shorter ranges, a standard M14 worked just as well. The M14 worked even better, in fact, with running targets since the target kept running out of the Winchester scope and you couldn't follow it. Half of the rice field shots we subsequently made in the Da Nang enclave could have been made better with the open sights on an M14.

Although Marine Corps field use of the M1903A1 Springfield and the M1 Garand sniping rifles has been thoroughly documented, information pertaining to the Model 70 Winchester in the role of a "Marine sniper rifle" has been relegated to obscurity. Therefore in the interest of providing the reader with the official viewpoint of the Model 70, as intended to enlighten Marine sniper candidates, information contained in *USMC, FMFM 1-3B, SNIPING*, October 1967, the initial draft edition of the Vietnam-era sniper training manual, is presented as follows:

> The two models of telescope-mounted rifles in use by Marine snipers are the M70 Winchester and the 7.62mm M700 Remington. They are similar in characteristics and appearance. Each is manually operated (bolt action), has a 5-round capacity, and a medium heavy barrel for improved accuracy. Although the tabulated data for these rifles cites their maximum effective range as 1000 meters, snipers have achieved point target accuracy at ranges in excess of 1000 meters.

Rifle, Caliber .30, Model 70, Winchester

The Model 70 is a caliber .30, bolt operated, shoulder weapon capable of mounting a telescope or iron sights. It is operated manually by means of a bolt handle which is an integral part of the bolt.

Cycle of Operation

From a closed bolt position, the bolt handle is rotated upward approximately 90-degrees and pulled to the rear until action is terminated by the bolt stop. This movement uncovers the topmost round in the magazine, allowing the follower and follower spring to force the cartridge up into the path of the bolt. As the bolt is pushed forward, it strips the top cartridge out of the magazine and slides it up the feed ramp and into the chamber. When the cartridge is fully seated, the bolt is rotated down engaging the locking lug, completing the cycle.

Safety

A safety lever, located on the top rear of the bolt sleeve, when locked, prevents firing the rifle until ready. On early models the weapon is safe when the lever is forward and to the left, and an arrow points in the direction of movement of the safety for firing. On recent models the weapon is safe when the lever is to the rear, and the word "fire" indicates the position of the lever for firing.

Bolt Removal

The bolt stop release is situated on the left rear of the receiver bridge. When depressed, it allows the bolt to be pulled straight to the rear and out of the weapon.

Floor Plate Release

The floor plate release is at the forward end of the trigger guard. When depressed, it quickly releases the rounds in the magazine by allowing the floor plate to snap out.

Telescope Mounting Blocks

The top of the barrel and the top of the receiver are drilled and tapped to accommodate the telescope mounting blocks.

Iron Sight Mounting Block

The barrel is also drilled and tapped at the muzzle end for receiving a block on which a front sight can be mounted. The left side of the receiver bridge is drilled for a rear sight.

Tabulated	Data
Caliber	30.06
Length	44 inches
Weight	10 lbs.
Weight with Unertl telescope	11 lbs. 9 oz.
Barrel length (medium heavy)	24 inches
Lands and grooves	4
Twist, right hand	1 turn in 10 inches
Trigger weight (recommended)	3 to 5 lbs.
Magazine capacity	5 rounds
Maximum effective range	1000 meters

Though the section describing the Model 70 safety lever does make reference to the safeties as "early" and "recent" models, a concise review of the different "safeties" found on the pre-1964 Winchester rifles and their relationship to this reference ("early" and "recent") appeared in Whitaker's *The Model 70 Winchester: 1937–1964*:

Safety Configuration

Three different standard safeties were fitted to the Model 70 during the years of production. These are known as the "Pre-War," the "Transition" and the "Late" safeties. As the names imply, the different safeties were fitted to rifles manufactured during the respective production eras. The "Pre-War" unit was utilized from 1936 until sometime shortly after World War II, around serial number 63,000. The "Pre-War" safety was located on the rear of the bolt, atop a flat, milled surface on the bolt sleeve. This positioning was convenient for use with iron sights, but was very cumbersome when a telescopic sight was mounted over the receiver.

The "Transition" safety was introduced shortly following World War II, around serial number 63,000. This safety was designed to accommodate the installation of telescopic sights without interference and was positioned so that the "fire" position was attained by rotating the lever forward in a counter-clockwise movement.

The "Transition" safety was utilized for approximately 2 1/2 years, being phased out sometime during 1948, around serial number 87,000, although it was installed sporadically for several years after 1948, until the production inventory was exhausted.

The "Late" safety was fitted on most rifles from late 1948 to the final production in 1963. Located on the right rear side of the bolt, similar to the "Transition" model, the "Late" model differs in shape from the "Transition" model, being endowed with an "L"-shaped lever and more generous surface area.

Of perhaps equal importance to defining the safety differences and their point in time in this case is the insight Whitaker's account provides into the approximate serial number ranges of the USMC Model 70 sniper rifles employed in RVN.

As for the field use of "iron sights" with the Model 70, however, although target sights (metallic sights) could be readily attached to the barrel and receiver of a typical Model 70 target rifle, with possible exceptions, they do not appear to have seen sniper use with the Model 70 in South Vietnam.

Even though there would be no way of determining when the last Model 70 was withdrawn from Marine Corps service in Vietnam, examples of the venerable Winchester/Unertl sniping system were still encountered long after the Remington M700 rifles were fielded in quantity.

Though many of the original Vietnam-era .30-caliber sniper rifles were reportedly in "bad shape" by that time, the weapons—and the scopes for that matter—had seen continuous combat in the hands of any number of Marine snipers in a tropical environment best described as "hostile" and still performed as well as could be expected.

Few men tasked with using the Model 70 for sniping purposes have voiced any serious complaints about this system. When opinions on the Winchester Model 70 are solicited, responses such as "a very reliable weapon" and "absolutely no problems" are usually in order.

The "Winchesters" had met the challenge and proven their worth in Southeast Asia.

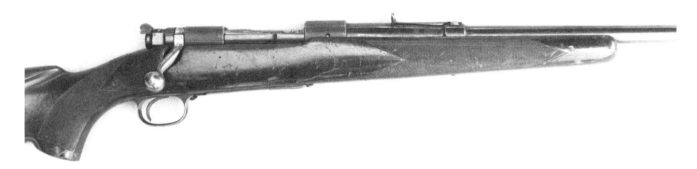

Winchester Model 70 "Standard Rifle," serial no. 46918, manufactured in 1941. The venerable .30-caliber (.30-06) rifle still has the original 24-inch standard barrel (.600-inch muzzle diameter) and hand-checkered "Standard Grade" stock. The unique specimen served as a "Base Special Services" rifle and was used for recreational purposes at Camp Pendleton, California. Although weapons of this type have been mentioned elsewhere, this is the first time photos of an original "BSS" rifle have been published. The rifle is part of the Marine Corps small-arms collection. (Hijar-Gluba-Griffiths.)

A close-up view of the Marine Corps Model 70 Standard Rifle (no. 46918). The matted surface of the receiver ring and bridge was typical of early Winchester production. Note the "clip-feeding slot," a feature found on most of the early Model 70s regardless of style. (Hijar-Gluba-Griffiths.)

A close-up view of the butt stock of USMC Model 70 no. 46918. The legend stamped into the stock stands for "Property of Camp Pendleton Base Special Services." At one time the rifle was used for target shooting and hunting at the MCB in California. Note the typical "Standard Grade" pistol-grip checkering. Although "BSS" rifles were reportedly sent to Vietnam as supplemental sniping equipment, the quantities involved and the circumstances surrounding their combat use have not been disclosed. (Hijar-Gluba-Griffiths.)

A typical "clip-feeding slot" machined into the receiver bridge of a "Transition" Model 70 Winchester. Although clip-slots were originally included on most of the Model 70 rifles, this feature was eventually eliminated on all configurations except the target/competition models. A clip-feeding slot could be obtained on a special order basis; however, the clip-slots found on Winchester and Remington rifles were virtually identical. (Dean H. Whitaker.)

Marine sniper sighting over a sandbag rest. Snipers were encouraged to use "artificial support" to steady their aim. The illustration provides a close-up view of the Model 70/Unertl system employed in Vietnam. The Winchester barrel markings are clearly visible in the original photograph. According to the III MAF caption (January 1966), "The Marine Corporal [Ronald A. Szpond] has been a sniper since November 1965." (U.S. Marine Corps.)

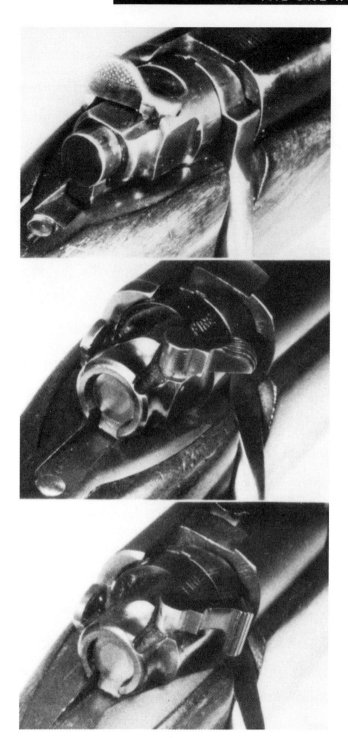

Safety configurations found on USMC Model 70 rifles. A typical "Pre-War" safety (top), a "Transition" safety, and a "Late" safety. According to Winchester authority Dean H. Whitaker, "Three different standard safeties were fitted to the Model 70 during the years of production." The safety differences and their operation were described in the draft edition of *USMC FMFM 1-3B, SNIPING* (October 1967). (Dean H. Whitaker.)

A close comparison of a solid and hollow Model 70 bolt-handle knob. The hollow variation began appearing "sporadically" on rifles serial numbered in the 215,000 range (1952). Though less obvious, the "sweep" or angle of the bolt handle was altered during the course of production as well. (Dean H. Whitaker.)

Marine marksmen practice firing from the sitting position. One of the four basic shooting positions used for sniper training. Snipers were taught to fire from the prone, sitting, kneeling, and standing positions. According to USMC training doctrine, "A sniper must assure the steadiest position possible which will allow observation of the target and target area and provide some cover and/or concealment." (U.S. Marine Corps.)

Another view of the Marine sniper (R.A. Szpond) firing from a sandbag rest. Note the early safety, solid bolt-handle knob, and "cloverleaf" receiver tang. The weapon characteristics are consistent with Model 70 rifles categorized as "early production." (U.S. Marine Corps.)

A comparison of the fore-end profiles of the Model 70 Winchester "standard stock" (top) and the "target stock." The broad base of the target/marksman stock fore-end ("beavertail") served to support the rifle and eliminate canting when fired from a rest. Target stocks remained virtually unchanged during the course of Winchester production. (Dean H. Whitaker.)

Winchester, Caliber .30, Model 70 Van Orden Sniper serial no. 254544 (1953) with "standard stock" (uncheckered) and 12-power Lyman Super Targetspot telescopic sight. The rifle was purchased from Evaluators Ltd. by the U.S. Army in August 1953 for tests involving various telescopic-sighted .30-caliber rifles, special long-range .50-caliber antitank rifles, and Browning (M2) machine guns, under the direction of Capt. William S. Brophy. The rifles marketed by Evaluators Ltd. were based on "special order Model 70s" obtained from Winchester. A highly respected organization catering to the weapon and equipment needs of law enforcement agencies and the military, Evaluators Ltd. was owned and operated by George O. Van Orden and his wife, Flora Mitchell Van Orden. The firm was located in Triangle, Virginia, near the Marine Corps base at Quantico. (U.S. Army.)

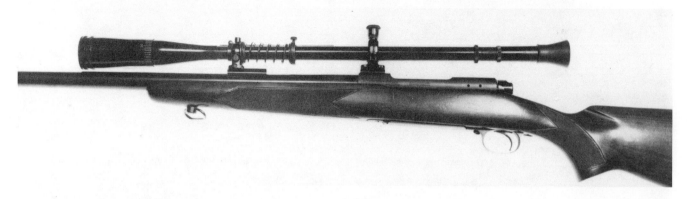

Winchester, Caliber .30, Model 70 Van Orden Sniper serial no. 272958 with checkered "standard stock" and 20-power Lyman Super Targetspot telescopic sight. According to a shipping manifest (Service Transport) signed by George O. Van Orden (3 August 1954), this rifle was part of the equipment sent to Camp Perry, Ohio, by Evaluators Ltd. for the 1954 National Matches. (Rosenbaum Collection.)

An original "Van Orden Sniper" target rifle with Army rifle team service to its credit. Model 70 no. 272958 is fitted with a 24-inch medium-heavy barrel dated 1954. The bolt assembly is polished and serial numbered to the rifle. "U.S. PROPERTY" markings are etched (electric pencil) on the left side of the receiver. The Lyman target scope (no. 21384) makes use of a Unertl "recoil absorber." The rubber eye cup, a Lyman accessory item, was often used on Unertl target scopes. (Rosenbaum Collection.)

A 20-power Super Targetspot telescopic sight (no. 17515) furnished to the Marine Corps by the Lyman Gunsight Corp. in 1949. A contract sight in this case, its tube is marked "USMC PROPERTY." The Super Targetspot came with a "3-point suspension" 1/4-minute click rear mount. The scope weighed 25 ounces and measured 24 3/8 inches long. The standard reticle was an extrafine cross hair; normal eye relief was 2 inches. A rubber eye cup, hardened steel bases, dust caps, and a wooden carrying case were included with each sight furnished to the Marine Corps. Storm Queen molded rubber lens covers were eventually offered as standard equipment. Of all the Targetspot scopes in the Lyman line, the Super Targetspot was the most successful. Introduced in 1937, the "Super" model was manufactured until 1978. In original form, the sight was available in 10-, 12-, and 15-power models. A 20-power version in 1949 and a 30-power model in 1953. Although Lyman target scopes were reportedly fielded in RVN by Army and Marine Corps marksmen, the specific models and the circumstances behind their use have not been clearly defined. (Peter R. Senich.)

SPECIFICATIONS FOR THE VAN ORDEN SNIPER

RIFLE, 30-06 SNIPER: 24 inch medium heavy barrel, precision grade, mounted in the Winchester M70 special clip-slotted receiver: barrel mounted with bases for Lyman 77A Front Sight and Lyman SuperTargetSpot Sighting Telescope (telescope not furnished); barrel and action hand bedded in dense walnut 4-Position Sniper Stock with length of pull, drop and pitch approximating that of the U.S. Rifle cal 30 M1903A1; stock smooth finished and drenched to saturation with linseed oil, without checkering or lacquer; 1 1/4" selected sling swivels with 1 1/4" first quality leather military sling; rifle equipped with Lyman 48WH 1/4' Micrometer Receiver Sight with Target Disc and Lyman 77A Front Sight with 9 interchangeable discs; triggers and actions finished to target standards with allowances for wear in training to result in durable smooth final performance without further adjustment; overall weight approximately 10 pounds; tested with Western 30-06 Super-Match 180gr Boattail Handload to assure zero and grouping within requirements of national competition; final assembly, inspection and test under supervision of experienced ordnance and target practice technicians; delivered complete with operating instructions, ammunition handbook, metallic and telescopic sight manuals, and warranted ready as received for competition without further modification or adjustment other than the determination of the user's zero.

George O. Van Orden
Brig.Gen., U.S.M.C., Ret'd
President

An original copy of the Evaluators Ltd. "Specifications for the Van Orden Sniper." The special M70s were reportedly among the USMC team rifles sent to South Vietnam as supplemental sniping equipment early in the war; when the rifles reached Vietnam, however, they were just issue sniper equipment. There is no way of knowing how the Van Orden Sniper performed in a combat environment. The extent of Marine Corps involvement with Van Orden and his Winchester rifles remains a topic of some debate. The Van Orden rifles were purchased by a variety of individuals and military organizations for match shooting purposes. (Blair M. Gluba.)

A close-up view of the Lyman Super Targetspot "split-frame" aluminum alloy 1/4-minute microclick rear target mount. When bases were installed on 7.2-inch centers, one click changed the group center 1/4 inch (1/4 minute) at 100 yards. The 3-point suspension mount was provided with nonrotating nylon "rocker-bearings" to hold the tube without marring. The front mount was also fitted with nylon bearings. The mounts were designed to fit all "standard dimension" target bases. (Peter R. Senich.)

A close-up view of a typical "USMC PROPERTY" marking on the Lyman Super Targetspot contract sight. Apart from the factory applied markings, Marine Corps target scopes were often marked "USMC PROPERTY" and eventually "U.S. PROPERTY" after 1962 with an electric pencil. Although some target scopes were procured by the military on a contract basis, most were apparently random purchases. (Peter R. Senich.)

An example of the typical wood "scope box" furnished with the Marine Corps 20-power contract sights. This is a standard commercial box with "USMC PROPERTY" markings applied (stamped) at the Lyman factory. The wooden box was 26 inches in length with electroplated hardware. The 20-power target scopes were intended for match shooting purposes. They were not procured with sniper use in mind. (Peter R. Senich.)

CHAPTER 7

SNIPER PLATOON

A Good Example

The Vietnam experiences of M.Sgt. William D. Abbott, USMC (Ret.), the Third Marines Scout-Sniper Platoon Commander (25 December 1966–14 October 1967), provide valuable insight into one Marine regiment's efforts to employ Scout-Snipers to its best advantage.

The problems encountered and the measures necessary to pull the Third Marines sniping program together are indicative of the difficulties Marines like Bill Abbott faced in Vietnam. As the Corps was quick to learn, training snipers was one thing; employing them effectively was another problem altogether and the key to successful sniper operations.

The discipline required of a successful match shooter was one of the major reasons for the use of competitive marksmen as the organizational foundation of the Marine Corps sniping program in Vietnam. In this case, however, rather than being an accomplished rifle and/or pistol shooter, as most of the Marines involved with the sniper program were, Sergeant Abbott had earned the title of "Distinguished International Shooter" for his trapshooting skills before he was posted to Southeast Asia.

The principal arteries in the I Corps Tactical Zone, the Marine Corps area of responsibility in RVN, were Routes 1, 4, and 9. Camp Carroll, the Headquarters for Third Marines, was located on Route 9 approximately 12 miles west of Dong Ha in Quang Tri Province. The camp was situated about 6 miles south of the demilitarized zone (DMZ).

Though barely a dirt trail for much of its length, Route 9 passed through, or in close proximity to, such places as Cam Lo, The Rockpile, Ca Lu, Khe Sanh, and Lang Vei on its way to the Laotian border. For the Marines who were there, these were names and places not likely to be forgotten.

Bill Abbott describes in his own words the activities of Third Marines Scout-Sniper Platoon during 1967 as follows:

When I arrived at Camp Carroll in the Republic of South Vietnam on Christmas Day 1966, I was assigned to Headquarters 3rd Marines. On reporting I was assigned the duty of Platoon Commander of the 3rd Marine Scout-Snipers. I was instructed to report to Regimental Commander Colonel John P. Lanigan.

The colonel informed me that their "snipers were scattered from hell to breakfast" and "were not being used for what they were trained to do." He said he would give me "just 30 days" to round them all up; retrain and refit them for duty as Scout-Snipers. The colonel wanted a unit he could call on to plug the holes as needed.

As I went to the various companies in the regiment I found the snipers being used on mess duty, guard duty, burning and every other dirty task that needed to be done.

One of the company commanders who had a two-man team assigned to him told me "I don't give a damn who you are, you don't get these men until they are off mess duty." I asked to use his field phone and he said "go right ahead, call anybody you want to, but you aren't getting them." I told the phone operator to call "Starboard 6" (Col. Lanigan), and when the "6" came on the line I stated my problem. He said to put the company commander on the phone. I handed the company commander the phone and told him "Starboard 6" wanted to talk to him. He turned white as he took the phone and didn't have much to say except "Yes Sir, Yes Sir, I understand Sir, I'm sorry Sir." When he got off the phone he told his 1st Sergeant to get those men to regimental headquarters on the double. He then turned to me and said "I owe you one."

While assembly of the snipers was going on, I had my Platoon Sergeant and squad leaders putting together a training program that included a refresher course in all aspects of Scout-Sniper duties. We set up a long distance range and conducted dawn till dusk shooting practice for a minimum of 6 hours per day. The training included hand-to-hand combat, physical exercise, the use of radios for artillery and air-strikes, map reading, etc.

With training set, I took a squad leader, rations for 15 days, maps of our entire A.O., and we went on a scout mission from Camp Carroll east to the ocean. We moved at night, slept a little, and studied the terrain during the day. When we reached the ocean north of Dong Ha we crossed the Ben Hai River and proceeded west in the DMZ to Laos. We crossed the river to the south side of the DMZ and made our way back to Camp Carroll.

There were several reasons for this trip:

1. To learn the A.O. we would be working in.

2. I took plastic playing cards with me to prove to my troops that I had been there. The cards were hidden in fairly easy locations so that the patrol leaders could find them. I would sign a card, date it, hide it, and mark the location on my map. The patrol was told the location of the card, but not which card it was. When they found it they knew damn well I had been there. The former platoon commander would not go on patrol, nor did he check on the men assigned to the infantry companies.

3. To locate the routes the NVA were using to head south.

4. To determine the best locations to set up interdiction teams.

After the training was completed and the sniper weapons were brought up to as good a condition as they could be, we were assigned the task of clearing snipers ("the bad guys") from Route 9 from Dong Ha to Khe Sanh. Our convoys were taking sniper fire on a regular basis.

We set up a system consisting of two Scout-Sniper teams in two jeeps with a squad leader and radio operator that would work together as a team. We formed a total of 10 teams and stationed them as follows; 2 at Khe Sanh, 1 at The Rockpile, 4 at Camp Carroll, 1 at Cam Lo, and 2 at Dong Ha. When a shot was fired at a convoy we responded from the east and west of the convoy and sent an additional 2 teams from Camp Carroll. The way this was set up we could have a team respond in not more than 30 minutes anywhere along Route 9. This worked very well and we secured the road from enemy sniper fire.

During this time I also visited our battalion and company commanders and gave each one a run-down on the best way to employ Scout-Sniper teams. This turned out to be a nearly full-time job due to combat injuries and rotation of officers. It proved to be worthwhile, however. When teams were assigned to go with a battalion or company on a combat sweep, in most cases, the snipers were used correctly and effectively.

The major problems we had to overcome were:

1. Being treated like a bastard at a family reunion. No one wanted to be responsible for our equipment or rations.

2. There was no schooling at company or higher level on proper employment of Scout-Snipers.

3. All of this was taking place when the Corps was really just starting to gear up in RVN.

For all of the difficulties we experienced, however, with the help of Colonel Lanigan and the S-3, things did improve a great deal before I left in October 1967. We received the Remington M700s with the 3-9 scopes, the AR15, and Starlight Scopes as well.

The rotation of snipers with two-thirds in the field and one-third being held in reserve for rest and refit worked very well. We relieved one-third every 30 days which meant 60 days in the field and 30 days R&R. When the troops came in for R&R they cleaned their equipment first and the rest came after that. While they were in base camp they were subject to being called out for Route 9 patrol or any other problem that came up.

I had 20 months combat in Korea as a squad leader and platoon sergeant and I had some very good men. I do believe the special training the Scout-Snipers had gone through gave them a better edge, that is, the men were trained for known missions and were equipped to carry out the missions both mentally and physically.

These were the most highly motivated Marines I had ever commanded in combat. I am indeed a very lucky man to have had that honor. They were the best!

The official position regarding the Sniper Platoon was set forth in "Division Order 3590.3A," 5 July

1967. The order "promulgated instructions and information concerning the activities of Sniper Platoons within the 3d Marine Division."

As it was then stated:

Policy

a. The unique capabilities of the Scout-Sniper Platoon are at the disposal of the Regimental and/or battalion commanders. The platoon may be employed as a unit, or it can be broken down into squads or teams which may be attached to any size tactical unit of the regiment/battalion.

b. Snipers should wherever possible, be employed in pairs to minimize eye fatigue from incessant surveillance. The two members relieve each other in performing the duties of sniper and observer.

c. A squad (10–14 Marines) built around a Sniper team is generally considered as the smallest unit which should be employed on missions beyond sight or direct communications from parent units. However, where the situation, terrain, and reaction capability permits the commander to reduce this force to exploit stealth and surprise, the calculated employment of smaller groups (4–8 Marines) is authorized out to 2,000 meters from friendly positions. These forces may be made up primarily or even exclusively of scout/sniper personnel provided appropriate arms and equipment augmentation is provided. Again with appropriate situation, terrain and reaction capability commanders are also authorized to employ single scout-sniper teams out to 500 meters from friendly positions.

d. Under all conditions of employment scout-sniper teams/units will be provided with appropriate communications, artillery and mortar fire support on an "on-call" basis.

e. RTE armorers, MOS 2112, will be the only armorers authorized to perform second echelon maintenance. Weapons and telescopes requiring third echelon maintenance will be evacuated to FLSG.

Mission. The mission of the Scout-Sniper Platoon is to support the Infantry/Reconnaissance Battalions by providing a specially trained and equipped unit capable of rendering sniper support in combat operations, by providing personnel trained to kill individual enemy soldiers with single rifle shots from positions of concealment.

Organization. Reference (b) [Allocation Change Number 753-65] promulgated detailed instructions concerning the organization of the Scout-Sniper Platoon within the Infantry Division.

a. Infantry Regiment organization consists of 3 squads of 5 two-man teams and a squad leader each, an NCOIC, an RTE armorer and an Officer-In-Charge with a total strength of 1 officer and 35 enlisted.

b. The Reconnaissance Battalion organization consists of 4 squads of 3 two man teams and a squad leader each, an NCOIC, an RTE armorer and an Officer-In-Charge with a total strength of 1 officer and 30 enlisted.

Considerations for Employment
a. Conventional Offensive

(1) The capability of snipers to support infantry offensive action by precision destructive/neutralizing fire is invaluable. Snipers with telescopes have the distinct advantage of being able to see as much as nine times better (with a 9x scope) than the infantry personnel being supported. Neutralization of enemy automatic weapons and defensive positions is facilitated by the utilization of optics. As advancing infantry elements continue in the advance, snipers must displace to forward echelon to effectively support the offense by fire. Depending upon the size of the objective, snipers may be massed to render proportionately more support. Upon seizure of the objective, pursuit by fire phase is enhanced by the presence of snipers.

b. Conventional Defensive

(1) The effective range and optical advantage of sniper rifles used in defensive situations causes premature deployment of enemy elements and unquestionably creates a tremendous psychological, demoralizing impact upon the enemy. Officers, NCO's and crew-served weapons are likely targets. Variable telescopes with magnification at low power possess the capability of acquiring targets at ranges up to 600 meters when a full moon is evident, over rice paddies. While the ability to penetrate heavy foliage and tree lines is limited, distinct objects such as monuments, pagodas, etc. may be identified. Conventional iron sights do not have this capability. With telescopic sights, an additional hour of effective shooting time with accuracy, is possible. This capability denies the enemy movement during first light and at dusk.

c. Attachment to Patrols

(1) Experience has shown that the Viet Cong invariably take patrols under small arms fire from concealment. Firing is sporadic, of short duration, and because of the dense foliage it is extremely difficult to detect the source. Snipers, attached to patrols, with telescopic sights have the capability of acquiring targets more readily than other patrol members without benefit of optics. Additionally, their long range accuracy denies the enemy the ability to close and therefore minimizes the accuracy of the weapons. In built up areas, targets frequently cannot be taken under fire by area type weapons because of the proximity of innocent civilians. The capability of the sniper in delivering precision, long range fire is a tremendous asset to the patrol.

d. Daylight Ambush - Extended

(1) This type employment is used in selected areas where there is a likelihood of encountering Viet Cong. The concept of employment provides for the sniper team, with infantry protection moving to a pre-selected ambush site under cover of darkness and being in position by first light.

Surveillance is maintained throughout the day. Withdrawal is made after darkness. Snipers, with the dual capability of adjusting artillery fire, take identifiable targets under fire with artillery or sniper rifle depending upon the size of the target. Survivors of observed artillery missions are taken under fire by the sniper.

e. Daylight Ambush - Close

(1) Close ambushes are those sniper team ambushes within approximately 300 meters of friendly positions. To avoid possible capture or destruction the sniper team is covered by friendly fires. The 300 meters, coupled with the 1000 meter range of the weapon theoretically denies the enemy movement within 1300 meters of friendly positions and accordingly minimizes the effect of enemy sniper fire and surveillance. This type of employment also involves assumption of the pre-selected ambush site prior to daybreak and withdrawal after darkness has followed.

f. Counter-Sniper

(1) In situations wherein friendly positions receive small arms fire on successive days from the same general location, snipers are employed to decrease the enemy's effectiveness by delivering accurate counter-sniper fire. The distinct advantage lies in the sniper weapons precision fire capability when firing into built-up areas which normally precludes the utilization of automatic weapons or supporting arms.

g. Blocking Positions

(1) Sniper teams attached to infantry elements in blocking positions have been used extensively and effectively in conjunction with search and destroy operations. The enemy is taken under fire when driven into the blocking positions or while attempting to evade capture. The sniper rifle's accuracy, range and telescopic sights permit long range fires at targets which normally are too far distant to allow positive identification. This capability, in effect, precludes indiscriminate firing at innocent indigenous who have inadvertently wandered into the area of operations.

Employment of Attached Snipers

a. Employment of snipers in both an offensive and defensive role is generally limited only by the imagination. Types of employment for which snipers are suitably equipped and trained are as follows:

(1) Execution of long range (500–1000 meters) daylight ambushes.

    (a) To kill and harass the enemy by precision fire.

    (b) Striking fear in the enemy by the psychological aspects derived from long range accurate small arms fire.

(2) Daylight patrols - Provided the terrain is suitable for long range accurate fire in support of patrol activities.

(3) Blocking forces - Cover likely avenues of escape.

(4) Offense

    (a) Provide accurate covering fire for advancing maneuver elements.

    (b) Attack prime targets such as: crewserved weapons, bunker apertures and personnel in trench lines or fighting holes.

    (c) Pursue enemy by long range fire

(5) Defense

    (a) Take enemy under fire at distances up to 1000 meters with accuracy.

    (b) Deny the enemy freedom of movement in approach to friendly positions.

    (c) Counter-sniper fire - decrease enemy effectiveness through accurate counterfire.

b. Supported Unit Requirements. Units employing sniper teams must insure that the following principles are adhered to in employing snipers:

(1) Always employ in teams (pair) to increase their capability.

(2) Always cover by a security element (one fire team and a radio operator).

(3) Do not employ as a security element to front, rear, or flanks in column movements.

(4) Do not employ in ambushes, patrols or listening posts during the hours of darkness.

(5) Always insure snipers are informed of any friendly forces within their operating area.

   c. Control of Teams

      (1) Units desiring sniper team augmentation submit request to this Headquarters. Request to include number of teams desired and estimated duration of utilization.

      (2) Sniper Platoon personnel when deployed will be under the OPCON of the supported unit and under ADCON of Headquarters Company Regiment. The supported unit will provide logistical support to sniper personnel under their OPCON.

   Reports

      a. Units participating in normal operations include the following information in 1800 SITREP to cover the period 0001-2400H that day.

      b. Units submitting 24 hour SITREPS include the following information for consolidation into Division Daily SITREP.

   c. Format & Example

CMD GRU/OP	No. of Teams	No. Deployed	Method of Employment	Results
A/1/4	3	2	Outpost Security	1VC KIA

      d. Additionally, a copy of enclosure (1) [Sniper Report Form] will be forwarded to this Headquarters on a weekly basis for evaluation of Scout-Sniper teams.

   Action

      a. Commanding Officers will implement the instructions contained within this order upon receipt.

      b. The Assistant Chief of Staff (G-3 Training) will provide staff cognizance of the Scout-Sniper Platoon performance and questions/problems will be directed to this Headquarters as they occur.

      c. A copy of this order will be placed in the Commanders Continuity file.

   In addition to his duties as platoon commander, while serving with Third Marines, Sergeant Abbott initiated a highly successful civic action program for the Vietnamese and Montagnard children in the Third Marines' Tactical Area of Responsibility. The program, named Operation Red Wagon, was described as follows in the January 1968 issue of *Trap & Field* magazine:

   Operation Red Wagon is a program begun in May 1967 by the Amateur

Trapshooting Association to encourage the Vietnamese people to be self-sufficient, healthy individuals and to help our boys in Vietnam. The program was conceived by MSgt Bill Abbott (our ATA man in Vietnam at the time) and then-ATA President Ralph Taylor.

The goal of 1000 red wagons—awarded to Vietnamese children on the basis of achievement in schools and also offered as incentives for families in crowded refugee areas to maintain high standards of personal cleanliness and hygiene—was reached in November 1967. When it became apparent that the enthusiasm and efforts on the part of trapshooters would carry the fund over the $4000 goal, the ATA checked with Bill Abbott and asked, "What else can we offer the kids that will do you and them a lot of good?" The answer was obvious to Bill: "Blue bib overalls—coveralls. The kind every kid in the United States has. Many of these little ones don't have anything to wear. And it's hard to go to school under these circumstances."

Though it is rarely noted by the media, there was considerably more to American involvement in Southeast Asia than death and destruction. The efforts of Bill Abbott are just one example.

● ● ●

"There were 77,729 Marines in South Vietnam at the end of 1967."

—United States Marine Corps

Brigadier General Metzger (left) and Master Sergeant Abbott, Camp Carroll, 1967. The Commanding General, Ninth Marine Amphibious Brigade, Metzger became assistant division commander, 3d MarDiv, in May 1967. Sergeant Abbott served as Third Marines Scout-Sniper Platoon Commander (25 December 1966–14 October 1967). Said Abbott, "Even generals got their faces dirty in Vietnam." The photograph was taken immediately after a Viet Cong mortar attack. Both Marines were as close to the ground as they could get. (William D. Abbott.)

Third Marine Regiment (3d MarDiv) Scout-Sniper personnel shown "sighting-in" their equipment near Camp Carroll. The rifles are Model 70 Winchesters with 8-power Unertl telescopes. (William D. Abbott.)

The Commandant of the Marine Corps Gen. Wallace M. Greene Jr. (left) and Third Marine Regiment Commander Col. John P. Lanigan are shown during an inspection tour of Camp Carroll (1967). Note the 175mm powder canisters lining the path. According to Marine Corps information, at one point "there were 14 U.S. Army 175mm long-range guns [support artillery] operating from Camp Carroll." The area was also referenced as "Artillery Plateau" in Army and Marine Corps documents. (William D. Abbott.)

Members of the Third Marines Sniper Platoon, February 1967. The Model 70 Winchester and the M1D, the mainstay of the Marine Corps sniping program during the early months of the war, served Third Marines until the Model 700 Remington rifles arrived in April 1967. (William D. Abbott.)

Purple Heart award ceremony, Third Marines Scout-Sniper platoon, Camp Carroll (1967). While not disproportionate to those earned by American combat forces at large, awards and decorations were earned in significant numbers by Army and Marine Corps snipers during the war in Vietnam. As a matter of interest, Camp Carroll was named in honor of a Marine officer (Capt. Joseph J. Carroll) killed in action while leading an assault on Hill 484. (William D. Abbott.)

Third Marines snipers, Camp Carroll 1967. The Marine (foreground) is using a 20-power M49 observation telescope for spotting targets. The others are sighting Unertl-equipped Model 70 Winchesters. (William D. Abbott.)

A Third Marine Regiment Scout-Sniper Platoon sergeant during operations near Cam Lo (March 1967). The sniper rifle is an M1D mounting a M84 telescope. (William D. Abbott.)

Veteran USMC rifle team member 1st Lt . Don L. Smith, the CO for HQ Company, Third Marines, at the battalion command post at The Rockpile, August 1967. A Distinguished Marksman, Smith competed with a Van Orden Model 70 Winchester, winning the Wright Memorial Trophy at the 1953 National Matches (Camp Perry, Ohio). The same rifle was among the Model 70s shipped to RVN as supplemental sniping equipment early in the war. (Don L. Smith.)

The "Rockpile," a 700-foot-high hill described officially as "a cork to the valleys leading down from North Vietnam from the north and west" (major North Vietnamese Army infiltration routes). "Mutter's Ridge" is at the right, the "Razor Back" on the left. As Don L. Smith related, "An OP could look across the DMZ directly into North Vietnam from The Rockpile." The photograph was taken "looking north" from the battalion command post (1967). (Don L. Smith.)

Marine Sgt. Bjorn A.G. Dahlin, from Sweden, a squad leader with Third Marines Scout-Sniper Platoon at The Rockpile, 1967. The "Swede," as Dahlin was known, had served with an elite Swedish commando unit in Africa and Cyprus with United Nations Emergency Forces before enlisting in the Marine Corps. (Don L. Smith.)

SNIPER REPORT FORM

Mail to: OIC, Div Sniper Project - 3d MarDiv G-3 Tr. Inter-Island

Date:_____

1._____
   NAME   RANK

2._____
   NAME   RANK

_____
 Unit Attached To   Coordinates of Location Employed

How Employed:_____

_____

_____

_____

Sightings   Yes   No   How Many   Range

Moving   Stationary   Did You Fire   How Many Rds

Results:_____

_____

_____

Killed   # Wounded   # Bodies Recovered

Confirmed By -_____
              NAME   RANK   BILLET

Condition of Rifle   Scope

Comments: (Such as Terrain, Weather etc.)

_____

The 3d MarDiv Sniper Report Form cited in Division Order 3590.3A, 5 July 1967. (U.S. Marine Corps.)

M.Sgt. William D. Abbott is pictured with one of the early-issue Remington sniper rifles and wagons destined for Vietnamese children as part of Operation Red Wagon (May 1967). According to Abbott, the first M700 rifles reached his unit (Third Marines Scout-Sniper Platoon) in April. The Redfield telescope is fitted with the soft (pliable) plastic lens covers; the rifle has a web sling. (William D. Abbott.)

The logo for Operation Red Wagon was used to generate interest in the project conceived by Bill Abbott. The program was sponsored by the Amateur Trapshooting Association and *Trap & Field* magazine in the United States. (Abbott Collection.)

This illustration was part of an article describing Operation Red Wagon in the 30 June 1967 issue of *SEA TIGER*, a publication of the III MAF, Vietnam. Its caption read as follows: "WAGON SWAP—Marine M.Sgt. William D. Abbott (left) holds a Vietnamese boy's homemade wagon after trading it for a new red wagon. Abbott is working with the Amateur Trapshooting Association, in the United States, to supply Vietnamese youngsters with wagons donated by members of the Association." (U.S. Marine Corps.)

One of the countless souvenirs brought back from Vietnam, *The Charlie Ration Cookbook*, a "tongue-in-cheek" approach to "C-Rats" with Tabasco sauce (a product of the McIlhenny Co., Avery Island, Louisiana) as one of the main ingredients. The 10-page booklet featured such recipes as "Fox Hole Dinner for Two," "Patrol Chicken Soup," "Breast of Chicken under Bullets," and similar culinary delights all made with basic C Rations. Fred Rhoads, the illustrator for the booklet, was the author of the "Gizmo" and "Eight Ball" series in *Leatherneck* magazine. (McIlhenny Co./Fred Rhoads.)

CHAPTER 8

THE UNERTL SCOPE

The 8-Power Model

The Unertl 8-power Sniper Scope employed with the Model 70 Winchester in RVN was the same target-type telescope purchased by the Marine Corps during World War II. The Unertl scopes were made for the Marine Corps beginning about late 1942 and were used primarily to fill the equipment requirements of newly organized Sniper-Observer-Scout Teams (Scout-Snipers) destined for action against the Japanese in the Pacific. While most of the Unertl scopes were mounted on the USMC M1903A1 sniper rifle, some were reportedly used with Model 54 and Model 70 Winchester rifles. These were not official issue, however.

Regardless of their 8-power marking and reference, all sights were actually 7.8-power. A 1/8-inch-wide (±) "Pope-rib" located on top and in line with the tube prevented the scope from rotating in its mounts. The front clamping ring was used to reposition the sight after the weapon was fired (when the rifle was fired, the scope slid forward in the mounts and was pulled back into firing position by hand). A second ring behind the front mount was simply a spare, rather than an effort to limit the recoil of the tube.

The rear mount provided an adjustment of approximately 200 minutes, with each division on the graduated thimble representing 1/2 minute and each click a 1/4-minute adjustment. Later scopes were reportedly modified for 1/2-minute adjustments for each click. Both the front and rear mounts were known as "3-point suspension mounts."

Although telescope carrying cases were furnished with the Unertl sights when they were originally issued, the cases were not used in Vietnam. In keeping with Marine Corps practice, telescopic sights were not removed from the rifles unless it was absolutely necessary. Even though a telescope carrying case was considered "essential equipment" by some, a suitable cover would have proved far more practical, especially in South Vietnam. Despite ordnance measures to supply carrying cases for telescopic rifle sights through the years, few were ever carried into combat.

The initial operation and maintenance instructions for the Unertl telescope were set forth by U.S. Marine Corps Headquarters, Washington, D.C., in *Ordnance Maintenance Bulletin No. F-(Telescope)-1,* (15 December 1943). The "General Data" for the USMC sniper sight were listed as follows:

Magnification 8X
Objective size . . . . (effective) 1 1/4 inches
Exit pupil 4.2mm
Field of view at 100 yards . . . . 11 feet
Luminosity 17.6
Eye relief . . . . 2 1/4 to 2 3/4 inches
Length . . . . 24 inches
Resolution . . . . 3/32 inches
Reticle angle . . . . 1/4 minute

Medium-size Crosswire with Center Dot:
Weight . . . . 24 ounces
Maximum O.D. . . . . 1 1/2 inches
Main tube diameter . . . . 3/4 inch
Eyepiece adjustable for individual eye.
Target type, 1/4-minute click anodized, duraluminum mounts
with hardened steel bases and screws.

[The telescope tube was made of steel with a "blued" finish. The aluminum alloy mounts were anodized black; the lenses were not coated.]

NOTE: The operation and maintenance instructions for the Unertl Sniper Scope, a four-page pamphlet, were published on 27 December 1943. An 8-1/2 x 11-inch three-page version (31 August 1949) was circulated within the Marine Corps some years later.

As a point of interest in this case, whereas the aforementioned documents had served the Marine Corps sniping effort during World War II and Korea, in anticipation of continued field use of the Winchester/Unertl system, details concerning the Unertl sight were included in the initial draft edition of *USMC FMFM 1-3B, SNIPING* (October 1967).

NOTE: Though *USMC FMFM 1-3B, SNIPING* was originally intended to instruct USMC sniper candidates in the operation and maintenance of the Model 70/Unertl system and the Model 700/Redfield combination, all reference to the Model 70 Winchester and the Unertl scope was deleted from the draft editions that followed. The draft editions of the USMC sniper training manual were used for review and correction purposes. They were not intended for training and/or field use.

The draft copy of *FMFM 1-3B, SNIPING* (October 1967) provided the following information on the 8-power Unertl telescope:

Telescope, Rifle, Unertl, USMC Sniper, 8X

The Unertl Telescope, USMC Sniper was developed for use by Marine Corps snipers during World War II. It is a precision instrument that requires skill in manipulation, mounting, and use. The Unertl telescope features a crosshair reticle and external adjustment mounts with audible click movements. The telescope is generally carried mounted to the rifle on most sniper assignments; however, the sniper must know how to remove and remount the telescope. The Unertl telescope is currently issued for use with the Winchester Model 70 rifle only.

Adjustments

It is vitally important that the scope be properly adjusted to obtain the optimum focus, parallax, reduction, and eye relief.

Focus

In order to properly focus the Unertl telescope, both the optic (rear) and the objective (front) lenses must be adjusted.

Optic Lens

The rear lens is focused by rotating the eyepiece counterclockwise until the reticle (crosshair) is out of focus. The scope is then properly focused by pointing it at a bright background and adjusting the eyepiece clockwise until the reticle appears sharp and clear at a glance. (Quick glances simulate actual field shooting. Slow study of the reticle allows the eye to adjust to it, a situation which is seldom possible under field conditions.) The eyepiece is locked in focus with the eyepiece lock ring.

Objective Lens

The objective lens is focused by pointing the telescope at a fixed target at approximately 500 yards (457 meters) and rotating the objective lens until the target is distinct.

Parallax

Parallax is the apparent motion of a nearby object (sight reticle) in relation to a distant object (aiming point) when viewed from different positions. To test the mounted telescope for parallax, the rifle is placed on a rigid support and the sight is aligned on an object not less than 500 yards away. The head is moved slightly from side to side and up and down. If there is any movement of the reticle in relation to the distant object, parallax is present. A small amount of parallax may be tolerated at short ranges but not at ranges normally used. When an adjustment for parallax is required, IT WILL BE DONE BY AUTHORIZED PERSONNEL ONLY.

Eye Relief

Eye relief is the distance from the eyepiece to the eye and each sniper must adjust for his own eye relief. A distance of two or three inches is normal. To find the correct eye relief, the clamp stops are loosened, the telescope is moved back and forth until the field of view fills the eyepiece, and the "picture" in the telescope seems to "lock" in position. After the correct eye relief is found, the front clamp stop is tightened against the front mount to prevent further movement to the rear.

Mounting the Unertl Telescope

The Unertl telescope is designed to be mounted on the M70 Winchester rifle. Each of the two mounting blocks are attached to the rifle by two screws which should be checked periodically for tightness to prevent a zero change. The telescope has two movable mounts for mounting the telescope to the rifle. Each mount has a mount locking screw for attachment to the mounting blocks.

Marine Corps sights, furnished by Unertl under World War II contracts, bore the following legend on the tube directly in front of the eyepiece:

J. Unertl

USMC-SNIPER

2299

Unertl contract sight numbering appears to have started at serial number 1001. So far as it is known, a total of 3,500 scopes were actually ordered by the Marine Corps, the initial order being for 1,000 and the second for 2,500. However, according to USMC records, 1,750 Unertl telescopes had been accepted by the Marine Corps by April 1945, and, as then stated, this figure represented the "total delivered." Though additional deliveries may have taken place before the war ended a few weeks later, considering the status of the war at that point, further deliveries are believed to have been highly unlikely.

Although some Unertl sights were disposed of as surplus following the war in the Pacific, an unspecified number remained in Marine Corps service and were fielded again in Korea with the USMC M1903A1 and an occasional Model 70 Winchester.

When the call went out for sniping equipment in South Vietnam in 1965, Unertl telescopes were drawn from stores and shipped to Southeast Asia for use against the Communist forces in Vietnam. Ironically, the Unertl Sniper Scopes were still serving the Marine Corps more than 20 years after they were purchased.

By any measure or standard, the 8-power Unertl telescope was a superb sight, with the only genuine question being its durability for sustained use in a combat environment.

As events transpired, for that matter, the Unertl telescopes were subject to the same problems in Vietnam as they had experienced in Korea and World War II. Though more than capable of bringing down enemy personnel at extended ranges, the sights were susceptible to moisture, and to a lesser extent, reticle damage as well. Although problems with the reticles (crosshair damage) were duly attributed to the rigors of combat and, in some cases, to careless handling, insofar as optical manufacturers had not perfected the art of optimum lens sealing when the scopes were made, the temperature, humidity, and rainfall extremes found in South Vietnam combined to create "lens fogging" and "moisture retention" problems in varying degrees. In total fairness to the Unertl scopes, however, most, if not all, of the telescopic sights fielded in Southeast Asia would experience the same difficulty.

Interestingly, correspondence between John Unertl and a U.S. Army officer (16 July 1952) regarding combat use of Unertl target telescopes in Korea left no doubt that Unertl was well aware of the moisture problem. Commenting that "a scope should not be a complicated piece of machinery," Unertl went on to describe what took place with the "sniping scope" his firm had furnished to the Marine Corps in World War II as follows:

> When the man had it wet or, filled with water, the whole thing could be taken apart, the water shaken out, lenses wiped and the scope was ready for service again.

Judging from the comments of USMC snipers who used the Unertl scope in the Pacific, Korea, and South Vietnam, given the capability and inherent simplicity of the Unertl telescope, "drying the damn thing out," if need be, was a trade-off many of the more experienced Marine marksmen were prepared to accept.

NOTE: According to Walt Sides, the platoon sergeant for the Fourth Marines Sniper Platoon (1966), Gy.Sgt. Lawrence Dubia, in addition to serving as the platoon commander, performed maintenance on the telescopic sights fielded by the unit. With moisture problems as severe as they were, Sergeant Dubia fashioned what many referred to as a "hot locker" (a small box fitted with two or three 200-watt bulbs) to dry out the telescopes without damaging them. Additional measures intended to seal the scopes against moisture included the use of ordinary fingernail polish applied to the joints. For all of that, however, as any Marine with sniping experience in Vietnam will attest, there was no foolproof means of waterproofing the telescopic rifle sights fielded in Southeast Asia.

As a matter of reader interest, Major Russell, the officer-in-charge of the sniper program in RVN during its formative stages, was asked various questions pertaining to combat use of the target telescope. Major Russell's responses, which follow, came during the preparation of this book:

Q. What was your opinion of the target scope in a combat environment?

A. "As you know, you will encounter many different opinions about telescopes. However, with the 8-power Unertl at that time—it was great! Except, it was very vulnerable to humidity, sensitve to rough handling and not as versatile as a variable-power scope under varying light conditions."

Q. If there was any genuine problem associated with this type of rifle scope in Vietnam, what was it?

A. "It was susceptible to moisture and high humidity."

Q. Were commercial Lyman and Unertl target-telescopes fielded in RVN as part of the Marine Corps sniping effort?

A. "Not to my knowledge."

NOTE: Although small quantities of Lyman and Unertl commercial target scopes were reportedly fielded by Army and Marine Corps marksmen during the course of the war in Vietnam, equipment of this type was not viewed as "official issue." The extent of such use remains unconfirmed at present.

Q. In your opinion, which type of rifle scope (hunting or target) performed best in Vietnam?

A. "I really have mixed feelings here. The 8-power Unertl was an excellent scope for an accomplished sniper. Perhaps a 6-power would have been better, but, all in all, the Unertl was a good choice. For the average Marine sniper, however, I would choose a hunting telescope."

Q. If you could have personally selected a telescopic sight for use in RVN at that time, what would it have been?

A. "For the Marines in my crew, I would have chosen the 8-power Unertl."

Adding to our perspective in this matter, M.Sgt. Donald G. Barker, an original member of Major Russell's "crew" (sniper-instructor) had this to say about the telescopic sights he used in RVN:

At the start we were using 3X9 variable-power scopes trademarked "MARINE." It was difficult to establish a zero for a given range as they were strictly hunting scopes. The first time it rained the lenses on several of the sights fogged-up and they were virtually useless. It gives you a weird feeling to be ready for action and find out that your rifle scope is fogged-up.

[**NOTE:** For the sake of clarification, there are, in effect, two types of "fogging" (tiny water drops) common to telescopic sights—that which occurs on the outside of the lenses and, the more serious of the two conditions, that which occurs on the lens surface inside the telescope, the latter being a direct result of moisture entering the scope.]

We took the sights to the FLSG optic shop [the Force Logistic Support Group small arms and optics repair shop was based near the air strip at Da Nang], had them water-proofed and that took care of the problem.

After a couple of months we received the Unertl Sniper Scopes from the Supply Center at Albany, Georgia, which, according to the markings on the boxes, had been last inspected in August 1946. They were apparently inspected after World War II and placed in storage.

The Unertl scopes were sent to the optics shop where new crosshairs were fitted and water-proofing was applied [according to Barker, measures to waterproof their telescopic sights had included the use of "candle wax" and a "black sealing compound," which proved "very effective"].

The scopes were all 8-power with 1/4-minute adjustments for both elevation and windage. With the arrival of the Unertl telescopes, things really started to happen.

We zeroed some at 100-yard intervals from 100 to 1200 yards, and we also had several zeroed out to 1500 yards. The reason we did not zero all out to 1500 yards was that some of the people we trained were not capable of holding a group tight enough to consistently hit a man-sized target at that range. The Model 70 I carried, until I had to give it up to someone we trained, was zeroed out to 1500 yards. The only scopes we mounted on the Model 70 Winchesters were the 3X9 Japanese variable-power sights and the 8-power Unertls.

NOTE: As noted in an earlier chapter, the Marine Corps used a limited number of 3X-9X variable-power rifle scopes manufactured in Japan (the scopes were trademarked "MARINE"; the brand name and Marine Corps use were coincidental in this case) with the Model 70 for early sniping activity beginning in 1965. While hardly an optimum rifle sight, its ranging capability (variable-power adjustment) was seen as a "desirable feature" in a field scope at that time. The Japanese hunting sights were purchased on Okinawa as a supplemental measure. So far as it is known, this was the first time a variable-power rifle scope had been employed by Marine snipers in combat. The use of a variable-power hunting scope in this case had a direct bearing on the ultimate selection of the Redfield 3X-9X model.

When asked, "Having used both commercial target and hunting scopes with the Model 70, did you prefer one type over the other?" Barker responded as follows:

I prefer the 8-power Unertl USMC Sniper Scope. You take this scope and mount it on any rifle that is capable of holding a minute of angle and put it in the hands of an experienced marksman and you have a deadly killing machine at work.

Like all telescopes even this one would have a cross-hair break but, this was not a major problem. The people in the optics shop taught us how to take the scope apart, make new cross-hairs by pulling a couple of hairs from your head, wrap it around the screws, tighten them gently, put the scope back together, and you were in business.

As soon as we came in from patrol we would take the scopes over to the optics shop and have them checked and re-waterproofed if it was necessary. This procedure did not alter the zero of the rifle and scope.

NOTE: John Unertl, discussing the simplicity of his target-scope reticle some years earlier (1952), remarked, "In case of damage, a human hair, nylon, or similar fiber will be a good substitute and can be installed with a pocket knife or a small screwdriver."

Although "some" of the Unertl telescopes sent to RVN as supplemental sniping equipment early in the war were reportedly "still in use" when the Marine Corps began reducing troop strength in South Vietnam in late 1969, with sniper use in Vietnam to its credit (even though the "USMC-SNIPER" sights were not fielded in any significant numbers), the venerable target-scope had served the United States Marine Corps in three major conflicts—a feat no other telescopic sight can boast of at this juncture.

The military version of the Unertl 1 1/4-inch objective commercial target sight known as the "Combination Target Scope," an 8-power Unertl "SNIPER" sight as furnished to the Marine Corps during World War II. In addition to combat use in Korea, the Unertl scopes served the Marine Corps during its involvement in Southeast Asia as well. As a matter of interest, the following Unertl telescopes were fielded in RVN for Marine sniper use: 2006, 2113, 2197, 2223, 2243, and 2355. The telescope serial numbers were recorded by a member of the 3d MarDiv sniper-instructor team. So far as it is known, the sights listed are the only Unertl telescopes with confirmed combat use in South Vietnam. (Peter R. Senich.)

The military version of the Unertl "patented 3-point suspension mount" introduced in 1940: the target-type, USMC contract, 1/4-minute click, black anodized duraluminum mount with hardened steel parts and base locking screw. Machined from a single piece of aluminum alloy, the mount provides an adjustment of approximately 200 minutes, each division on the graduated thimble representing 1/2 minute, each click a 1/4-minute adjustment. The micrometer "thimbles" were black enamel with graduations in white. Later-model scopes were modified with each click a 1/2-minute adjustment. (Peter R. Senich.)

Marine Gy.Sgt. Marvin C. Lange instructs novice snipers in the operation and care of the Unertl telescopic sight. Even though the Unertl sights were just as susceptible to the moisture and humidity in South Vietnam as they were during the island campaign against the Japanese in World War II, with proper care, the Unertl target scopes performed "extremely well" for Marine snipers in Vietnam. (U.S. Marine Corps.)

Typical Model 70 Winchester target telescope mounting blocks. The base (left) attached to the receiver ring, the other to the barrel. When positioned on the rifle, the beveled mill cuts (mount locking notches) provided both 6-inch and 7.2-inch spacing for the target mounts. Although target telescopes could be fitted to a Model 70 Standard Rifle (standard barrel), it was necessary to use a different front base. The base shown was sized to fit on a target barrel. (Peter R. Senich.)

Marine Corps armorer preparing a Model 70 rifle for a Unertl telescope, Vietnam, 1966. In the eyes of the Marine Corps, the armorer was an integral part of the Sniper Platoon, "responsible for the maintenance and security of the weapons and equipment." Regardless of his training, however, like all Marines, the armorer was a combat rifleman first. (U.S. Marine Corps .)

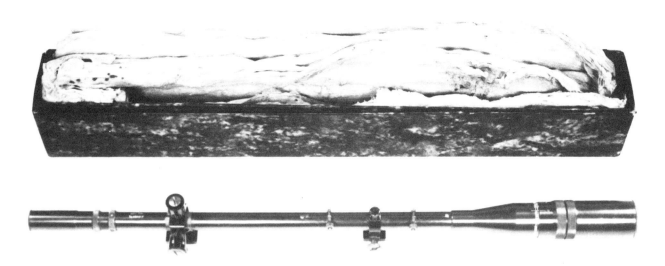

An 8-power Unertl USMC "SNIPER" sight with an original shipping carton (cardboard container) used to protect the sights in transit. The scope is shown as it was furnished to the Marine Corps during World War II. The USMC "Unertl 8-power Sniper" sight was not procured after 1945. Although some of the telescopes remained in service, a small quantity were placed in storage following the war. (Peter R. Senich.)

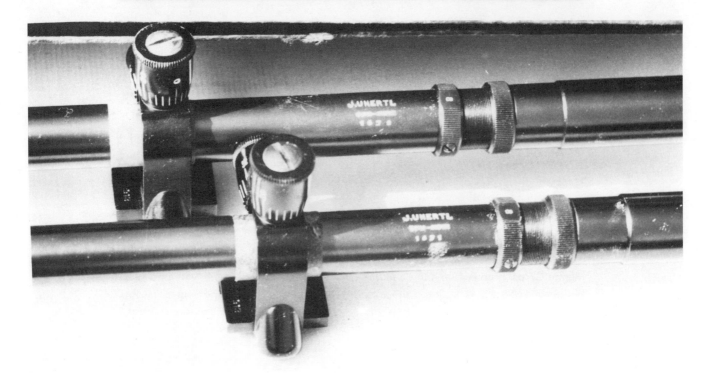

A close-up view of two consecutively numbered Unertl USMC contract sights (1670–1671) provides a good look at the typical manufacturer's legend and the left side of the rear mount. The number "8" stamped on top of the eyepiece locking ring (right) indicates the power, or magnification of the sight (7.8X). Steel parts of the Unertl telescopes were given a lustrous blue/black finish (blued) characteristic of a commercial sight rather than a military model. Although "parkerized" Unertl telescopes alleged to have been "rebuilt" by USMC ordnance have been reported, without suitable confirmation, such claims must be viewed with reservation. In ordnance circles, parkerizing was not an acceptable method of finishing a precision instrument such as a telescopic sight, even on an expedient basis. As a matter of record, ordnance specifications called for "black oxide" for finishing and/or refinishing military telescopes made of steel. The 2.2-power M84 telescope is a good example; the finish is black oxide. The use of certain metal finishing procedures for one part or another was no accident. (Peter R. Senich.)

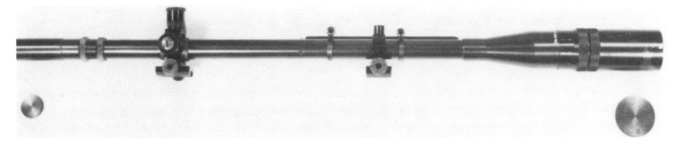

A typical USMC contract sight as furnished by the John Unertl Optical Company for Marine Corps sniper use. The 8-power scope was 24 inches in length with a 3/4-inch main tube diameter. Threaded dust caps were provided for both ends of the scope. Though reasonably effective, the end caps were frequently lost. The 1/8-inch rib located on top of the tube prevented the scope from rotating in its mounts. The front clamping ring was used to reposition the sight after the weapon was fired. A second ring behind the front mount served as a spare rather than an effort to limit the recoil of the tube. Both front and rear mounts were known as "3-point" suspension mounts. Although telescope carrying cases were originally included with the Unertl sights, the cases were not issued for use in Vietnam. (Peter R. Senich.)

Marine Corps snipers selecting "their mark" during early action against the Viet Cong. According to intelligence sources, "killing" the enemy at ranges so distant the report of the shot was barely audible was particularly unnerving to many of the "borderline" Communist insurgents (Viet Cong). By some estimates, the effect of snipers or the threat of their presence proved to be a greater psychological deterrent than a squadron of American heavy bombers. The snipers are armed with Model 70 Winchesters mounting 8-power Unertl telescopes. (U.S. Marine Corps.)

L.Cpl. Donald Allen (Second Battalion, Third Marines, 3d MarDiv) holds the objective end of a Unertl telescope hit by a bullet during an encounter with the Viet Cong (6 August 1966). The Model 70 has a "five-digit" serial number in the 40,000 range (the rifle was manufactured during the 1940s). Note the sealing compound at various points on the telescope. A variety of sealing agents were used to waterproof the Unertl scopes in Vietnam. (U.S. Marine Corps.)

Browning .50-caliber machine gun mounting an 8-power Unertl telescopic sight. The weapon served Marine sniper Carlos N. Hathcock for a "2500 yard kill" near Duc Pho during Operation Desoto in Quang Ngai Province (January 1967). The size and weight of a Browning machine gun (approximately 128 pounds with the M3 tripod) necessitated selecting an appropriate location and sandbagging the weapon carefully if serious long-range work was contemplated. The .50-caliber machine gun was not readily moved from one place to another. Sniping was carried out from a fixed, or relatively static, position. (Edward J. Land Jr.)

Another view of the Browning machine gun employed by Hathcock and others during operations near Duc Pho (January 1967). The Marine opposite the weapon is scanning the area for Viet Cong activity with an observation telescope. Note the commanding view from the hilltop position. A steel block with a dovetail to fit the sight base and the Unertl mounts was used to adapt the telescope to the .50-caliber machine gun. (Edward J. Land Jr.)

A comparison between a .50-caliber cartridge (left), .30-caliber (.30-06) M72 match cartridge (center), and a 7.62mm (.308) M118 match cartridge (right). Any benefit derived from employing the Browning machine gun for sniping rested with the long-range capability of the .50-caliber round. There was no questioning the authority of the 2.310-inch-long, 709.5-grain bullet (Ball, M2) at any range. (Peter R. Senich.)

CHAPTER 9

SNIPER RIFLE

The Marine Corps Choice

So far as the efforts to provide Marine combat personnel with suitable sniping equipment in Vietnam were concerned, when the Marine Corps deemed it necessary to replace the Winchester/Unertl combination with a lighter rifle and a scope that would aid the sniper in getting off a "quick first round," Headquarters, USMC directed the Marksmanship Training Unit to come up with a bolt-action sniper rifle for use in Southeast Asia.

The MTU then conducted comparative testing of "off-the-shelf" commercial rifles and telescopes during December 1965 and January 1966, concluding that the Remington Model 700-40X rifle and the Redfield Accu-Range 3X-9X variable-power telescopic sight were "superior to items now in use."

The results of the evaluations were detailed in a letter of recommendation to the Commandant of the Marine Corps from the Officer in Charge of the MTU, Weapons Training Battalion, Quantico, Virginia (9 February 1966).

As the letter relates:

Subject: Sniper Rifle/Telescopic Sight; Recommendation of

1. In December 1965, verbal instructions

were received from Colonel H.A. York, USMC, Code A03M, directing that the Marksmanship Training Unit recommend for procurement a rifle and telescopic-sight suitable for use by Marine Corps snipers. An early recommendation was required, but no deadline was established. No further guidelines or limitations were provided.

2. The indicated urgency for an early recommendation dictated that evaluation be limited to presently available commercial items. Accordingly, such evaluation was made within the following self-imposed assumptions:

a. The cartridge to be used would be cal. 7.62mm.

b. Most targets would be presented at ranges less than 600 yards.

c. The telescopic sight must be capable of adjustment at ranges up to and including 1000 yards.

d. The rifle/scope/ammunition combination should be capable of shooting within two (2) minutes of angle.

e. The rifle/scope combination must be simple, sturdy and explainable with minimum amount of instruction.

f. Areas of probable use would present conditions of high humidity, requiring a well sealed scope.

3. The following equipment was evaluated:

Rifles	Comment
2 Remington, Model 600	These are too light and produce excessive recoil. Modification is required to suitably mount telescope.
2 Remington, Model 700-ADL and BDL	Somewhat heavier than above, but still too light. No floor-plate in ADL Model.
2 Harrington and Richardson Ultra-Rifle	These rifles are assembled from components of 3 manufacturers including a foreign made action.
2 Winchester, Model 70	This rifle built on an action designed for .30-06 cartridge. Magazine blocked to accept shorter 7.62mm cartridge. Trigger not adjustable. Somewhat difficult to bed.

2 Remington, Model 700-40X

This rifle built on an action designed for the 7.62mm cartridge. Trigger is internally adjustable. Relatively simple to bed.

Telescopes	Comment
Weaver K4	Insufficient power, marginal sealing.
Bushnell Scope Chief 3X-9X	Foreign manufacture, marginal sealing, difficulty in mounting with available mounts.
Unertl Vulture 8X	Receiver mounting in relation to eye relief is unsatisfactory. Inadequate sealing.
Bausch & Lomb BALVAR 8A 2 1/2-8X	No internal adjustment, no satisfactory externally adjustable mounts.
Lyman All-American 6X	Insufficient power, insufficient internal adjustment.
Leupold 3X-9X	Insufficient internal adjustment, otherwise excellent.
Redfield Accu-Range 3X-9X	Well-sealed, adequate in-ternal adjustment, built-in range finder to 600 yards.

4. Based upon physical examination and use of the above equipment, coupled with the personal experience of testing-personnel with the above and similar equipment, it is believed that the Remington Rifle Model 700-40X, in combination with the Redfield Accu-Range 3X-9X variable-power telescopic sight in Redfield mount, is the most suitable equipment now available for the purpose expressed in paragraph 1, and to support the assumptions of paragraph 2.

5. The presence in the Marine Corps Supply System of a number of Winchester Model 70 Rifles was considered. However, these are all chambered for the .30-06 cartridge. Modification to the 7.62mm cartridge could be accomplished, but would be expensive and not especially desirable. Additionally, rifles that are nominally "Winchester Model 701, are now found, due to factory modifications made over the years in 3 different types. Many of the parts are not interchangeable.

6. It is recommended that:

a. Remington Rifle, Model 700-40X, cal. 7.62mm be procured as a Sniper Rifle.

b. The stock have a dull oil-finish and no fore-end tip or checkering.

c. Swivels be non-removable, military type.

d. Finish of action and barrel be dull, non-glare.

e. Barrel to be 1 in 10" twist.

f. Barrel to be free-floating.

g. Action to have clip-slot.

h. The rifle be capable of shooting 2 minutes of angle, 5 shot groups, measured center-to-center when fired from a device and using Remington Match grade ammunition.

i. The Redfield Accu-Range 3X-9X variable-power telescopic sight be procured.

j. The telescope be provided with special sealing to assure maximum protection from moisture.

k. The finish be dull, non-glare.

l. The telescope be mounted in Redfield mounts modified to afford maximum use of the internal elevation adjustment.

m. A hard carrying-shipping case with protective foam-padding containing desiccant and fungicide be provided for each rifle/scope unit.

n. Action be taken to insure availability of match-grade ammunition for use in the rifle.

W.R. Walsh

NOTE: This is the first time the letter recommending the Remington/Redfield system be procured for Marine Corps sniper use has seen publication. The Marine officer responsible for the evaluations, Col. Walter R. Walsh, USMC (Ret.), had directed the original "East Coast" Scout-Sniper School during World War II. Colonel Walsh is recognized as one of the "top" Marine marksmen of all time.

Even though the Remington M700, with modifications deemed necessary, would serve as the Marine Corps sniper rifle, the test weapons furnished by Remington were actually based on 7.62mm 40X target actions (so marked), complete with charger guides in the receiver (clip-slots).

The charger guide was referenced in military nomenclature as a "stripper clip charger guide." The clip-slot, as it was commonly known, was also referred to as a "clip-feeding slot," "charger slot," or just plain "slot" in many cases. By 1966, a receiver with a clip-slot was usually associated with a rifle intended solely for match-shooting purposes. The presence of this feature had nothing to do with overall weapon performance. A clip-slot did not enhance or detract from the accuracy or reliability of a rifle in any way.

Even though the requirement for a charger guide in a combat rifle mounting a telescopic sight directly over the receiver was considered unnecessary in some quarters, in a move viewed by various historians as a concession to the "rifle team influence," Model 700 sniper rifles furnished to the Marine Corps were to include a clip slot machined into the receiver bridge.

NOTE: Ironically, with the telescope mounting base covering the clip-slot as it did, few Marines tasked with using the Scout-Sniper Rifle in RVN would ever see the M700 charger guide.

Of further interest in this matter, in efforts to expedite initial shipments to the Marine Corps, early USMC Scout-Sniper rifles, though appropriately marked "Model 700" directly beneath the "Remington" script (logo) on the left side of the receiver, were reportedly assembled using receivers originally manufactured and intended for the 40X target rifle. In view of the fact that Remington receivers were machined, inspected, and accepted before the nomenclature (model designation) and serial number were added, such reports, though unconfirmed, are worthy of consideration.

NOTE: The Remington 40XB target rifle replaced the various 40X models in 1964. The "repeater version" of the 40XB target rifle formally introduced in 1966 made use of a M700-type action with a clip-slot for use on the National Match Course. Most shooters continued to refer to this rifle as the "40X" regardless of when it was manufactured.

The involvement of Remington in the Vietnam-era USMC sniper rifle was noted by John F. Lacy in his definitive work on the Model 700 rifle, *The Remington 700* (John F. Lacy 1989):

> M40 Marine Sniper Rifle—Around the beginning of 1966, Remington entered the competition for a bolt operated sniper rifle to be used by the U.S. Marines. The test rifles were built in the Custom Shop and based on the 40X target action. . . .
>
> The rifle was designated as the M40, and it, along with the original 40X test rifles, saw wide use in Vietnam. Possibly the M40 designation referred to the original 40-X action. The production model was based on the Remington 700 action and was rolled-marked as such on the receiver in the same manner as the commercial 700s of that era. Marine personnel commonly refer to it as a 700 Sniper Rifle.

NOTE: The "Custom Shop" at Remington (Ilion, New York), served to manufacture target, custom, and special-purpose rifles for civilian, military, and law enforcement applications.

For the sake of clarification, although early USMC/Remington 40X-marked ("Model 40-X") test rifles and commercial 7.62mm 40X target rifles with 27 1/4-inch heavy barrels may have made it to Vietnam as some contend, except for the addition of a "U.S." property marking above the serial number on the receiver, the USMC sniper rifles procured under contract from Remington were marked essentially the same as the commercial M700 rifles. There was no "40-X" or "M40" marking on the Vietnam-era Marine Corps sniper rifle.

Although the Marine Corps had stated that it was seeking a sniper rifle rather than a target rifle, there was an extremely fine line separating the characteristics of the M700 Remington and the Winchester Model 70 (the Model 70 rifles with the 24-inch target barrel and the standard stock shipped to RVN as supplemental sniping equipment were similar to the M700 sniper rifle with its 24-inch heavy barrel and sporter stock). Nevertheless, by Marine Corps definition, "A target rifle is expected to put all of its shots into a very small group after some adjustments to the sight. The sniper's rifle must put the first shot of any day into the same spot as the last shot of any other day. A free-floating barrel allows this with very few adjustments. A sniper gets no sighting-in shots, and he doesn't intend to put ten shots into the same target."

The Marine Corps wanted a 7.62mm bolt-action rifle with a medium-heavy barrel and a sporter stock, and the Remington organization made every effort to accommodate it.

Consequently, on 7 April 1966 the Model 700 Remington and the Redfield telescope were adopted for Marine Corps sniper use in Vietnam. According to the Marine Corps, the new sniping system utilized "regular production components" and, as further stated, "there were no unique specifications, just the right combination of parts."

In retrospect, however, even though the "Fiscal Year 1966" Marine Corps "Consolidated Procurement Execution Shopping List" (4 March 1966) had apparently moved the equipment evaluations to the procurement stage, a formal "Letter of Adoption and Initiation of Procurement for Scout-Sniper Rifles" from the assistant chief of staff, G-4, to the quartermaster general of the Marine Corps (7 April 1966) detailed the planning, budgeting, procurement, and funding phases for the Remington rifle and the Redfield telescope.

The specific "nomenclature" for the new sniping system was listed as "Rifle, 7.62mm, Sniper, Remington, M700, w/Heavy Sniper Barrel." The system was briefly described as follows:

> 7.62mm (.308) bolt-action Remington Rifle with short action receiver and heavy sniper barrel. Rifle has magazine capacity of five rounds, dull oil finish stock, military finish, military sling swivels, clip slot in receiver, and aluminum butt plate.

In conjunction with the procurement process, an "Acquisition Objective" of 700 (scout-sniper rifles) was cited with a "Planned Phase-in" of 250 rifles during fiscal year 1966 and 450 more in fiscal year 1967 and, while overly optimistic, a "planned in-service for use by WestPac Forces by 30 June 1966" was specified. Of further interest in this case, the telescopic sight, the weapon, and the exact method of identification were discussed as well.

As it was then stated:

> Rifle to be equipped with Redfield Scope and Mount.
>
> Unit cost includes installation of mount and Redfield scope and calibrating and test-firing of mount and scope with 550 weapons. Remaining 150 weapons will have mounts installed.
>
> Weapon, mount and scope will be identified with matching numbers utilizing rifle serial numbers on 550 calibrated weapons.
>
> U.S. property to be stamped on receiver in vicinity of weapon serial number.

The "life expectancy" of the system was listed as "10 years," with a "life of type" of "5 years." The sniper rifle would be manufactured in entirety by Remington Arms Co., "which owns the proprietary rights," and "Government Furnished Equipment" would include "carrying cases, rifle scopes, mounts, slings, basic issue items, and 35,000 rounds of 7.62mm match ammunition of the same lot." The ammunition would be used for "calibrating and test firing."

NOTE: Though minor details of the USMC planning process for the Scout-Sniper rifle would change before the contracts were finally placed with Remington and Redfield, it is interesting to note that the total of 700 rifles, which included 550 weapons with scopes and mounts, and 150 weapons with just the mounts (base), remained the same. This was in keeping with the "550 weapon" requirement originally specified (new procurement) in the comprehensive Headquarters Staff (HQMC) memorandum of 27 November 1965.

One of the earliest known illustrations of a Vietnam-era USMC M700 sniper rifle. This is a Remington Arms Co. photo (May 1966) of rifle serial no. 168346. Officially referenced as the "Rifle, 7.62mm, Sniper, Remington M700" in original form, the Vietnam-era USMC sniper rifles were produced at the Remington Custom Shop at Ilion, New York. Although procurement activity had begun earlier in the year, the Marine Corps formally adopted the M700/ Redfield system on 7 April 1966. (Remington Arms Co.)

An alternate view of the early USMC Remington Model 700 sniper rifle (serial no. 168346). The telescope is a first-generation commercial finish (black gloss) Redfield 3X-9X variable-power model. Note the soft plastic lens caps and the leather sling. The lens caps would serve as issue items with the USMC/Redfield contract sights; "leather or web slings" were furnished with the sniper rifles. It was common practice for arms manufacturers to photograph (record) one or more rifles during the initial or early stages of production. The weapon shown represents one of the first USMC M700 sniper rifles made for Marine Corps use in Vietnam. (Remington Arms Co.)

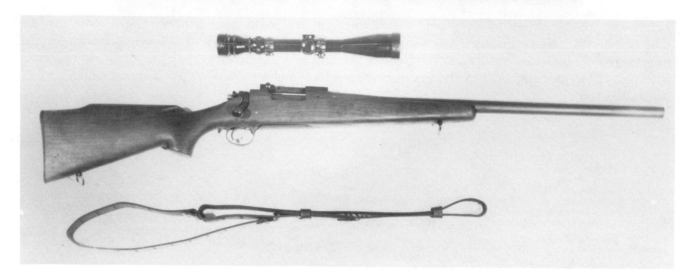

The early USMC Remington Model 700 sniper rifle (no. 168346) with the telescope removed (May 1966). The Marine Corps sniper rifle was referenced by Remington as the "Model 700 Precision Rifle," "Model 700 Sniper," "M700 Military Sniper Rifle," and the "Special Purpose M700" during the course of development and subsequent production. The names appear in Remington documents dating from this era. (Remington Arms Co.)

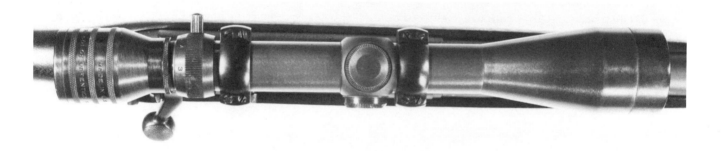

A top view of the Remington M700 sniper rifle with an original issue USMC/Redfield telescopic sight. The telescope was centered on the receiver; sights were positioned forward in the mounting rings at the factory. Even though sights could be moved up to 1 1/2 inches to the rear, the chances of the eyepiece contacting the forehead during recoil increased significantly. The Redfield scope was known to "leave its mark" on any number of unsuspecting shooters. Eye relief was listed at 2 to 3 inches. The sniper was instructed to move his head back and forth on the comb of the stock until there was a full field of view through the telescope. (Peter R. Senich.)

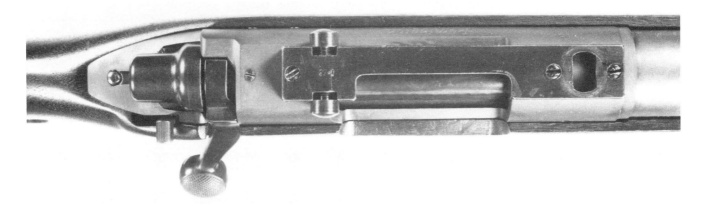

A top view of the M700 receiver with the telescope removed. The Redfield Junior (JR) one-piece bridge-type mounting base ("rotary dovetail system") was originally intended for the commercial market. The telescope mounting hardware employed with the USMC sniper rifle was not developed for this application. The "square-end" machined steel base fastened to the receiver with three screws. A lug beneath the front scope ring was inserted into the base opening, eyepiece to the right, and rotated 90 degrees clockwise to position the sight. Two slotted screws (windage screws) threaded into the base clamped the rear scope ring from both sides. After basic lateral zero had been established by adjusting the left screw, the right screw was tightened, locking the telescope in place. Internal scope adjustments were used for final zeroing. Although "40X" and "1-66" markings have been noted on bases considered original, there is no way of telling if all of the Redfield mounting bases furnished for Marine Corps use were marked in this manner. (Peter R. Senich.)

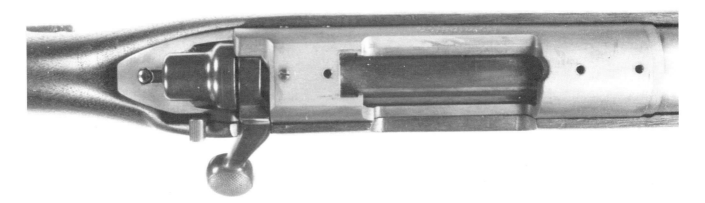

A top view of the Model 700 USMC sniper rifle with the telescope mounting base removed; the clip-slot, or charger guide, is clearly visible. According to contract specifications, a clip-feeding slot was machined into the receiver of every Model 700 sniper rifle furnished to the Marine Corps. Though previously unreported, there are at least two variations of clip-feeding slot found on the Vietnam-era M700/M40 sniper rifles: the type referenced here as the "square-cut" version (shown) and what is generally known as the "standard" clip-slot with small semicircular reliefs ("eyebrows") machined into the sides of the opening to facilitate entry of the stripper clip. Although Marine Corps armorers familiar with the system have acknowledged the difference, it is not known if this was a planned modification (a simplified machining process, perhaps) or a production oversight that occurred on a random basis. One thing is certain—unless someone can say he's seen the clip-slot on every M700 receiver made for the Marine Corps, there is no way of knowing the extent of this anomaly and how many receivers were involved. With the telescope mounting base covering the clip-slot as it did, few Marines tasked with using this rifle in combat have ever seen the M700/M40 charger guide. The telescope mounting base covers the opening completely. (Peter R. Senich.)

An early issue USMC M700 sniper rifle at Weapons Training Battalion, Quantico, Virginia (8 February 1967). The rifle is equipped with a USMC specification 3X-9X variable-power Redfield sight (green anodized finish) and a web sling. The weapon is ready to fire; the safety is set (back). The telescope power selector ring is positioned at or near 5-power. The USMC Scout-Sniper Rifles were not fielded in any appreciable quantity until early 1967. The rifle shown was among the very first furnished to the Marine Corps. As a matter of reader interest, both the rifle serial number (224237) and the Federal Stock Number (FSN 1005-930-5444) were included in the original photo caption. (U.S. Marine Corps.)

Another view of the early-issue M700 Remington sniper rifle serial no. 224237. (U.S. Marine Corps.)

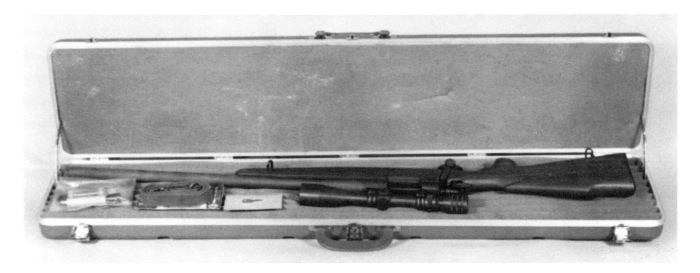

Marine Corps M700 sniper rifle serial no. 224237 (8 February 1967) with cleaning gear and accessory items. The molded plastic carrying case was intended to protect the weapon in transit. (U.S. Marine Corps.)

A portion of the machining facilities at the Remington Custom Shop during the early 1960s. The work table holds various Remington target rifles. The technician is examining an International Match Free Rifle. Note the barrel blanks on the machine opposite. In addition to target and custom sporting rifles, the Custom Shop "handcrafted" special purpose rifles for law enforcement and military applications. (Remington Arms Co.)

A 1960s Remington photograph shows a Custom Shop technician "air-gaging" a target barrel. Equipment of this type was considered indispensable for determining dimensional characteristics of the rifling (the same equipment was used by military marksmanship training units). The Custom Shop was responsible for a wide variety of "non-standard rifle production" through the years. The Vietnam-era Marine Corps sniper rifle was among these. (Remington Arms Co.)

Marine Corps combat photo with caption that reads, "A sniper of 'E' Company, Second Battalion, Seventh Regiment attached to First Platoon zeros in on a Viet Cong during Operation Arizona 25 miles southwest of Da Nang." Note the field gear carried by the sniper, the flak vest and the helmet serving as a rifle rest. The photo was taken on 20 June 1967. (U.S. Marine Corps.)

Marine sniper team (Cpl. O. Trujillo and Pfc. J. Trevine, 3d MarDiv) during combat in South Vietnam. The M14-equipped rifleman provides "security" for the sharpshooter. An M14 with iron sights was as important to the sniper-spotter team as the telescopic-sighted rifle. Various sniper platoons fielded M14s glass-bedded and accurized to improve performance; the match ammunition used with the sniper rifle was also fired in this weapon. An untold number of "kills" were made with the M14 in Vietnam. (U.S. Marine Corps.)

First Marine Division (Fifth Marines) sniper-spotter team L.Cpl. M.E. Berry and Pfc. R.E. Josey during a practice firing session, 19 June 1967. The spotter is equipped with an M16; note the glasses (corrective lenses) on the ground to his left. (U.S. Marine Corps.)

Marine sniper Pfc. D. Taylor "sights in on an NVA rifleman harassing Marines during operations south of Phu Bai" (15 August 1967). The spotter is Cpl. B. MacDonald. (U.S. Marine Corps.)

Left: A Marine marksman uses an old tombstone as a rest for his M700/M40 Scout-Sniper Rifle during an isolated encounter in RVN. (U.S. Marine Corps.)

Below: Marine rifleman (1st MarDiv) with an M16-mounted AN/PVS-1 Starlight Scope taking aim at dusk during Operation Shelby south of Da Nang, September 1967. Although Marine marksmen were known to employ Starlight Scopes for sniping purposes, their night vision equipment was used with conventional M14 and M16 rifles. The M16 is an early model; the bipod helped to steady the weapon with the Starlight Scope in place. (U.S. Marine Corps.)

Scout-Sniper Pfc. Dennis L. Caudle on Hill 689 west of Khe Sanh. (Dennis L. Caudle.)

The first Starlight Scope fielded for combat use in Southeast Asia, the AN/PVS-1 (Army-Navy/Portable Visible-Light Detection Series Number 1), is a portable, battery-operated, electro-optical instrument intended for passive visual observation and surveillance at night. It uses natural light, moonlight, or starlight for target illumination. The 4-power night vision sight was 18.50 inches long and 3.375 inches wide and weighed 6 pounds. The telescope was fitted with a conventional mount assembly. The unit was issued with a carrying case and accessories. (Excalibur Enterprises.)

The classic photograph of Marine snipers taken during the battle for Khe Sahn appeared in the February 23, 1968, issue of *LIFE* magazine in a feature article entitled "Khe Sanh" by David Douglas Duncan. According to the original caption, "The snipers of Khe Sanh work in three-man teams. . . . Here L.Cpl. Albert Miranda, 19, of El Paso, Texas, squeezes off a shot at a North Vietnamese soldier so far away as to be invisible without the help of glasses or exceptionally keen sight. His fellow sniper, L.Cpl. David Burdwell, 20, of Wichita Falls, Texas (center), calls the shot together with their platoon lieutenant, Alec Bodenwiser of Portland, Oregon, the third member of the team. For hours they sit motionless, stalking with their telescopic sights a quarry who, at the fatal moment, may feel alone—and safe."

David Douglas Duncan is widely known for his memorable photographs of Marine Corps combat personnel. From the Korean War on, when he was with the Marines in North Korea in 1950, Duncan has shared the same fate as the Marines he has recorded on film. This photograph is presented with the kind permission of the copyright holder, David Douglas Duncan. (David Douglas Duncan.)

Third Marine Division Scout-Sniper L.Cpl. James L. O'Neill is pictured with his Remington sniper rifle (serial no. 224192) in the Dong Ha area (1968). (James L. O'Neill.)

Third Marine Division L.Cpl. R. Moore "sights in on an enemy soldier" (19 October 1968). (U.S. Marine Corps.)

Marine sniper D.L. Caudle is pictured with a modified M14 rifle. The rear portion of the stock was removed, and a foregrip was added to control the weapon during automatic fire. Note the night vision sight bracket on the receiver. Even though unauthorized modifications were normally prohibited, a variety of altered weapons saw combat use in Southeast Asia. The unit and the type of operations usually had a direct bearing on the level of tolerance for this type of activity. (Dennis L. Caudle.)

A Scout-Sniper attached to Delta 1/5 selects an NVA target during the battle for the Citadel, 22 February 1968. The Marine marksman is equipped with an M700 Remington sniper rifle. (U.S. Marine Corps.)

Marine Corps rifleman during impromptu sniping activity near Dong Ha. The Army M14 sniper rifle was "liberated" from a Special Forces camp near Khe Sanh. According to Thomas F. Swearengen, retired chief warrant officer (USMC) and noted combat shotgun authority, "There was no match ammunition available to us; it was necessary to strip cartridges from M60 ammo belts. The rifle was used on targets in the 400–500 yard range. There were always three of us, one shooter and two with glasses [binoculars] and M16s for backup." An Army M14, in any form, was considered "fair game" to Marine Corps combat personnel. (Max Crace.)

CHAPTER 10

THE REMINGTON-REDFIELD SYSTEM

With the planning process completed and funding approved, formal contracts for the USMC sniping system were placed with Remington and Redfield during May 1966.

According to Marine Corps "Supply Contract" NOm-73565, dated 17 May 1966, a total of 700 Redfield 3X-9X variable-power Accu-Range riflescopes ("Scope, Special USMC Model") along with Redfield JR (Junior) 1-inch split-rings (low) and Redfield "Base, Special, JR 40X" were ordered from the Redfield Gun Sight Company, Denver, Colorado, for use with the Remington M700 Rifle.

The contract specified that shipment of the telescope and mounting hardware be made as follows:

- 29 each of the telescope, rings, and instruction booklet were to be sent to Marine Corps Supply Center, Albany, Georgia.

- 121 each of the same items were consigned to the Marine Corps Supply Center, Barstow, California.

- 550 each of the telescope and rings and 700 of the Redfield base and instruction booklet were to be shipped directly to the Remington Arms Company, Ilion, New York.

The contract also stated that shipments were scheduled to begin on or before 20 June 1966, with final shipment on or before 29 August 1966.

In addition to the Redfield order, Headquarters, USMC placed a parallel contract with the Remington Arms Company, Bridgeport, Connecticut ("Supply Contract" NOm-73566, 17 May 1966), for the Rifle, 7.62mm, Sniper, Remington M700, with requirements as follows:

- 550 each, Redfield scope and base installed, calibrated and test-fired.

- 150 each, Redfield base only installed.

In accordance with the contract specifications, in this case, shipments were to be made as follows:

- 123 of the rifles with telescopic sights and 29 without the sights (base only) were consigned to Marine Corps Supply Center, Albany, Georgia.

- 427 of the rifles with telescopic sights and 121 without the sights (base only) were destined for shipment to Marine Corps Supply Center, Barstow, California.

The time of delivery for both the telescope and the rifle was coordinated through 29 August 1966 in the contract as well.

NOTE: As a matter of interest, information circulated by the Ilion Research Division (Remington) during February 1966, more than three months before the contracts were placed, listed part numbers and component parts for the "Remington M700 Military Sniper Rifle." Such preproduction planning was considered "standard procedure" in American industry and served to decrease the amount of lead-time (the time between a firm commitment and the actual start-up of the manufacturing process) necessary to produce the Marine Corps sniper rifle.

Efforts to protect the rifle and scope when the system was shipped or transported (hand carried) from one duty station to another by sniper personnel included procurement of a special carrying case fabricated from molded plastic. The routine transfer of rifle team equipment, though packed and shipped as required, had proven less than satisfactory on numerous occasions. The equipment was often damaged in transit, especially when it was shipped overseas. The adoption of a special case was intended to eliminate this problem.

Marine Corps Supply Contract NOm-73564, 18 May 1966, awarded to Protecto Plastics, Inc., Wind Gap, Pennsylvania, specified the following:

Case, Carrying, Rifle, molded plastic, size 46" long, 9" wide, 3 1/2" deep, with luggage-type carrying handles and locks, interior lined with polyurethane cushioning foam, light-weight, scuff-proof, spot, stain and impact resistant, hardware and trim to be non-rust metal.

A total of 550 units were ordered; 100 cases were to be delivered on or before 20 June 1966, the balance by 1 July 1966. The carrying cases were shipped directly to Remington Arms Co. in Ilion, New York.

Marine Corps specifications for the principal component of the new sniping system, the rifle, were duly noted as follows in Supply Contract NOm-73566:

Rifle, 7.62mm, Snipers, Remington M40 (M700). 7.62mm bolt action Remington M700 Rifle with short action receiver and heavy sniper barrel. Rifle magazine capacity of five rounds, stock to have dull oil finish, metal to have military finish (parkerized), military sling swivels, clip slot in receiver, aluminum butt plate, hand operated repeater. Solid frame with take down stock. Rifle cocks as bolt handle is lowered to lock action closed. Extract and eject as bolt is opened. Direct action trigger.

Two stop safety. FIRE position on forward—SAFE position rearward. Action must feed, fire, extract and eject (include extraction and ejection without firing) satisfactory with all varieties of ammunition listed as standard length for listed calibers in SAAMI manual. Barrel to be round tapered to breech and crowned, twist 1 in 10 inches R.H. Chamber to be basic 7.62 NATO. Ejector-plunger type spring loaded and pin assembled in bolt head. Extractor-circular, clip type assembled inside bolt rim with rivet. Firing pin spring retracted in bolt. Receiver—cylindrical, alloy steel with 6 holes drilled and tapped for Redfield scope and mounts. Stock—American Walnut with Monte Carlo cheek piece—Pistol grip with comb. Weight approximately 9 lbs.

Accuracy
Range 100 yards—Accuracy 300 yards - point of impact
Point of Aim—Center on target
Center of impact—1 - MOA
Group size 100 yards E.S. one inch (1") 5 shot center to center
with bench rest
Ammunition—7.62mm Ball XM118 Match

NOTE: The specific mention of "6 holes drilled and tapped" (receiver) in the contract specifications referred to 4 holes directly on top of the receiver and 2 holes on the left side. In this case, the threaded holes (2) were intended for mounting receiver sights. Though rarely used, this feature is found on M700 rifles predating the USMC contract rifles. Remington continued this practice with the M700 until the early 1980s. At this juncture (1966), the receiver for the USMC sniper rifle was essentially a 40X target rifle receiver with Model 700 markings.

Although subtle variations (minor changes that did not affect performance or reliability) appear to have been part of the 700 rifle order procured by the Marine Corps, the principal characteristics of the Vietnam-era M700/M40 USMC sniper rifles (with exceptions noted) were essentially the same.

The 7.62mm (.308 caliber) Remington Model 700 sniper rifle made use of a standard action (clip-slot in receiver) fitted with a tapered free-floating (free-floated back to the receiver; approximately .035-inch clearance between the barrel and stock) 24-inch barrel (.830-inch muzzle diameter). The barrel was referenced as a "varmint weight" or "medium-weight" barrel in Remington collateral documents.

The walnut stock, a sporter-type with an integral cheek rest (Monte Carlo style with cheekpiece), was described by Remington as a "ADL type for 5-round BDL-type magazine, no fore end tip or grip cap, 13-3/8 inch length of pull (factory standard), no checkering, non-detachable swivels, oil finish."

The action on the original USMC sniper rifles was not glass-bedded at the factory. The system was defined by Remington as a "hand-bedded action and a free-floating stock."

The receiver ring and bridge were drilled and tapped for mounting the Redfield telescope base. The telescopic sight mounted directly over the centerline of the receiver. The receiver was also drilled and tapped (left side, rear) for a receiver sight; there was no provision for a front sight.

An inspection/date/assembly stamp appeared on the barrel of the rifles categorized as "early production"; a "7.62 NATO" stamping was substituted later. The left side of the receiver bore the designation

"Remington" (logo) and "Model 700" (model number), as well as "U.S.," which appeared over the six-digit serial number.

The barrel and receiver were parkerized (green), the aluminum butt plate and trigger guard assembly were anodized (black), and the bolt assembly was given a black oxide finish. The rifle serial number was placed on the underside of the bolt (electric pencil) when the weapon passed final inspection. The rifle weighed 9 1/2 pounds with the telescope in place, and the overall length was 43 1/2 inches.

When it came to bringing the rifle and telescope together, Ludwig P. (Paul) Gogol, a Remington design engineer and custom shop foreman when the USMC M700 sniper rifles were manufactured, offered the following:

> Ordnance inspectors witnessed all operations including targeting, final inspection and packing procedures. The rifles were sighted-in and targeted at the Ilion Fish and Game Club facilities. After targeting and acceptance, the rifles were placed in a hard case with their accessories, packed in cardboard containers, and palletized for shipment.

NOTE: The USMC contract requirements specified the following, in part: "The rifle, scope and base shall be identified with matching numbers utilizing the rifle serial number." This procedure took place following targeting and final acceptance of the rifle and scope as a "matched assembly." So far as it is known, the rifles shipped from Remington without telescopic sights did not have the serial number engraved on the receiver base.

As Gogol added, "The rifles left Remington as a complete package, ready for use."

The contract also specified that the "Preservation, Packaging and Packing" of the rifle with the scope and base installed (550) was to be carried out in the following manner:

> Rifle shall be coated with rust preventative and placed in vapor sealed bag (Springfield Armory Dwg. #B7265933 dated 15 May 1964).

> Vapor sealed bag shall be placed in Protecto Carrying Case.

> Protecto Carrying Case shall be repacked and taped in original shipping carton.

> Five (5) cartons shall be placed in one (1) outer container (3V-C) which shall be sealed with waterproof tape.

> Six (6) 3V-C containers to be palletized in accordance with MTL - STD - 147A, Figure 3, Load type 1.

The following material was packed with the rifle and telescope assembly in the special carrying cases ("one each [1] per end item"): the "Redfield commercial telescope manual, Sling, leather or web, and Kits of Basic Issue Items."

NOTE: The "Kits of Basic Issue Items" were referenced as "Government Furnished Material" (GFM) and contained the following:

> Brush Cleaning Small Arms (FSN 1005-556-4174)

> Brush Cleaning Small Arms Chamber (FSN 1005-690-8441)

Case, Cleaning Rod (FSN 1005-650-4510)

Case, Lubricant (FSN 1005-791-3377)

Extractor, Ruptured Ctg. Case (FSN 4933-652-9950)

Holder Cleaning Patch (FSN 1005-726-6110)

Rod Section Cleaning Small Arms (FSN 1005-726-6109)

The rifles with just the base installed (150) were prepared for shipment "in accordance with Military Specification MIL - P - 14232B (28 January 1965) Level A." The Redfield commercial manual and a leather or web sling were packed with this equipment. The special carrying case and the basic issue items were not included.

Provisions were made for "Repair Parts" for the system, and "factory training for five (5) Marine Corps personnel" (armorers) was specified as well.

Even though most of the rifles and telescopes from the original contract were ultimately shipped to South Vietnam from the West Coast (California), details concerning the quantities involved, the shipping dates, and the final destinations have not been disclosed.

On the other hand, subsequent orders of USMC sniping equipment are known to have been shipped from the Remington plant in Ilion, New York, to Force Logistic Command, Chu Lai, Republic of Vietnam.

Contrary to the fact that Remington "Production Tables" for 1966 include "700 Marine Rifles" in the yearly total, and veteran Marine Corps ordnance personnel insist that M700 sniper rifles reached Vietnam in late 1966, from all indications, the USMC Scout-Sniper Rifles were not fielded in any appreciable quantity until early 1967.

Though the exact "in-service" dates and locations in RVN were undoubtedly recorded on a clipboard as most things official were in the Marine Corps, this information has not surfaced thus far. In any event, however, judging from the information contained in Marine Corps Order (MCO) 8110.1, Advanced Logistics Data for the Scout-Sniper Rifle, Headquarters, USMC (3 January 1967), distribution activity for the M700 sniper rifle did not begin in earnest until early 1967. As it was then stated, the document was intended to "provide advance logistic information for placing the Scout-Sniper Rifle immediately in-service." According to the MCO:

> Adequate stocks of the Scout-Sniper Rifle are in the supply system to support authorized allowances. . . .
> Initial issue of the Scout-Sniper Rifle and repair parts will be accomplished by CMC directed shipment to the First and Third Marine Divisions and appropriate supporting units. The rifle also will be furnished the Second and Fifth Marine Divisions as well as Reserve Activities by CMC directed shipment. . . .
> This Order constitutes authority to initiate service with the Scout-Sniper Rifle. . . .
> An in-service target date is hereby established as 1 February 1967. Report the actual date on which the subject Scout-Sniper Rifle is placed in service use to the Commandant of the Marine Corps (Code A04).

NOTE: According to personnel involved with the USMC sniper training program at Camp Pendleton, California, the initial shipment of M700 sniper rifles (50) arrived during the "first week of January 1967." Camp Pendleton emerged as the principal Scout-Sniper training facility in the United States. The first sniper class started in January 1967.

The following information was listed under "Logistical Planning Data" in MCO 8110.1:

Stock No.	FSN 1005-930-5444 (Identifies the Remington, M700, Sniper Rifle with Redfield Scope and Mount)
	FSN 1005-999-8807 (Identifies the Remington, M700, Sniper Rifle without Redfield Scope)
	FSN 1240-937-0825 (Identifies the Redfield Scope, 3X-9X Variable)
Unit Cost	$266.00 (FSN 1005-930-5444)
	$149.00 (FSN 1005-999-8807)
Publications	
Commercial	Technical and Parts Lists will be furnished by the manufacturers.
Commercial	The Operation, Function and Care of Your Redfield Scope.
Military	SL 3-05539A and SL 4-05539A will be distributed 15 January 1967.

The Marine Corps practice of issuing match-grade ammunition for sniping purposes in RVN would continue with the Scout-Sniper Rifle. The 7.62mm (.308-caliber) ammunition furnished with the M700/M40 rifle was described as follows: "The cartridge caliber 7.62mm M118 MATCH is the sniper's standard cartridge."

The characteristics of the M118 match cartridge were listed as follows in the Vietnam-era USMC sniper training manual *FMFM 1-3B, SNIPING* (5 August 1969):

> Caliber 7.62mm M118 is identified by the word MATCH stamped on the head, the last two digits of the year of manufacture, and arsenal identification letters (e.g., L.C. identifies Lake City). The M118 has a 173-grain boat-tailed bullet, a velocity of 2,550 feet per second, and an accuracy specification of 3.5 inches mean radius at 600 yards.

NOTE: As a matter of reader interest, .30-caliber (.30-06) and 7.62mm match ammunition resemble each other in every way except length. The .30-caliber cartridge is 3.34 -inches in overall length, and the 7.62mm version is 2.83 inches long overall. The .30-caliber match ammunition (M72) was issued with the Model 70 Winchester and the M1D. Although 7.62mm match ammunition (M118) was intended primarily for the Scout-Sniper Rifle, Marine riflemen were known to secure match-grade ammunition for their M14 rifles whenever the opportunity presented itself. The government arsenal match-grade ammunition used by Army and Marine Corps snipers in Southeast Asia was manufactured at Frankford Arsenal (FA) and Lake City Arsenal (LC).

Although regular-issue ball ammunition could be utilized with this sniping system, conclusive Army and Marine Corps studies had determined the M80 round to be unsatisfactory for sniping purposes. Both Army and Marine Corps snipers were admonished to use standard ammunition only if it was absolutely necessary. Beyond the infrequent use of tracer ammunition, standard ball and armor-piercing cartridges were rarely employed by American snipers in Southeast Asia.

Unlike the Army's XM21 sniping system, which allowed the sniper to interchange the ART with a Starlight Scope for night operations, the Scout-Sniper Rifle possessed only a daylight capability except for rare occasions when conditions enabled a Marine sniper to use a riflescope at night.

Even though Marine Corps ordnance documents mentioned "an adapter bracket for the Remington M700" as early as 1967, efforts to broaden the night vision capability of the USMC sniper rifle did not take shape until late 1969 or early 1970.

NOTE: The Ordnance School, Quantico, fabricated an MTU-designed aluminum mount for the M700/M40 to accept the current ART and Starlight Scopes. The special mount extended down the left side of the receiver to form the same mounting area as the M14 rifle. In addition to at least two variations of MTU mountings, the U.S. Army Night Vision Laboratory fabricated a "low profile" steel version for USMC testing as well.

Although measures to adapt night vision equipment to the USMC sniper rifle were actively pursued, mounting a Starlight Scope on a bolt-action rifle proved to be a difficult proposition. Furthermore, the Marine Corps was not entirely convinced that replacing one sighting system with another in a combat environment was in the best interest of optimum accuracy. The Scout-Sniper Rifle was not equipped to mount night vision sights during Marine Corps involvement in Southeast Asia. When equipment of this type was necessary, the M14 or the M16 served in this capacity.

In view of the fact that the Vietnam-era USMC Scout-Sniper Rifle was alternately referenced as the "M700" or "M40" sniper rifle, in the interest of avoiding any possible confusion in this matter, when the system was selected for Marine Corps sniper use in Vietnam, the Remington rifle was, for the most part, referenced as the "M700 sniper rifle." The "M40" designation would not see widespread use until much later.

Though Supply Contract NOm-73566 (17 May 1966) also lists the rifle as the "Remington M40 (M700)" in the specifications, with few exceptions noted, Marine Corps documents referenced the Remington sniper rifle as the "Rifle, 7.62mm, Sniper, Remington, M700," the "Model 700 Rifle," "Model 700," "M700," or the "Scout-Sniper Rifle" during the early phases of procurement and combat use.

The Remington firm, on the other hand, referred to the Marine Corps rifle as the "Model 700 Precision Rifle," "Model 700 Sniper," "M700 Military Sniper Rifle," and the "Special Purpose M700."

Though later officially designated as the "Rifle, 7.62mm, Sniper, M40," with proper regards to official changes in nomenclature in this case, the alternate use of the M700 and M40 reference would continue until the emergence of the M40A1 sniper rifle some years later.

For most of the Marines with combat duty in RVN, the weapon they carried as snipers will always be known to them as "the M700 sniper rifle."

Even though Remington production records indicate a total of 995 7.62mm Model 700 sniper rifles were manufactured from 1966 to 1971, Remington completed the 1966 Marine Corps order (700 rifles) that same year (550 rifles with telescopic sights, 150 rifles without telescopes). The yearly total of Model 700 sniper rifles is noted as follows:

1966	1967	1968	1969	1970	1971
700	62	87	137	8	1

In addition to a small quantity of rifles the Marine Corps obtained for combat and subsequent development purposes following the initial order, the U.S. Navy and the Air Force reportedly obtained an unknown number of the Vietnam-era Remington sniper rifles as well.

NOTE: With Remington holding the "proprietary rights" to the Model 700 rifle as it did, even though the Marine Corps sniper rifle was made to USMC specifications, a similar weapon could be sold to whomever the Remington firm deemed worthy. In addition to those indicated, Sionics, Inc., the silencer and suppressor firm, purchased a small quantity of 7.62mm M700 sniper rifles (identical to those furnished to the Marine Corps) during this period.

In any event, veteran Remington staff members insist that "the M700 sniper rifles produced during this era [995] were made to USMC specifications."

According to Remington information, the "first" Model 700 serial number series began at 1000 in 1962 and ended with the 1968 model year at or near 387000. The second block began on or about 26 November 1968 at 6200000. The "second series" (rifle serial numbering) began as a result of the 1968 Federal Gun Control Act. A small quantity of M40 sniper rifles with serial numbering in the early "second series" was, in fact, procured from Remington for USMC test and evaluation purposes following the difficulties encountered with the system in Vietnam. Except for the rifles mentioned, it is important to emphasize that all but a few of the Model 700 Remington sniper rifles furnished to the Marine Corps were assembled and shipped before 1969, and these, of course, will bear "six-digit" serial numbering. The Vietnam-era USMC M700/M40 sniper rifles with seven-digit serial numbers are categorized as being part of the "product improvement series." Although quantities were extremely limited, Marine Corps ordnance documents from this era do list rifles used for evaluation purposes with seven-digit serial numbers.

It is important to note that even though a seven-digit serial number would tend to suggest a previously unknown serial number range for the USMC M700/M40 sniper rifles, in view of the limited number of rifles procured for evaluation purposes, any weapon categorized as a Vietnam-era USMC development rifle without proper documentation should be viewed with reservation.

Furthermore, when the remaining M700/M40 sniper rifles were eventually reconfigured by the Marine Corps following the Vietnam War, many of the principal components (barrels, stocks, trigger guards, etc.) were scrapped, while some of the parts were retrieved and circulated as souvenirs. Unfortunately, many of the same parts have been used to transform standard M700 rifles into "original Scout-Sniper Rifles" for the collector trade in the years since. As hell would have it, there are no machining and/or assembly operations (clip-slot included) on the USMC M700/M40 rifle that cannot be duplicated by a competent gunsmith using the equipment available today.

Even though a partial list of M700 sniper rifle serial numbers categorized as Marine Corps issue has seen publication, without the benefit of knowing the specific serial numbers for all of the rifles purchased by the Marine Corps, an incomplete listing, as common sense dictates, serves no practical purpose in this case. Therefore, it is important to understand that any Vietnam-era Marine Corps sniper rifle offered as "authentic" should be viewed with extreme caution.

In any event, however, by 1973, as official documents attest, of all the rifles procured by the Marine Corps (the exact number remains unknown), there were only 425 ("total density") Remington M700/M40 sniper rifles remaining in the Marine Corps worldwide.

While it appears that at least half of the sniper rifles procured by the Marine Corps were lost or rendered unserviceable for one reason or another, this cannot necessarily be attributed outright to combat losses as some contend. Rather, according to Marine Corps ordnance personnel with firsthand knowledge of the situation, USMC sniper rifles were, in some cases, depending on their availability, "issued" to any combat units that could prove a valid need for equipment of this type.

By all accounts, in addition to supplying U.S. Navy personnel, Marine Corps sniping hardware was also furnished to Vietnamese Marines (VNMC), Korean Marines (ROKMC), and U.S. Army Special Forces.

By way of partial explanation, rather than tracking sniper equipment by the rifle serial number, as took place later in the war, for a time, the practice of using the Federal Stock Number (FSN) as the principal means of identifying this equipment made "accountability" less of a problem for ordnance personnel in South Vietnam. As a veteran Marine ordnance officer summarized it:

The scale and tempo of operations called for decisions and the use of equipment that would have never taken place during peace-time or back in the United States. If putting some of our goods in the hands of people who could help us is what it took, then that's what we did and we didn't think twice about it either. With the level of combat operations as they were in the I Corps area, we were supporting the equipment needs of more than just Marines.

For the lack of a better description, an unknown quantity of USMC sniping equipment simply "fell through the cracks" in South Vietnam. At this juncture, there is no way of accurately determining what actually happened to a large portion of the Vietnam-era Scout-Sniper Rifles. The figure cited earlier (425) came as a direct result of Marine Corps efforts to locate and determine exactly how many rifles would need to be reconfigured in conjunction with official measures to improve the system.

In retrospect, however, the Remington sniper rifles were well received at the Stateside training centers. The reports of problems with the system in Vietnam did little to dampen the enthusiasm for the new equipment. So far as the typical sniper candidate was concerned, this was issue equipment and if there were any flaws in the system, they were rarely encountered during the time spent in training. The rifles used for training purposes remained in the United States, and the men trained as Scout-Snipers received their sniping rifles in Vietnam.

Drawing on the fresh perspective of an experienced rifleman during his sniper training at Camp Pendleton, California, Sgt. Douglas Mark de Haas, winner of the 1,000-yard Leech Cup Match at the 1966 National Rifle and Pistol Matches, offered the following impressions of the Scout-Sniper Rifle in an article entitled "Letter from a Marine Sniper" in the April 1968 issue of *American Rifleman*:

> The rifles really look good. They are new Model 700 Remingtons with 3X-9X Redfield scopes with the Accu-Range finder. They have the regular stock with medium weight barrel. We will be sighting these rifles in for 500 yards only, and holding either high or low for all other ranges, as the scopes have internal adjustments which cannot be adjusted quickly.
>
> This rifle is a modified version of the Remington Model 700 Varmint rifle in .308 caliber. It has a heavy 24" tapered barrel and a light sporter-type stock with a non-reflecting oil finish (like the stocks on all military rifles). . . .

NOTE: According to Remington authority John F. Lacy (*The Remington 700*), "The M40 closely resembles the 700 Varmint Special. In fact, the 700 Varmint Special was introduced in 1967 and had been developed from the M40 instead of the other way around. The Varmint Special retains the pressure point between the fore-end and the barrel rather than being free-floated as on the M40." The Remington "Varmint Special" was not available in .308 caliber (7.62mm) until 1976.

> The scope is a standard Redfield 3X-9X variable with Accu-Range finder attached to the rifle with the Redfield Jr. mount. We were instructed to keep the black plastic scope caps on all the time except when firing, as the sun shining into the scope might melt the plastic range finder. Even so, we did not use the range finder in our training with this rifle.
>
> Unless I was careful in sighting through the scope, parallax was a problem at the longer ranges. We did all our firing with the scope set on 9X magnification.
>
> Now, as for the rifle's accuracy, I thought it was very good, all things considered. All firing was done from the prone position over sand bags. Imagine shooting 100-150 rounds through a cal. .308 bolt-action rifle in this position with no recoil pad on the rifle and wearing only a thin, unpadded shooting jacket! To protect my shoulder, I stuck a rubber shower shoe under the jacket to help absorb recoil [though the practice was viewed with disfavor by the typical instructor, more than one Marine sniper recalls "using a shower shoe" to cushion the recoil of his sniper rifle during training]. This position called for the use of a

high sand bag under the forearm and nothing but the clenched fist under the toe of the buttstock. It is not a rock steady position, even if all other conditions are perfect. Besides the rather high position and recoil of the rifle, we had to contend with wind, mirage, and changing light conditions.

Even with all this I could still consistently hold all the shots within a 12" circle at 500 yards, with most of the shots even tighter yet. We fired at silhouette targets 19" high by 26" wide, with a pistol target repair center stapled on the front to give us a 6" aiming bull. We sighted-in at 500 yards, then held off when firing at 200, 300, and 600 yards. We did not make any sight corrections at all after we were sighted-in at 500 yards, as making quick and reliable adjustments with the scope was not possible. So we had to aim approximately 18" low at 200 and 300 yards, and approximately 26" high at 600 yards.

Here I fudged a little. After firing for a couple of days, I found it was pretty tricky aiming that high at 600 yards. So I sighted-in at 500 yards, aiming at the bottom of the silhouette. That way I only had to hold about 3"-5" over the head, which was much easier to see than holding a foot or more over. Anyway, it worked fine, as on qualification day firing in a switching 1 o'clock to 11 o'clock wind, I ended up with the only perfect score in our class.

Sergeant de Haas went on to serve as a sniper instructor in South Vietnam.

Even though the Model 700/Redfield combination possessed the characteristics sought by the Marine Corps, the system was plagued by a number of difficulties with both the telescope and the rifle.

A Marine Corps M700 sniper rifle mounting a 3X-9X variable-power Accu-Range USMC/Redfield contract sight. An original "matched assembly" in this case, the telescope and receiver base are engraved with the rifle serial number (no. 224353). The barrel and receiver are parkerized, and the bolt assembly was given a black oxide finish. The aluminum trigger guard and floorplate were "colored black." The Redfield sight was anodized (olive green) to match the barrel and receiver; telescope mounting hardware was finished in black. (Otte Collection.)

A close-up view of Marine Corps M700 sniper rifle no. 224353. The Remington logo, model designation, "U.S.," and the serial number were "roll marked" into the receiver. Except for a small quantity of Model 40-X target rifle receivers (so marked) used for evaluation purposes, the receivers of Marine Corps sniping issue categorized as "production rifles" were marked as shown. Note the barrel markings and the matching number telescope and mounting base. In this case, the barrel markings (U E N 41) indicate the rifle was assembled in October 1966. (Otte Collection.)

A close-up view of a matching number USMC M700/Redfield sniper rifle produced during the Vietnam War. The rifle serial number (no. 322764) was applied to the left side of the receiver mounting base and the telescope tube directly behind the objective bell. The numbering was done with a "hand-held engraving tool" (electric pencil) when the weapon passed final inspection. The rifle serial number was also placed on the underside of the bolt. A review of Vietnam-era USMC M700/M40 rifles and sights indicates that the numbering was consistent in form and artfully applied. The "7.62 NATO" barrel stamping (left) appears on rifles categorized as "late production." Remington met its obligations by serial numbering the sight assemblies, but with telescope mounting hardware toleranced and manufactured as it was (i.e., the use of interchangeable components), and as long as the rifle and scope were both in working order and zeroed properly, it made little difference if the parts were numbered or not. When problems beset the weapon system in Vietnam, the rifles and scopes were "switched" on a routine basis in an effort to keep sniping equipment in the field. Few of the remaining matching number ("factory matched assembly") Remington/Redfield sniper rifles were ever subjected to combat use in Southeast Asia. (Scott Collection.)

The "business end" (muzzle) of a medium-heavy barrel from a M700 Remington sniper rifle. The tapered, free-floating barrel (free-floated back to the receiver; approximately .035 inch clearance between the barrel and the stock) was also referenced as a "varmint weight barrel" in Remington documents dating from early 1966. (Peter R. Senich.)

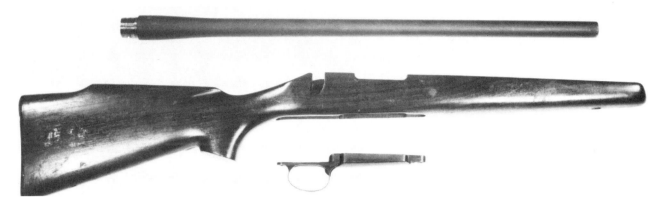

An original Remington barrel, stock, and trigger guard assembly removed from a Marine Corps M700/M40 sniper rifle when it was reconfigured to M40A1 specifications during the late 1970s. The barrel was made of a proprietary alloy Remington chose to reference as "ordnance steel." The rifle stock, a sporter-type with an integral cheek rest, was made of American walnut. The trigger guard and the floorplate are die-cast aluminum alloy. As a matter of interest, despite claims that "steel floorplates were used," the Vietnam-era Remington sniper rifles purchased by the Marine Corps were fitted with aluminum trigger guards and floorplates. (Peter R. Senich.)

A close-up view of the barrel markings on the Vietnam-era USMC M700/M40 sniper rifles. The triangle stamp (left) denotes magnaflux testing. The "R.E.P." marking (Remington English Proof) surrounded by an oval was usually placed on the factory-installed M700 barrels. The

heart-shaped "gallery stamp" signified function and accuracy testing. The markings appear on the right side of the barrel near the receiver. Barrels fitted to the original Marine Corps sniper rifles were all made by Remington. The heart-shaped stamping does not indicate a Hart barrel as some contend, a point verified by both Remington and the Hart organization. (Peter R. Senich.)

An example of Remington barrel markings (left side) that appear on M700 sniper rifles categorized as "early production." In this case, the "U D N 41" stamping represents the inspector (U), the month (D), and the year (N). The two-digit number (41) next to the recoil lug/receiver is an assembler's stamp. With the barrel stamped as indicated here, the rifle was assembled in September 1966. The coding was a routine part of the Remington production process. (Peter R. Senich.)

An inside view of a Vietnam-era Remington M700 sniper rifle stock. The action on the original USMC sniper rifles was not glass-bedded at the factory. The system was defined by Remington as a "hand-bedded action and a free-floating stock." The recess for the recoil lug is clearly visible. (Peter R. Senich.)

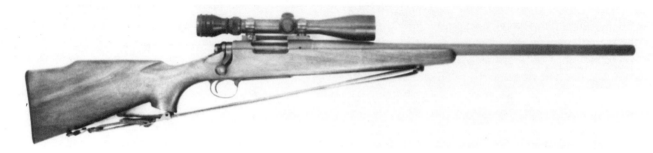

An original Vietnam-era Remington M700/M40 sniper rifle (serial no. 314165) mounting a second generation 3X-9X variable-power Redfield Accu-Range rifle scope (black satin finish). The rifle is part of the small-arms collection at Springfield Armory. (Springfield Armory NHS.)

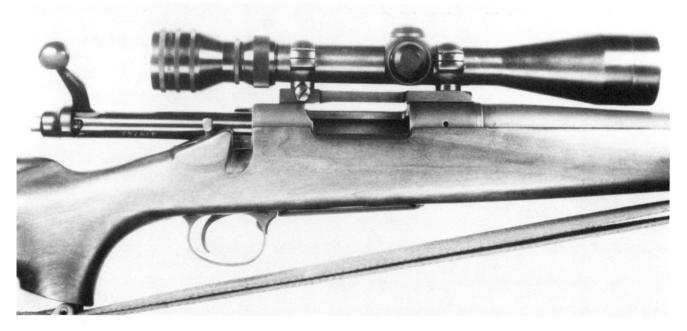

The Remington sniper rifle (no. 314165) with the bolt drawn back. Note the rifle serial number engraved (electric pencil) on the underside of the bolt. The entire serial number was applied to the M700 bolt body on a routine basis; the numbering took place when the weapon passed final inspection. Only the last four digits were used beginning in early 1969. The rifle and scope have been at Springfield Armory for more than 20 years. When examined during the early 1970s, the weapon and telescopic sight appeared to be unused. (Springfield Armory NHS.)

A close-up view of Remington sniper rifle serial no. 314165. The receiver markings are typical; the barrel is stamped "7.62 NATO." There are no rifle numbers on the telescope or the original mounting base. A closely numbered rifle (no. 314169) is part of the Remington small-arms collection at Ilion, New York. In this case, an original USMC/Redfield contract sight is mounted on the rifle. The telescope and the mounting base are not numbered, however. Rifle no. 314165 and no. 314169 are believed to have been "set aside" as representative examples during the final stages of production. (Springfield Armory NHS.)

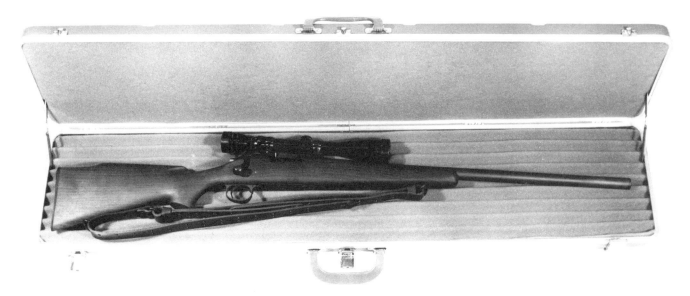

A "factory fresh" USMC Remington Model 700 sniper rifle (May 1966) and "special carrying case" intended to protect the weapon system in transit. Even though Marine Corps documents indicate "lightweight metal containers" were considered, so far as it is known, only molded plastic was used for this purpose. Cleaning gear and accessory items necessary for supporting the system were packed with the rifle and scope. When they hand-carried the weapon system from one duty station to another, Marine snipers were often referred to as "hit men" by their comrades in arms. The specialists were instructed to position the rifle with the telescope opposite the handles to lessen the chance of damage if the case was dropped. The brown plastic cases were manufactured by Protecto Plastics, Inc. (Remington Arms Co.)

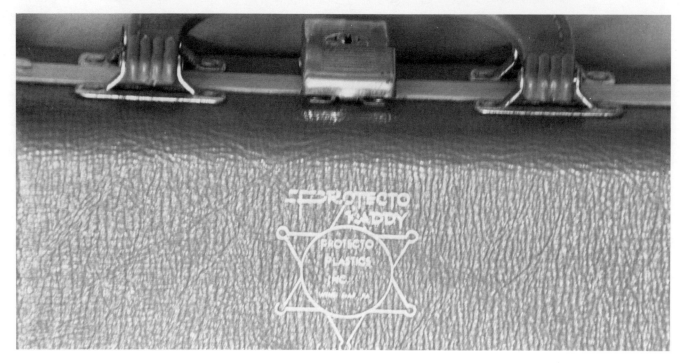

A close view of the factory markings on a Vietnam-era Protecto Plastics carrying case. The logo appears on the side of the case beneath the handles. The case illustrated was originally issued with rifle no. 224233 (so marked). (Laine Collection.)

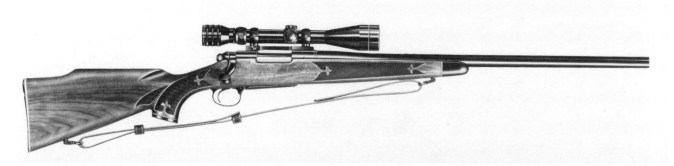

Remington Model 700 BDL Varmint Rifle and 3X-9X variable-power Redfield telescopic sight circa 1967. According to Remington information, "The ADL and BDL designations were originally acronyms for A Grade Deluxe and B Grade Deluxe rifles." The 24-inch heavy barrel "Varmint Special" introduced in 1967 was based on the M700 Marine sniper rifle. At this point, the principal differences between the USMC sniper rifle and the Varmint Special were the stock and the cartridge chambering. A 7.62mm (.308-caliber) version was not available until 1976. The BDL stock shown has what Remington referenced as "custom quality fleur-de-lis checkering." (Remington Arms Co.)

Marine Corps Scout-Sniper rifle serial no. 221276. The USMC/Redfield contract sight (green anodized finish) is not numbered (no rifle serial number). The telescope mounting base was originally fitted to rifle number 221587 (so marked). The symbol found on the right side of the M700/M40 telescope mounting base is a Redfield logo—a letter "R" superimposed on a crosshair telescope reticle. The barrel markings (U D N 41) indicate the rifle was assembled in September 1966. (Cors Collection.)

M118 7.62mm match cartridge dating from the Vietnam War. (Peter R. Senich.)

An aluminum alloy mounting used to evaluate the Adjustable Ranging Telescope (ART) and Starlight Scopes with the M700/M40 sniper rifle. At least three different mounts were tested during the early 1970s. (Peter R. Senich.)

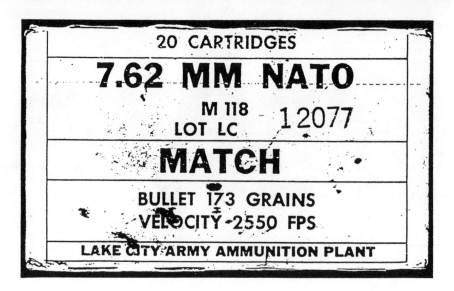

M118 7.62mm (.308) match ammunition of the type fielded for sniper use in Vietnam. The cartridges were manufactured at the Lake City Army Ammunition Plant in 1968. The front (top) and the back of the cartridge box are shown. The M118 cartridge served Marine snipers with the Remington M700/M40 system and the M14 rifle. With .30-caliber and 7.62mm sniping equipment in the field, the Marine Corps was obligated to supply both M72 and M118 match ammunition to its snipers in Vietnam. (Lau Collection.)

A Scout-Sniper from Alpha Company, First Battalion, Twenty-sixth Marines at Hill 557 near Khe Sanh (10 January 1968). (U.S. Marine Corps.)

For those who insist Marine snipers "never used" steel helmets or flak vests or carried a great deal of field gear while plying their trade in Vietnam, the Marine Corps combat photos presented in this book will put such claims to rest. In this case, a sniper attached to the First Battalion, Fifth Marines is wearing a steel helmet and a flak-vest. The Remington M700/M40 rifle is fitted with a 3X-9X variable-power Redfield telescope (16 February 1968). (U.S. Marine Corps.)

Right: Marine sniper Joseph T. Ward, dubbed "the man who wasn't there" by some, with an M16 and AN/PVS-2 Starlight Scope at An Hoa, the Fifth Marine Regiment combat base southwest of Da Nang. Not only did Joe Ward serve as a sniper, the Marine combat veteran went on to author *Dear Mom: A Sniper's Vietnam* (Ballantine Books 1991), dealing with his experiences as a Scout-Sniper in South Vietnam 1969–1970. The same photograph appears on the front cover of Ward's book. (Joseph T. Ward.)

Below: A First Marine Division sniper team (Corporal T. Romo and Private J. McConnell) operating in Vietnam, April 1968. Twenty-power observation telescopes (M49) permitted sighting well beyond the capability of 7 X 50 binoculars. Although bulky, the spotting scope was carried whenever the mission justified its use. Note the use of only one lens cover on the Redfield sight. An M16 Rifle lies opposite the spotter. (U.S. Marine Corps.)

Left: One of three towers used for observation and sniping purposes at An Hoa, the Fifth Marines combat base (1969). In some cases, a large NOD, AN/TVS-4 (Night Observation Device) Starlight Scope was employed with snipers using M14 rifles and a tracer-match ammo mix for night work. One of the towers could be lifted with a Sky Crane helicopter (CH-54) and moved to different points on the base. Although most sniper "kills" in Vietnam were made in the field, a number of VC and NVA personnel were eliminated by Marine snipers "working the lines" at one combat base or another. (Joseph T. Ward.)

Below: Scout-Sniper team, Company D, First Battalion, Fourth Marines (3d MarDiv) during Operation Nanking (14 October 1968). The Marine (left) is armed with an M14 rifle. (U.S. Marine Corps.)

Members of the Seventh Marines Scout-Sniper Platoon, Lance Corporals A. Kogelman and L. Bridges are pictured with a Unertl-equipped .50-caliber machine gun "southwest of Da Nang." The weapon was positioned on top of the bunker for photo purposes; the Brownings were normally "sandbagged" to keep them in place. Even though the exact location is not mentioned in the original caption, the 1968 photo is believed to have been taken at the Seventh Marines command post on Hill 55. Note the flash hider attached to the barrel. Unlike most heavy machine guns, the Browning possessed both automatic and semiautomatic fire option as well as provisions for mounting a telescopic sight. Semiautomatic fire could be obtained by unlocking the bolt latch release and alternately pressing the trigger and the bolt latch release. It was also possible to fire single rounds (single shot) with the weapon in an automatic mode by manipulating the trigger with a deft touch. The practice was known as "touching off a round" to the experienced "machine gunners." (U.S. Marine Corps.)

CHAPTER 11

SCOUT-SNIPER RIFLE

Rough Edges and All

However suited for combat the Remington/Redfield system may have been, as the level of combat exposure increased, the newly adopted Scout-Sniper Rifle was encountering difficulties in the field.

When various problems beset the rifle and the telescope early on, initial optimism gave way to impatience with the system and those responsible for fielding it.

Even though the Remington M700 sniper rifle and the Redfield variable-power scope were arguably "the best" commercial bolt-action rifle and telescopic sight available in the United States, the value of the system had been placed in doubt as a direct result of unsatisfactory field reports.

The Remington/Redfield system was evaluated and procured on an accelerated basis under circumstances deemed "urgent." Despite this, however, in view of the fact that eminently qualified Marine Corps personnel (Walter Walsh, Jim Zahm, Al Hauser, and others) were directly involved with the rifle and telescope evaluations, the phrase "the most suitable equipment now available" used in conjunction with the Remington/Redfield selection in the letter of recommendation to the Commandant, HQMC (9 February 1966) summarized the situation best.

When the need for snipers in Vietnam became a certainty, the task of fielding suitable equipment was approached on the basis of "immediate requirements," which resulted in the .30-caliber sniping rifles (Model 70 - M1D) being sent to RVN and new rifles and telescopic sights being procured ("new procurement," as referenced by the Marine Corps).

As a matter of historical interest, the reasons for the course of action taken by the Marine Corps during the rifle and telescope selection process are outlined as follows by Maj. William K. ("Kam") Hayden, USMC (Ret.), the assistant head of the Marksmanship Branch, G-3 (HQMC) at the time.

> We realized we were putting obsolete equipment in the field and turned our attention to coming up with a readily procurable, modern rifle in the standard caliber [7.62mm]. We did not spend any time considering items of foreign manufacture, noting the comments of the Van Orden-Lloyd study regarding the importance of avoiding items which could be made unavailable by the exigencies of war. Nor did we consider developing new equipment for this purpose with the urgency of the matter as significant as it was.
>
> After weighing such things as foreign manufacture of major components of some items being sold by domestic manufacturers, and the long-term survival factor of the same manufacturers, the final choice of vendors came down to Winchester and Remington for the rifle, and to Redfield and Leupold for the scope.
>
> Although Remington did not make their Varmint Special at that time, it was a simple matter for them to build a rifle with these characteristics [according to personnel then involved, the Remington test rifles were based on the 40X target action and made use of a heavy barrel in a standard or sporter stock]. Winchester submitted a similar rifle for evaluation.
>
> Both performed well and the final decision was based on a number of relatively minor points. As I recall, some of us leaned towards the Remington because we could foresee confusion from having two incompatible Model 70s in the supply system.
>
> [**NOTE:** Winchester began marketing a modified version of the Model 70 in 1964. The new design became known as the "New Model 70," while the rifle it replaced became the "pre-64 Model 70." The new rifle was different from the model it replaced. Although "small quantities" of M70 rifles procured as supplemental equipment were reportedly sent to RVN during 1966, at the time of the selection process (late 1965–early 1966), the USMC Model 70 rifles categorized as "sniping issue" in South Vietnam were "pre-64" rifles.]
>
> The decision between Redfield and Leupold was also very close and was based largely on the greater amount of elevation adjustment in the Redfield scope.
>
> The Remington/Redfield combination was accepted as the Marine Corps sniper rifle. Remington was the prime contractor for the assembled sniper equipment and delivered each rifle complete with the Redfield scope and mount, sling, cleaning kit, and carrying case.

Despite impressions that the weapon and telescopic sight suffered from inherent design deficiencies, in total fairness to Remington and Redfield, neither the rifle nor the telescope had been developed with the ability to withstand the rigors of combat in a hostile climatic environment as a design prerequisite. Regardless of the measures taken to adapt this equipment to military use, both items were essentially commercial products intended for the civilian market.

The problems that surrounded the Remington/Redfield system were characteristic of those experienced in the past when commercial equipment had been pressed into military service. Despite claims to the contrary, the Remington/Redfield combination was a fundamentally sound sniping system. There had been nothing wrong with the selection process that brought the USMC "Scout-Sniper Rifle" to South Vietnam.

Contrary to the established practice of pointing out only the deficiencies this system encountered in RVN, the comments of veteran Marine Corps snipers would indicate that the Remington sniper rifles and the Redfield scopes, when given the care and concern prevailing conditions and circumstances warranted, performed as intended for months on end in the hands of more than one sniper.

Although USMC sniper personnel returned ("rotated back") to the United States when their tour of duty was completed, their sniper rifles remained in Vietnam. As a result, in numerous cases, the same sniper rifle served two or more Marine specialists with only "routine armorer maintenance" necessary during the time the rifle remained in service in RVN.

Beyond basic adjustments made by the sniper, the job of maintaining the Remington/Redfield system in the field was one Marine Corps armorers (gunsmith in civilian parlance) were tasked with.

NOTE: According to Vietnam-era Marine Corps information:

> The Rifle Team Equipment (RTE) Repairman is responsible for the maintenance and security of weapons and equipment.
>
> RTE armorers, MOS 2112, will be the only armorer authorized to perform second echelon maintenance. Weapons and telescopes requiring third echelon maintenance will be evacuated to FLSG.

The "echelons of maintenance" extended from First echelon through Fifth echelon and were defined by the military as follows:

> 1st Echelon: This is the responsibility of the user. The soldier to whom the rifle is issued or who is using it. It consists of cleaning the rifle and maintaining it with care to prevent excessive wear or damage.
>
> 2nd Echelon: The using unit armorer makes 2nd echelon repairs, consisting of replacement of minor parts and minor adjustments.
>
> 3rd Echelon: The ordnance unit assigned to support the using unit conducts 3rd echelon repairs and inspections for serviceability.
>
> 4th Echelon: Conducted by the ordnance unit assigned to support one or more forward ordnance companies. Such units have a greater supply of maintenance parts and are capable of more technical and complicated repairs.
>
> 5th Echelon: Ordnance Depot rebuild and Arsenal overhaul are the highest echelon of repair. Replacement of major parts as well as inspection, repair, and refinishing of parts. Rifles overhauled at this level are usually done on a maintenance order directed by higher authority, and large numbers of rifles are involved on a production basis.

NOTE: According to Marine Corps information:

> From the onset of operations in RVN, the concept of logistic support provided centralized control of supplies and services. This was considered essential in order to maintain the flexibility required to retain an amphibious assault capability. The initial maintenance concept for the ground units provided for first-through-third echelon maintenance in-country, fourth echelon at 3d Force Service Regiment on Okinawa, and all depot or fifth echelon rebuilding in the continental United States. However, because of the unexpected deterioration of equipment

resulting from the climatic conditions of South Vietnam and the effect of years of under-procurement, by 1966, the demand forced FMFPac to initiate fourth echelon repair in-country and to establish a fifth echelon capability offshore. . . .

The 3d Force Service Regiment in Okinawa, with funds and guidance from FMFPac, would accomplish all the fifth echelon repair and rebuilding within its capability and then contract with other facilities for the remainder.

The activities described took place during the period 1966–1970.

Even though maintenance for the rifle and telescopic sight and the levels of responsibility were clearly defined by the Marine Corps, many snipers were known to make what were viewed officially as "unauthorized" repairs and adjustments to their equipment. For the most part, however, any significant repairs or alterations to the rifle or the scope were usually performed by the unit armorer.

Subsequent remedial modifications to the Remington rifle, such as increasing the clearance between the barrel and stock ("the float"), glass-bedding, and waterproofing the stock when basic measures (linseed oil) proved ineffective, were performed by RTE armorers, for example.

The "care and cleaning" of the USMC sniping issue was a routine part of Scout-Sniper training (the formal Syllabus of Instruction allotted 1 1/2 hours for this purpose). Both "Rifle Maintenance" and the "Care of Optical Equipment" were detailed in the Vietnam-era USMC sniping manual *FMFM 1-3B, SNIPING* (5 August 1969). As the manual stated in part:

> Rifle maintenance is any measure taken to keep the weapon in top operating condition. It includes inspection, repair, cleaning, and lubrication.
>
> Inspection – Inspection reveals the need for repair, cleaning, or lubrication. A weapon sheltered in garrison and infrequently used, must be inspected often to detect dirt, moisture, and signs of corrosion, and must be cleaned accordingly. A weapon in use and subject to the elements, however, requires no inspection for cleanliness since the fact of its use and exposure is sufficient evidence that it requires repeated cleaning and lubrication. The sniper couples his daily cleaning chores, however, with a program of minute inspection for damage or defect.
>
> Repair – The sniper, himself, can accomplish only the most superficial repair tasks, such as screw tightening or replacement. He has no disassembly authority (except that he may strip the bolt to clean or lubricate it), nor does he have a required variety of tools or parts. Field repair of the rifle is the responsibility of the rifle team equipment repairman.

In addition to taking preventative measures such as maintaining the clearance between the barrel and the stock ("clearing the float") with emery cloth, sandpaper, strips of sheet metal, or wire—all of which some snipers recall using for this purpose—Marine marksmen were also known to "readjust" the Remington M700 trigger mechanism (trigger pull) to suit their individual shooting requirements. (According to Remington information, the recommended "Trigger Weight" for the M700 sniper rifle was "3 to 5 pounds.")

Aside from being "good at their work," taking proper care of their equipment (first echelon maintenance) was not as important to some Marines as it was to others. While many gave the "tools of their trade" the best treatment possible, others were not as concerned as they might have been under the circumstances. Having seen the best and the worst in this respect, a veteran RTE armorer noted, "It was just a matter of human nature."

It is in the interest of providing the best possible insight on Marine Corps use of the Remington/Redfield system in South Vietnam that the following observations of Marine Sgt. Douglas de Haas, an experienced rifle team member and Scout-Sniper instructor, are presented. It is interesting to compare the comments of Sergeant de Haas following his exposure to Vietnam and the Remington/Redfield system in a combat environment with his initial impressions of the system as noted in another chapter. In this case, the information was written in 1968, following his discharge from the Marine Corps. It originally appeared in the publication *Bolt Action Rifles* by Frank de Haas (Digest Books, Inc. 1971):

For an entire year, as an instructor in the Marine scout-sniper school in Vietnam, I had an opportunity—indeed, it was part of my job—to check on the activities of the several platoons of marine scout-snipers stationed throughout the First Marine Division area around Da Nang and Phu Bai. Besides being an instructor, part of my time was taken up in gathering and keeping records of the kills made, keeping tabs on the sniper rifles, helping the individual snipers keep their rifles properly in order and sighted-in, obtaining replacement rifles and scopes, and doing anything else to aid the snipers in their work. Thus I had the opportunity to evaluate our present sniper rifle.

The standard sniper rifle now being used by the Marines in Vietnam is the Model 700 Remington. . . . It is equipped with the Redfield 3-9x variable-power scope, in Redfield Jr. mounts, and fitted with the rangefinder reticle. This rifle gave a very good account of itself in the last two years in Vietnam, and it is, almost without question, the best sniper rifle ever issued. However, after having fired, examined and kept tab on a number of these rifles in use in Vietnam, I could not overlook the number of weaknesses that showed up.

The average sportsman owning the counterpart of this sniper rifle, scope and mount, could expect to use it for many years without ever having any trouble with it. But wartime combat conditions are something entirely different. In one year in Vietnam, the sniper rifle may be subjected to more use and abuse (not from the sniper, but from weather and other conditions) than it would from a lifetime of use by a sportsman. For example, in one month it may be used in an area or during a period that is very hot, dry and dusty. It may next be used in the swampy areas under conditions of rain, mud and high humidity. High elevations present other climatic hazards. Probably the worst hazard occurs when troops are transported in trucks; in the crowded box of a truck the sniper cannot very well cradle his rifle in his lap, and resting it butt down in the hard riding truck certainly does it no good.

Marine snipers are taught to always make the first shot count. That is certainly the most important shot, and it may be the only one he'll get before he is shot at. Since an accurate first shot is so essential, the sniper rifle must be properly sighted-in and just as important, stay zeroed-in for the entire time the sniper is afield.

Even though the Remington 700 sniper rifle is considered the best sniper rifle now in use, I have seen too many of them put out of commission by the weather, a ride in a truck, or by some unavoidable mishap, and not always the fault of the sniper. . . .

In my visits with the snipers in my area, I learned that more sniper rifles were put out of action because of scope failure than from all other causes combined. In one such trip, during which I obtained records of some 17 sniper rifles, 10 were out of commission because of some type of scope failure. . . .

Practically all of the Marine snipers I've talked with set their scopes at the highest power, and leave them so set. Few of them ever had the need to use a lower power. Some of them were set at 7x or 8x because the scopes would be slightly out of focus when set at 9x. Quite often, after a scope was fixed for some time at one setting, it would freeze at that setting. The variable power feature has only been a source of trouble. . . .

While Marine scout-snipers were taught to use the range-finder, most of them seldom bothered with it in combat. Like the variable power feature, the rangefinder was just another mechanical device that could, and often did, get out of order. For example, the rangefinder post was evidently made of plastic and, if the scope was in a position to let the sun shine into it, or through it, this post would become distorted or "wilt". . . .

It has been found that lens caps are a useless accessory; the mechanical ones with flip-open covers soon get out of order and are discarded; the slip-on types are soon lost or discarded by the sniper. . . .

After examining many sniper scopes that had been in use for some time, I noticed that the fluoride coating, on both eyepiece and objective lenses, was usually well-scratched or partially removed. This is understandable—the lenses get dirty and the sniper usually has only his shirttail to clean them with. On sighting through these scopes it seemed to me that the damaged coating had affected definition. . . .

[**NOTE**: Even though the Redfield variable-power scope had been maligned for one reason or another during the span of USMC combat use in RVN, in addition to Marine Corps acceptance, Vietnam-era rifle and telescopic sight evaluations conducted by the U.S. Army Marksmanship Training Unit had concluded, "The Redfield 3-9 Power is considered the best of the variable scopes for sniper use whether it be on a standard mount or the Leatherwood self-ranging mount. . . . Our findings are that Redfield telescopic sights are the finest of American made telescopes." In retrospect, with the Army and the Marine Corps drawing parallel conclusions with respect to the Redfield telescopes, it would certainly appear that this was indeed "the best" rifle scope available to the Marine Corps at that time.]

Although the Redfield scope mount is quite well made and rugged, I don't think it's as rugged as a sniper scope mount should be, it requires too much maintenance. For example, the base screws are too small. If these screws become loose (and they often do), or if the sniper or armorer merely wants to check them for tightness, the scope and rings have to be removed first before these screws are accessible. Of course, every time the scope and rings are removed and replaced on the base, the rifle has to be sighted in again, and each time the scope is removed the front ring becomes looser in its base opening. . . .

The M700 Remington Sniper rifle has performed well in Vietnam, but there was a major problem with the stock. The stocks were not waterproofed, which caused bedding problems if the fore-end warped to contact the barrel. The armorers solved this by opening up the barrel channel to give at least 1/8 inch space between the fore-end sides and the barrel. As originally issued, the rifles were not glass-bedded. I found many rifles in which the barrel and the receiver had loosened in the stock, or rifles whose guard screws had been tightened so often that the front screw contacted the bolt. I was convinced that glass-bedding would largely eliminate these problems and, in my reports, I recommended that this be done. Glass-bedding was eventually authorized and the armorers supplied with materials and instructions to do it. The glass-bedding did help keep the rifles accurate and in zero. . . .

Though few Marine snipers serving in RVN had the opportunity to make an effective comparison between the Model 70 Winchester and the Remington M700 (M40) on the basis of actual combat experience, there are exceptions. Noted Marine marksman Carlos Hathcock, when asked to comment on the performance factor, stated there was essentially "no difference between the two rifles." But, given the option, Hathcock stated, he "would prefer the Model 40."

By all accounts, the collective judgment on the Remington/Redfield system came down to this: when everything was working the way it should, accuracy was certainly no problem.

First Marine Division sniper-spotter team (L.Cpls. G. Levandoski and G. Willite, Third Battalion, Fifth Marines) during action south of Da Nang (October 1967). The proximity of the barrel to the stock is obvious in this view of the M700 rifle. Strips of sandpaper or emery cloth were often used to maintain clearance ("the float") in the field. According to Remington, the rifles left the factory with .035/.040-inch clearance between the barrel and the stock. Remedial measures saw the clearance increased to .125 inch or more in Vietnam. In this case, the spotter is armed with an M16; the rifle is barely visible. (U.S. Marine Corps.)

Marine Corps sniper-instructor Sgt. Douglas Mark de Haas shown sighting in the Model 700 Remington sniper rifle, Vietnam 1968. (Reproduced from *Bolt Action Rifles*, by Frank de Haas, DBI Books.)

Marine Corps riflemen with Starlight Scope-equipped M16 rifles prepare for night activity in Vietnam. Both AN/PVS-1 (top) and AN/PVS-2 units are mounted on the rifles. Even though USMC combat personnel made routine use of rifle-mounted and hand-held Starlight Scopes, by all accounts, Marine snipers employed night vision equipment only when it was absolutely necessary. (U.S. Marine Corps.)

The second in the series of Starlight Scopes fielded for combat use in Southeast Asia. The 4-power AN/PVS-2 was 17.50 inches in length and 3.50 inches wide and weighed 6 pounds. Though similar in appearance to the AN/PVS-1, the improved model offered better focusing characteristics and a clearer reticle. The system came with a mount assembly for "boresighting" the sight to the rifle. A carrying case and accessories were issued with the unit. The AN/PVS-2 Starlight Scope saw extensive combat use in SEA. The AN/PVS-1 and the AN/PVS-2 Starlight Scopes were categorized as "first-generation" individual-served weapon sights. Despite some use by the Army and Marine Corps with the M14, the vast majority of rifle-mounted Starlight Scopes employed in Vietnam were mounted on the M16. By some estimates, however, Starlight Scopes were most commonly used as "hand-held units" in Southeast Asia. (Excalibur Enterprises.)

An original Remington M700 sniper rifle with an unusual history. The weapon was obtained at an estate sale long after the war in South Vietnam had ended. The Marine Corps sniping rifle had been transformed into a varmint rifle with a stainless-steel barrel. Rifle no. 221319 was restored to near issue condition by Maj. Edward J. Wages, USMC (Ret.) over an extended period. (Laine Collection.)

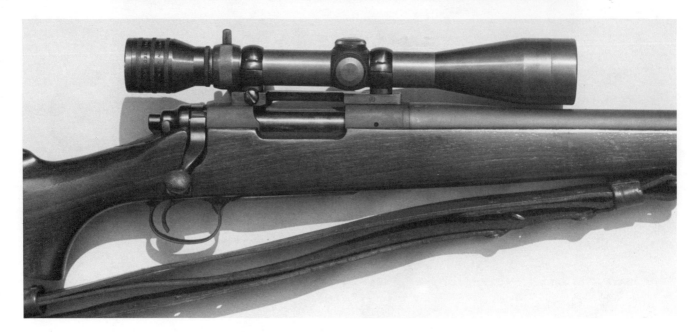

A right-side view of USMC sniper rifle no. 221319. The 3X-9X variable power Redfield telescope (green anodized finish) was obtained during the restoration process. The barrel, stock, and many of the parts used to restore the rifle came from one of the M700/M40 rifles reconfigured to M40A1 specifications. The parts were known as "takeoffs" to Marine ordnance personnel. (Laine Collection.)

A left-side view of USMC sniper rifle no. 221319. The original telescope mounting base is number-matched to the rifle; the Redfield scope is not numbered. Considering how few Vietnam-era USMC/Redfield contract sights were left unnumbered (no rifle serial number), telescopes such as this are highly prized by collectors. Although severe pitting has reduced their clarity, the receiver markings are consistent with the M700 Remington sniper rifles furnished to the Marine Corps. The receiver has a standard clip-slot. (Laine Collection.)

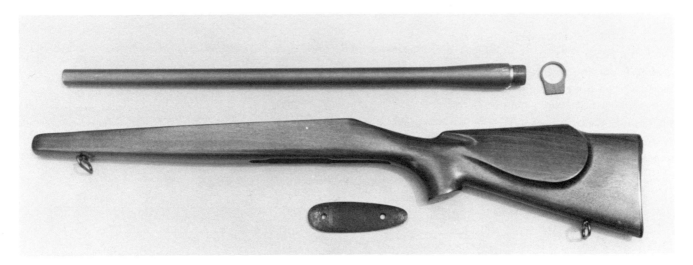

Vietnam-era M700 Remington barrel, stock, and parts used to restore USMC sniper rifle no. 221319. Note the recoil lug behind the barrel. (Laine Collection.)

Ammunition within easy reach, an M40-equipped Marine sniper (Pfc. B. Slipman, 1st MarDiv) takes careful aim during the battle for the Imperial City of Hue in February 1968. Even though flip-up lens covers proved effective, most Marines chose to use their scopes without lens caps of any kind. (U.S. Marine Corps.)

Marine sniper L.Cpl. James L. O'Neill (H BLT 2/4, April 1968) with his M700 sniper rifle. Note the Redfield sight wrapped with a towel. According to O'Neill, "The scope was covered to keep the rifle disguised and protect the lenses. Even though we had lens covers, it took too long to pop them open when everything was falling apart." Though barely visible, the barrel is plugged at the muzzle. A wrapper from a "C-Rat spoon" was used and simply shot through when necessary. The bandoleers carried "reserve" match ammunition in M14 stripper clips and 5.56mm cartridges in 20-round magazines—the latter, said O'Neill, "in case we were over-run and I had to use an M16 someone left on the ground." A rifle sling "was not used" during operations; the field gear shown here was carried for the time of "total movement." The photographs were taken at Dai Do in the Dong Ha area. (James L. O'Neill.)

Another view of L.Cpl. J.L. O'Neill (April 1968). Note the field gear and ammunition carried by the sniper. The cylindrical object (right) is a carrying case for the M49 observation telescope. O'Neill was credited with 24 enemy kills during action east of Dinh To on 2 May 1968. The feat earned the Marine sniper a Bronze Star Medal with Combat-V (the "V" was awarded with some medals to denote valor in combat). A part of Jim O'Neill's sniping activities is covered in *The Magnificent Bastards: The Joint Army-Marine Defense of Dong Ha*, 1968, by Keith William Nolan (Presidio Press, 1994). (James L. O'Neill.)

Third Marine Division sniper shown "searching for enemy soldiers" during operations in the Demilitarized Zone (DMZ) 20 September 1968. The Marines operated from a series of combat bases just below the DMZ from Dong Ha west along Route 9 to Khe Sanh for most of the war. (U.S. Marine Corps.)

A Marine sniper at work (L.Cpl. B. White, Ninth Marines, 3d MarDiv) during a sweep of the DMZ, September 1968. The towel provided protection from the sun and camouflage for the rifleman's head. The rifle is a USMC M700 Remington with a 3X-9X Redfield variable-power sight. Note the telescope power selector ring set at "7." Although many snipers preferred to leave the power ring at "9," some scopes were slightly out of focus at this setting and 7 or 8-power was used instead. (U.S. Marine Corps.)

A unique combination: a Scout-Sniper (Fourth Marines) and a Marine combat photographer pictured in the same photo, 10 October 1968. Even though Marine sniper personnel made it a point to avoid "the media" as the war progressed, a significant amount of information concerning the Marine Corps sniping program in Vietnam would have been relegated to obscurity were it not for the efforts of the service correspondents and combat photographers. (U.S. Marine Corps.)

Scout-Sniper Joseph T. Ward (First Battalion, Fifth Marines) shown "scoping the area," "Arizona Territory," 1969. According to Ward, the region was "a persistent thorn in the sides of the Fifth and Seventh Marine Regiments. . . . Charlie would hit us coming and going and constantly peck away at us while we were there." The Marine Corps defined the region as "a piedmont agricultural area located between the Vu Gia and Thu Bon Rivers northwest of An Hoa." The serial number for Ward's M700 sniper rifle was 221552. (Joseph T. Ward.)

First Marine Division sniper J.T. Ward with full field gear and Remington M700 sniper rifle (An Hoa, 1969). Although many Marine snipers chose to carry as little as possible while they were working, the amount of field gear a sniper carried usually depended on the type of mission and the length of time he expected to be in the bush. To say, as some have, that "all" Marine snipers "traveled light and fast" is not correct. The "way it was" for one Marine wasn't necessarily the way it was for another. (Joseph T. Ward.)

A Marine from Delta Company, First Battalion, Fifth Marine Regiment shown "sighting in" a 106mm recoilless rifle north of An Hoa (1969). The recoilless rifle, though used for various tasks, was considered to be the ultimate antisniper weapon by many Marines. Depending on the mount, "the rifle" could be used as a ground weapon or mounted on utility vehicles. Note the spent .50-caliber spotting cartridge case to the front and right of the weapon. A "spotter-tracer" round was used in the semiautomatic spotting rifle (top) for "pinpointing targets" before firing the main weapon. From all indications, the only problem with the 106mm recoilless rifle was "there simply weren't enough of them." (U.S. Marine Corps.)

First Marine Division sniper-spotter team (Mawhinney and Kihs) near Liberty Bridge, 1969. The 825-foot Seabee-constructed span was located just south of Dai Loc. The strategic bridge carried the highway link between Da Nang and An Hoa over the Thu Bon River. Note the improvised lens covers made from an inner tube. The strips of rubber connecting the ends (covers) were taped to the Redfield telescope in two places without interfering with the power ring and adjustment turrets. (Charles B. Mawhinney.)

A unique photo taken through a USMC/Redfield telescopic sight. Even though the subject is barely visible as reproduced here, the scope is focused on an AK-47-equipped Viet Cong rifleman intent on watching the unit command post. In this case, "Charlie" did not have an opportunity to report back. The VC observer had returned to his vantage point (Liberty Bridge, 1969) one time too often. (Charles B. Mawhinney.)

For those who believe South Vietnam was made up largely of rice paddies and tropical jungles, a USMC field photo shows Marine combat personnel (Company A, First Battalion, First Marines) making their way through rocky terrain "on a search and clear operation" (27 April 1970). According to the Marine Corps, the coastal areas of the I Corps Tactical Zone (the five provinces in the northern part of South Vietnam) were relatively flat, the inland areas mainly mountainous. (U.S. Marine Corps.)

SNIPER TRAINING AND EMPLOYMENT

In late 1965, as sniper activity and training were gaining momentum in South Vietnam, Headquarters, U.S. Marine Corps was formulating plans to establish schools for training "Scout-Sniper Specialists" in the United States.

According to Marine Corps documents dating from November 1965:

> A training program should be established in CONUS. Such a program envisions the creation of a Scout-Sniper Course as part of the Basic Specialist Training at Camp Pendleton and Camp Lejeune. This school will operate on an approved syllabus for a time specified to properly train an individual in scouting techniques as well as the marksmanship skills required to become a highly qualified sniper. Recommended syllabi as submitted by Camp Pendleton and Camp Lejeune are currently being reviewed by Marksmanship Branch, G-3 Division with the view towards the development of a standard syllabus for this training.

Even though III MAF was training snipers in Vietnam, the stateside training program did not take shape until the latter part of 1966 when the

Commandant, USMC, directed the Commanding General, Marine Corps Base, Camp Pendleton, California (4 October 1966), to commence specialist training for Scout-Snipers.

In addition to outlining the general requirements, the Commandant stipulated that the "Standard Training Syllabus" included with the directive be implemented "upon receipt of sniper rifles and related equipment." The "Syllabus For Scout-Sniper Training Course," as the enclosure was entitled, was based on the training and methods of employment formulated in South Vietnam during the early months of the USMC sniping effort.

The requirements for sniper candidates were stated as follows:

> This basic specialist training will be conducted at the completion of the two week basic specialist training for individuals assigned MOS 0311 [infantryman]. Commanding General, Marine Corps Base, Camp Pendleton will assign 25 individuals per month to this training. Selection of personnel will be based on the following criteria:
>
> A. Expert Riflemen 225 or higher [qualified as expert riflemen with the M14 service rifle—a score of 225 or better out of a possible 250; 225 was ultimately considered a "minimum" satisfactory score for a trained sniper].
>
> B. Excellent physical condition.
>
> C. Demonstrated maturity.
>
> D. Volunteers desired, but not mandatory [no Marine was assigned to the school if he had any reservations about sniper duty].

As noted in another chapter, according to Marine Corps personnel involved with the early sniper training program at Camp Pendleton, the "first" shipment of Remington M700 rifles and Redfield telescopic sights arrived the first week of January 1967. The first sniper class held at "Pendleton" began that same month.

Marine sniper candidates were provided with the skills necessary to effectively eliminate the enemy and remain alive in the process. In time, 30 or more Scout-Snipers were graduating from the Camp Pendleton school on a monthly basis.

The Marine Corps Stateside sniper training program was summarized as follows:

> Only men who volunteer, are expert riflemen, are mature, are above average in physical and mental ability, and have good vision are accepted for Scout-Sniper training.
>
> Prior to transfer to Vietnam, the selected individual is placed in the Scout-Sniper School for a duration of approximately 15 days. There, he is taught the skills of a Scout-Sniper. Instruction includes movement by day and night, map reading and the use of a compass, camouflage, cover and concealment, and finally, training with the sniper rifle and equipment and firing on the range. The shooting problems consist of many types of situations, firing on targets located at varying ranges. Above all else, the Scout-Sniper learns to score consistent hits on targets the size of a man's head at 300 meters and the torso at 600 meters. He also develops the ability to hit man size targets at ranges up to and beyond 1000 meters. This accuracy stems from his thorough knowledge of ballistics, of his rifle, and of his equipment, allowing him to "hold off" or adjust sights, depending on the situation at the time of firing. Upon completion of the Scout-Sniper School, the Marine is given an additional MOS of 8541 and usually assigned to the First or Third Marine Divisions.

Even though sniper training, in one form or another, took place at other installations in the United States, Camp Pendleton served as the principal Scout-Sniper training facility during the war in Vietnam.

Though it is rarely noted, an "independent" Marine Corps Reserve Scout-Sniper School was conducted periodically by Lt. Col. William C. Dickman, USMCR, Fourth Reconnaissance Battalion, Fourth Marine Division (-) FMF, USMCR, San Antonio, Texas (Camp Bullis).

In addition to training snipers for eventual combat duty in RVN, Colonel Dickman and his staff would evaluate equipment relative to sniper training and equipment.

Reporting to HQMC at the conclusion of the Scout-Sniper School held at Camp Bullis in August 1969, Colonel Dickman, along with recommending that the AN/PVS-3 Starlight Scope be considered for Marine sniper use, had this to say about a range-finding reticle made by the Redfield firm:

> Extensive tests have been conducted by myself on the Redfield multiple circle reticle scope. This has been over the period of one year and in conjunction with the Redfield Gun Sight Company. Results have been excellent. Several Marine officers and key men in our law enforcement agencies have fired the Remington Model 700 with this scope, all are very enthused on the accuracy and simplicity for range finding. I will recommend after a report to the Marine Corps that we adopt this scope for our Model 700 Remington Rifles (M40).

NOTE: According to information provided by M.Sgt. William D. Abbott, USMC (Ret.), a veteran of the USMC sniping program and Redfield contact in RVN in 1967, various range-finding reticle patterns based on the multicircle idea were developed by Redfield with Marine Corps use in mind. Maj. Robert A. Russell was involved initially; at least "two scopes" were evaluated in South Vietnam in 1967.

Although design efforts appear to have commenced in late 1966 or early 1967, it is not entirely clear if work on a multicircle reticle was initiated at the request of the Marine Corps or as part of Redfield's desire to "improve the sniper capability." The special reticles were fitted to "military specification" USMC/Redfield 3X-9X variable-power sights, otherwise known as "the green scopes."

Redfield summarized the "multicircle idea" as follows:

> The circles are spaced vertically, with the sizes of each circle determining range, according to which circle the target best fits in, and the location of the circles vertically automatically compensating for elevation. . . .
>
> We can make any size circle diameter and we can provide for range in feet or in meters. . . .
>
> The advantage would be the complete elimination of either holdover or elevation adjustment changes. Range finding is automatic when a circle fits and proper elevation of the rifle is made at the same time.

Despite the fact that the unique sighting system was "favorably received," the Redfield multicircle reticle was not adopted by the Marine Corps.

Even though the contributions of Lt. Col. W.C. Dickman have remained relatively obscure, judging from the comments of veteran Marine officers who were familiar with his work, Colonel Dickman was "well respected" for his efforts to further the Marine Corps sniping program during this era.

Measures to coordinate and maximize the benefits of Scout-Sniper training in the United States and South Vietnam would include what was then referenced as an in-country "Scout-Sniper Refresher Training Course." The purpose of the course, as it was then stated, was to ensure that "Scout-Snipers are qualified in all of the requisite skills demanded of them in a combat environment such as is presently the situation in RVN."

The "refresher courses," or "requalification," as many of the Marine snipers called it, were held at the First Marine Division Headquarters at Da Nang, and Third Marine Division Headquarters at Quang Tri/Dong Ha. The "Student Prerequisites" were noted as follows:

> Be assigned as a Scout-Sniper MOS 8541 or assigned on-the-job training with a Scout-Sniper Platoon.

> Have a minimum of six months service remaining on current tour.

The course was given to individual Marines and Scout-Sniper teams. It was recommended that "both members" of a Scout-Sniper team be at the same training session whenever possible. The five-day course was conducted on a regularly scheduled basis.

Of all the documents generated during the war in Southeast Asia, those that were recorded at that time, by the personnel so involved, are especially noteworthy. One such document, a report by the First Marine Division entitled "The Organization, Training, and Employment of 1st Marine Division Snipers in Combat, Da Nang, RVN, July 1969" provides insight on Scout-Sniper training and employment at the height of Marine Corps involvement in RVN. The measures described in this report are representative of Marine Corps sniping operations in Southeast Asia. As the report stated in part:

Background

> A sniper is a highly trained and skilled sharpshooter equipped with a telescope-mounted rifle capable of accuracy at extended ranges. The primary mission of a sniper in combat is to support combat operations by delivering precision fire on point targets from a concealed position. Secondary missions include collection of intelligence and acting as a forward observer.

Organization

> The Scout-Sniper Platoon organic to the infantry regimental headquarters company consists of a platoon commander, a platoon sergeant, and three squads of five two-man teams supported by a rifle team equipment armorer (MOS 2112). The Reconnaissance Battalion Scout-Sniper Platoon organic to the headquarters and service company, consists of a platoon commander, platoon sergeant, four squads of three two man teams, and an armorer. The basic element of the Scout-Sniper Platoon is a team composed of two men, each trained as a sniper and an observer, team members alternate in performing their duties.

> [**NOTE**: As an aside, the program was under the staff cognizance of the G-3 section. The 1st MarDiv G-3 at the time (July 1969), Maj. W.M. Greene was the son of the Commandant of the Marine Corps (1964-1967), Gen. Wallace M. Greene Jr.]

Equipment

> Each sniper team is equipped with one Model 700 Remington 7.62mm sniper rifle with a Redfield 3X9 variable telescope and an observation telescope which the observer uses for seeking targets. The observer is armed with an M16/M14 rifle and provides personal protection for the sniper.

Maintenance

> a. The sniper rifle with telescope is a delicate instrument. Unless his equipment is properly cared for, a sniper will be ineffective regardless of his expertise as a sharpshooter.

b. The individual sniper will perform first echelon maintenance on his equipment daily. This consists of care and cleaning of the rifle and optical equipment. No further maintenance will be performed by the sniper.

c. The rifle team equipment armorer, will be the only person to perform second echelon maintenance on sniper rifles.

d. All rifles requiring third echelon or higher maintenance will be turned into the appropriate repair facility.

Selection of Personnel

Personnel will be selected from organic resources and will possess the following qualifications:

a. Expert rifleman with demonstrated superior marksmanship ability.

b. Volunteer for the program.

c. Above average physical and mental ability.

d. 20/20 uncorrected vision.

e. Six months remaining in country or extend to qualify.

f. Recommended by commanding officer.

Training

a. The training of each scout-sniper team must be vigorous, progressive, and continuing. The end product must be a team which can live and work together in harmony; move with stealth; and find and kill the enemy with single shots. Organizations possessing Scout-Sniper Platoons will insure that the necessary training is accomplished to maintain their platoons at maximum efficiency.

b. The Division Scout-Sniper School, under the direction of the G-3 section, will conduct periodic classes to assist units in maintaining desired standards of proficiency. Class convening dates and unit quota assignments will be published by separate directive. The Division Scout-Sniper School is collocated with the Division Schools, Camp Perdue, Da Nang.

c. The basic syllabus utilized by the Division Scout-Sniper School will be modified periodically to conform with specific needs of the students. It will be updated as new techniques and tactics are developed.

Employment

Methods of employing snipers are limited only by the initiative and imagination of the commander whose unit is supported by snipers. Since the primary mission of snipers is operational in nature, sniper teams are best employed under the cognizance of the unit S-3.

Action

Scout-Sniper teams are valuable asset to the combat capability of the Division. Commanding Officers will insure:

a. That this asset is profitably utilized.

b. That sniper rifles as authorized in current Table of Equipment are on hand and in serviceable condition.

c. That there is effective utilization of school trained snipers by screening Service Record Books for MOS 8541 (Scout-Sniper) and by assigning these individuals, when feasible to Scout-Sniper Platoons.

Report

In order to monitor and evaluate the scout-sniper program a Monthly Scout Sniper Platoon Report will be submitted by the 5th day of each month for each infantry regiment and the Reconnaissance Battalion. This report will cover operations during the preceding month.

The format for the "Monthly Scout-Sniper Platoon Report" follows:

MONTHLY SCOUT-SNIPER PLATOON REPORT

From: Commanding Officer
To: Commanding General, 1st Marine Division (Rein.), FMF (Attn: G-3 Training)
Subj: Scout-Sniper Platoon Report for the month of _____
Ref: (a) DivO 3590.1B

1. The following report is submitted in accordance with reference (a):

a. Roster of personnel with rank, service number, MOS, and RTD. List KIA and WIA credited each individual for month of report and cumulative KIA and WIA credited each individual since joining platoon.

b. Cumulative KIA and WIA for platoon for month of report and for calendar year.

c. Number of teams available for employment.

d. Number of teams employed.

e. Equipment on hand (rifles, observation telescopes, starlight scopes) and condition.

f. Remarks.

The following information was part of the preceding First Marine Division report:

SUGGESTED EMPLOYMENT OF SCOUT-SNIPERS

General

a.   The importance of the sniper and his rifle is measured in both terms of the casualties he inflicts and the fear his presence instills in the enemy. A sniper team enhances a unit's firepower by providing that unit with an additional supporting arm. The sniper's role is unique in that it is the sole means by which a unit can engage point targets at distances beyond the effective range of the service rifle.

b.   Snipers are trained to operate in teams of two. As a team they can maintain continuous observation over an area; assist one another in shooting by averaging their range estimations, by observing each other's fire, and by offering adjustment information; and they provide for each other's protection. The sniper team should never be split up.

c.   The sniper team should not be used as a substitute for other riflemen. The team should be in addition to the normal force employed, not in place of it.

Offensive Employment

a.   Approach March

(1)   Moving with the point – a sniper team can provide the point with additional observation and reconnaissance by fire capabilities. However, since the sniper is armed with a single shot weapon, he should not be the point man, nor should he be utilized with the point if the unit is moving through heavy vegetation where observation is limited.

(2)   As rear security – snipers can be extremely effective when utilized as stay behind elements to engage any attempting to follow a unit on the move.

(3)   With flank security – if terrain is such that the flank security is on high ground, or has exceptionally good observation to the front of the unit, snipers can be used effectively with the flank security to engage long range targets.

(4)   With the main body – a sniper team is the best counter-sniper weapon available to a unit on the march. With his knowledge of sniper modus operandi, his optical equipment, and his ability to engage long range targets, the sniper can seek out enemy snipers independently, thus negating the need for premature deployment by units to destroy snipers harassing their movement.

b.   In the Attack

(1)   Snipers can support a frontal assault by directing fire from carefully concealed positions at exposed enemy troops; delivering fire into apertures of enemy bunkers; destroying enemy crew-served weapons positions; delivering long-range fire at targets located beyond the objective, but directly opposing the advance; and by providing flank protecting fire at targets threatening an exposed flank or at small, isolated pockets of resistance that have been bypassed.

(2)   Snipers can be used effectively in pursuit by fire and in providing security during consolidation of an objective.

(3) In a daylight assault, snipers can cross the line of departure under cover of darkness and be in position near the objective to engage targets of opportunity during the confusion caused by preparation fire and the initial phases of the assault.

(4) Snipers can be positioned to the flanks or rear of an objective to block enemy attempting to escape from the objective area. This is usually effective in a village sweep.

(5) In river crossing operations, the sniper team, utilizing its optical equipment, can conduct a visual reconnaissance of the opposite river bank. During the crossing, snipers can provide covering fire. This technique applies equally well when a unit must cross any type of danger area.

c.   Patrolling

The capabilities of the sniper team in terms of reconnaissance, intelligence gathering, and as forward observers can be most effectively utilized in patrolling. Employment techniques such as covering, blocking, and counter-sniper fire, previously discussed, also apply equally well during patrol activities.

d.   Ambushing

(1) The sniper team employed with a larger force ambush provides long range observation and kill capability. If only one or two enemy approach the ambush site, they can be engaged by a sniper. In this way the ambush does not compromise its position.

(2) The sniper team itself can constitute a long range ambush. As a lay-out element, this ambush can be used to cover roads and trails as a counter-booby trap measure; to cover known enemy river crossing sites; or to cover any other area where enemy movement is known or suspected.

e.   Defensive Employment

In the defense the sniper provides long range observation, and the capability to engage targets before they reach the defensive position. This capability can be especially effective when the sniper is employed with an outpost, or in a tower. The sniper covers avenues of approach and any obstacles protecting the position. In a temporary defensive position, the sniper should not be placed with the command group, but on the perimeter where he can utilize his observation capability. This is particularly true during first and last light when enemy movement is prevalent.

Interestingly, in addition to training Marines for sniping in Vietnam, with as many "allied" and U.S. Army units as there were operating in the I CTZ, Marine Corps instructors reportedly trained an unknown number of ARVN, ROK, and Army personnel as snipers during the course of the war.

With proper regards to the officers and men of the First Marine Division and the Third Marine Division, it is important to emphasize that the training and employment of snipers, particularly during the later stages of the war, was essentially the same in both divisions. Whatever differences did exist can be rightfully attributed to the exigencies of war.

For all of the plans and training, however, perhaps the greatest problem associated with Army and Marine Corps sniping operations in RVN was the improper use of snipers.

A close view of the Redfield 3X-9X variable-power Accu-Range sight in use with the M700 rifle. According to the Marine Corps caption, the sniper is making "sight adjustments" (3d MarDiv Sniper School, 1967). The power selector ring is set at 9 power, and the caps are removed from the elevation and windage adjustment turrets. The rifle is ready to fire. (U.S. Marine Corps.)

Right: The business end of an M700 sniper rifle—a view seldom seen or survived (Pvt. R. Josey, Second Battalion, Fifth Marines, First Marine Division, June 1967). Although some Marine officers were reluctant to accept personnel with corrective lenses for sniper training, snipers wearing glasses proved no less effective than those without. However, a chance reflection and the loss or damage to the glasses was always a genuine concern for any Marine wearing corrective lenses in combat. (U.S. Marine Corps.)

Below: Fourth Marines Scout-Sniper team Lance Corporals Ortega and Moore (7 October 1968). (U.S. Marine Corps.)

Marine Corps field photo (July 1969) with caption that reads, "Marine and Army personnel make final adjustments prior to qualification at the 3rd Marine Division Sniper School in Quang Tri, Vietnam." In many cases, Army marksmen received their sniper training at Marine facilities and Marines at Army centers. The demand for snipers in Vietnam was always greater than there were sniper schools available. The men on the firing line are equipped with M14 rifles. (U.S. Marine Corps.)

A sniper instructor (Gy.Sgt. J. Vance) and a student on the firing line at the Third Marine Division Sniper School at Quang Tri, Vietnam (July 1969). After four years of combat, Third Marine Division redeployed to Okinawa from Vietnam in late 1969. (U.S. Marine Corps.)

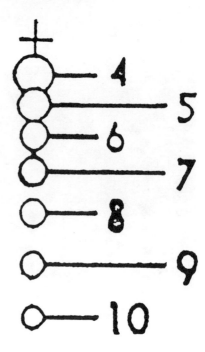

An example (enlarged) of a Redfield "multicircle reticle" evaluated by the Marine Corps during the Vietnam War. At least three or four versions of the unique reticles were developed and tested by Redfield; the reticle pattern was applied to "Milar film," and the film, in turn, was applied to the lens surface. The small cross (top) served as a point of aim, point of impact for ranges out to 300 yards, with the circles beneath covering ranges from 400 to 1,000 yards. The diameters of the circles represented a certain number of inches on the target. The relationship remained the same at the ranges indicated. The special reticle was intended for use with the USMC/Redfield 3X-9X variable-power scope in conjunction with the M700 sniper rifle and 7.62mm M118 match ammunition. The Redfield multicircle reticle predated the range-finding and trajectory compensating reticle system marketed by Shepherd Scope Ltd. The Shepherd reticle was not available commercially until the late 1970s or early 1980s. (Peter R. Senich.)

While deployed, the snipers' choice and mode of concealment was a matter of discretion. Elaborate camouflage was rarely used by U.S. snipers in Southeast Asia. Though barely noticeable, the sniper-spotter team (Cpls. W. Alfred and L. Bridges, Seventh Marines, First Marine Division) have "stick camouflage" applied to their faces and hands (October 1969). The personnel noted here were named in the original Marine Corps photo caption. (U.S. Marine Corps.)

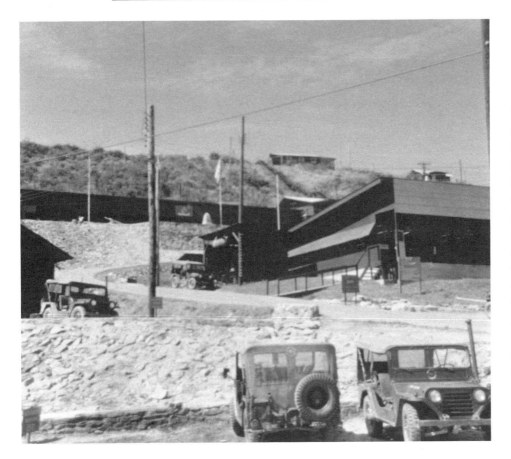

First Marine Division headquarters, Da Nang, 1968. The hillside complex was known as "the Bunker" to countless Marines. (The division command post was located approximately two miles west of Da Nang. The 300-foot-long concrete and timber bunker was designed to absorb a direct hit by a 120mm mortar without damage.) The First Marine Division relocated to Da Nang from Chu Lai in October 1966. The site had served as Third Marine Division headquarters until their move to Phu Bai near Hue. (Robert L. Goller.)

Gy.Sgt. Robert L. Goller, the noncommissioned officer in charge (NCOIC) of the First Marine Division's Scout-Sniper School, at a point overlooking the harbor at Da Nang, with the ESSO storage terminal to the left. The sniper rifle is a M700 Remington; the photo was taken during a training session in late 1968. An accomplished marksman, Goller served the Marine Corps sniping program in RVN with the Third Marine Division and the First Marine Division. As a chief warrant officer assigned to the Marksmanship Training Unit during the late 1970s, Goller was the head coach of the Marine Corps Rifle Team. (Robert L. Goller.)

Sergeant Goller (right) with Scout-Sniper candidates at the division known distance range near Hill 327 (a measured known distance range was used for zeroing sniper rifles and practice firing under ideal conditions). At this juncture, the First Marine Division sniper range was located between Hill 327 and what was known as "the Pass." (Robert L. Goller.)

An expanded view of the firing line at the 1st MarDiv known distance range. M.Sgt. Paul Dudash is seated at the left, with Corporal Yount, an instructor, to his right. Sergeant Goller relieved Dudash as NCOIC, 1st MarDiv Scout-Sniper School, in mid-1968. The other Marines are unidentified. (Robert L. Goller.)

A rifleman's view from the 1,000 yard line at the First Marine Division sniper range near Hill 327. The firing line is at the bottom of the photograph, the target area beyond the road near the base of the hill. As a matter of interest, a small part of the Twenty-sixth Marines encampment can be seen at the right. The tube pointing down-range (upper right) is the objective end of an M49 observation telescope. The known distance range was a part of this facility. The photo dates from late 1968. (Robert L. Goller.)

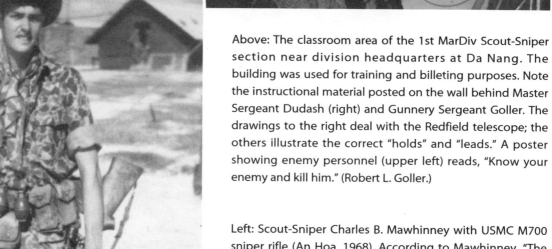

Above: The classroom area of the 1st MarDiv Scout-Sniper section near division headquarters at Da Nang. The building was used for training and billeting purposes. Note the instructional material posted on the wall behind Master Sergeant Dudash (right) and Gunnery Sergeant Goller. The drawings to the right deal with the Redfield telescope; the others illustrate the correct "holds" and "leads." A poster showing enemy personnel (upper left) reads, "Know your enemy and kill him." (Robert L. Goller.)

Left: Scout-Sniper Charles B. Mawhinney with USMC M700 sniper rifle (An Hoa, 1968). According to Mawhinney, "The rifle stock was painted green when the weapon was issued." (Early efforts to waterproof sniper rifle stocks in Vietnam included "sealing measures" involving the use of paint. USMC ordnance papers indicate gray or green were "acceptable colors.") As an aside, note the camouflage fatigues worn by Mawhinney. The camo pattern was variously referenced as "dapple-style" or "leopard-spotted" camouflage. The pattern is similar to the distinctive five-color utility uniform worn by Korean Marines (ROKMC) in Vietnam. Despite Army and Marine Corps regulations designed to ensure uniformity, a wide variety of camouflage clothing was worn by U.S. combat personnel in Southeast Asia. First Marine Division sniper Charles B. Mawhinney left Vietnam with 103 confirmed kills to his credit. (Charles B. Mawhinney.)

Scout-Sniper Charles B. Mawhinney with two "3-Star" Marine Corps lieutenant generals (center and right) during his Meritorious Combat Promotion at An Hoa. The promotion, from private first class to lance corporal, came a few days after Mawhinney registered his 101st confirmed kill on 20 April 1969. While on patrol with a small contingent from D Company, First Battalion, Fifth Marines (D/1/5) approximately 15 miles northwest of An Hoa, Mawhinney fired on three North Vietnamese regulars. The action resulted in two probable and one confirmed enemy kill, an NVA payroll officer—Mawhinney's 101st as a Marine sniper. Although Chuck Mawhinney had received Scout-Sniper training at Camp Pendleton and in Vietnam, his field skills and knowledge of firearms came from the experience gained as an avid hunter. Mawhinney had literally grown up learning to handle and care for hunting rifles and telescopic sights. His success in Vietnam came as a result of his inherent ability and, as Mawhinney put it, "learning Oriental habits and adapting to Charlie's domain." The Marine marksman logged "two more confirmed" on the lines at An Hoa before returning to the United States. When asked about his final score, Mawhinney replied, "I turned in a tally of 103 confirmed kills to the top before I left. I had 216 sniper probables." Mawhinney left the Marine Corps in 1970 as a sergeant, the decorations and awards recorded on his discharge papers (DD 214) include the Bronze Star Medal with Combat-V, Navy Achievement Medal, Navy Commendation Medal with Combat-V, the Republic of Vietnam Gallantry Cross with Palm, and the Purple Heart Medal. (Charles B. Mawhinney.)

A significant memento from the war in Vietnam: Vietnamese currency recovered from the NVA payroll officer rendered KIA by Marine sniper Chuck Mawhinney—his 101st confirmed kill. (Charles B. Mawhinney.)

First Marine Division Scout-Sniper team during operations in the bush. Pfc. R. William provides sniper security for team member Pfc. L. Mock (21 January 1970). Note the M14 fiberglass stock and hand-grenade pin-rings decorating the tropical hat ("boonie hat"). Even though the fiberglass stocks were durable and impervious to moisture, if left in the sun for extended periods the stock would absorb enough heat to burn a rifleman's hands or cheek if care wasn't taken. (U.S. Marine Corps.)

A .50-caliber machine gun manned by Corporal Martin, a member of the Twenty-sixth Marines Scout-Sniper Platoon, during operation Eagle Eye (1969). The Browning was positioned at a hilltop observation post in the Elephant Valley approximately four miles west of the Nam O Bridge (Cu De River) northwest of Da Nang. An AN/PVS-2 Starlight Scope and a Redfield 3X-9X variable-power scope are mounted on the machine gun. Note the flash-hider attached to the barrel and camouflaged (pattern-painted) M16 rifle at the lower right. A flash-hider was essential with the early night vision equipment. The muzzle flash would cause the Starlight Scope to be saturated with light and literally shut down as a result. When the attachment was not available, wet towels or blankets were often placed over the end of the barrel to minimize the muzzle flash. At this juncture, the platoon leader for the unit (Twenty-sixth Marines sniper platoon) was CWO2 D.I. Boyd; the platoon sergeant was W.W. Wiseman. Although many snipers were not exposed to this activity, some Marine units in particular were known to employ the Browning machine gun for various forms of sniping on a routine basis. The availability of suitable equipment, the area of operations, and the circumstances at hand were deciding factors, however. Any number of Vietnam-era Marine snipers recall "taking their turn" with the Big Browning at remote combat bases, hilltop outposts, in towers, and in the lines at various places in the I Corps Tactical Zone. (U.S. Marine Corps.)

First Marine Division sniper (L.Cpl. J. Carroch, Scout-Sniper Platoon, H&S Company, First Battalion, First Marines) "checks out the zero on his rifle, while L.Cpl. F. Gerdon spots his rounds" in the Charlie Ridge area 15 miles southwest of Da Nang (April 1970). Even though a number of problems were encountered with the M700/M40 system in Vietnam, a great many VC and NVA personnel were "taken out" with this weapon. (U.S. Marine Corps.)

A Marine rifleman armed with an M16A1 rifle during the closing stages of the ground war in South Vietnam. The telescope is a 3-power "Colt Scope" made by Realist. Even though a wide variety of fixed-power and variable-power telescopic sights were fielded with the AR15 and M16 during this era, the Colt/Realist model remained a popular choice. Many combat personnel favored the Colt scope for no other reason than its diminutive size. The compact sight saw duty in diverse applications, including combat use by the various U.S. "special mission groups." While hardly a sniper sight, the Colt telescope was considered "effective enough" in the 200-300 meter range. (Max Crace.)

CHAPTER 13

THE REDFIELD TELESCOPE

The Redfield 3X-9X variable-power telescopic sight, the rifle scope that served as the principal Marine Corps sniper sight in Vietnam, was introduced to the commercial market in 1962. The constantly centered nonmagnifying reticle, variable-power, and range-finding capability offered with the highly rated scope proved to be what the Marine Corps was seeking for combat use in Southeast Asia. According to Redfield information:

> The constantly centered nonmagnifying reticle was developed in 1957. The design placed the reticle behind the erector lens system so it would stay on center and at one size as power was varied. This feature placed the Redfield telescope at "the top of the list" of the variable-power telescopes of the day and had a great deal to do with its selection by the Marine Corps and the U.S. Army. By combining the Redfield 3X-9X variable-power sight with its constantly centered nonmagnifying reticle and Jim Leatherwood's auto-ranging principle, the Adjustable Ranging Telescope (ART) fielded for Army sniper use in SEA came to pass.

Acting on the recommendation of the MTU, the Marine Corps adopted the Remington Model 700-40X and the Redfield 3X-9X variable-power Accu-Range Telescope.

With range estimation as big a problem as it was for the average sniper, the Accu-Range system Redfield offered was considered essential for effective sniping in Vietnam. (The Accu-Range reticle was offered as an option beginning in 1965. Redfield referenced this as "the first built-in distance finder in a telescopic sight.")

NOTE: With regard to the difficulties associated with training and fielding snipers early on, Major Russell, the officer tasked with establishing the Marine Corps sniping program in South Vietnam in 1965, said, "One of the more significant problems we encountered in Vietnam was the individual sniper's inability to estimate range accurately." Even though the Marine Corps selected the Redfield 3X-9X variable-power commercial sight with the Accu-Range range-finding feature for sniper use with this concern in mind, instructing sniper candidates in range estimation and correct "holds and leads" remained an essential part of the USMC sniper training syllabus during the war in Vietnam.

As Redfield then stated, "The Accu-Range feature provides an accurate means of determining the distance from the shooter to the target." The power selector ring located in front of the eyepiece controlled the power of magnification and the range-finder functions of the scope. Though later detailed in *FMFM 1-3B, SNIPING* (5 August 1969), the range-finding system was explained as follows by the Redfield Gun Sight Co. in the instruction booklets it furnished to the Marine Corps (the initial USMC procurement documents reference this booklet as the "Manual, Commercial Type"; it was subsequently listed as a "Commercial Publication" with the title *The Operation, Function and Care of Your Redfield Scope*):

> The three related elements in a Redfield Accu-Range Variable are the "stadia" wires, located near the top of the sight picture, a power selector ring for enlarging or reducing the image, and a range scale located in the lower righthand quadrant, marked in yard increments.
>
> To find the range to a target, position the target between the upper parallel (stadia) wires and begin to turn the power selector ring. Continue to turn the power selector ring until the stadia wires bracket the target from shoulder to belt. Read the number at the bottom of the range indicator scale—this is the distance from you to the target. Once the range is known, you determine the holdover necessary for an accurate shot with the weapon and the load you are using.

NOTE: The term "holdover" is the procedure used to hit a target at ranges other than the range for which the rifle is zeroed. The correct use of "holds and leads" enabled the sniper to hit his target without holding his sights directly on the target.

The Marine Corps specifications for the Vietnam-era Redfield 3X-9X variable-power Accu-Range rifle scope ("Scope, Special USMC Model") were listed as follows in "Supply Contract" NOm-73565, dated 17 May 1966:

	At 3X	At 9X
Actual Magnification	3.3X	9.1X
Clear Aperture of Objective Lens	38.6mm	38.6mm

	At 3X	At 9X
Exit Pupil	12.6mm	4.3mm
Relative Brightness	159	19
Field of View at 100 yards	37 ft.	12 ft.
Eye Relief	2 3/4 – 3 1/2 inches	
Overall Length Focused to Infinity	12 3/4 inches	
Diameter of Tube	1 inch	
Outside Diameter of Objective End	1.820 inch	
Outside Diameter of Eyepiece	1.494 inch	
Weight	12.5 oz.	
Internal Adjustment Graduation in Minutes (Inches at 100 yards)	1/2 minute	
Reticle Adjustment	Internal	
Minimum Reticle Adjustment	1/4 minute	
Finish	Anodized Military Finish	
Mount and Rings	Special JR Mount and Rings for Remington M700 Sniper Rifle	
Reticle	Accu-Range w/Special Fine Cross Hair	

NOTE: As a point of interest, according to Maj. William K. Hayden, the assistant head of the Marksmanship Branch, G-3, HQMC, at the time, "Since the range of elevation adjustment was an important factor, it was requested that the telescope mount [base] be tapered to provide the maximum amount of elevation adjustment at the ranges where it was needed most."

The letter of recommendation (Sniper Rifle/Telescopic Sight) to the CMC (9 February 1966) listed the following among its recommendations:

> The telescope be mounted in Redfield mounts modified to afford maximum use of the internal elevation adjustment.

The difference between the highest point of the receiver ring and the receiver bridge at its centerline on the Vietnam-era USMC-M700 sniper rifle was .117 inch (±).

The height of the one-piece JR base furnished by Redfield ("Base, Special, JR 40X") was .200 inch

(±) at the front and .345 inch (±) at the rear. As such, the base was approximately .028 inch (±) higher at the rear ("tapered") when attached to the receiver.

By comparison, according to information provided by the Redfield firm, the standard one-piece JR base intended for the Remington Model 700 short-action rifle (pre-1974) was .196 inch (±) at the front and .322 inch (±) at the rear, a difference of .009 inch (±) when the base was mounted.

The dimensions for the Junior (JR) base used with the original USMC M700/M40 sniper rifle were established by Redfield. It is not known if a similar base was made available to the general public.

Although USMC/Redfield telescopic sights were made and finished to Marine Corps specifications, there were no unique features, characteristics, or markings to indicate military service in this case. Except for their green anodized finish (simply referenced as a "military finish" by the Marine Corps), the sights were essentially the same as the commercial models sold over the counter.

Rather than an attempt to "camouflage" the scope, according to Redfield records, "the external finish was matted and colored to match the parkerized finish of the Remington M700 rifles on which they were mounted." Fabricated from aluminum alloy as they were, the sights were "anodized" to protect them from the elements. CAI Technologies, the company responsible for anodizing and color-finishing the original USMC/Redfield contract sights (and which still provides the anodizing and finish work for the Redfield line), provided the following insight on the process used with this system:

> The coloring of aluminum anodized components is achieved in much the same manner as that of dyeing an Easter egg. The clear anodized finish is put on first, electrolytically, then the parts are immersed in a hot bath of the desired color organic dye. The anodized coating is very porous and absorbs the dye. . . . The coating is then chemically sealed to prevent the dye from leaching back out.

A radical departure from most telescopic sights of the day with their typical black finish, the "green" rifle scopes were considered unique in appearance when first issued. Furthermore, following extended field use in Southeast Asia, many of the USMC/Redfield scopes took on an unusual hue, which CAI Technologies attributed to "prolonged exposure to sunlight."

As CAI explained further:

> The nature of organic dyes is such that they are sensitive to degradation by ultraviolet radiation. Prolonged exposure to sunlight causes damage to the dyes. This often results in the dye color changing from one color to another. For example, as a brown dye is damaged, it turns pink, and as a black finish degrades it often turns blue or purple. The burnished copper or bronze look was a degradation process on the green scopes.

As an aside, the camouflage-pattern rifle scopes available on the market today are created by using special painting techniques. They are not anodized.

NOTE: Judging from the comments of various Army and Marine Corps ordnance personnel with service in South Vietnam, in addition to problems affecting coatings, aluminum alloy "did not hold up very well" in Southeast Asia. By all accounts, a form of "metal cancer" (exfoliation) would attack the aluminum on an M16 rifle or a telescopic sight, for example, and literally dissolve small parts and/or portions of the surface. Though rarely noted, miscellaneous equipment, including "some M16 rifles and telescopes," were reportedly "painted black" as a remedial measure.

In addition to concerns regarding the finish, a number of other problems with the Redfield system resulted from exposure to the rigors of combat, Marine snipers, and the weather extremes in South Vietnam. The scenario was all too familiar. Though more than adequate for general field use in the hands of a civilian rifleman, commercial rifle scopes, when pressed into military service in an "as manufactured" state, rarely held up in a combat environment.

Although a number of Redfield 3X-9X variable-power telescopic sights fielded in Vietnam were rendered inoperative for one reason or another, many were still in service when the last Marine combat units left Southeast Asia. According to one Marine veteran, an armorer with firsthand experience in RVN, "It was a lot like buying a new car. It seemed you either got a good one or you didn't."

In deference to the Redfield system, even though most of the problems encountered in Vietnam were rightfully attributed to "design inadequacies" exacerbated by combat use, an untold quantity of Redfield sights were literally beat to hell due to negligent and/or careless handling. Their length of field service was hardly more than a matter of time in the hands of some Marines.

However, concurrent with difficulties affecting both the rifle and the telescopic sight, Marine Corps ordnance documents summarized the Redfield situation as follows:

> The scope is easily damaged, subject to fogging, and inadequately sealed against moisture.
> The body of the sight cracks under the variable-power adjustment ring.
>
> [**NOTE:** A lateral opening or slot in the tube (approximately 180 degrees) beneath the power selector ring was necessary for the "power-ring" to move the erector lenses to change magnification. As such, there was a tendency for "cracks" to form when the tube was stressed].
>
> The range scale melts. Rays of the sun are reflected through the objective lens and are magnified, thereby causing the range finder to melt and/or lose adhesiveness which in turn results in the scale dropping into the tube rendering the scope less effective.
>
> [**NOTE:** The range scale was held to the internal lens surface with a "clear mastic adhesive." The sunlight, magnified as it was entering the tube at certain angles, caused the adhesive to melt and the range scale would then slip out of place, if it didn't melt in the process. Even though the scope remained functional, the Accu-Range feature was useless. Many Marine snipers referred to this as "losing the reticle."]
>
> The lense covers provided with the sight loosen in the heat and fall off.
>
> [**NOTE:** Redfield furnished soft (pliable) plastic lens covers with each sight assembly. Though intended for field use, the plastic covers were more effective protecting the telescopes in transit than in the field. When subjected to elevated temperatures of direct sunlight, the lens covers softened and simply fell from the tube. The plastic lens caps were part of the original equipment package. As a matter of interest, the same type was later issued with the Army AR TEL sighting system with the same results. Separate telescope carrying cases or covers were not furnished with the USMC M700/Redfield system in Vietnam.]

Though it is rarely noted, it was not uncommon for the "point of impact" to shift significantly when the power settings were changed in the variable-power sights. Whenever possible, Marine snipers were known to "pick through" whatever sights were available "to find one that worked properly." Marine snipers were taught to replace damaged reticles (cross hairs) and perform routine maintenance and basic repairs on the Unertl target scopes during early combat activity in RVN. But as complex as the Redfield variable-power system was by comparison, there were practical limits to the repairs a Marine sniper or a trained armorer could make, even under the best conditions.

Because the Redfield was a first-generation variable-power sight, only basic design improvements separated the Marine Corps model from those introduced to the commercial market a few years earlier. An "improved" 3X-9X variable-power sight described by Redfield as a "beefed-up" version was available in 1968. However, except for a "limited quantity" of this version reportedly sent to Southeast Asia for combat evaluation during the final months of Marine Corps involvement, the vast majority of the M700/M40 sniper rifles Marine snipers employed during this era made use of the first-generation 3X-9X variable-power Redfield sights commonly known as "the green scopes." (Marine Corps ordnance personnel have verified that second-generation "black" Redfield 3X-9X variable-power scopes saw combat use in RVN beginning in late 1969.)

When it came to remedial measures taken in response to problems encountered with the Redfield sighting system during stateside sniper training and combat use in South Vietnam, one of the most effective solutions was the procurement and issuance of "flip-up" lens covers to counter the problem with sun-damaged range scales. An accessory item originally intended for commercial use, the lens cover protected both ends of the telescope and popped open instantly when the sight was needed.

NOTE: For the sake of clarification, even though they have been mentioned elsewhere as having been made and furnished by the Redfield firm, for the record, the flip-up lens covers ("flip-open covers") originally fielded with the USMC/Redfield contract sight as a remedial measure were made (and so marked) by the E.D. Vissing Company, a plastics firm based in Idaho Falls, Idaho. As a Redfield supplier, in addition to eventually producing the Redfield "Supreme" flip-up covers, Vissing also made the soft plastic lens caps furnished with the Vietnam-era USMC and Army Redfield sights. The Vissing firm was sold to the Butler Creek Corporation in 1974.

The following admonition was eventually added to the instruction booklet furnished with the Redfield Accu-Range sights:

> IMPORTANT: Avoid letting the sun shine directly into the objective lens. This lens can act as a "burning glass," causing deterioration of the Accu-Range scale.

Reflecting on the selection and subsequent field use of the Redfield telescope, Major Hayden added the following:

> We went to a 3X9 variable thinking we had achieved the perfect compromise between high power and the corresponding ability to resolve small, indistinct targets in a cluttered background, and the superior brightness and field of view that go with low power. As it turned out, it appeared that we had wasted our money on the variable feature and unnecessarily complicated the scope. Reports from the field indicated that the scopes were routinely set on the highest power and left there. The variable mechanism, of course, introduced another joint and increased the chances of problems with moisture and fogging.
>
> We had also specified the Accu-Range feature for the scopes. It was soon found that, if the objective lens was left uncovered, the sun entering the tube would literally melt the plastic Accu-Range strip. Even though this did not make the scope unserviceable, it seems few Marines were using the range-finding feature anyway.

Although no one can say for certain when the first reports of trouble with the Redfield Accu-Range scale actually occurred, Veteran Marine sniper Donald G. Barker provides the following insight on his experience with the Redfield sights while serving as an instructor at the newly formed sniper school at Marine Corps Base, Camp Pendleton, California:

> We received our first shipment of Remington rifles and Redfield scopes [50] during the first week of January 1967. . . . The first sniper class held at Camp Pendleton experienced difficulty with a few of the scopes [melted range scales].

And, as Barker continued,

> One phone call to Redfield and they had a representative out there. . . . After finally admitting we were not "nuts," he wanted to know if I had any ideas for a quick fix. Something that would protect the reticles from the sun. A spring-loaded lens cap was suggested and the rest is history.

When it came to the improved model, whether significant changes to the Redfield 3X-9X variable-power sight came as a result of the Marine Corps problems in Vietnam or were scheduled improvements has not been substantiated. In any case, what Redfield referred to as "improving the line" emerged as a redesigned second-generation 3X-9X variable-power sight.

Even though the two models appeared similar at first glance, the improved version displayed some notable differences. The turret housing, adjustment turrets, and caps were completely redesigned, as Redfield stated, "to make adjustments easier." (The scale on each turret [elevation-windage] was changed from 33 to 48 index lines. The graduation adjustment values [1/2 minute of movement] remained the same.) The tube was reinforced at the opening beneath the power selector ring, and the ring itself was reconfigured. Instead of a "jointed tube" (screwed together), the objective bell and the main tube were eventually formed from a single piece of aluminum alloy. While this was essentially a "one-piece tube," the eyepiece assembly still threaded to the end. (According to Vietnam-era Redfield technical information, "the main tube with its objective end is hydraulically formed in one piece. The eyepiece bell is separate to allow for reticle focus." This design change was noted in 1968 U.S. Army ordnance documents as a "significant improvement." The first "one-piece" rifle scope was not introduced by the Redfield firm until the early 1980s when the entire telescope tube, including the turret housing, was machined from an aluminum alloy extrusion). The eyepiece assembly was enlarged, and the field and ocular lenses were resized accordingly. The range scale (Accu-Range reticle) yard markings and divisions were also changed.

NOTE: From all indications, Redfield made use of at least three different range scales (yard markings) with their commercial Accu-Range telescopes during this era. At least two versions were used in the original USMC/Redfield contract sights. A random sampling of "green" 3X-9X variable-power Redfield sights issued with the Vietnam-era USMC Remington M700/M40 sniper rifles indicates some use of range scales normally found in the second-generation scopes. Whether these represent sights "rebuilt" by Redfield (as many of the original issue scopes subsequently were) or manufactured as such remains unknown.

Commercial sights were available with a black gloss or black satin anodized finish. Though few in actual number, the variable-power telescopes procured as replacements for first-generation sights that were lost in combat or beyond repair made use of the satin finish.

Both first and second-generation 3X-9X variable-power Accu-Range telescopic sights (green-black) remained in Marine Corps service during the 1970s.

While it seems that the Marine Corps experienced considerable difficulty with the Redfield system while the Army apparently did not, as an Army spokesman summarized the matter in retrospect, "The improvements made to the Redfield sighting system [1968] did make a significant difference in their reliability."

NOTE: According to Marine Corps information, in keeping with its contractual obligations, the Redfield firm absorbed the expense of repairing any telescopic sight with defects relating to design flaws or the manufacturing process.

Whereas the USMC/Redfield contract sights were first-generation variable-power scopes, the adjustable ranging telescopes fielded by the Army, beginning with those sent to the Ninth Infantry Division in late 1968, were based on the improved second-generation model.

As a matter of historical interest, the Limited Warfare Laboratory Adjustable Ranging Telescopes evaluated by the Army Concept Team in Vietnam (ACTIV) during 1967 were based on first-generation 3X-9X variable-power Redfield sights. The Adjustable Ranging Telescopes sent to South Vietnam as part of the emerging U.S. Army sniper program (Ninth Infantry Division), were second-generation 3X-9X variable-power sights. In this case, however, the Army scopes were manufactured as such at the Redfield plant (1969) to ART specifications.

In one form or another, the Redfield 3X-9X variable-power telescope served as the principal Army and Marine Corps sniper sight during the war in Vietnam.

A typical first-generation 3X-9X variable-power Redfield Accu-Range rifle scope issued with the USMC M700/M40 sniper rifle during the Vietnam War. The scope was colored green (anodized) to match the parkerized finish of the rifle. The power selector ring (numbered 3 to 9) located in front of the eyepiece assembly controlled the power of magnification and the range finder functions of the scope. The elevation and windage adjustment turrets were identical in appearance and movement; the turret caps tightened against small rubber rings to form a moisture seal. Commercial markings appeared on the eyepiece, a factory serial number beneath the turret housing. According to Redfield, "Except for the green finish, the Marine Corps rifle scopes were the same as the standard model available in sporting goods stores." The sights were not marked to indicate military service. Marine Corps contract specifications defined the telescope and mounting hardware as, "Scope Special USMC Model, Item No. 112035, w/JR I" Low Ring, pr Item No. 523503" and the receiver base "Base, Special, JR 40X, Item No. 511153." The telescope rings used with this system were made of steel. The four-screw ("access screws") 1-inch split rings are .625 inch wide, and the ring height is .152 inch. The lug beneath the front scope ring engaged the mounting base opening. In this case, the serial number of rifle 221394 is engraved on the left side of the telescope tube. (Peter R. Senich.)

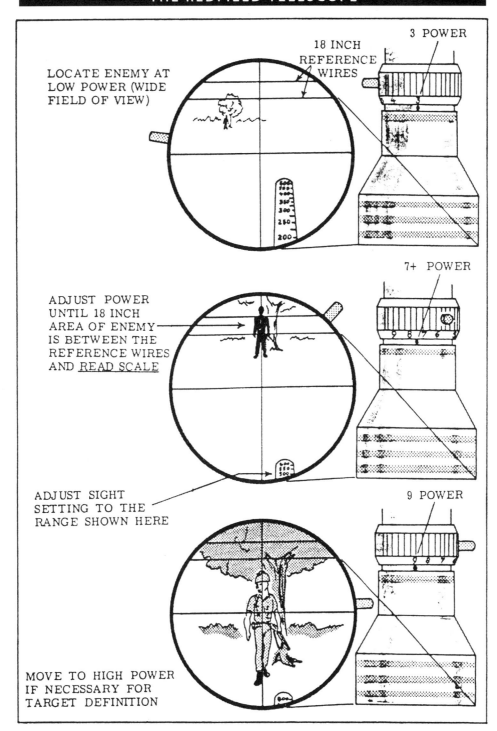

An illustration from *FMFM 1-3B, SNIPING* (August 1969), the Vietnam-era USMC sniper training manual, provides a view of the Accu-Range reticle and the range-finding reference lines (stadia wires). The range scale pictured is different from those used with the USMC/Redfield contract sights. It is not known if this version actually existed, or if the illustrator simply took some latitude with his drawing. The same illustration also appears in the 1967 and 1968 draft editions of the USMC sniping manual. (U.S. Marine Corps.)

An actual range scale (enlarged) from a Redfield Accu-Range telescopic sight. The scale was held to the internal lens surface with a clear mastic adhesive. In this case, the thin plastic strip is .040 inch wide at the base and .200 inch in length. The original adhesive is clearly visible. The Accu-Range reticle was offered as an option beginning in 1965. From all indications, Redfield made use of three or possibly four different range scales (yard markings) with their commercial Accu-Range telescopes during this era. At least two versions were used in the USMC/Redfield contract sights: the range scale shown here and what some choose to refer to as an "earlier version." (Peter R. Senich.)

Right: The Redfield turret assembly as pictured in *FMFM 1-3B, SNIPING* (August 1969). The assembly was described as follows: "The elevation and windage turrets within the assembly are identical in appearance and movement. Each turret has a dial with an arrow indicating the direction of movement; the elevation dial reads 'UP'; the windage dial reads 'R' for right. Each turret contains an adjusting screw for making elevation and/or windage adjustments. The elevation adjusting screw affects the strike of the bullet vertically, while the windage adjusting screw affects it horizontally. There are no audible clicks when the adjusting screws are turned, making it necessary to set the sights by eye. The elevation and windage adjustments are graduated in 1/2-minute of angle." (U.S. Marine Corps.)

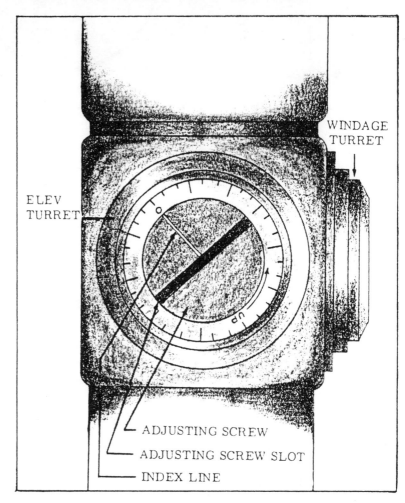

Below: A Vietnam-era Redfield 3X-9X variable-power Accu-Range Marine Corps contract sight. The serial number of rifle no. 221358 is engraved (electric pencil) on the side of the tube. (Nelson Collection.)

An original Marine Corps issue M700/M40 sniper rifle mounting a second-generation 3X-9X variable-power Redfield Accu-Range sight. Although Vietnam-era M700/M40 rifles were reconfigured eventually (M40A1), the Redfield scopes remained in service until replaced by the Unertl 10-power Sniper Scope in the early 1980s. The extended bolt shroud (shown) was introduced by Remington in late 1968/early 1969. Although original Marine Corps contract rifles (the initial order) made use of the shorter, earlier style, the extended bolt shroud was apparently retrofitted to various M700/M40 rifles during the course of Marine Corps service. (Peter R. Senich.)

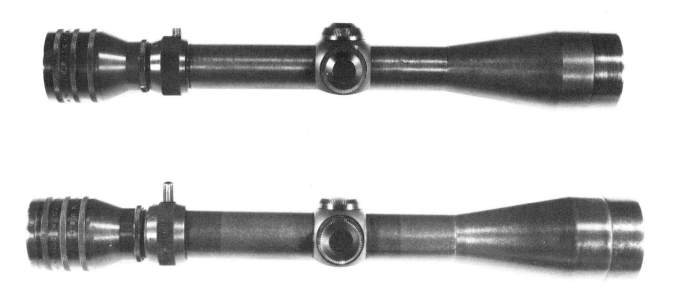

A direct comparison between two Redfield 3X-9X variable-power rifle scopes with Marine Corps service to their credit. The second-generation model (top) has a black satin finish. The green anodized scope was originally issued with a M700/M40 sniper rifle. The second-generation telescope is not numbered. (Peter R. Senich.)

A close comparison between the elevation and windage adjustment turret housing on the first-generation (top) and the second-generation 3X-9X variable-power USMC/ Redfield rifle telescopes. The entire assembly was redesigned, as Redfield stated, "to improve adjustments." Note the change from "Redfield 1" Tube" to an updated version of "Redfield." The "3X-9X" model designation remained the same. As a matter of interest, the small markings on the turret housing (bottom) served as reference points for elevation and windage adjustments. The practice was known as "marking the sights" to many Marine marksmen, with either nail polish or paint used for this purpose. (Peter R. Senich.)

A typical second-generation 3X-9X variable-power Redfield Accu-Range rifle scope. The most obvious differences between this and the first-generation Redfield sights were the turret housing and the power selector ring. The early USMC scopes were green; the newer model has a black satin finish in this case. Even though veteran USMC ordnance personnel have verified that second-generation Redfield 3X-9X variable-power telescopic sights ("the black scopes") were fielded in RVN during the latter part of 1969, the extent of their combat use remains unconfirmed at present. (Peter R. Senich.)

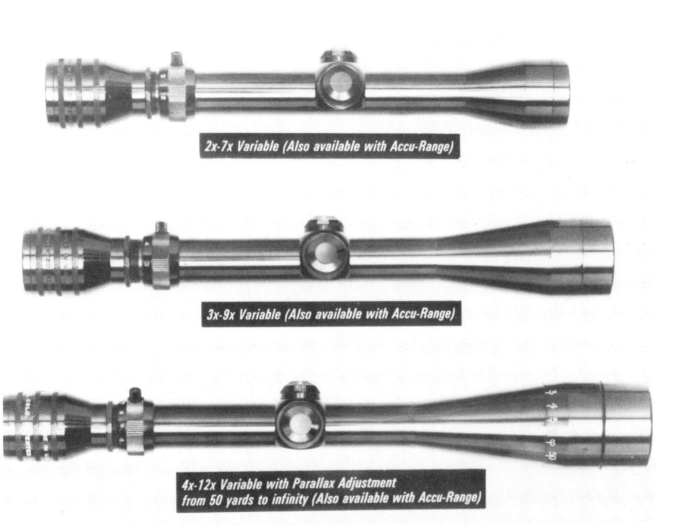

2x-7x Variable (Also available with Accu-Range)

3x-9x Variable (Also available with Accu-Range)

4x-12x Variable with Parallax Adjustment from 50 yards to infinity (Also available with Accu-Range)

A late 1960s illustration of Redfield variable-power telescopic rifle sights. The 2X-7X model was fielded with the AR15/Ml6 by U.S. military forces in RVN. The 3X-9X sight saw combat use in commercial trim and as procured by the Army and the Marine Corps for their respective sniper programs. The 4X-12X model saw only limited use in Southeast Asia. (Redfield.)

The flip-up lens covers ("flip-open covers") originally fielded with USMC/Redfield contract sights as a remedial measure were made by the E.D. Vissing Co. (so marked). The cover is pictured on the ocular end of a Marine Corps telescope. The illustration also provides a good view of the Redfield power selector ring; the ring is positioned at 3 power. (Peter R. Senich.)

E.D. Vissing lens cover fitted to the objective end of the Marine Corps sniper sight. The cover is shown in the open position in this case. An effective means of protecting the lens, the plastic covers were developed and patented by E.D. Vissing as an accessory item for commercial use. As a matter of interest, even though the Vissing soft plastic lens caps ("Black Cover Set") were listed and illustrated in the various Vietnam-era USMC Supply Activity "Stock Lists" for the M700/M40 sniper rifles, the flip-open covers pressed into service in RVN were not. There does not appear to have been a separate manufacturer's code or stock number for the flip-up lens covers at the time. (Peter R. Senich.)

An end view of the black plastic E.D. Vissing flip-up lens covers removed from the Redfield telescope. The cover left, is marked "Supreme"; the other bears the Vissing name and location. From all indications, many snipers chose to use only the objective cover on their Redfield telescope. Lens covers, in any form, were considered essential by some snipers and a nuisance to others. (Peter R. Senich.)

Plastic lens caps ("Black Cover Set") furnished with the Vietnam-era 3X-9X variable-power Redfield telescopic sights. The covers were made for Redfield by the E.D. Vissing Co. of Idaho Falls, Idaho. Though intended for commercial use, the caps were issued with the USMC/Redfield sniper sight and the Redfield Adjustable Ranging Telescope (ART) fielded by the Army. The covers were connected by a thin cord when issued; the lens cap for the ocular end of the second-generation Redfield sight was slightly larger due to design changes made by the Redfield firm. Though the caps were reasonably effective, direct sunlight or elevated temperatures would soften them, causing them to fall from the tube. (West Point Collection.)

An inside view of the Redfield lens caps showing the markings for the objective (right) and the ocular ends of the telescope. In addition to the soft plastic (pliable) covers, the E.D. Vissing Co. made flip-up lens covers for Redfield. The plastics firm was later absorbed by the Butler Creek Corp. in 1974. The caps shown were issued with an Army XM21/ART system during the Vietnam War. (West Point Collection.)

The "production model" of the Adjustable Ranging Telescope (ART) manufactured during the war in Vietnam with an ART mounting fabricated at Frankford Arsenal. Even though the sights were essentially second-generation 3X-9X variable-power rifle scopes, rather than adapting existing commercial sights, the production version with ART reticle, ballistic cam, power adjusting ring, and ring lock were made to ART specifications at the Redfield plant in Denver, Colorado. The sights were shipped to Frankford Arsenal, where they were mated with the mount assemblies. The scope and mount pictured are typical of the Adjustable Ranging Telescopes issued with the U.S. Army XM21 sniper rifle during the Vietnam War. (Peter R. Senich.)

An alternate view of the Redfield "AR TEL" Adjustable Ranging Telescope with elevation and windage adjustment turret caps removed. The raised mounting ridges were designed to engage the groove and screw recess on the left side of the M14 receiver. The mounting screw retainer ("E" ring) is barely visible; the spring-loaded telescope base is directly above the sideplate. The ballistic cam rested on a nonmagnetic hex bushing threaded into the cam base, an extension at the back of the mount. Production sights were given a black matte (anodized) finish to eliminate reflections. (Peter R. Senich.)

An XM21 Army sniper rifle in combat trim. The 3X-9X variable-power Adjustable Ranging Telescope (ART) was manufactured by Redfield. (U.S. Army.)

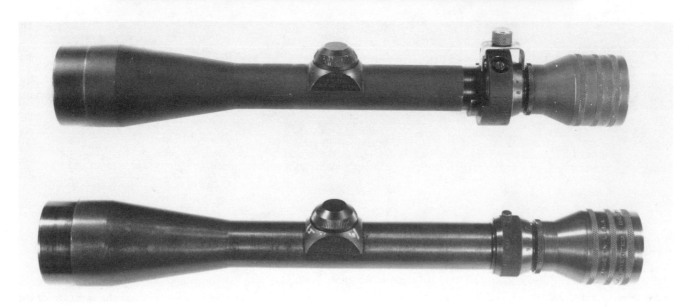

A comparison between a Redfield 3X-9X ART, a production AR TEL model, and a commercial Redfield 3X-9X variable-power Accu-Range sight. Both telescopes are second-generation variable-power sights. The ART was issued with an Army XM21, and the Accu-Range model was a Marine Corps replacement sight fitted to an M40 sniper rifle. The Adjustable Ranging Telescope bears military markings on the turret housing (3X - 9X AR TEL SER NO 0000). The conventional sight has standard commercial markings. Except for the finish, reticle, and power selector/adjusting ring assembly, the two rifle scopes are virtually the same. (Peter R. Senich.)

Adjustable Ranging Telescope carrying case developed for Army sniper use in South Vietnam. ART carrying cases were made from .062-inch-thick (nominal) 6061-T6 aluminum alloy, coated with olive drab vinyl paint, which had a tendency to peel and weighed in at 18 ounces empty, 40 ounces with scope and mount. The item name ("Case, Carrying") and the ordnance reference number (11729637) appeared on the side of the case. The aluminum container was listed as a "Basic Issue Item." As a matter of interest, the outline of the large Redfield "R" from the plastic lens caps issued with the ART system will be found impressed in the rubber gasket beneath the lid on many of the surviving cases. The lid pressed against the lens caps when the sight was in place. Even though the objective end of the telescope was intended to be placed into the case with the power ring set at "3" (power), manipulating the power ring one way or the other allowed the scope to go into the case in either direction. (Peter R. Senich.)

An alternate view of the ART carrying case. The 14 5/8-inch-long, 5 1/4-inch-wide case was fitted with a strap and keeper for attachment to the ammunition belt. Soft rubber inserts protected the telescope from shock; a gasket prevented water from entering the case. The earliest published reference to the carrying case appeared in the Limited Warfare Laboratory ART installation and operation manual (September 1968). The first carrying cases categorized as "production" were shipped to Vietnam with the Ninth Infantry Division sniper rifles in late 1968. Army Ordnance documents listed Frankford Arsenal as the manufacturer. Though effective for protecting the ART, the aluminum carrying cases were rarely used in combat. Telescope carrying cases or covers were not issued by the Marine Corps for sniper use in Vietnam. (Peter R. Senich.)

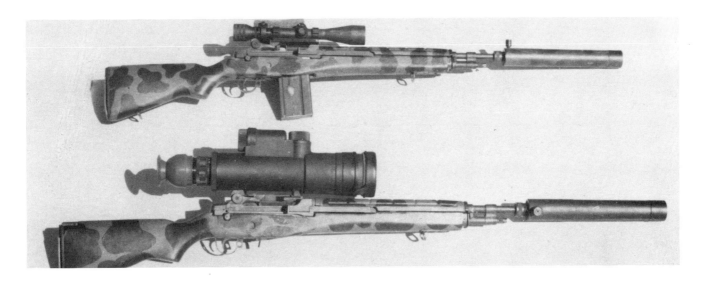

With a day and night capability, the Vietnam-era XM21 mounting the ART or a Starlight Scope in combination with the Sionics M14SS-1 Suppressors wrought havoc among VC and NVA combat personnel in Southeast Asia. The alternate use of the Adjustable Ranging Telescope, a Starlight Scope, and the Sionics Suppressor with the semiautomatic XM21 rifle provided the Army with an extremely versatile sniping system in Vietnam. Although some have come to regard sniper use of night vision equipment as little more than an "ambush," with a number of documented VC and NVA killed and wounded by Army snipers armed with Starlight Scope-equipped XM21 rifles at ranges of 500 meters or more, one slightly perturbed veteran Army sniper chose to respond in the following manner:

"All this crap about 'night shooting' and 'long-range kills being the mark of a true sniper' really pisses me off! The fact of the matter is they put me in the field as a sniper to kill the enemy as best I could. And, if I accomplished that by putting a slug in someone at close range, brought them down at 900 meters with one round, or beat them senseless with my rifle butt, it still counted as an enemy KIA no matter what time of the day this took place. Some of these people are out of touch with reality, especially the ones that were never in 'Nam. I only wish we could have had some of the night sights they are using now." (U.S. Army.)

CHAPTER 14

A SYSTEM IN TRANSITION

When the rigors of combat revealed flaws in the 7.62mm USMC sniper rifle that had not turned up when the system was evaluated at Quantico, reports citing one problem or another began filtering back to Marine Corps Headquarters in Washington.

Even though the rifle and telescope were performing extremely well in most cases, the system was experiencing difficulties that would require immediate attention. Consequently, not only would the system undergo remedial measures that would sustain it in Vietnam, but the Scout-Sniper Rifle was about to enter a period of transition that would extend well beyond Marine Corps combat involvement in Southeast Asia.

Despite only marginal official attention to snipers and sniping equipment in the years prior to Vietnam, the Marine Corps displayed a level of commitment to its Vietnam-era sniping program that can only be described as "total" in this case.

When the official focus on snipers and their equipment all but ended following the war, however, a resolute group of officers and men managed to "keep the sniper concept alive" in the Marine Corps and develop a first-rate sniper rifle (M40A1) in the process.

NOTE: As a matter of reader interest, development work on what eventually became the USMC M40A1 7.62mm sniper rifle actually began as a result of the problems the M700/M40 sniper rifle had encountered in RVN. Although various Marine Corps personnel were involved with an ongoing project between 1969 and 1977 when the second-generation M40A1 was formally adopted, the effort put forth by a relatively small band of Marines in the pursuit of an optimum sniper rifle during this time span was nothing less than remarkable. What started out as "product improvement" in 1969 culminated in 1977 with the formal adoption of the M40A1 sniper rifle (29 June 1977), a weapon system still employed by the Marine Corps.

Although countless equipment problems were dealt with effectively at the field level, as a matter of course, unusual and/or significant malfunctions were duly noted in an "Unsatisfactory Equipment Report" (UER) and forwarded to HQMC through proper channels.

In this case, various references in Marine Corps documents indicate "reports" involving the Scout-Sniper Rifle were directed to the Commandant of the Marine Corps beginning in late 1967.

NOTE: So far as can be determined, one of the earliest UERs from South Vietnam (lst MarDiv, 4 October 1967), recommended that the Remington M700 Sniper Rifle be glass-bedded "in a manner similar to the Winchester M70."

Except for early measures to keep the system in a state of combat readiness in RVN, however, any significant measures to improve the Remington/Redfield system would not take serious form until early in 1969 when III MAF focused attention on the mounting problems with the 7.62mm USMC sniper rifle.

Acting on the requirements and recommendations set forth in a series of "messages" (March–April 1969) from the commanding general III MAF to the commanding general FMFPac concerning "certain problem areas in existing sniper equipment," the CG, FMFPac, in a response forwarded to the CG, III MAF and the Commandant, HQMC, recommended a product improvement or weapon replacement program for sniper equipment and directed CG, II MAF, to submit an "all inclusive Unsatisfactory Equipment Report" on the rifle and associated equipment.

As then followed, UER No. 05-69 and No. 06-69, dated 6 May 1969, would serve as the official basis for a sweeping reevaluation of the Remington/Redfield system then employed in South Vietnam.

NOTE: Rather than leave the reader with the impression that the Marine Corps was slow to react to problems with the Scout-Sniper Rifle, it is important to note that while months would pass before official measures were taken to improve the system overall, remedial measures designed to keep sniper equipment in the field were instituted as soon as the proper course of action was determined. From all indications, by mid-1968, efforts to sustain the system in RVN were centered on "glass-bedding to retain accuracy," "stock waterproofing to prevent warping," and "the adequate supply of spare trigger guards" (according to early field reports, the cast aluminum M700 trigger guards were "easily damaged" in combat). Despite some discussion of "in-service rebarreling," there is no evidence that unserviceable barrels were removed and replaced in RVN as part of the early corrective measures.

The "all-inclusive" UERs pertaining to the Remington Rifle and the Redfield Telescope were prepared and submitted to HQMC by Headquarters, Maintenance Battalion, First Force Service Regiment, Force Logistic Command, FMFPac.

Report No. 05-69, 6 May 1969, for the "Telescope, Sight; Variable 3-9X, Redfield Gun Sight Corporation" read as follows:

> This maintenance activity provides RTE maintenance for the 1st Marine Division Scout-Sniper Teams. The following comments are offered to assist in the development of a Specific Operational Requirement for truly specialized sniper equipment. A large number of M700 rifles have been repaired during the past 24

months. It is obvious that the telescope sight is generally not sufficiently rugged for active combat use. The major deficiencies are:

    1. The body of the sight cracks under the variable power adjustment ring.
    2. The range finder scale melts.
    3. Small amounts of dust cause the variable power adjustment ring to freeze to the body of the sight so that no adjustment is possible.
    4. External lens faces are easily pitted by blowing dust and sand particles.
    5. Lens covers provided with the sight loosen with heat and fall off.

Recommendation: No concrete recommendation is offered as a solution. The deficiencies noted here are prevalent in all known commercial telescope sights. A possible solution is the development of a rugged sight suitable for Marine Corps use.

Report No. 06-69, 6 May 1969, for the "Rifle, 7.62mm, M700, Remington Arms Co." contained the following information:

This maintenance activity provides RTE maintenance for the 1st Marine Division Scout-Sniper Teams. The following comments are offered to assist in the development of a Specific Operational Requirement for specialized sniper equipment.

Since 16 February 1968, the Command has serviced 99 rifles. Of the 99, 54 have been declared unserviceable and in a Code "H" condition. At the present time, the 1st Marine Division has only 45 rifles in the field against an allowance of 82. A recent Limited Technical Inspection of the 45 rifles indicates that 23 are in serviceable condition and 22 are in questionable condition as to serviceability. It is anticipated that all 22 rifles will be totally unserviceable within the next six month period.

[**NOTE:** The figures cited in UER No. 06-69 (serviceable and unserviceable M700 rifles) have been quoted out of context on more than one occasion. In one case, for example, the "99 rifles" serviced since 16 February 1968 have been listed as the only 7.62mm USMC sniper rifles "in all of Vietnam" in 1969. The 23 rifles "in serviceable condition" have been noted as the "only" serviceable rifles "in use" in Vietnam.

Even though Marine Corps troop strength was in the process of being reduced, those who choose to believe there were only "23" Scout-Sniper Rifles in the field in RVN in 1969 should consider smoking something else! Moreover, discussion of this point with both 3d MarDiv and 1st MarDiv personnel tasked with Scout-Sniper "requalification" in mid-1969 have indicated there was "no perceptible shortage" of M700/M40 sniper rifles at that time.]

A breakdown of the major deficiencies of the rifle follow: the telescope sight has been treated separately in UER No. 05-69 and is not included in this breakdown.

1. Barrels become unserviceable due to heavy pitting in less than one (1) year service, or an average of less than 1000 fired rounds. This may be attributed to several factors:

    a. Lack of proper bore cleaning by the individual Marine
    b. High ambient humidity in Vietnam
    c. A scarcity of proper cleaning materials (bore brushes, patches and .30 caliber rods) at the using level since the introduction of the M16 rifle.

Recommended Solution: Adoption of stainless steel barrels.

2. Trigger mechanism fails to hold adjustment over a long time period. The adjustment screws are staked in place at the factory and are difficult to adjust.

Recommended Solution: Eliminate staking of adjustment screws. Rather, adopt the use of LOCTITE or a similar cement.

3. The stock warps at the forend, touching the barrel and adversely affecting accuracy. Additionally, as the weather conditions change, the stock tends to dry or absorb moisture causing the receiver to become excessively loose or tight, adversely affecting the zero and accuracy of the rifle. The brass pin to the rear of the magazine mortise is ineffective. The stock is not sufficiently waterproofed as the oil treatment is totally unsatisfactory in this climate. Comment: All rifle stocks have been fiberglassed locally through the receiver section and the barrel channels have been relieved to prevent stock warpage affecting accuracy.

Recommended Solution:
a. Adopt a high grade, pressure epoxy-impregnated stock.
b. Fiberglass the receivers and full-float the barrel channels at the factory. Waterproof the barrel channels.
c. Replace the brass pin with a Mauser-type special stock lock.
d. Adopt the use of a waterproof finish such as hard polyurethane varnish, then paint the stocks a dull-grey or non-gloss dark green to eliminate reflection.

4. While the Redfield Junior telescope sight mount used is satisfactory, beyond 600 meters the sniper must judge the distance and "hold over" the target. A recent development by the Realist Corporation incorporates the use of a ballistically matched cam that automatically places the proper elevation on the sight as the range finder is adjusted. This mount appears to be very rugged and can be used with the standard Redfield "Accu-Range" sight. It is recommended that this mount be investigated as a replacement for the Redfield Junior mount. [NOTE: Adapting an Adjustable Ranging Telescope to the M700 rifle involved more than what is indicated here. Also, the mount for the Realist ART could not be used with a Redfield scope.]

Of further interest in this matter, an addendum to the "all inclusive" UER drew attention to the lack of a night vision capability with the Marine Corps sniper rifle:

While not in the category of unsatisfactory equipment, the usefulness of the M700 Rifle would be greatly extended with the provisions necessary to utilize Sight, Night Vision, AN/PVS-3. The M700 is presently limited to daytime use only. A quick-release mount capable of being easily returned to zero after removal and upon reinstallation on the sight is a necessary adjunct.

NOTE: At this juncture, the "Sight, Night Vision, AN/PVS-3," otherwise referenced as the "miniaturized Starlight Scope," would have presented a logical choice for the bolt-action Scout-Sniper Rifle. Though beset by problems when first introduced, the diminutive night vision sight (3 pounds) was significantly lighter than either the AN/PVS-1 or the AN/PVS-2 models. The AN/PVS-3 was reportedly available for field use in RVN by late 1967. Although Starlight Scopes were eventually tested with the M700/M40 rifles, the AN/PVS-3 model does not appear to have been included.

As the situation evolved, the problem of adapting a Starlight Scope to the Marine Corps sniper rifle was centered on the method of mounting rather than the type of sight. The physical characteristics of a typical bolt-action rifle were not conducive to mounting equipment of this type. By comparison, an M14 or M16 rifle fitted with a bipod, for example, provided an excellent platform for the AN/PVS-1 or AN/PVS-2 Starlight Scopes in Southeast Asia.

Though some have chosen to ignore this fact, the Army's use of a Starlight Scope with its XM21 sniper rifle proved to be a residual benefit to its program in Vietnam. A number of Army sniper "kills" were made with the Starlight Scope during night operations.

Responding to the situation, the Commandant, HQMC, issued a project directive to the Commanding General, Marine Corps Development and Education Command (MCDEC), Quantico, Virginia, to:

> . . . continuously evaluate sniper equipment and to make recommendations for improvement. This will include:
>
> a. Use of a stainless steel barrel.
>
> b. Evaluation of the product improved Redfield 3X9X Telescope [the second-generation model] and U.S. Army Limited Warfare Laboratory variable telescope [Adjustable Ranging Telescope].
>
> c. Determination of the most effective means for impregnation of the stock to prevent warping.

NOTE: Impregnating wooden stocks with epoxy served as an effective means of waterproofing the stock and eliminating warpage. Although linseed oil, in various forms and mixtures, was employed for waterproofing sniper rifle stocks in Vietnam, according to a III MAF field report, "the use of linseed oil is not considered an adequate preventative measure."

For the sake of clarification, even though HQMC had also opened the door for a "weapon replacement program," if called for, during the course of establishing a project directive, although changes to the system were definitely in order, official emphasis was placed on the III MAF statement, "The Model 700 is considered adequate for its intended use as a sniper rifle."

NOTE: In view of the problems the Remington/Redfield system encountered in RVN, it is important to point out that III MAF considered the M700 sniper rifle "adequate" under the circumstances. Rather than push for a replacement system as it might have, the impetus was placed on finding a solution for the problems at hand. Without question, the III MAF position favoring the Scout-Sniper Rifle was instrumental in keeping the system in Marine Corps service.

Even though Marine Corps documents referenced pending changes to the Scout-Sniper Rifle, it is important to emphasize that the M700/M40 rifles fielded in South Vietnam remained essentially the same as they were manufactured by the Remington Arms Company.

Except for the remedial measures involving glass-bedding, stock waterproofing, and the replacement of trigger guards whenever necessary (other minor mechanical problems were involved and subsequently corrected), there were no significant changes or modifications to the 7.62mm USMC sniper rifles during the war in Vietnam. The same was also true for the Redfield sighting system.

NOTE: Appropriate instructions pertaining to glass-bedding and waterproofing of stocks were provided to the CG, III MAF in a CMC letter (8 May 1968), and to the field units in a bulletin dated 16 December 1968. In response to the recommendation that sniper rifle stocks be glass-bedded and waterproofed prior to shipment to Southeast Asia, the MTU, Quantico, Virginia, was tasked (6 June 1969) with "waterproofing and glass-bedding all Marine Corps sniper rifle stocks that are presently held in the supply centers."

The term "glass-bedding" is generally known as the process of using liquid fiberglass, epoxy, or similar materials to obtain an exact matching fit between the stock and the action/receiver. This procedure was considered essential in maintaining accuracy with a competition and/or sniping rifle. Various commercial bedding products were employed by the Army and Marine Corps MTUs for this purpose.

Of further interest in this matter, even though authorized bedding materials were eventually shipped overseas, according to a veteran RTE armorer, "We used steel epoxy from the AMTRAC repair kits for bedding M700 sniper rifles when nothing else was available." Measures such as this were indicative of the improvising that took place in Vietnam.

Officially categorized as an "Open End" evaluation, CMC Project Directive No. 44-69-03 (13 June 1969), "Marine Corps Sniper Rifle and Associated Equipment," tasked MCDEC with the following purpose and objectives:

> Purpose: To determine the suitability of the present sniper rifle and determine if there is in existence a telescopic sight that is more suitable for Marine Corps use than the one presently in use.

> Objectives:

> a. Evaluation of recommendations for improvement and unsatisfactory equipment reports from the field.

> b. Determine Marine Corps requirements for a sniper rifle and develop a recommended specific operational requirement.

> c. Determine Marine Corps requirements for a sight for a sniper rifle and develop a recommended specific operational requirement.

> d. Determine the suitability for Marine Corps use of two improved Redfield telescopic sights and the U.S. Army Limited Warfare Laboratory developed telescopic sight.

> e. Determine the suitability for Marine Corps use of a stainless steel barrel for the present sniper rifle.

> f. Determine the feasibility of utilizing non-wood stocks for sniper rifles.

> g. Determine the best available method of waterproofing wood rifle stocks.

> h. Continuously evaluate for Marine Corps use new items of sniper equipment as they become available.

NOTE: "Participating/Coordinating Agencies" were listed as "Fleet Marine Force Units as required, and the Marksmanship Training Unit/MCDEC."

In addition to the cooperation of the Remington firm and the Redfield Gun Sight Company, the U.S. Army Marksmanship Training Unit, U.S. Army Weapons Command, and the U.S. Army Night Vision Laboratory rendered support to the Marine Corps project at various times during the evaluations.

The Quantico-based MCDEC established a course of action that would involve an ongoing program to test and evaluate the Remington M700/M40 in conjunction with, or in comparison to, the following items and weapons:

Redfield 3X-9X variable-power Adjustable Ranging Telescope [Redfield ART or AR TEL]

Realist 3X-9X variable-power Adjustable Ranging Telescope [Realist ART]

Redfield 3X-9X variable-power Accu-Range Telescope [the second-generation model]

Special sight mounts and mounting brackets to allow interchangeability between the ART and night vision sights

Individual-served weapon sight AN/PVS-4 [Starlight Scope]

Crew-served weapon sight AN/TVS-5 [Starlight Scope]

Star-Tron [Smith & Wesson] passive night vision system [the commercial sight was included among the night vision equipment tested with the USMC sniping equipment]

Hand-held Laser Range Finder AN/GVS-5 [for range determination in sniper operations]

Free floating stainless steel barrels [free floating "chrome molybdenum" steel barrels were also considered]

Stamped steel trigger guards

Waterproofed and camouflaged wood stocks [fiberglass (nonwood) stocks were considered as well]

Bipod bracket [swivel] and detachable lightweight bipod

M2 bipod assembly ["modify sniper rifle stocks to allow use of a sling and the attachment of the bipod on an as required basis"]

7.62mm National Match Ammunition [recommend appropriate action to ensure consistent results and/or adopt a suitable replacement cartridge for sniper use]

Remington M700/M40, 7.62mm, USMC sniper rifle "Modified" [free floating stainless steel barrel, stamped steel trigger guard, bipod bracket and bipod, special sight mount and mounting bracket, waterproofed and camouflaged wooden stock]. The M40 "Modified" was also referenced as the "Product Improved Model."

Remington M700/M40, 7.62mm, USMC sniper rifle [standard issue rebuilt]

U.S. Army semiautomatic rifle, 7.62mm National Match [M14 accurized] XM21

Winchester Model 70, 7.62mm "prototype sniper rifle" [1971]

NOTE: According to USMC ordnance documents, a "heavy barrel M16 sniper rifle" was considered for Marine Corps sniper use. The rifle was dismissed as a candidate sniping weapon due to the range limitations of the 5.56mm M193 cartridge. Except for recommended use as a sniper support weapon in conjunction with the Starlight Scope, the M16 rifle did not receive further consideration as a USMC sniper rifle.

Inasmuch as the evaluations were expected to take an indeterminate amount of time, the specifications for Project No. 44-69-03 included the following statement: "Interim reports are required within 30 days of completion of significant events and not less than semiannually."

As then followed, efforts to sustain the flow of information resulted in a series of progress reports from the MCDEC to the attention of the Commandant, HQMC, during a period that extended from 1969 into early 1973. The reports detailed the rebuild and development activities encompassed by "Project No. 44-69-03: Marine Corps Sniper Rifle and Associated Equipment."

Even though HQMC was obviously committed to enhancing the reliability and performance of the Scout-Sniper Rifle, by the time the program finally shifted into high-gear back in the United States, the Marine Corps had already begun reducing troop strength in South Vietnam.

According to information from *The Marines in Vietnam: 1954–1973* (History and Museums Division, Headquarters, USMC January 1974):

> The year 1969 opened with substantial Marine forces still conducting large operations while supporting the South Vietnamese pacification efforts. By the end of June, however, President Nixon had announced the first redeployment of American forces. Beginning with the departure of the 9th Marines, the entire 3d Marine Division was out of Vietnam by the end of the year. Throughout 1970 and early 1971, other Marine units left Vietnam in succeeding increments. On 14 April 1971, III MAF headquarters departed for Okinawa, leaving behind the 3d Marine Amphibious Brigade. Two months later, the brigade was deactivated. Residual Marine forces in Vietnam consisted of approximately 500 Marines, most of whom were performing essential liaison, advisory, staff, and guard functions.

NOTE: Of further interest in this matter, the "official" return of the First Marine Division to Camp Pendleton was recorded as 30 April 1971.

With the exception of the "residual" Marine forces, the war in South Vietnam was over for the U.S. Marine Corps. From 1965 through 1971, nearly half a million Marines served in Vietnam. Ironically, even though many considered the I Corps Tactical Zone (I CTZ) to have been "a Marine Corps operation from start to finish," As *The Marines in Vietnam: 1954–1973* noted:

> At its peak in 1968, before the redeployments had begun, III Marine Amphibious Force had included two Marine divisions, two Marine regimental landing teams, a Marine aircraft wing, a large Force Logistic Command, a U.S. Army Corps headquarters, three Army divisions, and an Army mechanized infantry brigade.

Despite reports that the first half of 1968 had been marked by the "greatest combat activity of the war," the number of Marine infantry battalions had declined from 24 to 21 by the end of the same year. According to the Marine Corps, "Marine troop strength in RVN reached a peak of 85,755 in September 1968."

Although Marine sniper operations had more than proven their worth in Southeast Asia, when the redeployments made it necessary to reassess the long-term requirements of the Marine Corps in 1969, the CMC determined that Scout-Sniper Platoons would be deleted from the force structure.

As it was then stated:

> Employment as established for RVN, was one 36 man sniper platoon [one officer and 35 enlisted men] per Infantry Regiment and one 31 man sniper platoon [one officer and 30 enlisted men] per Reconnaissance Battalion. Seventeen M700/M40 rifles were located in the Infantry Regiment and 14 per Reconnaissance

Battalion. In light of the recent decision to delete sniper platoons from the force structure, the sniper capability will be maintained in the Marine Division.

Interestingly, even though efforts to correct the problems with the Scout-Sniper Rifle would continue as directed, MCDEC, in a project status report to the CMC (12 May 1971) requested:

> . . . information and guidance concerning the development of Marine Corps sniper equipment in light of the decision to delete sniper platoons from the force structure. . . . [The measure was due to take effect in 1972, the MCDEC recommended that] . . . no further evaluation of sniper weapon systems be conducted in the absence of requirements [Specific Operational Requirement or SOR].

And the Commandant responded (2 August 1971) as follows:

> The sniper capability will be maintained in the Marine Division. It is envisioned that sniper squads will be formed in infantry and reconnaissance battalions with Marines assigned on an additional duty basis. It is further envisioned that training will be conducted under the supervision of the Division Commander. Second echelon maintenance of sniper equipment will be conducted by the two Rifle Team Equipment Repairmen (MOS 2112) assigned to the Division Service Battalion; and third, fourth and fifth echelon maintenance will be conducted by MTU, Quantico, Virginia.
> A proposed Marine Corps Order is currently in staffing which will outline the Marine Corps sniper program and incorporate the guidance resulting from the decision to delete the sniper platoon from the Marine Division.
> In view of the above, it is deemed prudent at this time to continue evaluation of candidate sniper weapon systems and to develop a specific operational requirement for a sniper rifle and telescope.

Regardless of the intent, however, as time passed and the reality of war in Vietnam began to fade, matters such as "funding" and "budgetary constraints" would have more to do with determining a course of action than the exigencies of war. The prospects of sustaining a viable sniper/sniper training program during peacetime decreased significantly.

Responding to the inevitable recommendations that the Scout-Sniper Rifle improvement project be terminated as a result of the withdrawal from South Vietnam, an official statement from HQMC (Ordnance/A04F), dated 20 January 1972, countered with the following:

> The continuance of the subject project [No-44-69-03] will provide the required visibility for a program which otherwise may be relegated to a completely dormant state. This situation has occurred in the Marine Corps after each conflict and valuable time has been lost in regenerating an effective sniper program. The requirement for an SOR can be readdressed at the conclusion of the various studies currently underway which address the M40 sniper rifle. In the interim, the project directive will provide an economical monitorship of sniper rifle technology by the Marine Corps.
> Accordingly, it is recommended the subject project remain in effect and preparation of an SOR continue to be held in abeyance pending completion of the Infantry Weapon System Study (CMC Project No. 30-71-04).

Project No. 44-69-03 was eventually superseded by an even broader program referenced by the Marine Corps as:

> . . . an on-going Infantry, Organization and Weapons System Study (1973–1977). CMC Project No. 30-71-04 (30 September 1971) will analyze the requirements for snipers within the organization of the infantry battalion and will consider the present Marine Corps sniper rifle, the M40 rifle in this role.

The efforts of the Marine Corps Development and Education Command to develop acceptable rebuild standards for a "product improved Remington sniper rifle" based on the M700/M40 system would finally take shape in early 1973.

In view of the overlapping projects in this case, in the interest of avoiding any possible confusion, the official position regarding sniping equipment and the role of the sniper in the Marine Corps was stated during the Symposium on Sniper Weapons and National Match Ammunition (14 February 1973), a one-day affair attended by civilian and military experts concerned with marksmanship and sniper weapons systems. The symposium was hosted by the MCDEC at the Marine Corps base, Quantico, Virginia.

The Marine Corps position was summarized as follows:

> Commandant of the Marine Corps decisions in 1969 deleted Scout-Sniper units within infantry regiments and reconnaissance battalions effective in 1972. CMC Project No. 30-71-04, Infantry, Organization and Weapons System Study (1973–1977) has, as one of its objectives, the determination of sniper requirements within the infantry battalion.

> Sniper equipment is presently available within the Marine Corps and CMC Project No. 44-69-03, Marine Corps Sniper Rifle and Associated Equipment, is examining means to improve the capability of the equipment. Rifle improvement tests are expected to be completed in April 1973, with rebuild of the rifle to recommended standards to begin shortly thereafter. Improvement of the rifle's sighting system will continue until a suitable replacement for its present telescopic sight is found.

> A Tentative Specific Operational Requirement (TSOR) for the post 1980 Sniper Weapon System is being prepared. The post 1980 weapon system is expected to provide an increased first round hit probability, a day and night sighting and range finding system and improved reliability over the present sniper rifle.

> It is envisioned that infantry battalions will maintain teams of snipers within the organization for employment in combat or contingency situations. Personnel to be snipers will be those who have either participated in the marksmanship programs or who possess unusual skill with the rifle. Those snipers will primarily be infantry personnel whose sniper duties will be in addition to their regular jobs. During field exercises or combat they may be either employed as snipers or in their primary skills. Training will be conducted by Division rifle and pistol teams with support from the Marksmanship Training Unit, Weapons Training Battalion, Marine Corps Development and Education Command, Quantico, Virginia. Sufficient equipment will be maintained within the Division for training and contingency operations.

In due course, a memorandum from the MCDEC to HQMC (21 March 1973) concerning the "Rebuild Standards for the M40 Sniper Rifle" stated in part:

> During a meeting at HQMC on 7 March 1973 at which Remington Arms representatives, the Development Center Project officer for Sniper Rifles, and representatives of CMC were present, the following agreements were made:

> a. MCDEC will provide the rebuild standards.

b. Remington Arms will provide one proposal citing repair parts only, and one proposal citing rebarreling, restocking and replacing the trigger guard, with the USMC Marksmanship Training Unit to perform the accurizing and testing of rifles.

The rebuilt rifles will provide:

a. A heavier stock forearm to which a bipod can be attached.

b. Accuracy to 1.5 minutes of angle to 1000 yards (914 meters). This is comparable to the USMC's long-range competitive rifles and far exceeds the accuracy of the present M40.

As then followed, a formal presentation of the "Technical Specifications for the Rebuild of the M40 Sniper Rifle" was forwarded to the Commandant of the Marine Corps.

According to the information contained in Marine Corps Sniper Rifle and Associated Equipment, Project No. 44-69-03, Significant Event Report (30 March 1973):

> Rebuild standards for the M40 Sniper Rifle are being submitted as a significant event in the project. They are submitted at the request of the CMC to enable the rebuild of the Remington Rifle.
> Evaluation of associated equipment, i.e., sighting equipment, ammunition and bipod, will continue.

As the report stated further:

> The technical specifications pertaining to the rebuild of the M40 Sniper Rifle includes replacement of the barrel, stock, and trigger guard with accurizing and test firing as an integral part of the rebuild criteria. Completed rifles should include recorded test firing data specifying that the rifle has achieved 1.5 minutes of angle accuracy at 600 and 1000 yards.

The features that were considered "major improvements" to the M40 rifle were listed in the following order:

(1) A thicker stock forearm for mounting a bipod bracket and detachable bipod (to be evaluated with new sighting system) [Remington Model 40XB "Rangemaster" target stock. Straight grain American walnut impregnated with water resistant nongloss wood sealer].

(2) Increased accuracy through greater quality control in barrel manufacture.

(3) Increased accuracy through free floating barrel and glass-bedding barrel, receiver and trigger guard to stock.

(4) Improved durability through replacing aluminum trigger guards with steel guards [stamped steel trigger guard of the same configuration as the one presently in use].

(5) Improved reliability and durability through replacing ordnance steel barrels with stainless steel barrels [416 grade stainless steel 24 inch, free floating tapered barrel with a muzzle diameter of .900 inch (nominal) and a recessed crown].

(6) Insuring quality of rebuild through test firing of each rifle 1.5 minutes of angle accuracy is a minimum acceptable standard.

Of further interest in this case, the "accuracy requirements" were specified as follows:

> The accurized rifle will be fired at 600 and 1000 yards from the prone position, using a sandbag or similar support.
> National Match Ammunition with known ballistic characteristics will be used (pre-test for acceptable muzzle velocity and vertical dispersion characteristics).
> At 600 yards, rifle must achieve a nine inch average extreme spread (1.5 minutes of angle accuracy) from three ten-shot groups.
> At 1000 yards rifle must achieve a fifteen inch average extreme spread (1.5 minutes of angle accuracy), from three ten-shot groups.
> Rifles not achieving the desired accuracy will be returned to the accurizing facility for correction of deficiencies, i.e., bedding, barrel, head space, sights.

As comprehensive as the rebuild specifications were in this case (five pages detailing the barrel, trigger assembly, receiver, bolt, stock, trigger guard, and the accurizing, assembly, and inspection procedures), an RTE armorer armed with the necessary components and the proper test and support equipment would be in a position to reconfigure a standard M40 rifle into a "product improved Remington sniper rifle."

By Marine Corps definition, the M700/M40 sniper rifle was being reconfigured as a "highly refined combat version of the Remington Model 40XB target rifle."

So far as the telescope evaluations were concerned, with the quest for a suitable telescopic sight lagging behind improvements to the rifle, the Significant Event Report (30 March 1973) submitted to the Commandant addressed the matter in the following manner:

> The technical specifications package for the rebuild of the Model 40 Sniper Rifle has been completed. However, the rebuild criteria does not include a sighting system since the evaluation has not been completed. . . . It is recommended that the telescopic sight which was initially procured with the rifle and is presently standard issue [the Redfield 3X-9X variable-power Accu-Range Telescope] continue to be used on the rebuilt rifles until a suitable replacement can be found.

NOTE: Whereas the primary objective of CMC Project No. 44-69-03 had been realized with the emergence of the M40 rebuild standards, according to Marine Corps records, "the project was terminated in April 1973."

In an effort to determine the "optimum course of action" for rebuilding the Scout-Sniper Rifle, the MCDEC contacted the Remington Arms Company (24 May 1973) and requested a quotation ("estimated cost breakdown") for "replacement parts only" and "to rebuild the total Marine Corps density of 425 sniper rifles" based on the rebuild standards (Technical Specifications) they had formulated for this purpose. As the MCDEC letter stated in part:

> The Marine Corps is contemplating two possible courses of action for a rebuild of the rifle. The first course will require replacement parts only, since the rebuild will be performed at a Marine Corps facility. In this case, approximately 425 rifle barrels, stocks, and trigger guards will be required.
> The second course of action is to contract Remington Arms Company to

rebuild the total Marine Corps density of 425 sniper rifles. The Marine Corps will provide receivers, trigger assemblies and sling swivels. In this case, Remington Arms Company will rebuild and finish the exterior of each rifle. Thereafter, the rifles will be shipped to a Marine Corps facility for glass-bedding and accuracy firing.

To enable the Commandant of the Marine Corps to decide on a course of action it is requested that this Command be provided an estimated cost breakdown for each alternative.

Although Remington submitted detailed proposals ("Rebuild Program, Sniper System M40/Remington Model 700") to the MCDEC (1 August 1973), HQMC and the MCDEC ultimately decided against the plan to have Remington furnish replacement parts and/or rebuild the M40 sniper rifle as outlined. Except for their early support and a small quantity of parts, the Remington organization was not involved with the subsequent rebuilding of the USMC 7.62mm sniper rifles.

Consequently, when the Marine Corps decided to conduct the M40 modification program in entirety ("procure new components and commence the rebuild/modification of the subject weapon"), it requested that the Marine Corps Supply Center (MCSC), Albany, Georgia, comment on its ability to rebuild the M40 sniper rifle in accordance with the Technical Specifications submitted to the CMC by the MCDEC (30 March 1973). In response, MCSC identified several "problem areas" it believed would make rebuilding the M40 rifles difficult. MCSC's concerns were centered on "the requirement for additional mechanics/equipment and the lack of a qualified match shooter/rifle range."

As then followed, the MTU at Quantico, Virginia, was selected to conduct the M40 sniper rifle modification program on the basis of its ordnance capability and ready access to qualified personnel and the facilities (rifle range, etc.) integral to the Weapons Training Battalion, MCDEC.

NOTE: Despite frequent reference to the intended and/or pending "rebuild" of one quantity of rifles or another during the early 1970s, except for the weapons used to evaluate various concepts and components and the M700/M40 sniper rifles that were rebuilt as such for testing sighting systems and ammunition, the M40 rebuild/modification program did not begin in earnest until the M40A1 sniper rifle finally took shape.

The impetus to reconfigure the original Scout-Sniper Rifles came as a direct result of the CMC decision (CMC Ltr RD/POM33-JMK, 26 February 1976) to restore the Scout-Sniper capability within the Infantry Battalion. The recommendation was set forth in the final report of the Infantry, Organization and Weapons System Study (1973–1977), otherwise known as CMC Project No. 30-71-04.

A summation of Marine Corps efforts to improve the Scout-Sniper Rifle was provided by Maj. Robert J. Faught, USMC (Ret.), during the preparation of this book.

Major Faught, a veteran of Vietnam with Marine Corps Ordnance, was an active participant in the M40 product improvement program and was one of the Marines responsible for bringing the M40A1 sniper rifle to fruition.

As Major Faught relates:

> At the closing of the Marine Corps Ordnance School at Quantico, I was transferred to the Development Center [MCDEC] and assigned as an Infantry Weapons Project Officer.
>
> In addition to my involvement with various projects, I was also tasked with exploring means for improving the M40 sniper rifle. The evaluations took place over an extended period and included the M40 in both standard and modified form, the Army's 7.62mm M21 sniper rifle, ART scopes and night vision equipment.
>
> Among other things, the testing determined that the bolt-action M40 rifle

with a sight that remained in place was better for Marine Corps use than a semiautomatic sniper rifle and/or a removable scope.

We made several recommendations to Headquarters, Marine Corps at the time:

Retain the M40 as the Marine Corps Sniper Rifle.

Upgrade the system to correct Vietnam noted deficiencies (M40 rifles were tested with corrections for these deficiencies).

Initiate a rebuild program for the M40 rifle.

Conduct the rebuild program at the Weapons Training Battalion at Quantico using MTU armorers rather than rebuilding the rifles at the Marine Corps Logistic Support Base at Albany, Georgia or Barstow, California.

Procure a telescope to replace the Redfield model and design the new scope to meet Marine Corps requirements for durability, waterproofing, and sighting adjustments [this was later accomplished by the Unertl firm].

Adopt a special sniper round to replace National Match ammunition. The ammo intended for combat use was made up of lots that had been picked over for competition shooting. The sniper needed ammunition that was accurate.

[**NOTE**: Even though HQMC would approve virtually all of the recommendations made during the M40 evaluation process, according to Major Faught, when it came to special sniper ammunition the response was, "That will cost entirely too much. If you require single round hits at 1000 meters . . . use a tank."]

Retain the fixed, daylight scope rather than adopt the removable Army version [ART], and equip each sniper team with an M16 and a Starlight Scope for night operations. It was found that removing and replacing the telescopic sight under these circumstances did not provide the accuracy levels we were seeking.

In my estimation, the Marines at Headquarters who managed to keep the sniper in the Infantry Battalion Table of Organization deserve a lot of credit. There was a great deal of pressure to delete snipers from active Marine Corps units in those days.

The weapons Training Battalion/Marksmanship Training Unit at Quantico rates high on the list in this regard also. Some names I remember as being of significant value to the program are Dave Willis, Jim Land, and the M40A1 rebuild officer, Neil Goddard. I cannot recall the names of the shooters we used during the testing but, I do remember they were among the best long range marksmen in the Marine Corps. They were really good!

I have always been very proud of my involvement with the Marine Corps sniper program. I happened to be in the right place at the right time to do some good.

Major Faught was reassigned to HQMC in Washington, D.C., before the 40A1 sniper rifle was formally adopted, and while his responsibilities broadened as a result, Faught continued to support the revitalized sniper program in his capacity as the ordnance officer for the Marine Corps.

Above: An early "product improved" version of the M40 tested in 1970 with modifications described by the Marine Corps as "a 24 inch stainless steel barrel, water-proofed stock, and a lightweight bipod assembly" (the bipod mounted to a special swivel attached to the stock). The Ordnance School (Quantico, Virginia) fabricated a USMC/MTU-designed aluminum mount for the M40 to accept current ART and Starlight Scopes. The special mount extended down the left side of the receiver to form the same mounting area as the M14 rifle. In addition to at least two variations of the MTU mounting, the U.S. Army Night Vision Laboratory fabricated a "low profile" steel version for USMC testing as well. The sight is a Redfield "AR TEL" 3X-9X Adjustable Ranging Telescope (ART), the same model issued with the XM21 Army sniper rifle in Vietnam. Note the extended bolt shroud and the rounded safety thumb-piece, features characteristic of 1969 and later Remington M700/M40 production. The weapon is believed to be one of the "seven-digit" serial number rifles procured by the Marine Corps for test and evaluation purposes during the late 1960s and early 1970s. (U.S. Marine Corps.)

Left: A front view of the 1970 USMC test rifle. The lightweight bipod simply clamped to a swivel projecting from the bottom of the stock. Though it was well received in this form, it was decided to move the bipod mounting point forward to increase stability. (U.S. Marine Corps.)

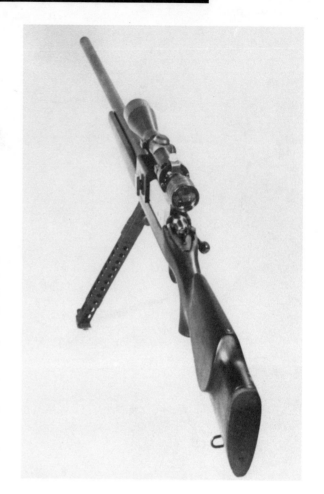

Right: A rifleman's view of the 1970 product-improved version of the USMC M40 test rifle. (U.S. Marine Corps.)

Below: The early product improved M40 sniper rifle mounting a commercial Smith & Wesson Star-Tron passive night vision sight. No matter what type of mount was used, the "sight line" of the M700 stock was considered "too low for some optics." Note the relationship of the sight to the cheek rest in this case. Although measures to adapt night vision equipment to the M700/M40 sniper rifle were actively pursued, the bolt-action rifle did not provide a suitable platform for mounting a Starlight Scope. In addition, the Marine Corps was not convinced that replacing one sighting system with another in a combat environment was in the best interest of optimum accuracy. To this day, the Marine Corps M40A1 sniper rifle does not possess a night vision capability. The telescopic sight is intended to remain in place on the rifle. (U.S. Marine Corps.)

A relatively unknown Starlight Scope fielded in Vietnam, the "Night Vision Sight, Miniaturized AN/PVS-3" was developed for use with the M14 and M16 rifles. Though well received because of its extremely light weight (3 pounds), the system had operational difficulties that prevented widespread use in Southeast Asia. The 4-power sight was 13.50 inches in length, 3.50 inches in width, and only 5.75 inches in height, complete with the "boresight" mount assembly. A carrying case and accessories were issued with the unit. The AN/PVS-3 was recommended for use with the M700/M40 USMC sniper rifle on two separate occasions during 1969. In some quarters, the diminutive Starlight Scope presented a logical choice for the bolt-action Scout-Sniper rifle. (Excalibur Enterprises.)

A left-side view of the product-improved M40 sniper rifle. The Star-Tron night vision sight was fitted with a boresight mount assembly from a AN/PVS-2 Starlight Scope. The USMC/MTU aluminum mount is clearly visible. Compare this mount with the one pictured on p. 254. (U.S. Marine Corps.)

A USMC/MTU aluminum alloy mount used to evaluate the ART system and night vision equipment with the "product improved" M40 sniper rifles during the early 1970s. The 5.875-inch-long, 1.440-inch-wide, machined mounting fastened directly to the top of the receiver. The left side was similar to the telescope mounting area on the M14 rifle. The vertical grooves are spaced .750 inch apart. The steel thread inserts beneath each groove have left-hand threads. The mounting screw is threaded to match. (Peter R. Senich.)

A side view of the special MTU aluminum mounting. The two holes at the back (right) were used to attach the mount to the receiver. The left side of the M700 receiver was already drilled and tapped for a receiver sight. There are no markings on this mount. (Peter R. Senich.)

According to Marine Corps documents, the crew-served weapon sight AN/TVS-5 (top) and the individual-served weapon sight AN/PVS-4 were considered for possible use with the "product improved" M40 sniper rifle. The second-generation Starlight Scopes were considerably smaller and lighter than the units fielded in Vietnam. (Excalibur Enterprises.)

Winchester, Caliber .308 (7.62mm) Model 70 sniper rifle serial no. G960443 with medium-heavy barrel, integral flash-suppressor, target telescope mounting blocks, and camouflage pattern fiberglass stock. The unique weapon was submitted to the Marine Corps in 1971 for consideration as a replacement for the M700/M40 system. (Hijar-Gluba-Griffiths.)

A close-up view of Winchester Model 70 no. G960443. Note the clip-feeding slot and telescope mounting block (the base is reversed). The barrel is "free-floated" to just forward of the receiver. The clearance between the barrel and the stock is clearly visible. A Winchester proof mark is stamped on top of the barrel. (Hijar-Gluba-Griffiths.)

A close-up view of the Model 70 flash suppressor. The 3-inch suppressor has five openings. The enlarged section of the barrel is 1 inch in length. The barrel, with the suppressor, is 24 inches long. According to Winchester information, the weapon was manufactured in 1971. Rifle no. G960443 is part of the Marine Corps small-arms collection. (Hijar-Gluba-Griffiths.)

A part of the post-Vietnam efforts to field an optimum sniper rifle for Marine Corps use. A 1973 test version of the M40 sniper rifle with bipod and Leatherwood/Realist Adjustable Ranging Telescope (ART). The weapon was an adaptation of the Remington Model 40XB 7.62mm target rifle complete with stainless-steel barrel and a heavy target stock. Although 21 1/4-inch barrels were considered, the 24-inch length was specified for this system. The lightweight bipod was intended to be attached on an "as needed" basis. The specifications for what the Marine Corps regarded as a "combat version" of the Remington target rifle were later used to reconfigure the M40 as the M40A1 sniper rifle. (U.S. Marine Corps.)

An alternate view (left) of the 1973 Marine Corps/Remington test rifle. In addition to addressing the major problems encountered in Vietnam (warped stocks and barrel erosion), the technical specifications pertaining to the improved M40 sniper rifles called for accurizing and test-firing as an integral part of the rebuild criteria (1.5 minutes of angle accuracy at 600 and 1,000 yards). Despite thorough testing of the Redfield and Realist Adjustable Ranging Telescopes, the ART system was not adopted by the Marine Corps. It decided to retain the 3X-9X variable-power Accu-Range Redfield sight until "a suitable replacement" could be found. (U.S. Marine Corps.)

Remington Model 40XB - BR (bench rest) target rifle with 20-power target scope circa 1971. The Remington "BR" target scope series (20-power or 24-power) was intended to "complement the bench rest rifles." At one point during the early 1970s, the Marine Corps had considered reconfiguring the Vietnam-era M700/M40 sniper rifles to Model 40XB specifications complete with heavy stainless-steel barrel and target stock. As then envisioned, the USMC sniper rifle would be "a combat version of the Remington 40XB target rifle." (Remington Arms Co.)

An early 1970s view of the Remington Custom Shop. Note the various heavy barrel target rifles (left) and "Model 40XBR" (so marked) rifles on the worktable opposite. (Remington Arms Co.)

A Custom Shop technician shown preparing a stock for a target action (1972). Note the "7.62 NATO" stamping on the stainless-steel barrel. The marking was applied to the .308-caliber (7.62mm) Remington target rifles on a routine basis. (Remington Arms Co.)

Suppressor-equipped Model 700 (M40) 7.62mm sniper rifle. According to Remington records, rifle no. 6257227 was shipped to Sionics, Inc. in December 1969. The telescope is an unnumbered (no rifle serial number) 3X-9X Redfield (green anodized finish) variable-power model with a multicircle reticle, the type developed by Redfield during the late 1960s. Except for minor details consistent with 1969 Remington production (extended bolt shroud and rounded safety thumb piece), the rifle is essentially the same as the USMC sniping issue. The barrel is marked "7.62 NATO"; the clip-slot is standard; the trigger guard and floorplate are made of aluminum. The barrel was machined and threaded to accommodate the Sionics M14SS-1 suppressor. The unit is typical of those fielded with the U.S. Army XM21 sniper rifle. The Sionics firm was known to have purchased a small quantity of Remington M700 sniper rifles for sale to the military and law enforcement agencies with their suppressors. The "seven-digit" M700/M40 sniper rifles produced by Remington are eagerly sought after by small-arms collectors. Any rifle categorized as such, without proper documentation, should be viewed with caution. (Bruce Nelson.)

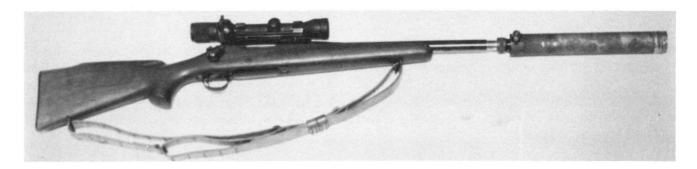

A Remington Model 700 sniper rifle with a 7.62mm Sionics suppressor dating from the Vietnam War. The telescope is a 1.5X-4.5X Leatherwood/Realist Adjustable Ranging Telescope; note the barrel machined and threaded to accommodate the noise suppressor. The 7.62mm Sionics suppressors fitted to the bolt-action rifles were the same as the standard M14 units. The weapon illustrated was modified for suppressor use by the Sionics firm. Though unsuccessful, Sionics had attempted to interest the Marine Corps in its 7.62mm and 5.56mm suppressors for sniping and general combat use in Vietnam. (Thomas Collection.)

RIFLE & AMMUNITION MARINE M-40 #6257338 ~~YARDS~~ SUPPRESSOR #983-B

M-118 MATCH LC 12073 — 300 METERS 17 FEB 1970

RIFLE NR.	TYPE WPN	TYPE AMMUNITION	ROUNDS THRU BARREL	1ST GROUP V	H	ES	2ND GROUP V	H	ES	3RD GROUP V	H	ES	AV GROUP ~~SHOOTER~~ ES
	M-40	M-118	?	6.9	4.9	7.4	6.9	4.8	6.9	6	6.4	6.5	BOUTIN
		W/ SUPPRESSOR		3	6.1	6.1	7.5	4.5	7.5	5	7	7.5	ORTON
	M-40	M-118	?	5.2	5.7	5.9	5.2	6.8	7.5				BOUTIN
		W/O SUPPRESSOR		4.9	6.2	7							ORTON

WEATHER OVERCAST LIGHT DULL REMARKS SAND BAG REST FROM BENCH

TEMP 50.° WIND N/A DIRECTION N/A

FT B (TUSAMTU) FORM 22 (10 DEC 59)

NOTE: LC 12073 AVERAGED 6" EXTREME SPREAD FROM THREE TEST BARRELS (5 GROUPS OF 10 RDS FROM EACH)

The U.S. Army Marksmanship Training Unit was continuously evaluating telescopic sights, rifles, ammunition, and noise suppressors during the Vietnam War in its quest for the optimum sniping system. In this case, the weapon testing involved a Marine Corps M40 sniper rifle (serial no. 6257338) fitted with a Sionics 7.62mm suppressor (no. 983B) at Ft. Benning, Georgia, on 17 February 1970. Testing such as this frequently involved one or more weapons on loan from one branch to another. The Vietnam-era USMC M700/M40 sniper rifles with seven-digit serial numbers are categorized as being part of the "product improvement series."

NOTE: In the interest of historical accuracy, however, without the benefit of Remington or Marine Corps verification in this case, it is not known if this weapon was loaned to the USAMTU by Sionics, Inc. or the Marine Corps. Even though the Marine Corps conducted its own silencer and suppressor evaluations, the Corps was not enthusiastic about employing ancillary equipment with its sniper rifles.) (U.S. Army.)

Remington Model 700 sniper rifle awarded to Marine marksman John W. Johnson for winning the National Trophy Individual Match at Camp Perry, Ohio, in 1981. The presentation rifle (serial no. 6257207) bears all of the characteristics of a USMC sniping rifle dating from 1969. At least three other Remington M700/M40 rifles were awarded under similar circumstances—in 1979, 1980, and 1981. (Johnson Collection.)

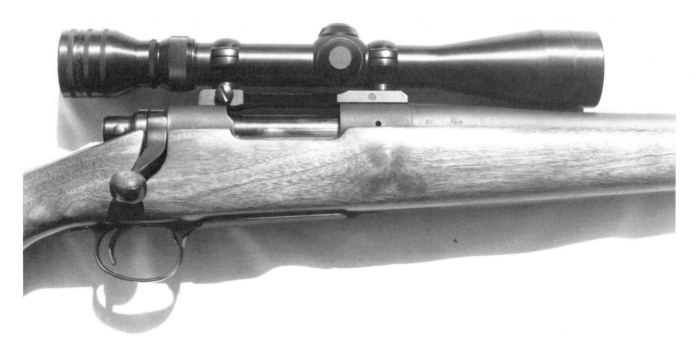

Another view of the Remington M700 sniper rifle serial no. 6257207. The 3X-9X Redfield variable-power scope is a second-generation model (black anodized finish). Except for 1969 production details, the rifle shown here was made and finished the same as the weapons categorized as Vietnam-era USMC sniping issue. (Johnson Collection.)

A close-up view (left) of the M700 Remington presentation rifle. Even though rifle no. 6257207 was not awarded to J.W. Johnson until 1981, the barrel markings and serial number indicate the rifle was manufactured and assembled in 1969. As a matter of interest, the other M700 sniper rifle presented in 1981 (serial no. 6257276) was also awarded to a member of the USMC rifle team. The plastic lens caps, though sized to fit the second-generation Redfield telescope, are essentially the same as those issued with the Vietnam-era "green scope." (Johnson Collection.)

An illustration of a well-used M40 sniper rifle and carrying case at the Marine Corps Development and Education Command (MCDEC) Quantico, Virginia. Though shown in original combat trim, the photo was taken long after the war in Vietnam. Note the stock wear in the area beneath the bolt handle. The finish is completely worn from the bolt-handle knob. The USMC M40 rebuild program had already started when this photograph was taken in June 1977. (U.S. Marine Corps.)

CHAPTER 15

SNIPER STANDARD

The M40A1

When the U.S. Marine Corps decided to conduct the M40 rebuild/modification program in entirety, instead of obtaining the necessary replacement parts from the Remington firm as first envisioned, it resorted to selecting what were deemed "the best components" from various commercial sources.

By mid-1976, according to USMC ordnance documents, the procurement process for the principal components of the new sniper rifle—the barrel, stock, and the trigger guard assembly—was proceeding as planned.

As it was then stated, the stainless-steel barrel and fiberglass stock

> . . . were obtained by competitive bid in the same manner as the barrels [and stocks] are procured for Rifle Team Equipment (RTE) competitive marksmanship rifles.

The steel trigger guard and floorplate ("magazine cover"), though modified for use with the M40A1, were essentially "over-the-counter" items and were purchased from existing commercial stock. Unlike the stainless-steel barrels and fiberglass stocks, which were categorized as "Marine Corps Peculiar," the trigger guard assembly was purchased and modified accordingly.

By the fall of 1976, the funding necessary to reconfigure the M40 was in place, an official project order had been initiated and, as further stated, "the rebuild of 216 M40 Sniper Rifles held by the Marksmanship Training Unit is hereby authorized." Consequently, nearly seven years after problems beset the Remington/Redfield system in South Vietnam, the Marine Corps was ready to begin rebuilding its 7.62mm sniper rifles.

NOTE: As a point of interest, the technical specifications pertaining to the rebuild of the M40 sniper rifle were the same standard submitted to the CMC by the MCDEC under date of 30 March 1973. Although changes were made, the original rebuild standards served the MTU during the initial rebuild activity.

The characteristics of the commercial parts procured for the new system were described by the Marine Corps (1976) as follows:

Stainless Steel Barrel

Length:	24 inches
Diameter in inches:	1.180 maximum, 1.175 minimum outside diameter at receiver. Barrel tapers approximately .01159 per inch to muzzle.
Muzzle Crown:	Smooth, free of burrs, and recessed. [According to MTU specifications, "The muzzle end of the barrel is faced off and a recess .100 inch deep is cut to a diameter of .700 inch. The muzzle is also crowned on the lathe.]
Land Twist:	One turn in 12 inches, right hand.
Bore Diameter:	Groove .3081 ± .0001 inch. Land .3002 ± .0002 inch with no more than .0002 variation in gradual taper toward the muzzle end of barrel (the grooves must be uniform in diameter throughout.)
Finish:	Outer surface of barrel is sand blasted and finished with black oxide. [Maintaining a finish on the M40A1 stainless-steel barrel proved to be a problem.]
Material:	#416 grade stainless steel.
Source:	Atkinson Gun Co., Prescott, Arizona.

Stock

Description:	Fiberglass, camouflaged, earth red with forest green as shown in U.S. Army TC 5-200 dated September 1974.
Configuration:	For Remington Model 700 Rifle.
Source:	Gale McMillan, Phoenix, Arizona

[**NOTE:** Marine Corps concerns over the ultimate effectiveness of waterproofing measures with conventional wooden stocks prompted the decision to procure fiberglass stocks for the new sniping system.

Although various means of waterproofing (coating, immersion, and impregnating the stock with epoxy) were experimented with during the course of the evaluations, the fiberglass stocks made by the McMillan firm proved to be exactly what the Marine Corps was seeking in this case. The stock was impervious to moisture, and it was virtually indestructible.

In the opinion of more than one USMC armorer with service in Vietnam, "warped stocks" and the resultant effect on weapon accuracy proved to be the greatest problems with the M700/M40 rifle.]

<u>Butt Plate</u>

Material:	Rubber
Color:	Brown
Source:	Pachmayr Gun Works, Inc., Los Angeles, Calif.

<u>Trigger Guard</u>

Description:	Steel trigger guard for Winchester Model 70.
Modification:	Modified by enlarging the hole for the trigger and by cutting off the front end by approx. one inch.
Source:	Winchester Division, Olin Corp. New Haven, Conn.

<u>Magazine Cover</u>

Description:	Steel magazine cover [floorplate] for Winchester Model 70.
Modification:	Cut off approximately one inch from the end that attaches to the trigger guard.
Source:	Winchester Division, Olin Corp., New Haven, Conn.

[**NOTE:** Although "steel trigger guards" made by the Remington firm were reportedly fitted to M700/M40 sniper rifles categorized as "late manufacture," so far as can be determined, the only steel trigger guards fielded with the 7.62mm USMC sniper rifles were a part of the evaluation process following the Vietnam War.]

The "Rifle, Sniper, 7.62mm, M40A1, USMC," as the reconfigured M40 rifle was officially designated ("full nomenclature"), was assigned the National Stock Number (NSN) 1005-01-035-1674 with equipment, and 1005-01-030-8020 without equipment.

According to MTU specifications, "all receivers" came from the original Remington M700/M40 USMC sniper rifles. The recoil lug and the magazine box were welded to the receiver as part of the measures to improve the system. The weld was made at the joint where the receiver mated with the recoil lug. The operation was carried out before the old barrel was removed. The magazine box was TIG welded to the receiver in three places—across the front and once on each side.

NOTE: The 425 7.62mm sniper rifles noted by the Marine Corps in early 1973 as the "total density" would provide the necessary M700 receivers for the ongoing M40 rebuild/modification program until 1991 when, according to Remington information, "replacement receivers [M700] were ordered by the Marine Corps."

Even though the first M40A1 rifles were reportedly reconfigured as such during the latter part of 1976, specific details concerning the initial rebuild activity remain unconfirmed at present. In any case, however, USMC ordnance documents dating from early 1977 make specific reference to the M40 rebuild program as being "well underway."

Logistics planning data for an emerging M40A1 Sniper Rifle made note of the following:

> The product improved M40A1 Sniper Rifle will serve as the replacement for the M40 Sniper Rifle. It incorporates the original Remington Model 700 action, a high grade stainless steel barrel, a camouflaged fiberglass stock with military swivels, rubber butt plate, and steel trigger guard. It is equipped with a military sling and a Redfield 3X9 variable-power telescope. This item is intended for use by Marine Corps combat snipers. . . .
>
> The original configuration M40 rifle will remain in the supply system and will be designated as Limited Standard. The M40 will remain in service until fielding of the new configuration is completed. . . .
>
> [**NOTE:** In spite of what USMC ordnance papers reference as "approximately three years" in this case (extended service), without proper documentation there is no way of knowing when the last of the original M700/M40 sniper rifles were officially withdrawn from Marine Corps service and/or whether these were recorded as M40 rifles in their original form or simply noted as weapons reconfigured to M40A1 specifications. From all indications, however, the last of the Vietnam-era M40 sniper rifles were not reconfigured until the early 1980s.]
>
> Rifle Team Equipment Repairmen, MOS 2112, are performing the reconfiguration within the Rifle Team Equipment Shop, Marksmanship Training Unit, Weapons Training Battalion, Marine Corps Development and Education Command. Maintenance training will be provided at that facility. This training will be provided to personnel during the performance of the reconfiguration, and by assigning the MOS 2112, personnel Temporary Additional Duty to the Rifle Team Equipment Shop prior to their permanent assignment to the intermediate level maintenance unit providing maintenance support for the rifles.
>
> Infantry Weapons Repairmen (MOS 2111) will be taught to inspect the rifle and its sight for serviceability as part of unit armorer's training provided in the Infantry Weapons Repair Course at the U.S. Army Ordnance Center and School, Aberdeen Proving Ground, Maryland.
>
> Optical Instrument Repairmen (MOS 2171) will be taught to inspect the rifle's telescopic sight for serviceability as part of the Fire Control/Instrument Repair Course at the U.S. Army Ordnance Center and School, Aberdeen Proving Ground, Maryland. . . .
>
> Redfield 3X9 variable-power telescopic sight. A commercial contract has been established, whereby unserviceable sights will be repaired by the manufac-

turer. The repaired sights will then be returned to stock awaiting a requisition from a secondary repairable float or the Weapons Training Battalion. Sights that have been declared unserviceable/unrepairable at intermediate level of maintenance will be reported for disposition instructions.

NOTE

The telescopic sight is a highly pilferable item that must be provided sufficient protection to prevent theft.

The formal "Letter of Adoption and Procurement" from the commandant of the Marine Corps for the M40A1 sniper rifle is dated 29 June 1977. The "Planning Data Sheet" contained in the letter called for the "phase-in" of 120 M40A1 rifles during fiscal year 1977 ("FY 77") with a "planned inventory objective" (total quantity) of 391 sniper rifles.

The "Allocation" for the M40A1 sniper rifle was listed as follows:

Unit Designation	Quantity
H&S Co. Infantry Battalion	8 per
MCDEC (The Basic School)	5 each
Aberdeen, MD, Marine Corps Det.	1 each
Operational Readiness Float (ORF)	6 per
5th Echelon Maint Flt (Barstow)	10 each
5th Echelon Maint Flt (Albany)	10 each
[MCDEC, Quantico (MTU)	10 each]

The "fielding of the M40A1" as the CMC letter stated would be incremental.

NOTE: The CMC Letter of Adoption and Procurement for the M40A1 sniper rifle (29 June 1977) superseded LAP 92-66 of 7 April 1966, the official Vietnam-era Letter of Adoption and Procurement for the original Scout-Sniper Rifle. At this juncture, the M40A1 had formally replaced the M40 sniper rifle in the U.S. Marine Corps.

With proper regards to official USMC planning data, specific quantities and/or projected in-service dates were known to change in matters such as this. As one ordnance officer summed it up, "This was simply the nature of the beast, especially when new weapon systems were involved or one item was replacing another."

Nevertheless, although early reconfigured weapon totals remain obscure (late 1976/early 1977), MCDEC correspondence to the CMC in November 1977 noted, "Currently there are 113 M40A1s issued to FMF Units. Another 20 are at the MTU." With the emergence of the M40A1 and the post-Vietnam Marine Corps sniping program tied to each other as closely as they were, although M40 rifles would continue to serve the Marine Corps on a limited basis, the first of the M40A1 sniper rifles were issued in conjunction with the new training program.

According to an article in the *Marine Corps News* Division of Information, HQMC, "Snipers Return to the Infantry" 6 April 1977:

The Marine Corps is moving to re-establish a sniper capability within the infantry battalion and regiments, giving an added option in modern warfare. . . .

[**NOTE:** For the record, CMC Project No. 30-71-04 outlined the post-Vietnam requirement for a sniper capability within the infantry battalion. The recommendation was subsequently approved on 26 February 1976 (CMC Ltr RD/POM33-JMK). The requirements were then delineated by HQMC in CMC Msg 301417Z, March 1977. The aforementioned directive served as the foundation for the Marine Corps sniper program as it exists today.]

> Under the planned program, each infantry battalion will be issued eight sniper rifles, the M40A1, a modified version of the M40. . . .
> Training of the first unit, the 2d Bn., 6th Marines, has been accomplished at Quantico. The new rifles have been issued to that unit.

NOTE: By all accounts, the personnel of Second Battalion, Sixth Marines were trained as Scout-Snipers at a level then described as "basic." The "first class" of the Scout-Sniper Instructor School (established in accordance with CMC Msg. 301417Z, March 1977, at Quantico, Virginia) did not begin until 1 June 1977.

A report entitled "Sniper Training in the United States Marine Corps" was forwarded to HQMC by the MCDEC in late 1977. The difference between the Division/Brigade Sniper School and the Scout-Sniper Instructor Course, as then envisioned, was described as follows:

> Sniper training within the Marine Corps is a two level affair. The first, most basic level is the Division/Brigade Sniper School. Here the basics of Sniper Marksmanship are learned, the bolt-action rifle, scope, holds, leads, etc. Camouflage and individual movement are given new meaning. Map and compass work are emphasized. Judging distance and techniques of observation are concentrated on. The use of supporting arms, particularly artillery, is taught as well. Finally, the tactical employment of snipers is learned and practiced. Successful completion of the course means receiving the 8541 MOS of Scout-Sniper. The highest level Scout-Sniper School is the Marine Corps Scout-Sniper Instructor Course, conducted by the MTU at Quantico, Virginia. Here students refine those basic skills learned at Division level. The objectives of the Division school had been to produce a basic sniper. The Objectives of the Scout-Sniper Instructor Course are to produce a sniper capable of teaching sniper skills and commanding a Sniper Section within the battalion.

As a matter of historical interest, even though the Marine Corps had fielded an effective sniping program in South Vietnam well in advance of the U.S. Army, the Army must be credited with developing the concept and establishing the first Sniper Instructor School (a formal course of instruction for training personnel who would then train snipers for combat) in late 1969.

The original U.S. Army Marksmanship Training Unit Sniper Instructor Group was assigned to the Ninth Infantry Division in RVN from June 1968 to June 1969. The U.S. Army Sniper Instructor School was established at Ft. Benning, Georgia, with Maj. Willis L. Powell serving as the school commandant. The "first class" graduated on 19 December 1969.

As for the Marine Corps program, however, information from the MTU had this to say about the original Scout-Sniper instructor course:

> There are eighteen Marines undergoing Scout-Sniper instructor training. They range in rank from First Lieutenant to Lance Corporal. . . . The final product will be the most knowledgeable and proficient scout-sniper instructors this unit's knowledge and experience can produce. [4 August 1977]

> On 26 August 1977, sixteen (16) of eighteen (18) Scout-Sniper instructor candidates were graduated from the first U.S. Marine Corps Scout-Sniper Instructor

Course. These Marines have returned to their units where they are establishing Division/Brigade level Scout-Sniper Schools. MTU in the meantime has reorganized its T/O to include a permanent Sniper Instructor Section. It is responsible for conducting the Scout-Sniper Instructor Course. [23 November 1977]

[**NOTE:** To begin with, CMC Msg 301417Z, March 1977, stipulated that "Scout-Sniper Instructors for the regular establishment will be trained by Team Captain, Marine Corps Shooting Team during 1977 Competition-In-Arms Program while participants are at MCDEC." Even though the Scout-Sniper Instructor School was tasked with providing Scout-Sniper instructors to the Fleet Marine Force (FMF), as the program evolved, few of the graduates were afforded the opportunity to serve as sniper instructors. Most were simply employed as Scout-Snipers in the infantry or reconnaissance units until their tour was completed.]

Though the USMC Marksmanship Training Unit is mentioned frequently in conjuction with the Marine Corps sniping program, its activities are rarely noted.

Therefore, as a matter of reader interest, a general view of the MTU during the late 1970s is presented here in the following excerpt from an article that first appeared in *Leatherneck* magazine (September 1979) entitled "The Marine Corps Rifle Team" by Nancy Lee White:

The Marine Corps rifle team is one of the various elements of the Marksmanship Training Unit (MTU) based at Quantico, Virginia. . . .

The MTU has a number of missions. One function is to field teams to represent the Marine Corps in interservice, national and international competition. Besides the high power rifle team, MTU consists of the pistol team and the international shooting team made up of international free rifle and international moving target shooters.

Other missions of MTU include a scout-sniper section, which conducts the only formal school [Scout-Sniper Instructor School] for scout-snipers in the Marine Corps; competition rifle and pistol management section, which provides competition weapons to all commands in the Marine Corps and Marine Corps reserve; competition rifle and pistol rebuild section; loading and reloading ammunition section; and the research and development section.

MTU is assigned to Weapons Training Battalion at Calvin A. Lloyd Range in Quantico. The unit is under administrative control of the Commanding General, Marine Corps Development and Education Command, and under operational control of Headquarters Marine Corps. Formed in 1956 at Camp Matthews, Calif., MTU moved to Quantico in 1962. In 1966 it picked up the competition rifle and pistol management and competition rifle and pistol rebuild shops. . . .

Technology-product improvement is found in the MTU loading room where ammunition for the rifle team is made, taking standard Lake City match ammo and re-working it to make a more precise and accurate ammunition for the intermediates (those who have been on the team a year or two) and experienced or "old-timers" (those who have been around and have won medals at several matches). Novice shooters (first year members) shoot only standard Lake City.

Technology-product improvement is also located in the test shed on Range Four at Quantico. The shed is primarily used for accuracy testing for the team, but once in a while, it is used to test weapons for outside organizations. . . .

There are 19 members of the rifle team who stay at Quantico year 'round. The rest are TAD. In addition to competition in the summer, lesson plans and rehearsals are conducted in the winter. The rifle team teaches advanced marksmanship training; holds seminars on coaching techniques; studies courses of fire and tries to devise ways to improve combat marksmanship; tests weapons, such as the new sniper weapon [M40A1] coming into use; builds ammunition for competition; and builds rifles and tests them.

From the time the M40 product improvement program took shape during the early 1970s to the adoption of the M40A1 sniper rifle and the emergence of the post-Vietnam USMC sniper program, there were, of course, a number of Marine officers and men involved with the weapon system and/or the sniper program.

Unfortunately, while many of the personnel then involved remain unknown, the following is a partial listing of those who played an active role in the development and subsequent fielding of the M40A1 sniper rifle and the resumption of Scout-Sniper training in the U.S. Marine Corps during the mid- to late-1970s:

R.J. Faught	W.W. Wiseman
D.J. Willis	C.N. Hathcock
E.J. Land Jr.	R. McAbee
J.C. Cuddy	G. Gregory
C.A. Reynolds	R. Killion
R.O. Culver	L. Wyatt
N.W. Goddard	R. Chadwick

An official Marine Corps photograph of an early M40AI sniper rifle (2 March 1977). The reconfigured M40 is fitted with an Atkinson stainless-steel barrel, McMillan fiberglass stock, and a modified Winchester trigger guard assembly. The telescope is a USMC/Redfield contract sight (green anodized finish). The two-screw 1-inch split-rings (medium) are replacements, and the "square-end" scope mounting base is original issue. The scope rings are not welded to the base. The weapon is a perfect example of the M40A1 USMC sniper rifle in original form. (U.S. Marine Corps.)

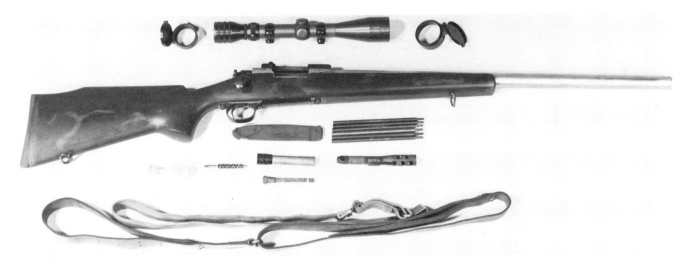

An M40A1 sniper rifle "with parts and accessories" (22 June 1977). The sight is a 3X-9X variable-power Redfield model (green). The scope rings and the mounting base are second-generation Redfield items. The flip-open lens covers are marked "Supreme." Note the web and leather slings. The steel cleaning rod issued with the M700/M40 system (shown) was replaced with a cleaning rod made of brass. In addition to the items pictured, "cleaning gear" used to maintain the system included bore cleaner, cleaning patches, a bore guide, alcohol, lens brushes, tissue, Neats foot oil, and a clean towel. In some cases, "all-weather cleaning kits" were made up and issued by the units fielding sniper personnel. The miscellaneous items were carried in a 7.62mm ammo can. The Marine Corps technical instruction booklet, *TI 05539B-12/1: Care and Cleaning of the Rifle, Sniper 7.62mm, M40A1*, provided instructions for the proper care and cleaning of the rifle and telescope. The lessons learned in Vietnam prompted the Marine Corps to stress the importance of proper care and maintenance of sniper equipment. The program designed to accomplish this included keeping detailed inspection and maintenance records for every M40A1 sniper rifle. (U.S. Marine Corps.)

The photographs in the following sequence represent the principal components used to reconfigure the M40 as the M40A1 sniper rifle. The "official" Marine Corps photos were taken at Quantico, Virginia, in June 1977. In this case, the stainless-steel barrels furnished by the Atkinson Gun Co. were shipped to the Marine Corps as shown. Machining operations involving the barrel shank and threads, chambering, the muzzle counterbore, and final sizing (24 inches) were performed by MTU armorers. (U.S. Marine Corps.)

The camouflaged fiberglass stocks used with the M40AI were procured from Gale McMillan (McMillan Fiberglass Stock Co.). The emergence of the McMillan fiberglass stocks ("a combination of epoxy impregnated, high-pressure laminated fiberglass cloths and chopped fiberglass strands") coincided with the Marine Corps quest for an optimum rifle stock. The stocks were delivered as a blank in an unfinished state (shown). Marine armorers machined-in the receiver and barrel channels and the magazine opening, and routed the stock for the epoxy steel-resin (receiver bedding) and the trigger guard assembly. The camouflage pattern (earth red with forest green) was impregnated in the stock. (U.S. Marine Corps.)

The 1 1/4-inch sling swivels fitted to the M40A1 stock were the same as those issued with the Remington M700/M40 sniper rifles. The parts were simply referenced as a "swivel assembly, non-detachable." The sling swivel mounting holes were drilled three inches from the front and two and one-half inches from the butt of the fiberglass stock. (U.S. Marine Corps.)

M40A1 brown rubber butt plate made by Pachmayr Gun Works, Inc. The "recoil pad," as it was also referenced in USMC documents, was not installed until the M40A1 was accepted for accuracy. (U.S. Marine Corps.)

Winchester Model 70 steel trigger guard. The steel trigger guard and floorplate were purchased from the Winchester Division, Olin Corp., and modified for use with the M40A1 rifle. Both components were essentially over-the-counter items. The part is shown in its original form. (U.S. Marine Corps.)

Winchester Model 70 steel magazine cover (floorplate). The part is shown in its original form. (U.S. Marine Corps.)

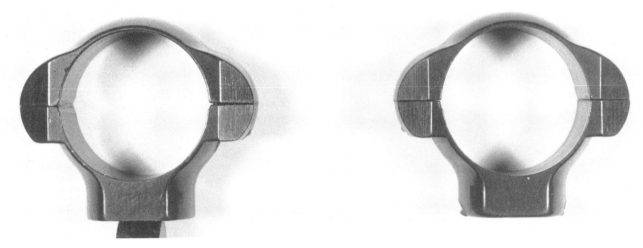

Second-generation Redfield 1-inch split rings (medium) purchased by the Marine Corps for use with the early M40A1 system (Redfield part no. 522605). The steel "scope mount rings" made use of two socket-head screws (recessed hex) in each ring. The ring height was listed at .272 inch. (U.S. Marine Corps.)

Redfield Junior "short action scope mount base" (JR 700 SA) purchased by the Marine Corps for use with the early M40A1 system (Redfield part no. 511227). Except for the "rounded ends," the second-generation telescope mounting base was essentially the same as the "square-end" version fitted to the Vietnam-era Remington M700/M40 sniper rifles. (U.S. Marine Corps.)

A view of the Redfield steel scope rings and mounting base used with the early M40A1 system. The difference between the Vietnam-issue and the second-generation rings and base is clearly evident in this illustration. The parts have a black commercial finish. (U.S. Marine Corps.)

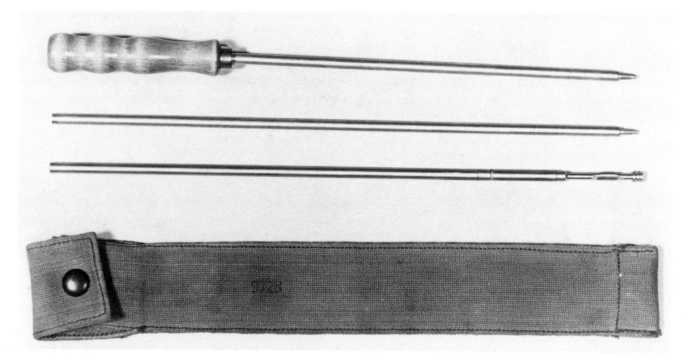

Marble Arms Corp. sectionalized brass cleaning rod issued with the M40A1 sniper rifle. The item was identified as the "Rod, cleaning (brass) 3 sections, w/case." The use of brass instead of steel was intended to minimize the effects of repeated cleaning (bore wear). (U.S. Marine Corps.)

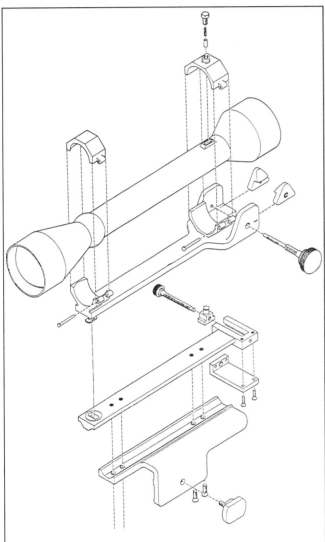

One of the original USMC M40A1 sniper rifles issued during the late 1970s with accessories and molded plastic carrying case. The Vietnam-era M700/M40 carrying cases were eventually replaced with cases made by the same firm (Protecto Plastics, Inc.). Although both carrying cases were virtually identical, the new cases were green. (U.S. Marine Corps.)

Of all the telescopic rifle sights considered by the Marine Corps during the transition from the M40 to the M40A1 sniper rifle, the Rand Systems Corporation (RSC) Dual Power Scope qualifies as the most unusual. The innovative telescopic sight offered the rifleman 3-power and 9-power "centered and tangential fields of view." According to the original RSC proposal, "The Dual Power scope is an optical device which presents a simultaneous static scene with two magnified fields of view. A low power background field [3-power] and a high-power center field of view [9-power]. A marksman can acquire a target with the wide field, low-power field of view, and without further adjustment shift the line of sight to the high power field of view which would contain the ultra-fine cross hair sight reticle. The riflescope should be fitted to a rugged and simple mount which will contain adjustment for zeroing the scope and subsequent adjustments for elevation and windage." A developmental version of the RSC Dual Power Scope is shown with an M14 mounting. At least two of the unique telescopic sights (serial nos. 001 and 002) were manufactured and delivered to the Marine Corps Base at Quantico, Virginia, for evaluation purposes in 1976. (U.S. Marine Corps.)

An example of the "simultaneous 3X Field and 9X Field" (field of view) from the RSC Dual Power Scope evaluated by the Marine Corps in 1976. As the feature was then described, "The higher power field can be placed anywhere within the field of view being much smaller than the wide field optics employed for the lesser power." (U.S. Marine Corps.)

The Redfield 3X-9X variable-power Widefield Low-Profile telescope with an Accu-Range reticle and black matte finish was among the rifle scopes considered for use with the M40A1 sniper rifle. The model shown here is the early version of the Widefield scope. The sight evaluated by the Marine Corps featured the low-profile configuration on both the objective bell and the eyepiece. (Bob Bell.)

According to personnel tasked with finding a suitable telescopic sight for the M40A1 sniper rifle, the Leupold M8 10-power scope (shown) was deemed satisfactory, but the Leupold organization would not make modifications to the scope for the quantity the Marine Corps planned on purchasing. (Bob Bell.)

Various Marine Corps Security Force (MCSF) organizations requested in 1977 that the M40A1 sniper rifle be furnished for use in antiterrorist operations. With the availability of the M40A1 "extremely limited" at that point and use of the 7.62mm NATO cartridge considered "not suitable for use in an urban environment because of the penetration capability and high ricochet potential," HQMC recommended M16 rifles mounting "Colt telescopic sights, or an equivalent" for "intermediate range" applications by MCSF units and Marine Corps commands operating a provost marshall activity. The "initial purchase" of "112 sights with mount" (Colt telescopic sight) was authorized in August 1977. As then stated: "Encounters in antiterrorist incidents will usually take place at ranges of less than 200 yards. The M16A1 with the Colt telescopic sight would appear to be more suitable for use by MCSF organizations." The illustration shows a typical post-Vietnam Colt Industries 3-power telescopic sight ("Colt 3X20"). The 6-inch-long aluminum alloy scope has a main tube diameter of 1.380 inch. The elevation adjustment turret is located on top; the windage adjustment is positioned on the right. Early reticle patterns consisted of an inverted post with crosshairs; a duplex reticle was added later. The scope and mount have a black matte finish. The mount assembly attached to an AR15 or M16 carrying handle with a spring-clip and latch ("mounting clamp assembly"). Lens covers were furnished with the scope. (Peter R. Senich.)

A unique view of a military marksman firing a sniper rifle with metallic sights. The M24 Sniper Weapon System (SWS) pictured was manufactured by Remington Arms Co. for the U.S. Army. The bolt-action 7.62mm (.308 Winchester) rifle was fielded as a replacement for the M21 (M14) sniper rifle in 1988. The Fifth Special Forces (Airborne) sniper is shown on the firing line at Ft. Campbell, Kentucky (1992). Though rarely noted, the Marine Corps made use of the M40A1 sniper rifle with metallic sights to win a major rifle championship in 1977. According to an article by L.Cpl. C.R. Dahl, in *The Navy News*, 21 July 1977: "History was made here recently at the Calvin A. Lloyd Rifle Range [Quantico, Virginia] as a team of Marines, firing the modified version of the new Marine Corps sniper rifle, won the Romanian Cup, a national high-power rifle championship sponsored by the National Rifle Association. The significance of the event is that this was the first time a sniper rifle has been fired in competition and the first time in 19 years that the Marine Corps has won the trophy. Firing against the finest match rifles available in the world, the Marine Corps M40AI sniper rifles not only equaled but exceeded all expectations." The team, all members of the MTU, included Lt.Col. Charles A. Reynolds, commanding officer, weapons training battalion, and officer in charge, Marksmanship Training Unit.

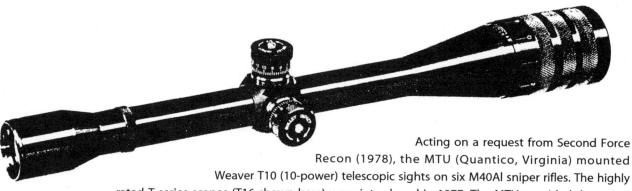

Acting on a request from Second Force Recon (1978), the MTU (Quantico, Virginia) mounted Weaver T10 (10-power) telescopic sights on six M40AI sniper rifles. The highly rated T-series scopes (T16 shown here) were introduced in 1977. The MTU provided the sniper capability (the personnel and weapons) for Second Force Recon; the "special purpose rifles" made use of "hand-loaded ammunition." As a matter of interest, the ultimate selection of a 10-power telescope for the M40AI rifle was no accident. Although 8-, 10-, and 12-power rifle scopes were considered, MTU testing had determined that "10-power was the best choice for Marine Corps use."

A USMC Marksmanship Training Unit, Weapons Training Battalion "weapon display." Display boards such as this were often used to promote Marine Corps marksmanship at public functions through the years. In this case, the weapons include a M1903A1 sniper rifle with a Unertl contract sight, an M1C with the Stith-Kollmorgen Model 4XD telescope, a Winchester Target Rifle mounting a Lyman Target scope, a Vietnam-issue M700/M40 with a Redfield sight, an early M40A1 and a "winter camouflage" M40A1, both mounting 3X-9X Redfield telescopes. (U.S. Marine Corps.)

CHAPTER 16

THE UNERTL SCOPE

The 10-Power Model

By the end of 1977, with the rebuilding of the M40 and a revitalized Marine Corps sniper program moving forward, the quest for an optimum rifle scope resumed in earnest. As it was then stated:

> The MTU is preparing to test and evaluate several scopes in an attempt to find a replacement for the current model Redfield 3X-9X variable-power telescope. One scope reticle under consideration was designed by the Sniper Instruction Section.

As events transpired, however, since Marine Corps procurement in matters such as this rarely involved more than a small quantity of one item or another, few rifle scope manufacturers were interested in developing a telescopic sight for the Marine Corps under the circumstances.

Developing military hardware from "scratch" was a costly proposition even under the best conditions, and the smaller the projected production quantities were, the less chance a manufacturer had to make a "reasonable profit" while producing a cost-effective item.

From all indications, the rifle scope manufacturers were not prepared to accept the task of building a telescopic sight for the Marine Corps, at least not in the numbers envisioned.

NOTE: Though rarely discussed, this had always been a major factor in the adoption of sniping equipment based on existing commercial hardware. The Remington M700 rifle and the Redfield 3X-9X variable-power scope are good examples. Make no mistake, the Marine Corps knew full well it was entering into an "expect the best" situation with the Remington/Redfield system, and while budgetary constraints were less of a factor during a shooting war, the time and expense necessary to develop sniping equipment from scratch left the Marine Corps with no other choice. Although many post-Vietnam "experts" have found fault with the decision to adopt the Remington/Redfield system, in the interest of putting an end to this argument once and for all, if there was a better option at the time (late 1965/early 1966), it has not been presented.

In this case, however, with the M40A1 arguably "an optimum sniping rifle," the officers and men responsible for this weapon were determined to complete the system with a telescopic sight that met their requirements in every respect.

After consulting with several firms, the Marine Corps turned to the John Unertl Optical Company, a relatively small but resourceful commercial rifle scope manufacturer that had served the best interests of "The Corps" for many years.

As then followed, the Unertl organization, led by John Unertl Jr., agreed to assist the Marine Corps in developing a suitable telescopic sight for the M40A1 sniper rifle.

Beginning in 1978, members of the MTU literally worked hand in hand with John Unertl Jr. for a period of several months, combining what experienced snipers and match shooters deemed both desirable and essential in a rifle scope with the expertise and manufacturing skills of the Unertl organization.

With appropriate Marine Corps specifications ("design criteria") serving as a guideline, the Unertl firm developed an entirely new telescopic sight, a fixed-power model intended for sniper use. The emergence of a Unertl telescope was the result of a "considerable number" of telephone calls and extensive travel between the MTU and the Unertl firm during the course of development. By all accounts, the entire process had been "a difficult proposition."

By late 1979 the 10-power Unertl USMC Sniper Scope, as the new sight was known, was all but ready for the Marine Corps.

Interestingly, even though the telescope design had been finalized, the initial lot of Unertl scopes (25) furnished to the Marine Corps featured a windage adjustment knob that was still in a transitional state. The windage knob was different in appearance than the Unertl prototype models and was changed again on the production version that followed.

From all indications, the initial shipment was used for evaluating the system under field conditions in the hands of Marine snipers over an extended period. The following shipments would reflect any changes deemed necessary.

NOTE: The "first" Unertl Sniper Scopes (25) from an initial order of 600 (±) were reportedly delivered in March 1980. So far as can be determined, the public unveiling of the 10-power Unertl USMC Sniper Scope took place at the 1980 (April) National Rifle Association Convention held at Kansas City, Missouri, when the weapon display board at the Marine Corps booth included an M40A1 sniper rifle mounting one of the original Unertl scopes.

According to Marine Corps information, the second shipment of Unertl scopes did not occur until January 1982. The windage adjustment knob had taken its final form, and from that point forward the telescopic sights furnished to the Marine Corps were categorized as "regular production."

In the absence of an official designation or reference in this case, the original Unertl sights (25) are collectively noted here as the "transitional model."

The transitional sight was pictured in *FMFM 1-3B, SNIPING* (28 January 1981), the contemporary USMC sniper training and equipment manual. (This publication superseded the Vietnam-era USMC sniper training manual with changes made through 7 April 1976.) The transitional model was also illustrated in the operation and maintenance manual for the M40A1 sniper rifle and the Unertl telescope, TM 00539-13/1, 30 November 1981 (Change 1 ["Pen Changes"] made this TM 05539-13/1).

It was standard practice to use items from an initial shipment (early production) for manual illustrations. To the chagrin of many, however, although it did not affect the instruction process, the portrayal of the Unertl sights in the sniper training and maintenance manuals did not accurately reflect the telescopes in general use.

Unlike the trend of development for telescopic sights of the day, the Unertl scope was made of steel instead of aluminum alloy. The rugged instrument was well suited for sustained combat in virtually any climate. Although few, if any, optical devices mounted on a rifle would qualify as "Marine-proof," by some estimates, the Unertl Sniper Scope "could hold its own" in this regard.

The optics are thick, strong, precision hand-ground lenses coated with a light-transmitting substance called HELR (high efficiency, low reflection film), a feature that allows more than 90 percent of the ambient light to pass through the scope, thereby providing better target definition at longer ranges in marginal light. (According to a veteran USMC sniper, "The Unertl scope allowed us to engage silhouetted targets under moonlight out to 600 yards, and a flare, depending on the type, could easily add another 100 or 200 yards to that.")

Tabulated data for the 10-power Unertl Sniper Scope circa 1981 was listed by the Marine Corps as follows:

UNERTL SNIPER SCOPE

Weight	2 pounds 3 ounces
Length	12 1/2 inches
Magnification	10X
Eye Relief	3 inches (fixed)
Adjustments:	
Elevation and Windage	1/2 minute
Main Elevation	Ballistic come-ups for M118 Lake City Match Ammunition (7.62mm) built in.
Fine Tune elevation	+ or - 3 minutes to adjust for differences in shooter's zeros, temperatures, and ammunition lots.
Windage	60 minutes main adjustment; + or - 4 1/2 minutes with stops on either end to allow shooter to run windage on and off in the dark.
Reticle	Mil dot duplex for range estimation and calculating leads on moving targets.

Lenses   HELR coating (high efficiency, low reflection film), gathers in over 90 percent of available light.

Steel tube with black chrome dull finish.

Capability of reading elevation and windage settings from the rear while shooting.

Scope allows shooter to shoot point of aim/point of impact back to 1,000 yards.

Capability of adjusting parallax.

ELEVATION AND WINDAGE

Once the scope is zeroed, all the sniper has to do is to estimate the range to a target and the windage, and apply those figures to the scope via the main elevation adjustment and the fine tune windage adjustment.

THE SCOPE WILL ALLOW THE SNIPER TO
SHOOT POINT OF AIM/POINT OF IMPACT BACK TO 1000 YARDS.

The main ballistic come-ups (for the M118 Lake City Match 7.62mm ammunition) are built into the main elevation adjustment. Once the scope is zeroed, the sniper has simply to dial the desired range on the scope and fire. The main adjustment on the elevation control is marked every 100 yards from 100 to 1000 yards. For ranges between these figures (example 650 yards), set the dial halfway between 600 and 700 yards. There is also a fine tune elevation control + or - 3 minutes to allow for different temperatures, ammunition lots, types of ammunition, and differences in shooters' zeros. The fine tune knob will allow any sniper to shoot point of aim/point of impact back to 1000 yards.

The windage fine tune knob allows the sniper to apply changes to allow for windage variations of + or - 4-1/2 minutes.

The scope settings for elevation and windage can be read from the rear while firing, and due to the distinctive clics and built-in stops, on all controls, the sniper can apply his elevation and windage in the dark.

The principal part of the system was a hand-crafted precision rifle produced by skilled armorers at Quantico, Virginia. As the Marine Corps described the weapon:

The sniper rifle used by the Marine Corps is a Marine Corps designed and produced bolt-action 7.62mm rifle with a stainless-steel barrel for improved accuracy. It weighs 14 pounds and has a maximum effective range of 1,000 yards. The rifle is fitted with a top-mounted telescope base, to which the sniper scope can be readily attached without special tools.

The M40A1 is capable of shooting a minute of angle or better at 300 yards with M118 Lake City Match Ammunition. With hand loads, it will shoot 1/2 minute of angle.

The principal characteristics of the M40A1 sniper rifle circa 1981 were noted as follows:

M40A1 SNIPER RIFLE

Overall length	44 inches
Caliber	7.62 NATO
Muzzle velocity	2,550 feet per second
Maximum effective range	1,000 yards
Chamber pressure	50,000 psi
Magazine capacity	5 rounds
Weight complete	14 1/2 pounds (approximate)
Barrel length	24 inches
Lands and grooves	6
Twist, right hand	1 turn in 12 inches
Stock	fiberglass with epoxy filler
Trigger weight	3 to 5 pounds

The free-floating heavy barrel, a product of the Atkinson Gun Company, is fabricated from No. 416 stainless steel, has a recessed crown, and is chemically treated to provide a dull black finish.

The heart of the M40A1 system, a Remington Model 700 (M40) action is "accurized" in accordance with Marine Corps specifications. The Remington trigger mechanism is retained and a steel trigger guard and floorplate from the Winchester Model 70 are adapted for use.

The special M40A1 stock, furnished by Gale McMillan, is made of pressure-molded fiberglass color-impregnated in an "earth red with forest green" camouflage pattern. Impervious to the effects of heat, cold, and moisture, the fiberglass stocks are considerably stronger and much lighter than wood. Machine-inletted for the Model 700 action, epoxy steel resin is used for bedding the receiver in the stock. Military sling swivels are provided and a brown rubber butt plate from the Pachmayr Gun Works is also used. For transportation purposes, a lightweight molded plastic carrying case (Protecto Plastics, Inc.) with a polyurethane foam liner is furnished for the M40A1 and its accessories.

NOTE: Although carrying cases were replaced as they wore out, the replacement cases were essentially the same as those originally furnished with the M700/M40 system when it was fielded for use in Vietnam.

An accurate, reliable weapon, the Marine Corps sniper rifle has proven to be an intelligent blend of uncomplicated, durable components. From the first combat use of the M40A1 in Beirut (1982) when Marines began their "peace-keeping operation" in Lebanon to the present day, whenever the use of snipers is necessary, the M40A1/Unertl system continues to serve the U.S. Marine Corps.

It is important for the reader to understand that the inclusion of the M40A1 sniper rifle and the 10-power Unertl Sniper Scope in a treatise covering the Vietnam War is intended to provide insight on the transition from what was intended to be an optimum sniping system (M700/M40) to one that arguably is (M40A1).

Even though a significant amount of factual information concerning the development of the M40A1 rifle and the USMC/Unertl telescope has been recorded in this volume, a comprehensive account of the contemporary Marine Corps sniping program will be presented in the next book in this series.

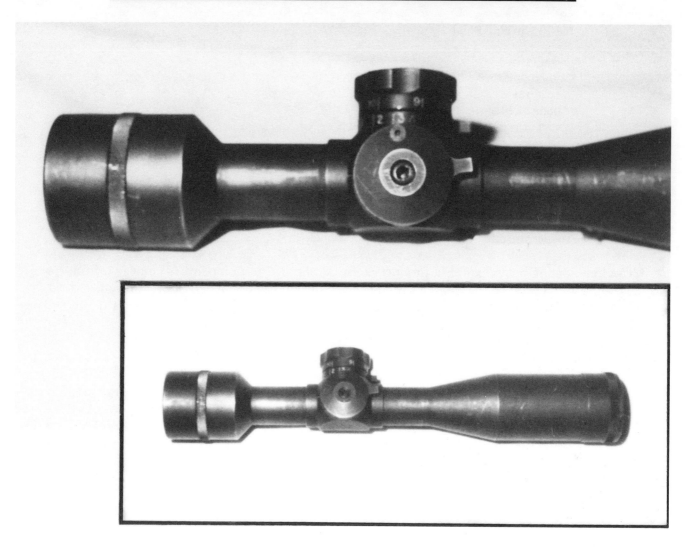

A prototype version of the 10-power Unertl USMC Sniper Scope developed for use with the M40A1 sniper rifle. Telescope no. 1003 (so marked) was one of five prototype sights made for the Marine Corps by the Unertl firm ("at no cost"). Serial numbering of the 10-power model began at no. 1001. The same numbering practice was used by the Unertl firm with the World War II-era 8-power USMC contract scope. The configuration of the windage knob (right side) was changed on the initial lot (25) of Unertl scopes furnished to the Marine Corps in early 1980. The left side of the turret housing bears the Unertl logo "USMC SNIPER" and the telescope serial number. The smaller inset photo provides an overall view of the same telescope. (Neil W. Goddard.)

U.S. Patent   Jan. 27, 1981   Sheet 1 of 2   4,247,161

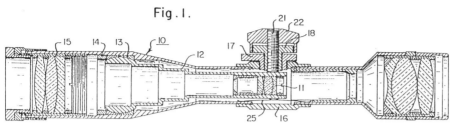

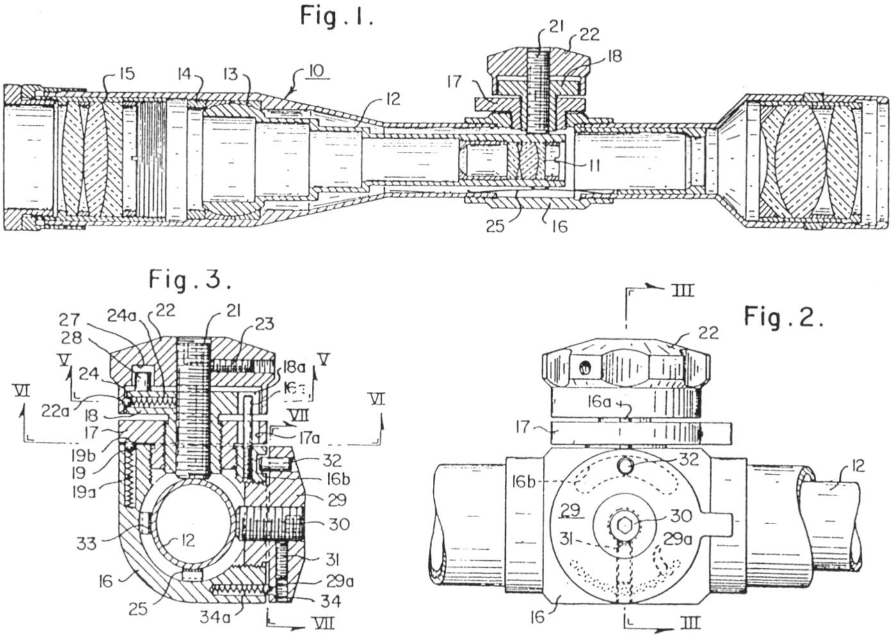

Fig. 1.

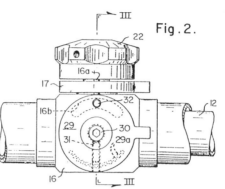

Fig. 3.

Fig. 2.

U.S. patent drawing of the 10-power Unertl Sniper Scope. The original patent application was filed by John Unertl Jr. on 9 May 1979. Patent No. 4,247,161 was granted on 27 January 1981. (Donald G. Thomas.)

U.S. Patent   Jan. 27, 1981   Sheet 2 of 2   4,247,161

Fig. 4.

Fig. 5.

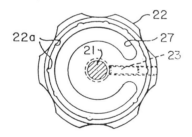

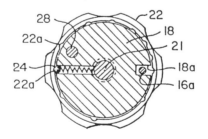

Another Unertl patent drawing provides a view of the original elevation (top) and windage adjustment knobs. Note the windage knob is the same as used on the Unertl prototype series. (Donald G. Thomas.)

Fig. 6.

Fig. 7.

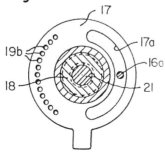

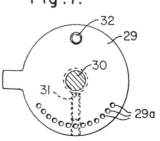

An illustration from the USMC operation and maintenance manual for the M40A1 sniper rifle and the Unertl scope (*TM 00539-13/1*, 30 November 1981) provides a close view of a transitional model of the 10-power Unertl Sniper Scope. The telescope shown here was one of the original 25 furnished to the Marine Corps in early 1980. Note the configuration of the windage knob; compare this with the prototype model. The transitional model is also pictured in *FMFM 1-3B, SNIPING* (28 January 1981). The windage knob was changed on the production version of the Unertl sight. For the sake of clarification, there were three versions of the Unertl Sniper Scope: the prototype, transitional, and production models. It is important to emphasize, however, that these were not Marine Corps designations. Note the Redfield scope rings welded to the base—an interim measure intended to prevent the rings from moving during hard use. In this case, the rings are second-generation Redfield; the base is an original M700/M40 "square-end" version. (U.S. Marine Corps.)

An early M40A1 sniper rifle as shown in the 1981 USMC sniper training and equipment manual *FMFM 1-3B, SNIPING*. Note the configuration of the windage knob. The telescope is a transitional model, one of the first Unertl sights furnished to the Marine Corps. At this juncture (1980), Redfield components (rings and base) were used to mount Unertl scopes on the M40A1 rifles. (U.S. Marine Corps.)

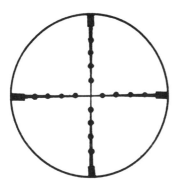

1 mil on the reticle is equal to 1 yard at 1,000 yards

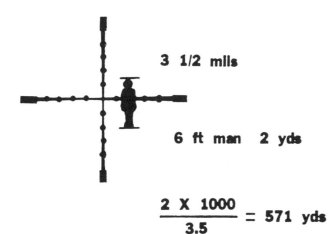

3 1/2 mils

6 ft man   2 yds

$$\frac{2 \times 1000}{3.5} = 571 \text{ yds}$$

Left: An illustration from *FMFM 1-3B, SNIPING* (28 January 1981) of the Mil Dot reticle used with the Unertl Sniper Scope. The reticle was described as follows: "The duplex reticle in the telescope provides the sniper with a range-finding capability. To determine the range, the following formula is used:

$$\frac{\text{Height of target (in yards)} \times 1000}{\text{Height of target (in mils)}} = \text{Range}$$

The dots on the fine crosshairs are 1 mil apart with a total of 5 mils from the center to the thick post in each direction. According to personnel involved with the original development project, the reticle was designed by the MTU, produced at Trueline Instruments in Englewood, Colorado, and sent to Unertl for assembly with the telescope. (U.S. Marine Corps.)

Below: Military magazine editor Jim Shults shown on the firing line at the Scout-Sniper Instructor School at Quantico, Virginia. The photograph was taken in early 1981 while Shults was gathering material for an article on Marine Corps sniping. The M40A1 is equipped with an early (transitional) Unertl model. The scope rings and mounting base are Redfield items. The rings are welded to the base. (Jim Shults.)

A 1981 photograph of a Marine marksman during a field exercise. The rifle is an M40A1 mounting one of the early 10-power Unertl telescopes. The sniper is wearing a "ghillie suit," an elaborate form of camouflage designed to alter the outline of the human form and blend with the surrounding natural terrain. Camouflage suits were adopted for training purposes when the Scout-Sniper program was revived. (Jim Shults.)

Marine Corps photograph with a caption that reads: "Beirut, Lebanon (October 1983) . . . A Marine sniper sights through the scope of his 7.62mm M40A1 sniping rifle from a sandbag rest in the Marine compound near Beirut International Airport." The Marines were deployed as part of a multinational peacekeeping force following confrontation between Israeli forces and the Palestine Liberation Organization (PLO). An outmoded mission concept and the unrealistic "Rules of Engagement" combined to make the Marine Corps venture in Lebanon one of their more difficult operations. (U.S. Marine Corps.)

A typical USMC M40A1 7.62mm sniper rifle and Unertl Sniper Scope. The rifle and telescopic sight are representative examples of contemporary Marine Corps sniping issue. The M40A1/Unertl combination has served the Marine Corps whenever Scout-Snipers have been employed during the 1980s and 1990s. The precision combat rifles are handcrafted by skilled armorers at the Marksmanship Training Unit, Quantico, Virginia. (U.S. Marine Corps.)

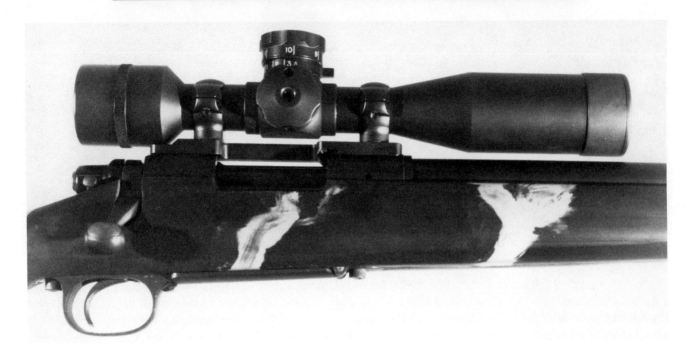

A close view of the M40A1 rifle and the Unertl telescope. The scope rings and mounting base are products of the Unertl firm. The bottom half of the scope rings are permanently attached to the base. A projection at the rear of the base fits into the clip-slot, and another rests against the back edge of the receiver ring. When mounted on the receiver, the unit remains locked in place. The Unertl telescope mounting was developed for this application during the early 1980s when problems were encountered with the Redfield components. Note the extended bolt shroud and the rounded safety thumb piece. Socket-head screws (recessed hex) were used to join the action, stock, and trigger guard assembly. A torque wrench (inch-pounds) was used to ensure uniform tightening to a predetermined setting. (U.S. Marine Corps.)

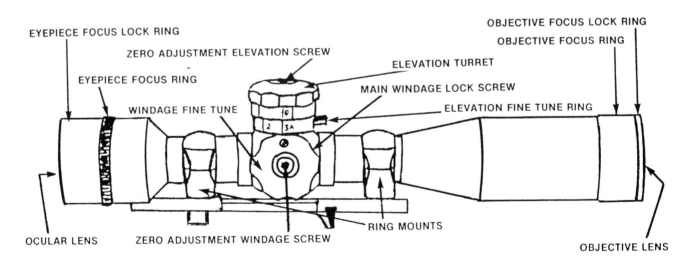

An illustration of the 10-power Unertl Sniper Scope (right side) from the Marine Corps operation and maintenance manual, *Fleet Marine Force Reference Publication (FMFRP) 0-11A* (13 April 1989), lists the principal parts of the Unertl scope and mount assembly. Note the projections beneath the base. (U.S. Marine Corps.)

A close-up view of the 10-power Unertl USMC Sniper Scope and mount assembly. Note the configuration of the windage adjustment knob. The telescope is a regular production model. In final form, the elevation and windage knobs were essentially the same in appearance. As a matter of interest, the scope is set on 600 yards with 2 minutes down +2 minutes left windage. (U.S. Marine Corps.)

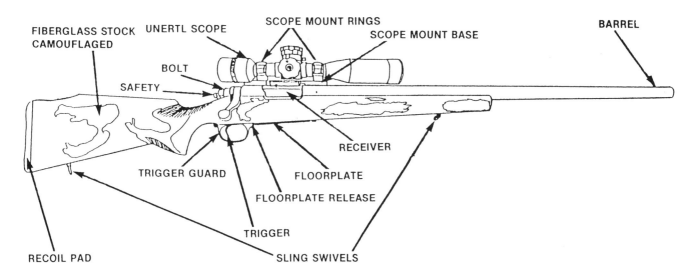

An overall view of the M40A1 sniper rifle from *FMFRP 0-11A M40A1 Sniper Rifle, 7.62mm* (13 April 1989). The illustration lists the principal components of the current M40A1/Unertl system. (Marine Corps.)

Marine sniper-spotter team during training exercises held in Hawaii, January 1985. (U.S. Marine Corps.)

Marine sniper team during training at Quantico, August 1987. The team member at left is armed with an M16A2 rifle; the other carries an M40A1 sniping rifle. According to the Marine Corps, a two-man team is the basic operational organization for the employment of snipers. Both members are trained Scout-Snipers; either member can fill the function of the sniper. (U.S. Marine Corps.)

Marine Corps photograph dating from late 1990 with a caption that reads: "Saudi Arabia . . . Two Marines from Surveillance and Target Acquisition (STA) Plt., Headquarters and Service (H&S) Co., 1st Bn., 3rd Marines, man an outpost during Operation Desert Shield. The Marine at left is armed with an M40A1 sniping rifle." Note the weapon and telescope camouflaged with flat-colored spray paint, a recommended procedure. (U.S. Marine Corps.)

A Marine sniper (Second Battalion, Second Marines) scanning his rifle scope at Cap Haitien, Haiti (1994). Note the M40A1 rifle and Unertl telescope camouflaged with spray paint. An improvised cheek rest has been taped to the stock. (U.S. Marine Corps.)

FLEET MARINE FORCE MANUAL

Sniping

In response to a mounting requirement for cohesive sniper training during the early stages of the Vietnam War, Headquarters, USMC assigned Landing Force Development Activities, Marine Corps Schools, Quantico, Virginia, the task of formulating "doctrine, techniques, and procedures for training and employing snipers in the Fleet Marine Forces" in late 1966.

Drawing from an information base involving "lesson plans, courses of instruction, and concepts of sniper employment" developed by the III Marine Amphibious Force in South Vietnam, the initial Marine Corps sniper manual emerged in October 1967.

NOTE: From all indications, the groundwork for a Marine Corps sniper manual and a standard training syllabus for Scout-Snipers actually began during the latter part of 1965. While documents categorized as "drafts," with different dates, in one form or another, emerged in the months that followed, in the interest of avoiding any possible confusion in this matter, the principal draft editions of *FMFM 1-3B, SNIPING* are referenced in this text as the "initial" and the "interim" versions.

The early or initial draft edition of Marine Corps field manual *FMFM*

1-3B, SNIPING (October 1967) served as the foundation for the Vietnam-era manual used for training Marine snipers. An interim draft edition followed in December 1968, and, in final form, *FMFM 1-3B, SNIPING* was published under date of 5 August 1969. The comprehensive publication was the first USMC manual intended specifically for "the training and employment of the Marine sniper."

With the equipment needs stabilized between the field use of the Model 70 Winchester and the Model 700 Remington sniper rifle in the early months of 1967, the initial draft edition contained information for training and employing snipers and detailed the operation and care of the "Rifle, Caliber .30, Model 70, Winchester"; "Rifle, Caliber 7.62mm, Model 700, Remington"; and the sighting system intended for each weapon respectively, the "Telescope, Rifle, Unertl, USMC SNIPER, Eight Power" and the "Telescope, Rifle, Redfield 3X9 Variable with Accurange."

The October 1967 edition of *FMFM 1-3B, SNIPING* consisted of 315 pages with seven chapters and eight appendices. The "Syllabus of Instruction" concerning sniper training was summarized as follows:

SUBJECT	HOURS
Introduction to Sniper Training	1
Sniper Equipment	1 3/4
Care and Cleaning of Equipment	1 1/2
Marksmanship Training	62 1/2
Target Detection	10
Range Estimation	8
Holds and Leads	8
Use of Map and Compass	8
Camouflage and Concealment	8
Individual Movement	8
Survival, Evasion, and Escape	8
Terrain Appreciation	8
Adjustment of Artillery Fire	24
Communications	11
Sniper Employment	85
Total Hours	252 3/4

The interim draft edition (December 1968) deleted all reference to the Model 70 Winchester and the Unertl telescope. The sniper training was also shortened to 203 3/4 "total hours" of instruction.

NOTE: As a matter of reader interest, whereas the officer in charge (OIC) of the 3d MarDiv sniper program in South Vietnam, R.A. Russell, had been tasked with developing the initial draft edition of *FMFM 1-3B* upon his return to CONUS, the OIC of the 1st MarDiv sniper program, E.J. Land Jr., was subsequently involved with bringing the USMC sniper manual to its final form following his return to the United States. In both cases, however, it is important to point out that many knowledgeable and experienced Marines, including some who were veterans of the sniping campaign in RVN, were also involved with this project.

The final version of *FMFM 1-3B, SNIPING* (5 August 1969), as adopted by the Marine Corps, contained 264 pages with seven chapters and six appendices. The "Scout-Sniper Training Syllabus" remained at 203 3/4 total hours; the subject and the time of instruction were listed as follows:

SUBJECT	HOURS
Introduction to Sniper Training	1
Sniper Equipment	1 3/4
Care and Cleaning of Equipment	1 1/2
Marksmanship Training	62 1/2
Target Detection	10
Range Estimation	8
Holds and Leads	8
Intelligence Collection and Reporting	3
Camouflage and Concealment	8
Individual Movement	8
Survival, Evasion, and Escape	8
Sniper Employment	85
Total Hours	204 3/4

For the sake of clarification, when it came to "training hours," as the Marine Corps expressed it, the sniper manual made note of the following:

> This syllabus is a guide for preparing training schedules. Training problems peculiar to a given unit or installation may necessitate modification or improvisation of some training objectives. . . .
> Hours of instruction allotted for each subject are maximum. The total hours may be reduced by concurrent training. . . .
> When additional training hours are available, emphasis should be on the marksmanship phase of sniper training. . . .
>
> THERE ARE NO SHORT CUTS IN MARKSMANSHIP TRAINING.

NOTE: It is important to note that lesson plans and training schedules ultimately contained in *FMFM 1-3B, SNIPING* were employed for training Marine Corps snipers in CONUS and RVN before the manual was published.

The "Definition" and "Mission" of the Scout-Sniper were stated in Chapter 1 of *FMFM 1-3B, SNIPING* as follows:

> A Marine Corps sniper is defined as a Marine who has been carefully screened and selected, has undergone comprehensive training in advanced infantry and marksmanship techniques, and has been assigned MOS 8541. The sniper's training, combined with the inherent accuracy of his rifle, firmly establishes him as a valuable addition to the weapons available to the infantry commander.
> The primary mission of a sniper in combat is to support combat operations by delivering precision fire on selected targets from concealed positions.

The Vietnam-era sniper training manual served the Marine Corps in published form until CMC changes to the role and use of the Scout-Sniper called for revisions to the manual. The first change ("Change 1") was dated 22 September 1971; the second change came on 7 April 1976. With the emergence of the M40A1 sniper rifle and the changes to the Table of Organization affecting Scout-Sniper training and employment during the late 1970s, an entirely new sniper training manual (*FMFM 1-3B, SNIPING*) was subsequently published under date of 28 January 1981. The completely revised manual included seven sections and seven appendixes dealing with sniper equipment (M40A1 sniper rifle with the 10-power Unertl telescope), and the selection, training, and employment of Scout-Snipers in the Fleet Marine Forces.

The 1981 Marine Corps sniper manual superseded the Vietnam-era version with changes through 7 April 1976. The new manual was intended to move the Marine Corps sniping program into the 1980s.

FMFM 1-3B

SNIPING

U.S. MARINE CORPS

The initial draft edition of Marine Corps field manual *FMFM 1-3B, SNIPING* (October 1967) served as the foundation for the Vietnam-era sniper manual. An interim draft edition followed in December 1968 and, in final form, Marine Corps *FMFM 1-3B, SNIPING* was published under date of 5 August 1969. The front cover of the 1969 manual is shown here; the publication is 4 3/8 inches wide and 6 11/16 inches in length. (U.S. Marine Corps.)

Remington HIGH POWER RIFLE BOLT ACTION REPEATER — MODEL 700

DU PONT

FIXED BOX MAGAZINE . . . ADL and BDL GRADES

INSTRUCTION FOLDER and PARTS PRICE LIST

Fig. 1

Fig. 2

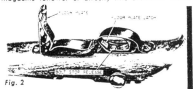

Fig. 3

Fig. 4

TO PUT BOLT IN RIFLE — Simply align bolt lugs to receiver properly, then push cocked bolt forward into rifle.

ON SAFE (Fig. 1) — Rotate side lever safety at right rear of receiver to rear stop position. Bolt handle will be locked down and trigger will **not** fire rifle.

FIRE—Rotate safety forward to front stop position. Trigger can be pulled to fire rifle or bolt handle raised to open action.

Caution: Before firing make sure barrel is clean, free of heavy oil, grease, or any obstruction.

TO SINGLE LOAD — Raise bolt handle to unlock bolt. Pull bolt handle back to open action. Load single cartridge upon magazine follower or directly into chamber. Close bolt and lower bolt handle to lock action closed.

TO MAGAZINE LOAD — Open bolt and load cartridges directly into magazine for ADL Grade model.

For BDL Grade, cartridges load in same way or close bolt and load from bottom of magazine. Push safety ON SAFE and turn rifle bottom upwards. Press floor plate latch to release floor plate (Fig. 2). Lift floor plate with attached follower and spring and load cartridges into magazine opening. Close floor plate and snap floor plate into position.

TO UNLOAD — Pull bolt rearward carefully and take cartridge from rifle. Then push bolt forward until next cartridge is released from magazine. Continue until magazine is empty. BDL Grade magazine may be unloaded from bottom with bolt closed and safety ON SAFE. Be certain also to empty chamber.

BARREL CARE—Use lightly oiled patch, cleaning from breech to muzzle. Remove bolt to make cleaning easier. Press upwards on bolt stop release (Fig. 2) and pull bolt from receiver. Scrub bore with cleaning solvent if necessary.

ACTION CARE AND DISASSEMBLY—Remove bolt and stock if necessary to clean action or replace parts. Unscrew, remove guard screws, and lift stock away from action and barrel. Clean bolt and action in solvent and wipe clean.

Before re-assembling stock to receiver, particularly on ADL Grade, **locate magazine fully into magazine recess** in bottom of receiver. This special care will prevent any damage to stock when stock is tightened against receiver.

Note: Re-assemble BDL Grade trigger guard assembly (includes floor plate, guard, magazine follower and spring) to stock before placing stock over assembled receiver.

TO DISASSEMBLE BOLT PARTS — Pull bolt from rifle. Pull firing pin head back until coin or similar piece can be inserted (Fig. 3). Hold bolt handle and turn bolt plug until entire firing pin assembly can be pulled from bolt assembly. Re-assemble in reverse order.

TO ADJUST TRIGGER — Remove trigger guard and stock. Cock bolt in receiver.

IMPORTANT: No adjustment or removal of the trigger engagement screw is recommended unless replacement is necessary. The trigger engagement screw is set at the factory to engage the trigger and provide the correct amount of supporting trigger connector surface beneath the sear (Fig. 4).

PULL OF TRIGGER: Is adjusted to the desired weight by turning the trigger adjusting screw clockwise for a heavier weight adjustment and counter clockwise for a lighter weight adjustment.

TRAVEL OF TRIGGER: May be reduced by turning the trigger stop screw clockwise until the firing pin will not fall when the trigger is pulled. Then while keeping pressure on the trigger, back off the trigger stop screw, counter clockwise, until the firing pin falls. Continue back off about 1/16 turn. This method of adjusting will allow the least amount of trigger overtravel.

Your **REMINGTON MODEL 700** will remain clean longer if little or no oil is used on action parts. Lubricate cam surfaces on bolt to prevent wear. Wash action and bolt parts with a good grade of petroleum solvent, dry, and re-oil **very** lightly.

HANDLING — Wipe barrel, receiver, and all steel parts to prevent rusting. Invisible "prints" of moisture can cause rust unless removed.

EXPOSURE — After using in wet weather always wipe steel parts with oil to prevent rusting. Abrupt changes in temperature can cause condensation and wetness. Therefore, special care is needed to interior steel parts to prevent rust. When shooting in freezing weather, remove excess oil for best results. Use dry graphite if necessary to lubricate metal parts.

REMINGTON ARMS COMPANY, INC. ● Ilion, N. Y., U.S.A.

CF–17

The front cover of the Remington instruction folder and parts price list for the Model 700 commercial rifle circa 1966. This folder served Marine Corps ordnance during the initial stages of the planning and procurement process for the Vietnam-era Scout-Sniper Rifle. According to USMC documents, subsequent changes ("new part numbers") were made at a conference held on 4 February 1966. (U.S. Marine Corps.)

COMPONENT PARTS

Remington

MODEL
700
SNIPER

BOLT ACTION -- HIGH POWER

7.62 NATO CALIBER

When ordering parts — Model No., Part No. and Part Name must be given.

View No.	Part No.	NAME OF PART	View No.	Part No.	NAME OF PART
1	16860	Barrel Assembly, 7.62 Cal. (includes Barrel, Barrel Bracket, Receiver)	30	22036	Rear Guard Screw
2	16861	Bolt Assembly (includes Bolt Body Assembly and Bolt Handle)	31	22560	Rear Swivel Assembly
			32	17034	Receiver Plug Screw
	16862	Bolt Final Assembly (includes Bolt Assembly, Ejector, Ejector Pin, Ejector Spring, Extractor, Extractor Rivet, Firing Pin Assembly)	33	26585	Safety Assembly (includes Safety, Safety Button)
			34	23222	Safety Detent Ball
3	17012	Bolt Plug	35	15368	Safety Detent Spring
4	17013	Bolt Stop	36	17043	Safety Pivot Pin
5	24475	Bolt Stop Pin	37	17044	Safety Snap Washer
6	15478	Bolt Stop Release	38	26590	Sear and Safety Cam Assembly (includes Safety Cam, Sear)
7	15224	Bolt Stop Spring			
8	16601	Butt Plate	39	24476	Sear Pin
9	25410	Butt Plate Screw	40	17047	Sear Spring
10	17017	Ejector	41	16865	Stock Assembly (includes Butt Plate, Butt Plate Screw (2), Stock, Stock Reinforcing Screw, Front Swivel Assembly, Front Swivel Nut, Rear Swivel Assembly)
11	17676	Ejector Pin			
12	17019	Ejector Spring			
13	16254	Extractor		18186	Stock Reinforcing Screw
14	27340	Extractor Rivet	42	15280	Trigger
15	22021	Firing Pin	43	17053	Trigger Adjusting Screw
16	22041	Firing Pin Assembly (includes Bolt Plug, Firing Pin, Firing Pin Cross Pin, Firing Pin Head, Main Spring)		26345	Trigger Assembly (includes Bolt Stop Release, Trigger Housing Assembly, Safety Assembly, Safety Detent Ball, Safety Detent Spring, Safety Pivot Pin, Safety Snap Washer, Sear and Safety Cam Assembly, Sear Spring, Trigger, Trigger Adjusting Screw, Trigger Engagement Screw, Trigger Pin, Trigger Spring, Trigger Stop Screw)
17	17022	Firing Pin Cross Pin			
18	16434	Floor Plate			
19	15291	Floor Plate Latch			
20	16451	Floor Plate Latch Pin			
21	16452	Floor Plate Latch Spring	44	19461	Trigger Connector
22	16453	Floor Plate Pivot Pin	43	17053	Trigger Engagement Screw
23	16859	Front Guard Screw	45	26375	Trigger Guard
24	16856	Front Swivel Assembly		26370	Trigger Guard Assembly (includes Floor Plate, Floor Plate Latch, Floor Plate Latch Pin, Floor Plate Latch Spring, Floor Plate Pivot Pin, Trigger Guard)
25	17682	Front Swivel Nut			
26	16857	Magazine			
27	15667	Magazine Follower			
28	15699	Magazine Spring	46	26655	Trigger Housing Assembly (includes Trigger Housing Spacer (3), Trigger Side Plate (2)
29	17058	Main Spring	47	24477	Trigger Pin
			48	15400	Trigger Spring
			49	15481	Trigger Stop Screw

DELIVERIES ARE F.O.B. ILION, N. Y.   PARTS SUBJECT TO CHANGE WITHOUT NOTICE

Above and following page: A sectional view from the instruction folder and component parts list furnished to the Marine Corps following its adoption of the Remington M700 sniper rifle in 1966. The document was adapted from information provided with Remington Model 700 commercial sporting rifles. The earliest instructional materials employed by USMC ordnance personnel were "marked-up" commercial folders with standard M700 part numbers simply typed over. The Marine Corps version (shown) was later incorporated into the Vietnam-era USMC Supply Activity "Stock List," the repair parts and components listings for the M700 and M40 sniper rifles. (U.S. Marine Corps.)

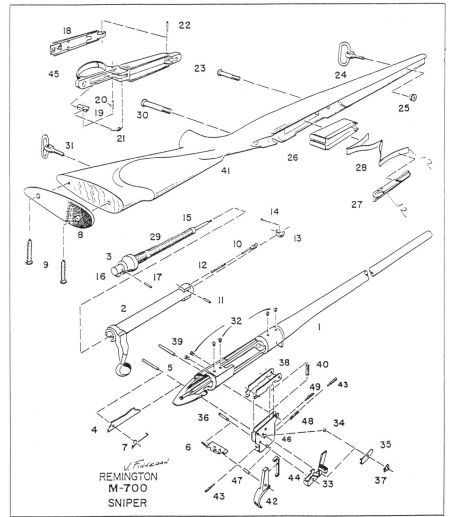

Send all guns for factory service and inquiries on
service and parts to
REMINGTON ARMS COMPANY, INC.
Arms Service Division
Ilion, New York 13357

All other inquiries are to be addressed to
REMINGTON ARMS COMPANY, INC.
Bridgeport, Connecticut 06602

MODEL
700
SNIPER

J. FINNEGAN
REMINGTON
M-700
SNIPER

REPLACEMENT PARTS

When ordering parts specify model, caliber, part name and serial number of the gun.

NOTE: The sale of barrel assemblies and breech bolts is restricted. When these parts are needed for replacement, the arm must be returned to the factory as the use of special tools and gauges is required to assure proper operation. All other parts will be shipped as ordered but, since they are made to close dimensions, the particular part may require slight adjustment or fitting to assure proper functioning of the arm.

NOVEMBER 1966

SL-4-05539A

MARINE CORPS STOCK LIST

REPAIR PARTS LIST

FOR

RIFLE, 7.62MM:

M700

FSN 1005-930-5444

An early (November 1966) Marine Corps Stock List (Repair Parts List) for the 7.62mm M700 sniper rifle. The Remington/Redfield system was referenced as the M700 during the early months of Marine Corps procurement and field use in Vietnam. The M40 designation saw increased use as the war progressed. (U.S. Marine Corps.)

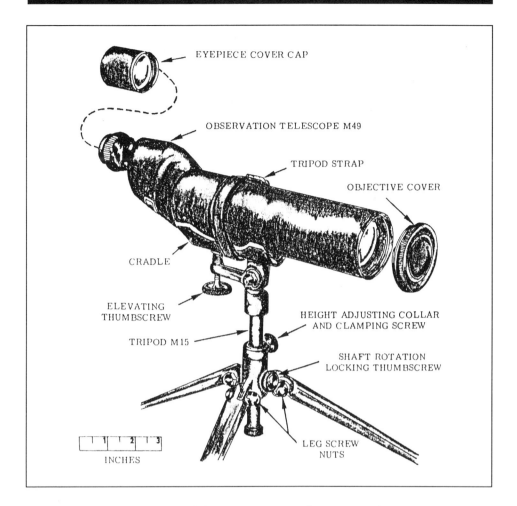

A sniping manual illustration of the 20-power M49 observation telescope with the M15 tripod assembly. The M49 telescope and 7X50 binoculars were issued to Marine Corps snipers for observation purposes in Vietnam. The spotting telescope and the binoculars are pictured in various USMC combat photos throughout this book. As a matter of interest, more than one Marine marksman has admitted to having used the M15 tripod assembly as a "rifle rest" with the observation telescope removed. (U.S. Marine Corps.)

AUGUST 1970

SL-3-05539A

P/C 123 055390 00

MARINE CORPS STOCK LIST

COMPONENTS LIST

FOR

RIFLE, 7.62 MILLIMETER:

M40

FSN 1005-930-5444

Marine Corps Stock List (Components List) for the 7.62mm M40 sniper rifle (August 1970). Even though the M40 designation was used officially, the USMC sniper rifle was also referenced as the M700 long after the war in Vietnam. To this day, many veteran Marine snipers and ordnance personnel refer to this system as the "M700 sniper rifle." (U.S. Marine Corps.)

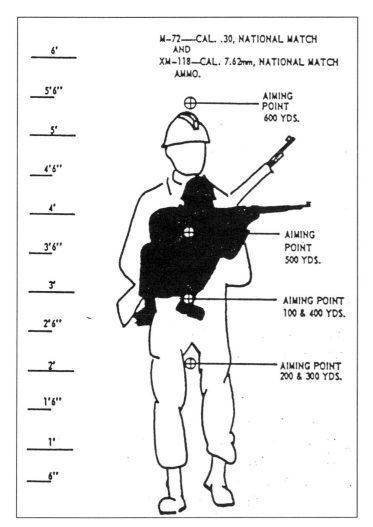

M-72—CAL. .30, NATIONAL MATCH
AND
XM-118—CAL. 7.62mm, NATIONAL MATCH
AMMO.

AIMING
POINT
600 YDS.

AIMING
POINT
500 YDS.

AIMING POINT
100 & 400 YDS.

AIMING POINT
200 & 300 YDS.

Left: Vietnam War USMC training illustration of an enemy soldier indicates the correct holds ("hold-off") for various ranges with the rifle sighted in for 500 yards (hold-off is the procedure used to hit a target at ranges other than the range for which the rifle is zeroed). In most cases, Marine sniper rifles were zeroed for 500 yards point of aim, point of impact and left unchanged. The practice was known as the "over the head and under the balls" firing technique to many of the Marine snipers. A similar illustration served the Army sniper program as well. (U.S. Marine Corps.)

Below: A sniper training illustration showing the correct "leads and holds at 90 degrees with sights set for 500 meters." The Marine Corps defined holds and leads as "advanced marksmanship techniques that enabled the sniper to hit his target without holding his sights directly on the target." The mastery of this technique required a thorough understanding of bullet trajectory and drop. Both "yards" and "meters" were alternately used to express distance in training documents dating from the war in Vietnam. (U.S. Marine Corps.)

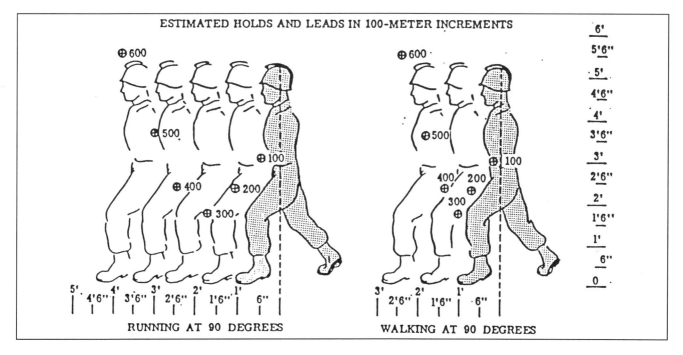

ESTIMATED HOLDS AND LEADS IN 100-METER INCREMENTS

RUNNING AT 90 DEGREES

WALKING AT 90 DEGREES

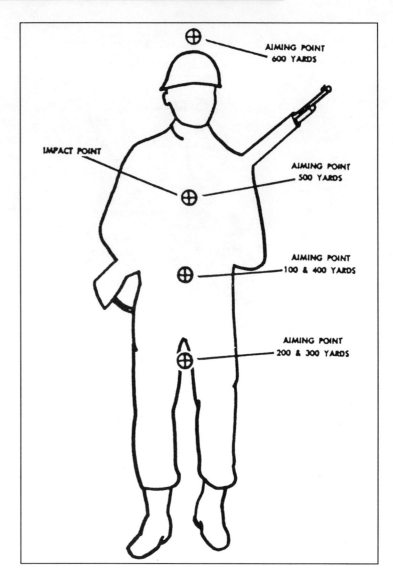

An early version of the "hold-off" illustration used to train USMC snipers for combat duty in Vietnam. (U.S. Marine Corps.)

Certificates signifying the satisfactory completion of Scout-Sniper School were awarded to Marine snipers in the United States and RVN. This form was used at Camp Pendleton during 1967 and part of 1968. (U.S. Marine Corps.)

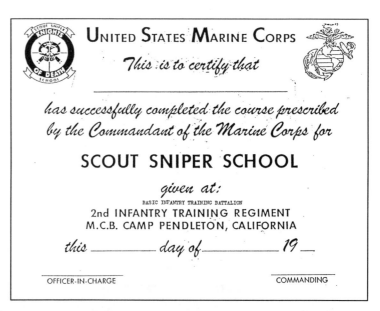

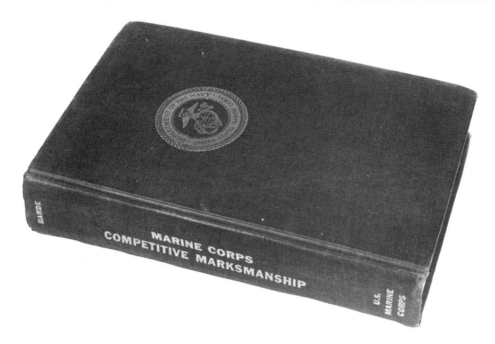

A copy of *The History of Marine Corps Competitive Marksmanship* by Maj. Robert E. Barde, USMC (Marksmanship Branch, G-3 Division, HQMC 1961). The "Red Book" as it is known in Marine shooting circles provides insight on nearly six decades of Marine Corps competitive marksmanship and the highly effective Competition-in-Arms program, described as follows: "The purpose of the Competition-in-Arms program is to increase the marksmanship proficiency and combat readiness of the Marine Corps by developing a base of Marines with high level skills in rifle and pistol marksmanship to serve as competitors and instructors in their units." Although members of the USMC shooting teams were deeply involved with the USMC sniping effort in World War II and again in Korea, the Vietnam War marked the first time that a concentrated effort was made to locate and assign experienced competitive marksmen as snipers and/or instructors. Without question, the vast majority of the personnel tasked with establishing and maintaining the USMC sniping program in RVN, especially during the formative stages, had been participants in the Competition-in-Arms program at one time or another. Though many of the Marines engaged with sniping and sniper training (sniper-instructors) in Vietnam are mentioned in the "Red Book," as it was published in 1961, the Marines distinguished with the rifle and/or pistol in the years immediately preceding the conflict in Southeast Asia are not included. (Laine Collection.)

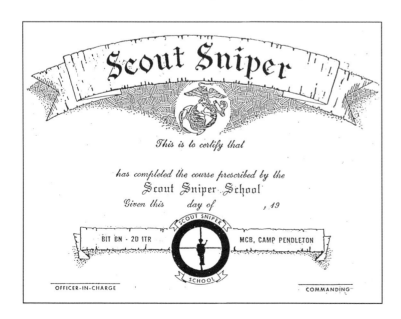

Scout-Sniper training certificate issued during 1968 and 1969 at Camp Pendleton, California. (The certificates pictured in this chapter were approximately eight by ten inches in original form.) (U.S. Marine Corps.)

FIFTH MARINE REGIMENT - SCOUT/SNIPER LOG

NAME: 1.   DATE:

2.

WEAPON NO.:   SCOPE NO.:   POSITION:

ELEVATION: WINDAGE:

TIME	NO. OF ENEMY	NATURE & TYPE OF WEAPONS	CO-ORD.	DIRECTION AND DESCRIPTION (DETAIL)

NO. OF ROUNDS FIRED _____ MATCH _____ BALL _____ TRACER _____

OBSERVATION OF ROUNDS:

1. HIGH _____ LOW _____ LEFT _____ RIGHT _____ ON TARGET _____

2. HIGH _____ LOW _____ LEFT _____ RIGHT _____ ON TARGET _____

3. HIGH _____ LOW _____ LEFT _____ RIGHT _____ ON TARGET _____

4. HIGH _____ LOW _____ LEFT _____ RIGHT _____ ON TARGET _____

RESULTS OF ROUNDS FIRED:

NO. _____ K. I. A.

NO. _____ P. K. I. A.

NO. _____ W. I. A.

An example of a Scout/Sniper Log typical of those used by Marine snipers in Vietnam. According to the Marine Corps, "The sniper log is a factual, chronological record of sniper employment which will serve as a permanent source of operational data. It will provide information to intelligence personnel, unit commanders, other snipers, and the sniper himself." In this case, the front (top) and the back of a Fifth Marine Regiment Scout/Sniper Log, or "kill sheet," as they were more commonly known, is shown here. The personnel, date, weapon/scope, location, activity, and the results of an encounter were duly recorded. The "kill sheet" was then signed by the officer in charge. The log was normally completed following a mission. The original sheet was approximately 6 1/2 inches wide and 9 1/2 inches long. (Joseph T. Ward.)

Scout-Sniper Instructor School Certificate of Proficiency circa 1977. The certificate served as "a symbol of achievement" for Marine Corps personnel completing the prescribed course of training. The document was based on the certificate awarded to Marines graduating from the World War II-era Scout-Sniper School at New River (Camp Lejeune), North Carolina. The contemporary certificate was designed to carry on the Scout-Sniper tradition in conjunction with a revitalized sniper program. (J.C. Cuddy.)

The Marine Corps Scout-Sniper School Certificate of Proficiency awarded to Marines completing the course of training at New River, North Carolina, during World War II. The document shown here served as "the reference," for the contemporary Scout-Sniper Instructor School Certificate of Proficiency pictured above. According to official records, The Marine named on this document, Walter C. Cuddy, graduated in the fourth class held at New River (20 August 1943). As a matter of interest, Walter Cuddy is the father of Marine officer Col. J.C. Cuddy, the OIC of the USMC Sniper School at Quantico, Virginia (1976–1980), and later the CO of Weapons Training Battalion. It should be further noted that Jack Cuddy was one of the Marines directly responsible for the fielding of the M40A1 and the 10-power Unertl telescope. (J.C. Cuddy.)

A 1970s photograph of Maj. Edward J. Land Jr. (left) and Col. Walter R. Walsh at Camp Perry, Ohio, the site of the National Matches. Major Land, a Distinguished Marksman and Pistol Shot, established the First Marine Division sniping program in Vietnam and was later instrumental in bringing about the adoption of the M40A1 sniper rifle and the reemergence of a viable USMC sniping program in the late 1970s. Colonel Walsh became the first Marine to

be "Triple Distinguished," winning the Distinguished Rifleman Badge, Distinguished Pistol Shot Badge, and the International Distinguished Badge. Walsh also commanded the first "East Coast" specialist school for training USMC Scout-Snipers in 1942 and, as OIC of the MTU at Quantico, Virginia, in late 1965, directed the evaluations that led to Marine Corps adoption of the Vietnam-era Remington M700 sniper rifle. Both Land and Walsh are prime examples of the strong ties that exist between the Competition-in-Arms program and Marine Corps sniping. (Edward J. Land Jr.)

A contemporary photograph (1994) of the Dale Bertoli Trophy awarded to the Scout-Sniper School's honor graduate (Quantico, Virginia). The front of the trophy is engraved with the words: "Dale Bertoli Trophy, died of wounds in June 1945, Okinawa, Japan."

According to a Marine Corps description of the award, "Dale Bertoli was a highly skilled sniper. He represented what a good scout-sniper should be."

The rifle and telescope are symbolic of the USMC sniping equipment fielded during World War II. The Bertoli Trophy was introduced to the Scout-Sniper Instructor School in the early 1980s. (U.S. Marine Corps.)

MAY 1978

SL-3-05539B
PCN 123 055391 00

MARINE CORPS STOCK LIST

COMPONENTS LIST

FOR

RIFLE, SNIPER, 7.62 MILLIMETER

M40A1

NSN 1005-01-035-1674

An early (May 1978) Marine Corps Stock List (Components List) for the M40A1 sniper rifle. (U.S. Marine Corps.)

FMFM 1-3B

SNIPING

U. S. MARINE CORPS

PCN 139 000107 00

With the emergence of the M40A1 sniper rifle came a new sighting system and changes to the Table of Organization and Equipment (TO&E) affecting Scout-Sniper training and employment during the late 1970s. An entirely new sniper training manual (*FMFM 1-3B, SNIPING*) was subsequently published under date of 28 January 1981. The 1981 manual superseded the Vietnam-era version that incorporated changes made up to 7 April 1976. The front cover of the 1981 publication is shown here; the manual is 8 1/2 inches wide and 11 inches long. (U.S. Marine Corps.)

"THOSE DAMN VIET CONG"

During early action in Vietnam when Marine Corps combat personnel were "taking out" an occasional Viet Cong sniper, the Communist insurgents equipped as snipers were using an assortment of telescopic sights and rifles.

Although much of this hardware was originally intended for this purpose, the Viet Cong mounted telescopic sights to a variety of bolt-action and semiautomatic rifles and carbines. The sights and weapons came from every nation that had been involved in Asia since World War II.

Intelligence reports categorized Viet Cong sniping activity as "more of a nuisance than a threat." At the field level, however, judging from the comments of various Army and Marine Corps combat veterans, "there always seemed to be a VC marksman who took his work too seriously."

Whether or not the damage done or intended came at the hands of a trained marksman using a telescopic sight or just an ordinary rifleman armed with a conventional weapon, the difference became academic when the firing started. There is no way of knowing if the American casualties attributed to snipers came as a result of enemy personnel acting in this capacity or from the small-arms fire invariably credited to "snipers."

Much of the Viet Cong sniping activity was reminiscent of the tactics the Japanese had employed against the United States in the Pacific theater.

A U.S. Army paper, "Tasks Trainfire III And IV," on 14 September 1955, summarized World War II Imperial Japanese Army sniping as follows:

> Some Japanese riflemen were referred to by many of our troops in the Pacific as "snipers," although these riflemen lacked many of the characteristics traditionally associated with snipers [no specific sniper training and/or telescopic sighted rifles]. These "snipers" operated in jungle areas remaining behind retreating Japanese forces or in front of defensive forces.

As one veteran First Marine Division sniper pointed out:

> What I saw of the Viet Cong in this respect was not what we would consider snipers in the true sense. They were usually a one or two man blocking force left behind to slow-down an approaching American force; a suicide mission, for lack of a better description. They would fire a few rounds and move-on, if they could. Their weapons were usually an AK-47 or the SKS.

NOTE: The AK47 (7.62 x 39mm selective-fire Kalashnikov Assault Rifle) and the SKS (7.62 x 39mm semiautomatic Simonov Carbine) served as the principal shoulder arms of the Viet Cong and the North Vietnamese Army during the Vietnam War. Although neither weapon was designed to mount telescopic sights, it was not uncommon for U.S. combat personnel to recover an AK-47 or SKS fitted with a riflescope of one kind or another.

Even though VC armed with telescopic sighted sniper rifles were killed and captured, Viet Cong snipers, for the most part, were ordinary riflemen on a harassing mission.

A Marine sergeant, reflecting on the Viet Cong snipers he had encountered in South Vietnam, had this to say:

> They would take these people, many without any education, train them to be snipers, and if we would capture them they couldn't tell you who they are. But here they were killing Marines and that was all they really knew. It was the craziest thing I've ever seen.

The Viet Cong, forced to travel light and fast as they were, made effective use of "prepositioned military supplies" during their campaign in South Vietnam. In some cases, large amounts of equipment were stored in underground complexes. In others, arms and ammunition were simply placed in trenches and carefully concealed to avoid detection.

When the war and the scope of combat operations expanded in Southeast Asia, search and destroy missions conducted by the Army and Marine Corps ("offensive operations designed to seek out and destroy enemy forces, headquarters, and supply installations, with the emphasis on destruction") began turning up significant amounts of arms and equipment. The Viet Cong weapon caches were also yielding "sniper rifles" in surprising numbers. In one instance, according to the following information provided by the U.S. Army:

> U.S. paratroopers 173d Airborne Brigade sweeping through a Communist stronghold north of Saigon discovered a huge supply dump. It included 62 long-range, Russian sniper rifles complete with spare parts and instruction booklets.

In another case, "More than 50 brand-new Russian sniper rifles were captured," and reports of "cases of Soviet sniper rifles still packed in their original cosmoline" were considered common after a time.

NOTE: Although most VC and NVA sniper rifles were supplied by the Soviet Union, other Communist-bloc countries were known to furnish sniping equipment as well. In terms of effective use, however, without the benefit of proper training, sniper rifles were of marginal value to the Viet Cong. Even though a significant number of "new-condition" Communist sniper rifles were captured in weapon caches, many of the rifles taken from killed or captured VC and NVA combatants were described as being in "poor condition." In many cases, the telescopes were not sighted in, and the weapons were in dire need of basic maintenance.

As the intensity of North Vietnamese combat involvement in South Vietnam increased, the level of sniping activity attributed to the North Vietnamese Army increased proportionately. Trained NVA snipers were taking an active part in military operations against American and South Vietnamese forces. Reports of "enemy marksmen with telescopic sights" became commonplace.

For the sake of comparison, when asked to differentiate between Viet Cong and NVA snipers, a Marine Scout-Sniper who had faced both replied, "The NVA snipers were a different breed of cat altogether. They were well-trained, and a formidable foe."

One of the earliest documented accounts of organized NVA sniping appeared in *SEA TIGER* (19 July 1966), a periodical published by III MAF in Vietnam. The article, written by Gy.Sgt. Jack Childs, USMC, offered the following:

> Da Nang—A North Vietnamese officer, who commanded an elite enemy sniper platoon, surrendered himself to a village chief 50 miles north of here.
>
> The officer, a 35-year-old lieutenant, carried with him a Russian made sniper rifle and scope [the weapon was a Model 91/30, 7.62mm (7.62 x 54R) sniper rifle with a 3.5-power PU telescopic sight].
>
> He was immediately turned over to Army of the Republic of Vietnam (ARVN) forces. He told them that his unit was operating in an area north of Phu Bai.
>
> Word of his surrender reached Major Robert A. Russell, officer in charge of the Marine Corps sniper school in Vietnam.
>
> Working through the ARVN's I Corps headquarters in Da Nang, the two snipers were brought together. Major Russell also inspected the enemy's weapon and scope.
>
> "I was extremely interested in obtaining information on their activities," said the major. Through an interpreter, the lieutenant told the major that his company had been formed in North Vietnam. They had been operating in the south for approximately nine weeks.
>
> The company, according to the lieutenant, consists of three, 30 man platoons and a company headquarters of an additional 30 men.
>
> "He was very cooperative," said Major Russell. "He told me that, with the exception of their officers—who are assigned to the company—each man is a volunteer. Their company is commanded by a junior captain."
>
> "When I asked why they volunteered, he said that it was because their families received extra rice and farm land. His family is still in North Vietnam."
>
> The prisoner disclosed that the average age of the North Vietnamese sniper was between 19 and 22. All of them are armed with the Russian 7.62 caliber rifle and a three-and-one-half power scope.
>
> "Their scope," said the Marine major, "enables them to get a good sighting even at night, if the moon is bright enough.
>
> "He told me that their training was for a period of three months. The first two were devoted to firing the standard rifle, and the last month for training with the sniper rifle and scope.
>
> "They spent eight hours a day snapping in. However, they were allowed to

fire only three rounds of live ammunition every five days. They practiced at ranges up to 1000 yards on man-sized paper targets."

The lieutenant added that throughout their training in the north, they were subjected to constant testing, to measure their progress and morale. If a man's morale was low, he was immediately transferred.

He freely volunteered the information that although their pay was low (20 piasters a month), their morale was high because they were considered elite troops.

Their 30-man sniper platoons are further broken down into three, 10-man squads. And, since they are elite troops, each squad is protected by a Viet Cong guerrilla platoon.

The squads stay widely dispersed. Each is separated by a three day march.

Each sniper was also trained to be his own armorer.

They also receive extensive training in camouflage and movement. Shooting at moving targets is confined to large targets such as trucks and helicopters.

"Their prime targets are NCOs, officers and radiomen," the major added. "He claimed that his platoon had, to date, killed several government troops. These kills were made at ranges of between 600 and 700 meters. Their rifle is considered extremely accurate at those ranges."

Major Russell said that the rolling terrain around Phu Bai is "an excellent area for snipers."

The North Vietnamese officer said that his platoon had not killed any Marines. [Of course not!]

He said that their primary mission was to kill Americans. But at the present time, he added, in an effort to battle-harden their young snipers they were confining their shooting to government (ARVN) troops.

"He told me that he didn't know when they would increase their activity towards the Marines," said Major Russell. "Nor does he claim to know if any more similar companies are being formed or trained in the north."

Asked for a comparison between the Marine and North Vietnamese sniper, the major said: "Their training can't begin to compare with ours."

In addition to effective countersniping measures developed in conjunction with the Army and Marine Corps sniper program in Vietnam, conventional means, such as air strikes, artillery, mortar fire and resourceful ground combat personnel, served to neutralize the vast majority of VC and NVA snipers.

NOTE: The extent of countersniper training (sniper versus sniper) was usually determined by the level of enemy sniping activity in a given area. Although sniping conducted by ordinary riflemen presented a problem to all combat forces and was dealt with accordingly, Army and Marine Corps snipers were known to "match skills" with North Vietnamese marksmen on numerous occasions. The opportunity to eliminate another sniper, especially one that had been trained and equipped for this purpose, was met with considerable enthusiasm by both factions.

Although a variety of weapons were employed against Communist snipers, by all accounts, the "all purpose" M60 machine gun proved to be an effective antisniper weapon in experienced hands; the .50-caliber Browning machine gun ("The Big Browning") and the imaginative use of 106mm recoilless rifles served this purpose as well.

Despite relatively good coverage of the effective use of the M60 and the Browning in contemporary publications dealing with the war in Vietnam, the recoilless rifle as an antisniper weapon is rarely noted. However, one good example of recoilless rifle use in this capacity was recorded in *The End of The Line: The Siege of Khe Sanh* (Ballantine Books 1983) by Robert Pisor (a correspondent for the *Detroit News*, Pisor spent 1967–1968 covering the war in Vietnam):

The Marines on 881 South hunted down North Vietnamese snipers with a 106mm recoilless rifle—blasting the sniper and the tree he sat in into bloodied splinters. When the North Vietnamese installed a rifleman who failed to hit a single Marine even with thirty shots a day, India Company let him live.

NOTE: The 106mm recoilless rifle was an air-cooled, breechloading, portable weapon designed to defeat heavy armor. Depending on the mounting system, it could be used as a ground weapon or mounted on a light vehicle. Other types (smaller caliber) could be fired from the ground or the shoulder. Recoil was eliminated by controlled escape of propellant gases to the rear through an opening in the breechblock.

Of further interest is the following excerpt from Pisor's book:

> The combat base also had a pet sniper. A North Vietnamese soldier had lugged a .50 caliber machine gun to a spider hole not much more than two hundred yards from the perimeter. Every day and night he fired at the Marines or at arriving and departing aircraft. The Marines actually caught glimpses of his face through the scopes on sniper rifles, but neither marksmen nor mortars nor recoilless rifles could knock him out. Finally, napalm was called in. For ten minutes the ground around the sniper's position boiled in orange flame and black smoke, the vegetation crisping and the soil itself seeming to burn. When the last oily flames flickered out, he popped out of his hole and fired a single round.
>
> The Marines in the perimeter trenches cheered. They named him Luke the Gook, and after that no one wanted anything to happen to him.

Whereas the Viet Cong had made use of a variety of ad hoc sniping equipment, as the North Vietnamese assumed control of the war in the south and the role of the Viet Cong diminished, the field use of Communist-bloc sniping hardware became more prevalent.

The principal weapon employed by Communist snipers in Southeast Asia was the Soviet Mosin-Nagant M91/30 sniper rifle mounting the 3.5-power model PU and, to a lesser extent, the 4-power model PE telescopic sights.

Although various documents recovered from the VC and NVA during the course of the war listed the effective range of the 7.62 x 54R Model 91/30 sniper rifle as "800 meters," the M91/30 (with possible exceptions) was not perceived as a serious threat beyond 500-600 meters. The limiting factors in this case involved the quality of the ammunition, the equipment, and the skill of the shooter. The Model 91/30 sniper rifle was utilized by Communist forces during World War II, the Korean War, and again in Southeast Asia.

Interestingly, even though a number of captured bolt-action sniper rifles and semiautomatic carbines were returned to the United States as legally documented souvenirs ("war trophies") by American servicemen, there were many U.S. combat personnel who, in their judgment, literally "got the shaft" when it came to gaining their share of the enemy small arms taken in Vietnam. Apart from the random weapons recovered by individuals in combat, materiel captured in quantity was either frequently destroyed or redistributed for use by "friendly forces." Although policy and practice varied widely, when combat personnel discovered an enemy arms cache, members of the unit responsible were occasionally permitted to keep "one weapon apiece" as souvenirs (bolt-action or semiautomatic rifles and carbines only—automatic weapons were considered contraband).

In many cases, captured weapons earmarked for distribution among combat troops as war souvenirs were frequently "redirected" to officers, noncombatants, or visiting dignitaries, many of who had faced no greater peril in South Vietnam than using the rest rooms in and around Saigon.

In addition to returning items to the United States by legal means, many servicemen simply took to shipping contraband in the parcels they were sending home. According to U.S. postal authorities, before remedial measures were taken, at least half of the packages selected at random ("50 percent") were found to contain items such as explosives, grenades, and the components necessary to assemble automatic weapons.

Although many have chosen to pay tribute to the "fighting spirit" and "tenacity" of the VC and the NVA in the years following the war in Vietnam, in the interest of balancing this point of view with a measure of reality, let it be said that countless American servicemen bore witness to the acts of brutality committed by the Viet Cong and the North Vietnamese Army against their own people and those they opposed in combat. Allowing for the exceptions, as there always are, the VC and the NVA were as savage as they were tenacious.

Marine Sgt. Douglas Mark de Haas with Model 91/30 Russian sniper rifle captured from the Viet Cong. According to Sergeant de Haas, the rifle was found to be "very accurate" at ranges of 500 yards or more. (Reproduced from *Bolt Action Rifles* by Frank de Haas DBI Books.)

A Soviet-manufactured Mosin-Nagant M91/30 sniper rifle mounting a PU telescope taken from an NVA sniper in the Khe Sanh area during the Tet Offensive (1968). In this case, the sniper was eliminated by a Marine (James C. Disney) with an M60 machine gun. The Soviet or Hungarian M91/30 bolt-action sniper rifles fitted with PU and, to a lesser extent, PE telescopic sights, served as the principal sniper issue for Communist forces in Southeast Asia. Except for markings, there was little difference between the Soviet and Hungarian M91/30 sniper rifles. (Carl J. Decker.)

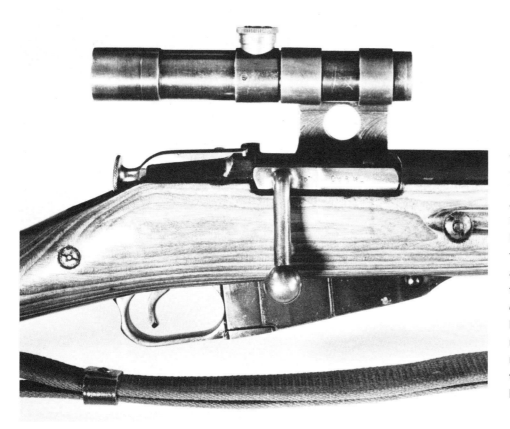

A typical Soviet Mosin-Nagant M91/30 sniper rifle with a 3.5-power PU telescopic sight. An adaptation of the basic Soviet infantry rifle, a turned-down bolt handle was used to clear the sight. The M91/30 served as the standard sniper issue for the Communist-bloc countries following World War II. The Mosin-Nagant sniper rifle, though antiquated by most standards, was extremely effective in capable hands. (Conway Collection.)

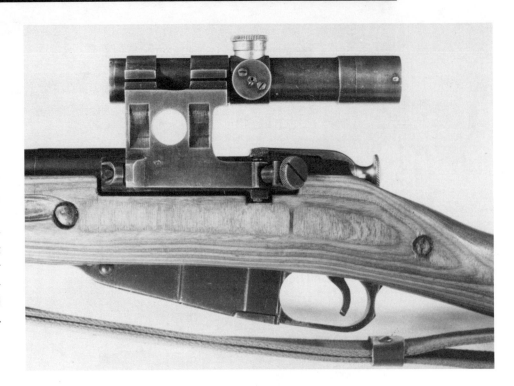

Another view (left) of the Soviet M91/30 sniper rifle. In addition to furnishing sniper weapons and instructional materials for their care and use, Soviet advisors reportedly trained Communist snipers in some cases. Leather lens caps, a sling, and cleaning equipment were issued with the M91/30 sniping rifles. (Conway Collection.)

A unique photo taken through a Soviet 3.5-power PU telescope illustrates the typical pointed post and horizontal side-bar reticle pattern used in Soviet telescopic sights. (Monty C. Lutz.)

A Hungarian-made M91/30 (7.62 x 54R) sniper rifle with a 3.5-power PU telescopic sight captured in Vietnam is typical of those employed by Viet Cong and North Vietnamese Army snipers in Southeast Asia. Although most weapons of this type were supplied by the Soviet Union, other Communist-bloc countries were known to furnish sniping equipment as well. (West Point Collection.)

A Soviet Mosin-Nagant M91/30 sniper rifle fitted with a 4-power PE telescopic sight with focus adjustment (a knurled collar with a diopter scale). The telescope mounting base attached to the top of the receiver (monobloc mounting). The PE telescope was specifically mentioned in captured Vietnam-era Soviet documents (Russian language) detailing the operation and maintenance of the M91/30 sniper rifle. In addition to providing directions for zeroing and adjusting both PU and PE telescopes, the instructions recommended the most suitable "enemy targets." As an aside, to this day it is difficult for the typical American serviceman to visualize himself as "the enemy." (V.J. Kirov.)

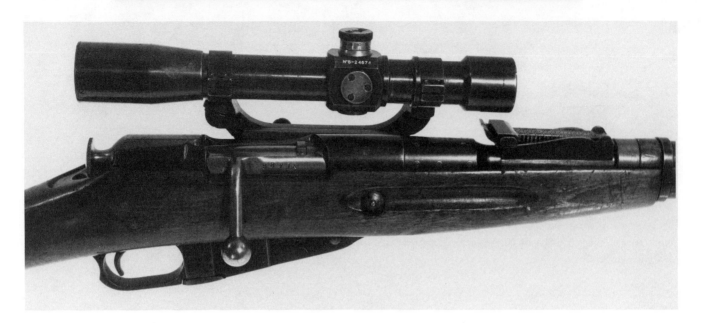

A Soviet Mosin-Nagant M91/30 sniper rifle with a variant 4-power rifle scope referenced by various Army intelligence documents as a "PE optical sight." In this case, the telescope mounting attached to the left side of the receiver. Though configured much the same as the other 4-power model, the variant sight does not have a focus adjustment. If this telescopic sight has separate nomenclature, the specific Soviet designation has not been clearly defined. Although both telescope types were recovered in Vietnam, the mounting attached to the top of the receiver was rarely encountered. The 4-power PE and the PE-variant pictured in this series were originally fielded by the Red Army during World War II. (V.J. Kirov.)

A comparison between a standard telescopic-sighted Mosin-Nagant M91/30 (top) and a 7.62X 54R Czech Vz57 sniper rifle mounting a 2.5-power telescope. (Charles W. Karwan.)

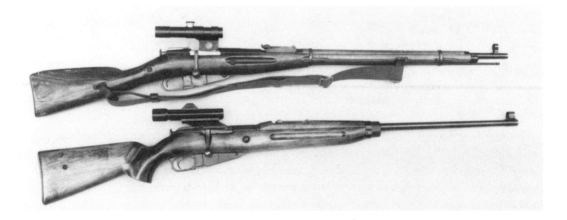

A close-up view of the Vz57 (or Model 1957) sniper rifle. The Czech system is based on the Mosin-Nagant action. The bolt handle was relocated to the top of the bolt's safety lug to clear the telescope and mount. The sight is mounted closer to the receiver than the PU model on a M91/30 sniper rifle. (Charles W. Karwan.)

An alternate view of the Vz57 Czech sniping rifle. The 2.5-power telescope is permanently attached to the mount. A dovetail base holds the two-piece scope mount to the left side of the receiver; the telescope is centered over the bore. The Vz57 is a refined version of the Vz54, a modified M91/30 with a PU telescope. Although both weapon types were reportedly captured in Vietnam, Vz54 and Vz57 Czech sniping rifles were rarely encountered in Southeast Asia. (Charles W. Karwan.)

A Vietnam-era Communist photograph of a relatively well dressed and equipped member of the Viet Cong. The VC were reviled by many and respected by others, and while opinions differed, the typical combat veteran would just as soon forget "Old Charlie." (U.S. Army.)

North Vietnamese Army personnel and Viet Cong captured by Third Marines (3d MarDiv) during action in the Demilitarized Zone, January 1967. The DMZ separated North and South Vietnam at the seventeenth parallel. A significant amount of combat took place in this region (northern Quang Tri Province) during the course of the war. (William D. Abbott.)

A Safe-Conduct Pass dating from the war in Vietnam. The brightly colored surrender leaflets, a part of the Chieu Hoi (I Surrender) or "Open-Arms Program," promised clemency and financial aid to the VC and members of the NVA who stopped fighting and agreed to live under South Vietnamese government authority. The program reportedly influenced the defection of thousands of VC and NVA "returnees" (Hoi Chanh). The three-by-six-inch leaflet and others like it were distributed throughout Southeast Asia. (Abbott Collection.)

The AK-47 (7.62 x 39mm selective-fire Kalashnikov Assault Rifle) and the SKS (7.62 x 39mm, semiautomatic Simonov Carbine) served as the principal shoulder arms of the Viet Cong and the North Vietnamese Army during the Vietnam War (the model designation for the assault rifle and the carbine depended on where the weapon was produced). In this case, an AK-47 captured by Company A, First Battalion, Fifth Infantry, First Air Cav Division, 22 February 1967 (Operation Thayer II). (West Point Collection.)

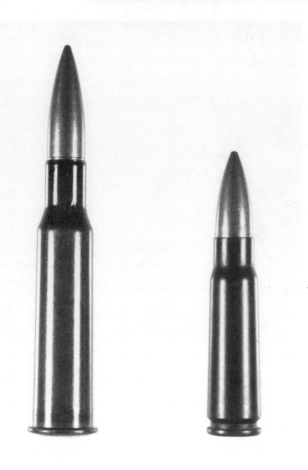

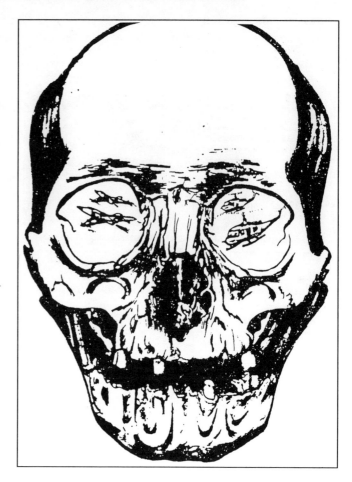

A comparison between a 7.62 x 54R cartridge (left) used with the Mosin-Nagant M91/30 sniper rifle and the 7.62 x 39mm cartridge for the AK-47 and SKS carbine. (Peter R. Senich.)

A variety of surrender leaflets were circulated during the war in Vietnam—in this case, a leaflet (4 by 5 1/2 inches) showing the universal symbol for death. Note the jet aircraft and helicopter gunships in the skull's eye sockets—a warning of the fate awaiting those who chose not to surrender. The leaflets were dropped from aircraft and strewn from vehicles. (Abbott Collection.)

An SKS semiautomatic carbine captured by Company C, First Battalion, Twenty-fifth Infantry, Fourth Infantry Division, 17 February 1967 (Operation Sam Houston). (West Point Collection.)

A Marine Corps recoilless rifle team is shown during the battle for Hue, February 1968. The 106mm recoilless rifle was one of the most effective countersniping tools the Marine Corps had at its disposal. The unique weapon was often called on to "vaporize" snipers and fortified sniper positions during the war. (U.S. Marine Corps.)

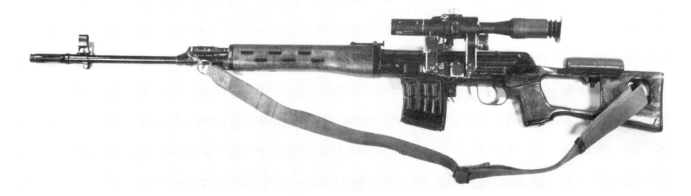

Vietnam-era (1972) Soviet manufacture 7.62 x 54R Dragunov sniper rifle. According to information provided by the U.S-Army Foreign Science and Technology Center, "The Dragunov, also known as the SVD, is a gas-operated, magazine-fed semiautomatic weapon fitted with a 4-power PSO-1 telescopic sight. The Dragunov (SVD) was developed by the Soviet Union as a semi-auto sniper rifle during the mid-1960s and entered Soviet military service in 1967." Intelligence sources list the "maximum range" for the Dragunov as "1300 meters." The SVD is considered effective out to 700-800 meters. There were no special accurizing measures taken with this system. (Landies Collection.)

A close-up view of the Soviet-made (1972) SVD sniper rifle. The PSO-1 optical sight has a six-degree field of view and contains an integral infrared detector and an illuminated range finder reticle. The SVD was employed in daylight for conventional targets or at night against active infrared emitters, such as night driving aids and weapon sights. Even though intelligence reports indicate "a small quantity" were eventually recovered by U.S. and Allied combat units during the later stages of the war, the extent of SVD field use in Southeast Asia by "Soviet advisors," or the NVA, for that matter, remains unconfirmed and subject to speculation. (Landies Collection.)

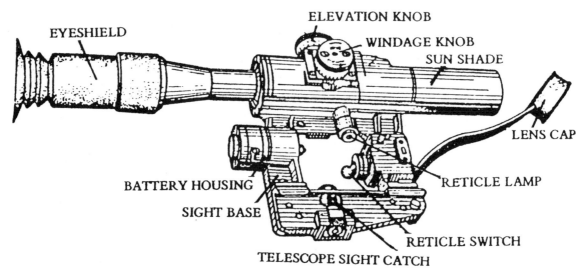

A Vietnam-era (1973) ordnance illustration of the Soviet PSO-1 telescope listing the principal parts of the sight and mount. (U.S. Army.)

A contemporary SVD PSO-1 telescopic sight. The former property of the Iraqi Army, the 4-power scope was "taken" by American combat forces (82d Airborne) in the Kuwait Theater of Operations (KTO) during the Persian Gulf War in 1991. The unique souvenir is in new condition and is shown as it left the optical works in the Soviet Union. Though numbered for an SVD rifle, the scope remained unused. (Peter R. Senich.)

An intelligence photograph of a Dragunov (SVD) sniper rifle dating from the Vietnam War. Although details surrounding the capture of this weapon have not been revealed, the rifle was taken in the final days of U.S. combat involvement in South Vietnam. Even though the U.S. and Allied intelligence community had focused its attention on recovering and evaluating the highly touted Soviet sniper rifle after it was introduced, as it turned out, the SVD was not an especially accurate or impressive weapon design. (Minnery Collection.)

CHAPTER 19

SNIPER AMMUNITION

The Match Cartridge

The use of special match ammunition was long considered an important aspect of rifle competition by the service teams. When the Marine Corps "team rifles" were shipped to South Vietnam for sniper use, National Match rifle ammunition was furnished with this equipment. Though this was viewed as a logical move by the Marine personnel tasked with establishing a sniping program in Vietnam, by so doing the Marine Corps set a precedent that has carried through to this day—the field use of match-grade ammunition for sniping purposes.

Even though military studies as far back as the early 1940s had recommended it, not until the war in Vietnam would match-grade rifle ammunition be introduced for combat purposes.

However indirectly, the Army followed suit, and use of National Match ammunition emerged as a requisite for sniper efficiency in Southeast Asia.

Though originally intended for use in competition, Cartridge, Cal. .30, National Match, M72 and Cartridge, Cal. 7.62mm, National Match, M118 were issued to Army and Marine Corps snipers during the war in Vietnam.

Of all the problems associated with fielding Army and Marine snipers during this hectic era, the combat use of match-grade ammunition appears to have caused the least concern. Judging from the comments of personnel involved with their respective programs, it was always available in sufficient quantities and, while performance was known to vary from one lot to another, overall, the match ammunition furnished by the military was considered more than adequate by all but the most demanding marksmen.

Highly skilled marksmen could usually detect variations in cartridge performance, though it required a considerable amount of shooting experience to do so.

In view of the circumstances and the manner in which a sniper operated, it was of paramount importance that his first shot—and frequently his only shot—find its mark. The use of match ammunition was intended to ensure consistent performance from one cartridge to the next.

For the sake of clarification, apart from the almost infinite cartridge variations and component combinations employed by civilian and military match shooters through the years, there were essentially three types of match-grade rifle ammunition used for competition purposes: the hand-loaded custom cartridges, the arsenal match ammunition, and the commercial match cartridges.

In a quest for optimum accuracy, the service marksmanship training units (MTUs) commonly "rebuilt" match ammunition by literally hand-assembling complete cartridges using commercial components or a mix of arsenal and commercial components. The use of such ammunition was usually limited to competition, testing, and/or "special applications," however.

With few exceptions, the National Match ammunition furnished for sniper use was strictly "off-the-shelf," as manufactured by the government (Frankford Arsenal and Lake City Arsenal).

In the interest of providing the best possible insight on the M72 and M118 National Match rifle ammunition issued for sniping in RVN, a description of the Vietnam-era government match ammunition is presented here. The following information was originally furnished by the U.S. Army Materiel Command, as part of its support for the National Matches held at Camp Perry, Ohio (1966):

CARTRIDGE MODELS

Two cartridge models manufactured especially for use in competitions are available for issue in the 1966 National Rifle Matches. Cartridge, Caliber .30, Match, M72 is for use in the M1 rifle and in bolt-action rifles chambered for it. This round is commercially identified as the .30/06 Cartridge. Caliber 7.62mm, Match, M118 is for use in the M14 rifle and in bolt-action rifles chambered for it. The round is identified commercially as the .308 Winchester.

The M72 cartridge is similar to that manufactured for the National Matches prior to World War II. The most significant change is the cartridge manufactured at the present time contains a noncorrosive styphnate primer (the primer does not leave a residue which causes rust). This reduces the cleaning required to maintain a rust-free bore from that when firing the M1903 rifle in the National Matches prior to World War II.

The M118 cartridge has similar performance characteristics to that of the M72 since it uses the same bullet design and the velocity is only slightly less. However, the case length is about one-half inch shorter. The propellant capacity is reduced, and this requires a different propellant charge from that of the M72 in order to produce a high velocity within a safe pressure level.

The M72 and M118 rounds are designed and manufactured to give better accuracy than other, caliber .30 and 7.62mm military cartridges. The boat-tailed bullet design produces a flatter trajectory and less wind drift. The manufacturing specifications for the match cartridge are significantly more rigid than those for other types of caliber .30 and 7.62mm ball cartridges with respect to accuracy characteristics.

Like other conventional ammunition, the M72 and M118 are composed of a bullet, a case, a primer, and propellant.

The principal components of a rifle cartridge (small-arms ammunition for military weapons) were defined by the Army as follows:

Cartridge. A complete assembly consisting of all the components necessary to fire a weapon once; i.e., the cartridge case, primer, propellant, and bullet.

Cartridge Case. A container designed to hold an ammunition primer and propellant to which a bullet may be affixed. Its profile and size conform to that of the chamber of the weapon in which the cartridge is fired.

Primer. An assembly which ignites the propellant.

Propellant. A low explosive substance of fine granulation which, through burning, produces gases at a controlled rate to provide the energy necessary to propel the bullet.

Bullet. A projectile fired, or intended to be fired, from a small-arms weapon.

According to the U.S. Army Materiel Command, the "testing" of M72 and M118 match ammunition was conducted in the following manner:

During production of the match cartridges the bullets and cartridges are subjected to daily quality control accuracy tests. This firing is conducted on a 600-yard outdoor range. Firing is done with an accuracy test rifle consisting of an M1919A4 machine gun type barrel and an M1903 rifle action. The barrel is secured in a slide which operates in a V block attached to a Frankford Arsenal machine rest. The barrel length for the rifle firing the M72 round is 24 inches and that for the rifle firing the M118 round is 22 inches. The accuracy requirements for both cartridges is similar. The acceptance test requirement is a mean radius of 3.5 inches for nine 10-shot groups from each of three test rifles at a range of 600 yards. The mean radius [MR] represents the average distance of each shot in the group from the group center.

[**NOTE**: Despite indications that U.S. Army Munitions Command (MUCOM) had relaxed or had planned on easing the accuracy requirements for match ammunition at the height of the war in Vietnam, discussion of this point with noted small-arms ammunition authorities William H. Woodin and Frank W. Hackley brought the following response (3 June 1993): "There was no change in match (M72 or M118) accuracy specifications in 1968. In fact, the basic requirement for 3.5 in. MR at 600 yards (550M) still exists today for the M118 Special Ball. It is true that the accuracy of the M118 has slipped somewhat over the years. During the late 1960s and 1970s, the MRs averaged 2.4 inches. During the 1980s and early 1990s, this was increased to about 3.0 inches. There are some reasons for this, which primarily have to do with lack of budget to properly maintain critical operations with bullet manufacture and loading.

In 1981, when the 7.62mm M852 Match Cartridge was adopted, its accuracy requirement was expressed in extreme spread (ES), first 8.5 in. at 550 meters, later increased to 9.5 in. However, this accuracy measurement (extreme spread) does not necessarily reflect a relaxation in performance, but in fact a tighter dispersion requirement, particularly when you consider the spread must not be exceeded for each 10 rd. group. A 9.5 in. ES, computed for each 10 rd. group, could be expected to produce about a 2.0 in. MR. Your composite 270 rd. target for M118 Lot LC 12072 loaded in 1967 is an example, with a MR of 1.7 in. and ES of 10.2 in. This was one of the most accurate machine loaded match lots made at Lake City AAP.

LC and FA were the only Government plants that produced Match Ammo during the Vietnam War. There were also government contracts with commercial producers for match grade cartridges during this period and some of this undoubtedly got to Vietnam for sniper use].

The velocity is calculated at a distance of 78 feet from the muzzle by measuring the time required for the bullet to pass over a known distance. Photoelectric screens are used to detect the passage of the bullet and signals are fed into a chronograph to start and stop the counting mechanism. The photoelectric screens are positioned at distances of 28 feet and 128 feet from the rifle muzzle to give a base distance of 100 feet. The velocity is then calculated from the formula v =100/t.

The maximum chamber pressure is calculated by means of copper crusher cylinders. Sample cylinders are subjected to a static load and their change in length is determined. A tarnage table is developed in this manner. The pressure gage consists of a test barrel with standard chamber and bore dimensions on which a hole is drilled through the chamber wall to accept a steel piston. A yoke permits a crusher cylinder to be positioned between the piston and a threaded anvil so that the cylinder is compressed on firing. The change in length of the cylinder is determined and this measurement is entered on the tarnage table to obtain a corresponding pressure in pounds/square inch. Since the load applied to the cylinder in developing the tarnage table was a static one and that applied when the round was fired was dynamic, this calculated result is not a true pressure reading. However, this system does provide an adequate measure of the safety of the cartridge.

Cartridge samples are further tested in the appropriate National Match rifle to assure proper functioning.

A bullet pull test is conducted to assure that the bullet will remain secure in the case during insertion and removal from the rifle. The requirement is a bullet-pull force of not less than 20 pounds.

[**NOTE:** In a quest for optimum accuracy, the arsenal match bullet was moved ever so slightly in the case to "break the seal" to ensure "better separation of the bullet and case" by many of the shooters for competition purposes.]

The Vietnam-era Department of the Army training circular *TC 23-14, Sniper Training and Employment* (October 1969) and Marine Corps field manual *FMFM 1-3B, SNIPING* (August 1969) both contained information on match, ball, armor-piercing, and tracer ammunition as they pertained to sniper use. The "Ammunition" section in the Marine Corps manual read as follows:

Whenever possible, the sniper will be supplied with match grade ammunition because of its great accuracy and reduced sensitivity to wind deflection. However, match ammunition may not always be available, or the situation may dictate the use of other ammunition. Therefore, the sniper must be familiar with all types. Ammunition he will use is caliber 7.62mm which is 2-13/16 inches long overall. The sniper will find that in ammunition other than match, both accuracy and point of impact varies among lots. He should try to identify an especially accurate lot number and use it exclusively as long as it is available.

Match

Caliber 7.62mm M118 is identified by the word MATCH stamped on the head, the last two digits of the year of manufacture, and arsenal identification letters (e.g., LC identifies Lake City). The M118 has a 173-grain boat-tail bullet, a velocity of 2,550 feet per second, and an accuracy specification of 3.5 inches mean radius at 600 yards.

Ball

Caliber 7.62mm M80 and M80E1. The M80 and M80E1 fire a boat-tail, 147-grain bullet. The head is stamped with date and arsenal identification letters. The M80E1 is the most accurate of the ball ammunition. Both have a velocity of approximately 2,750 fps.

Armor-Piercing

Caliber 7.62mm M61. The head is stamped the same as ball ammunition. Projectile tips are painted black. Velocities are between 2,700 and 2,750 fps.

Tracer

Caliber 7.62mm M62. The head is stamped the same as ball ammunition. Projectile tips are painted red or orange, and the velocity is 2,750 fps. The tracer element burns to a range of 900 meters.

Variance of Ammunition

Many shooters mistakenly believe that any ammunition of a given caliber, when fired from the same rifle, will impact in the same place. Differences in the weights of the projectiles or powder, in the diameters of the bullets, or even similar components manufactured by different arsenals will vary the strike of the bullet even though the rounds are fired through the same barrel. It is essential, therefore, that the sniper establish zeros for the various types of ammunition. The cartridge caliber 7.62mm M118 MATCH is the sniper's standard ammunition and is also the heaviest and slowest ammunition that will be encountered in the field; therefore, it is safe to assume that all other types used in combat will strike higher on the target.

The following explanation of "Ammunition Lots" was included in *TC 23-14*, the Vietnam-era Army sniper manual:

> Ammunition is manufactured in lots. To provide for the most uniform functioning and performance of all, the components in any one lot are manufactured under as nearly identical conditions as practicable. An identifying number is assigned to each lot at the time of manufacture. This lot number can be found on each ammunition case, can, bandoleer, or carton. The ballistic qualities of one lot of ammunition may be consistent and accurate in every respect, whereas the qualities of another lot may be inaccurate and unacceptable for sniping. It is quite possible that each type or lot of ammunition at your disposal may have a different center of impact, necessitating a different zero for each type or lot.
>
> If match grade ammunition is available it should be used.

NOTE: From the very beginning of the USMC sniper program in RVN in 1965, an integral part of sniper training included a relatively brief but thorough presentation on the performance characteristics of match ammunition. Unlike the Army, however, with .30-caliber (.30-06) and 7.62mm sniper rifles in the field, it was necessary for the Marine Corps to furnish both M72 and M118 National Match ammunition during the course of the war. As a matter of interest, even though *FMFM 1-3B, SNIPING* (October 1967) included information on the M72 and M118 match cartridges, with the Remington M700 sniper rifle emerging as the official USMC sniping issue, the ammunition section in the published edition of *FMFM 1-3B, SNIPING* (August 1969) only mentions the M118 match cartridge.

Though rarely noted, 7.62mm National Match rifle ammunition was also employed by many Marine sniper teams with the M14 rifles they used for sniper security.

Without question, the most significant action involving Vietnam-era National Match ammunition came as a result of "accuracy problems" encountered during the later stages of the war.

According to information contained in Project No. 44-69-03, "Marine Corps Sniper Rifle and Associated Equipment; 1972 Annual Report" (16 November 1971–12 December 1972), Marine Corps Development and Education Command:

> The National Match ammunition used by competitive shooters is also the ammunition used in the USMC M40 and U.S. Army sniper rifles. This ammunition's mean muzzle velocity was used when designing the ART sighting system. Recently it was discovered that muzzle variations as great as 100 feet per second had been experienced in a given lot of ammunition tested by the U.S. Army Marksmanship Training Unit at Fort Benning, Georgia. The Marine Corps Marksmanship Training Unit has also experienced serious accuracy problems with certain lots. In both marksmanship training units, it is common to disassemble, check and reload each round prior to use in competitive shooting. This creates a serious problem for a sniper since his sights are mated to National Match Ammunition as issued. To investigate the extent of the problem, the following action has been initiated or is being taken:
>
> (1) Frankford Arsenal is conducting a 7.62mm National Match Ammunition study to determine causes of inaccuracies. Completion date of the study is expected to be February 1973.
>
> (2) Headquarters, Marine Corps (Code CSX-3) is identifying National Match Ammunition in Marine Corps stocks by lot number.
>
> (3) Lake City Arsenal, the manufacturer, is being contacted by the U.S. Army Munitions Command (MUCOM) for possible retest of samples from each lot.
>
> (4) U.S. Army Munitions Command representatives have tentatively agreed to an Ammunition Accuracy Symposium to discuss 7.62mm National Match Ammunition accuracy requirements. U.S. Marine Corps and U.S. Army representatives involved in competitive shooting and combat sniping, plus manufacturer, quality control and ammunition management personnel are expected to attend.

The Sniper Weapons/National Match Ammunition Symposium was held at Quantico, Virginia, on 14 February 1973.

NOTE: This was the second Vietnam-era "symposium" hosted by the Marine Corps. The first (Sniper Rifle Symposium) was conducted in December 1969 when problems with the M700/Redfield system prompted the Marine Corps to determine exactly what its options were.

The Marine Corps "position" was stated as follows:

We realize that there is an immediate need for a better sniper rifle system for use in RVN. Thus, we want to find out what is currently available as far as sniper rifles and sights, both day and night, make a decision on a system, and get it out to the field ASAP.

We want to draft a realistic – state of the art requirement (SOR) [Specific Operational Requirement] for a sniper rifle and sight. I might add that we are always interested in a JSOR [Joint Specific Operational Requirement] with other services.

We then want to develop a sniper rifle and sight that will fulfill our SOR. We will call this the optimum sniper rifle.

Now we are getting down to the purpose of this symposium. We in the Marine Corps want to hear from you gentlemen. We are after input to find out what weapons are currently available. What these weapons' capabilities are, what their production cost may be and the same for sights of course, to again include both day and night. Further, we are interested in hearing your expertise on what weapon and sight approach you feel will give us this optimum sniper rifle. Do we have the optimum rifle now? Would a product improved version of what is currently available be the optimum sniper rifle? In other words we are after weapon characteristics, range requirements, first round hit probabilities at what range, and data of this nature to feed into an SOR. Thus, we feel that this symposium will be an excellent starting point to further educate us and guide us in the right direction.

The 1969 symposium was attended by a unique mix of Army, Marine Corps, and civilian ordnance figures.

The "Summary" from the Marine Corps Development and Education Command (6 April 1973) had this to say about the Sniper Weapons/National Match Ammunition Symposium:

> The purpose of the Symposium was to gather experts from military and governmental agencies who are interested in, or could contribute to, the development of marksmanship and Sniper Weapons Systems. The agenda was organized to provide a discussion of problems encountered with marksmanship/sniper ammunition and to provide insight into developments in ammunition, weaponry, sighting systems and laser range finders which could have possible sniper application. . . .

In effect, the "Symposium" amounted to a one-day World Series of military sniping as then practiced and contemplated by the U.S. Army and Marine Corps. The "Roster" (list of attendees) was a veritable who's who of prominent civilian and military ordnance figures of the day.

The "Problems/Recommendations" concerning "National Match/Sniper Ammunition" were addressed by the U.S. Army Marksmanship Training Unit, the U.S. Marine Corps Marksmanship Training Unit, and U.S. Army Munitions Command. Their respective positions were recorded as follows:

> Problems/Recommendations Concerning National Match/Sniper Ammunition (Lt. Col. C.E. Orr, U.S. Army Marksmanship Training Unit).
>
> My discussion will primarily be limited to the ammunition we have available for the Sniper Weapons and for the marksmanship program. Our shooters are consistently out-shooting our ammunition and weapons which are available for competitive marksmanship and sniper work. In the Army Marksmanship Training Unit we maintain and condition weapons, do a R&D effort and innovate in an attempt to field a weapon or ammunition which will outperform the shooter. Whether it be for the Olympics, National Matches or for

a sniper, we have not reached the point where we can produce a weapon which can out-perform the shooter.

One place we think a big improvement can be made is in the bullet for the M118 National Match Cartridge. Captain Faught and I discussed some of the problems that will occur if we try to engage targets out to 1200 meters [1300 yards ±] — I feel that the M21 system is capable of that, with the exception of the Sighting System's range estimation device and the ammunition. If we could accurately determine ranges and could hand load our ammunition we could reach 1200 meters effective range.

What we do in hand loading is change bullets. We have found that we can just about cut our group sizes in half by removing the bullet and replacing it with a Sierra Match bullet. I tested 100 rounds from Lake City Lot #20-7. The bullets were removed and concentricity tested by use of a dial indicator. There was an average of seventeen ten-thousandths difference between bullets. The diameter difference was nine ten-thousandths and weight difference was eight tenths of a grain.

In comparison, the Sierra bullets tested at the same time were four ten-thousandths different in concentricity; five ten-thousandths in diameter and about eight tenths in grain weight.

In shooting standard Lake City Lot #20-7 ammunition at 300 meters from a test cradle we achieved an average extreme vertical spread of 4.5 inches. By replacing the bullet we reduced the extreme vertical spread to 2.3 inches. As far as we are concerned the problem has been isolated to the bullet. In some Lake City lots we shot better; in some, worse. We suspect the problem lies in poor quality control during bullet manufacturing. Possibly a bad bullet swaging die.

The Army MTU also maintains the M21 Sniper Rifle and the only known sniper training program in the Army. We are the base from which a larger sniper program could expand.

Responding to a question from the audience concerning cartridge performance, Colonel Orr replied as follows:

> We have found no great difference in muzzle velocity from lot to lot. However, we have found differences in velocity between rounds in a given lot. We feel that the bullet is the cause of these variations. Diameter of the bullet affects the velocity. Our concern in marksmanship and sniping is not the mean or average variation; it is the extreme variation. If nineteen bullets go through the same hole but one is out of the circle, the mean radius is good but the competitor may have lost the match or the sniper may have failed to make a 900 meter kill.

> Problems/Recommendations Concerning National Match/Sniper Ammunition (CW03 Bartlett, U.S. Marine Corps Marksmanship Training Unit).

> Accuracy produced by the National Match, M118 Cartridge will not meet the requirements of the military competitive shooter or the combat sniper. This has caused extensive testing and reloading of national match ammunition prior to its use in competitive shooting. It is common for projectiles to be removed and discarded with commercially procured projectiles used in their place. For 600 yards and shorter ranges the Sierra "International," 168 grain hollow point bullet is used. For 1000 yard shooting the Sierra "Match King," 180 grain solid point bullet is used. This interchange is expensive, though feasible, for competitive shooting but is highly impractical for combat sniping.

Prior to use the Marksmanship Training Unit tests National Match Ammunition for:

a. Powder charge variation
b. Bullet weight variation
c. Bullet diameter and concentricity
d. Velocity variation
e. Extreme variation of shots in group
f. Group diameter at 600 and 1000 yards

If suitable performance is not obtained then disassembly, reloading, and retesting is necessary. For longer ranges (600 yards plus), the National Match Cartridge normally requires reloading to a heavier projectile to achieve increased accuracy through achieving higher remaining velocities at 1000 yards (thereby reducing yaw caused by velocity drop).

Another problem encountered is the variation in bullet release pressures when disassembling the National Match Cartridge for inspection or reload. The asphalt sealer used for waterproofing causes release of the bullet from the case at varying pressures. It is not known how this affects the bullet when fired, i.e., chamber pressure, muzzle velocity, etc. (It is recognized that waterproofing is necessary for military sniper ammunition, therefore some type of sealer must be used. The effect of asphalt sealer on bullet performance, however, is a matter of concern.)

The degree of boat tail on the bullet may affect long range performance. However, it appears that the 9-degree boat tail on the standard M118 National Match bullets will suffice for long range shooting since the 180 grain Sierra "Match King" bullet used for 1000 yards competitive shooting also has a 9-degree boat tail.

NOTE: As an aside, CW03 Bartlett was also involved with comparative testing (1971–1973) of the USMC M40 and the Army M21, the USMC/Redfield sight, the Realist Adjustable Ranging Telescope, and the Redfield AR TEL sighting system fielded with the M21. The test results helped the Development Center (MCDEC) with the decision not to replace the M40 with the M21 sniper rifle. The Quantico-based USMC personnel taking part in the "Symposium" were R.J. Faught, G.R. Hammond, E.J. Land, V.N. Behrens, J.A. Getchell, D.J. Willis, W.K. Rockey, and D.A. Ramsey.

Discussion of Problems/Recommendations Concerning National Match/ Sniper Ammunition (Mr. J.D. Henze, U.S. Army Munitions Command).

To improve the quality of National Match ammunition will require a cost increase. A justification for the cost increase will be required. A required Operational Capability statement will suffice from the Army. If the Marine Corps will specify the requirements in a MIPR and be willing to pay the increased cost a better round can be provided.

Problems discussed by MTUs are all state-of-the-art improvements but will require justification prior to action being initiated.

The bullet concentricity problem is for the most part a new one and will be explored. The problem should be able to be corrected on an automated basis without too much cost but Munitions Command will need a requirement stating what accuracy needs to be achieved.

U.S. Army Munitions Command and Frankford Arsenal engineers have discussed the problem of present acceptance standards for match ammunition. It is agreed that we will attempt to change the acceptance measure to extreme variability rather than average variability as done at present. To do this will cost extra money since there will be a rejection of ammunition which will have to be used for some other application. However, since the MTUs are presently reloading with different bullets to achieve the desired accuracy the added cost during initial production appears to be justified. The money now spent on reloading operations can be better spent during initial production.

If one round is to be used for sniper operations and another round for competitive shooting the problems are different. If one round is to be used for both, then make it match ammunition. The match/sniper ammunition combination will be a large program and will be more costly but will eliminate the problem of having to change bullets for competitive shooting and will serve the purpose of the sniper equally as well. This is a problem that the Marine Corps and the Army must address prior to coming to MUCOM for assistance.

The "Conclusions" drawn from the Sniper Weapons/National Match Ammunition Symposium were presented in the summary dated 6 April 1973:

A Sniper capability will be retained by the U.S. Marine Corps and the U.S. Army.

The National Match Cartridge should be capable of producing 1.5 minutes of angle accuracy at 600 and 1000 yards. This is equal to a 9-inch extreme spread at 600 yards and 15 inch extreme spread at 1000 yards. The present National Match M118 Cartridge will not provide the required accuracy without improvement in manufacturing and acceptance standards. The present per round cost for National Match M118 Ammunition is $.08 which is equal to M80 Ball used in the M14 Rifle and less than M80 Ball linked with tracer used in the M60 Machine Gun. To achieve the required accuracy for competitive and sniper shooting is an essential requirement which justifies a per round cost increase above the present $.08 round.

Product improvement of the M21 Sniper Rifle is not planned but is feasible.

Product improvement of the M40 Sniper Rifle is in progress, with rebuild of the rifle imminent (further evaluation of sighting systems will be conducted prior to replacement of the present telescopic sight being accomplished).

Even though a great deal of time would pass before measures to correct the problems with arsenal match ammunition were finally taken, from a historical standpoint, the Army and Marine Corps assessment of the M118 match cartridge, the principal ammunition employed for sniping during the war in Vietnam, and their recommendations for its improvement are noteworthy.

The 1966 edition of the U.S. Army Materiel Command brochure describing the weapons and ammunition "to be used in this year's competition." The U.S. Army's Materiel Command, Weapons Command, and Munitions Command provided ordnance support for the National Matches with materiel and trained personnel. The brochure provided detailed information on the M72 and M118 match ammunition and the M14 and M1 National Match Rifles. (U.S. Army.)

Standard small-arms ammunition has the manufacturer's initials and year of manufacture stamped in the metal in the head of the cartridge case (headstamp); the year is denoted by two figures. Match ammunition has the word "MATCH" stamped on the head as well. In this case, the M72 .30-caliber match cartridge was made at the Lake City Army Ammunition Plant (LC) in 1967 (67). (Peter R. Senich.)

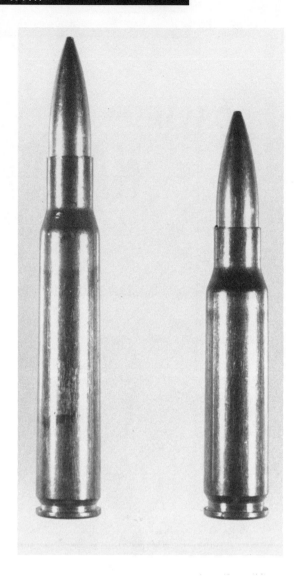

A comparative view of an M72 (left) and an M118 match cartridge dating from the conflict in Vietnam. Even though the Marine Corps and Army MTUs were well aware of the advantages offered by "hand-loaded" rifle ammunition, the exigencies of war necessitated the use of arsenal-produced match ammunition in Vietnam. Without the benefit of a second shot in many cases, it was of paramount importance for a sniper to know exactly what he could expect with his first shot. The use of match ammunition was intended to ensure consistent performance from one cartridge to the next. (Peter R. Senich.)

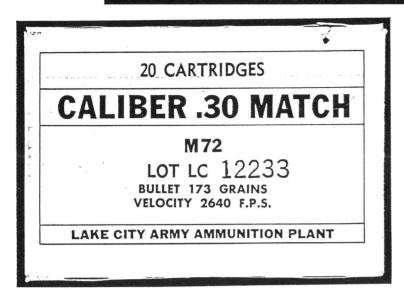

A typical box (20 cartridges) of CALIBER .30 MATCH cartridges (M72) manufactured during the Vietnam War (1967). The .025-inch-thick white cardboard box is 5 inches long, 3.50 inches high, and 1.060 inches wide. The printing is red and blue. (Peter R. Senich.)

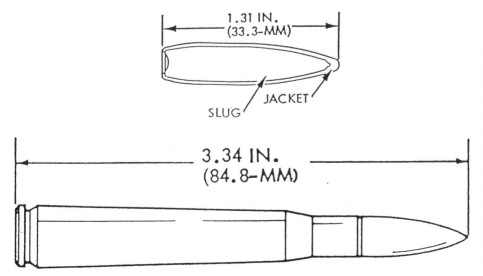

An ordnance illustration of the .30-caliber (.30-06) M72 match cartridge showing the principal dimensions. Though originally intended for use with match rifles in competition, the special cartridges were used against a wide range of targets in Southeast Asia. Of all the problems associated with fielding Army and Marine snipers during this hectic era, the combat use of match grade ammunition appears to have caused the least concern. (U.S. Army.)

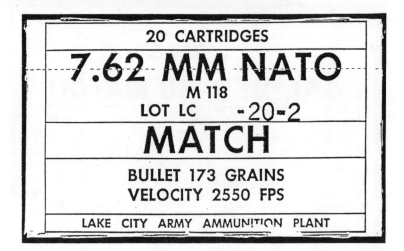

A typical box of 7.62mm match cartridges (M118) dating from the Vietnam War (1970). Except for the markings and the box dimensions, the 20-round M72 and M118 cardboard containers were essentially the same. Although Frankford Arsenal and Lake City were the principal source of match ammunition fielded by Army and Marine Corps snipers in Southeast Asia, according to cartridge authorities William H. Woodin and Frank W. Hackley, "There were also government contracts with commercial producers for match-grade cartridges during this period, and some of this undoubtedly got to Vietnam for sniper use." (Peter R. Senich.)

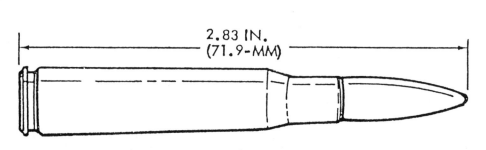

Ordnance illustration of the 7.62mm (.308) M118 match cartridges showing the principal dimensions. The bullets for both the M72 and M118 cartridges made use of a gilding metal jacket and a lead core. Compare the M72 and M118 cartridge and bullet dimensions. (U.S. Army.)

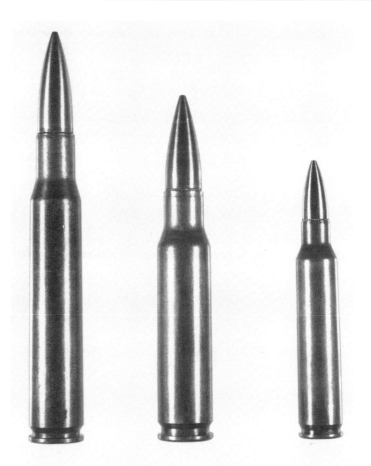

Left: A comparison of .30-caliber (7.62 x 63mm), .308-caliber (7.62 x 51mm), and .223 caliber (5.56 x 45mm) military small-arms ammunition (standard ball centerfire rifle cartridges) intended for use against enemy personnel and unarmored targets. (Peter R. Senich.)

Below: A Vietnam-era ordnance illustration of typical packing containers for small-arms ammunition. In this case, M72 .30-caliber match ammunition produced at Frankford Arsenal (FA) is packed in metal boxes (ammo cans) having hinged covers sealed by means of a rubber gasket. The containers are overpacked in wire-bound wooden boxes. Each outer shipping container and all inner containers down to the smallest unit container were marked to identify the ammunition. (U.S. Army.)

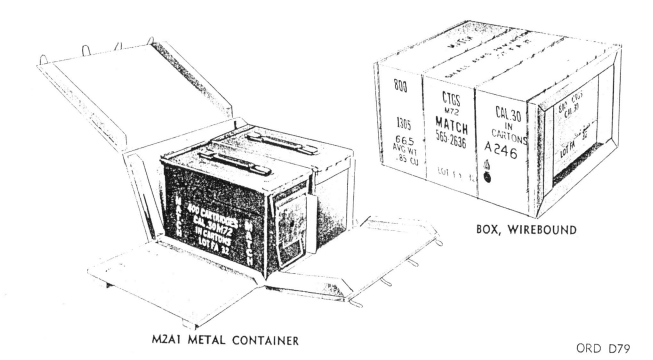

M2A1 METAL CONTAINER

BOX, WIREBOUND

ORD D79

| 20 CARTRIDGES |
| **7.62 MM MATCH** |
| XM 118 |
| LOT LC 12032 |
| **MATCH** |
| **BULLET 173 GRAINS** |
| **VELOCITY 2550 FPS** |
| **LAKE CITY ARMY AMMUNITION PLANT** |

Lake City 7.62mm XM118 match cartridges (Lot 12032 circa 1964), originally packed and shipped in the "ammo can" pictured below. (Lau Collection.)

460 CARTRIDGES
7.62MM, MATCH, XM 118
CARTONS
1964
LOT LC 12032

An example of a metal ammunition container (ammo can) used to provide protection during shipment and storage. The ammunition was packed to withstand conditions ordinarily encountered in the field. Metal boxes and cans were painted olive drab and marked in yellow. The container held XM118 7.62mm match cartridges produced at Lake City in 1964 (Lot 12032). XM118 match ammunition was standardized as M118 in 1965. ("XM" followed by an Arabic numeral was used to identify an item during its development. Upon the item's acceptance as an adopted type, the letter "X" was dropped, leaving the letter "M" followed by an Arabic numeral. The practice was not limited to ammunition.) (Lau Collection.)

CHAPTER 20

MILITARY MATCH CARTRIDGES

Adding to our perspective on the special rifle ammunition fielded in Vietnam, match cartridge authority Michael R. Lau prepared the information below for inclusion in this book.

Drawing from a wide range of documented sources, Lau describes the origins of the .30-caliber M72 and 7.62mm M118 match ammunition employed by Army and Marine Corps snipers during the war in Vietnam as follows:

> Competition shooters in the service did not have good military match grade ammunition available to them for the National or Interservice Matches in the early and mid-1950s. The National High Power Rifle Championships for 1951 were held at Camp Matthews, California, and the 1952 Matches were held at Fort Benning, Georgia. From 1953 on, the National High Power Rifle Matches were once again held at Camp Perry, Ohio. Up until 1957, except for small lots of International Match ammunition loaded in caliber .30, most competitors relied on service ball or commercial match ammunition.

In 1957 both Frankford Arsenal (Philadelphia, PA) and Lake City Arsenal (Independence, MO) began production of ammunition for the National Matches. Frankford Arsenal had produced match ammunition prior to World War II, but Lake City had not, the latter starting up during the war.

The new match cartridge (Cartridge, Caliber .30, Match, T291) was basically the M1 cartridge with the 173-grain bullet loaded to 2,640 feet-per-second (fps). The 1957 Camp Perry lot was packed in clips and boxes. The more accurate sublots were packed in the boxes and gave a MR (mean radius) of 2.6 inches, while the clipped ammo gave a 2.8 inch MR at 600 yards. This was manufactured by Frankford Arsenal.

The major change in the T291 match cartridge ["T" followed by an Arabic numeral was used to identify development type items prior to 1959] was the use of the new FA36 noncorrosive primer. Daily routine production tests at Frankford Arsenal noted a substantial improvement in velocity uniformity. The spread in velocity was decreased by 20 percent and the group size at 600 yards reduced by 10 percent. A second change in the new cartridge was made in the manner of case mouth waterproofing. This reduced the bullet pull by half with variations in pull from 5 to 10 pounds.

A total of 3,580,000 T291 cartridges were produced at Lake City Arsenal in 1957 [Lake City Arsenal, or Ordnance Plant, was later known as the Lake City Army Ammunition Plant].

On 9 January 1958, the T291 was standardized as the Cartridge, Caliber .30, Match, M72. To provide the best practical uniformity in accuracy, bullet lots of 8,000 each were grouped into three levels of accuracy and then used to create three lots of finished ammunition. Frankford Arsenal Lot 41B was set aside for the Small Arms Firing School and had a MR at 600 yards of 2.83 inches. Lot 41C was packed in clips for short range rapid fire and the Infantry Match and gave a MR of 2.78 inches at 600 yards. Lot 41A, for 600 yard and longer ranges, had an MR of 2.6 inches. At 1,000 yards the MR was 5.7 inches with an extreme vertical dispersion of 20.8 inches. Sight settings were also different than the M2 Ball and shooters had to adjust accordingly.

From then on, caliber .30 M72 match ammunition was fairly standardized with only minor changes through the following years.

In 1962 Frankford Arsenal's small-arms ammunition production was so reduced that it could no longer support the call for M72 National Match ammunition. As a result, all M72 ammunition requirements were shifted to Lake City AAP. Lake City tooling was all brand new and their ammunition over the next several years had superb 600 yard mean radius figures.

The development of 7.62mm match ammunition came about with the adoption of the M14 rifle. This established a requirement for 7.62mm match cartridges in order for the service rifle and free rifles to be used in the National and International Matches by competitors from the United States.

Prior to the 1956 Olympics, Frankford Arsenal was asked to develop 7.62mm ammunition to be fired in free rifles for the 300 meter Olympic match. The Arsenal had experience in producing limited quantities of .30 caliber match ammunition in 1953 and 1954 for International Match use, but most of the employees were only knowledgeable in producing cartridges used for war. The experienced, older employees, with the necessary expertise and knowledge of former production techniques, had retired following World War II. Because of these circumstances, it was decided to rely on components that were known best. The new 7.62mm match ammunition was designated T275. The primer was the standard FA26 with the corrosive chlorate composition (FA70), the powder was IMR 4895, and the bullet was the 172-grain, M1 .30 caliber type. Two lots were produced, one was loaded to approximately 2260 fps and the other to 2440 fps. Both were reportedly very accurate and were used in the 300 meter free rifle event of the 16th Olympiad held in Melbourne, Australia in 1956.

Several changes were made to the 7.62mm International Match ammunition at Frankford Arsenal, including changes in velocity and the use of the FA36 primer. The cartridge was designated T274E4 in final form; this ammunition was not produced after 1958.

In 1963 a new 7.62mm match cartridge, which was still under development, was designated XM118 and supplied to the National Matches that year. Frankford Arsenal produced several lots.

The developmental XM118 match ammunition was standardized in 1965 as Cartridge, Caliber 7.62mm, Match, M118. Frankford Arsenal stopped manufacturing 7.62mm match ammunition after 1965. Lake City Army Ammunition Plant continued to produce M118 match ammunition throughout the war in Vietnam.

As a matter of interest, due to the increased use of 7.62mm match ammunition, there was an excess supply of .30 caliber M72 National Match ammunition from the 1966 matches. As a result, no M72 cartridges were produced for the 1967 National Matches. However, some 1967 M72 lots were produced later; M72 was also manufactured in 1968.

In addition to defining the origins of M72 and M118 match ammunition, Lau also provided the following overview of the commercial and "White Box" match ammunition employed by civilian and military match shooters in the years preceding the Vietnam War:

In the 1950s and early 1960s there was no military match rifle ammunition available until the .30-caliber T291, 7.62mm XM118 and "White Box" ammunition was introduced. Standard service ball ammunition was used but it was not up to match standards. Commercial manufacturers were producing match cartridges for civilian shooters and some of this was also used by the military. The ammunition was of high quality, and while it was considered expensive, it more than served the purpose. The marksmanship training units (MTUs) made use of various commercially manufactured rifles chambered for the .300 magnum cartridges. The nonstandard calibers were employed for long range shooting in competition. International Matches called for reduced loadings in caliber .30 and 7.62mm for shooting at 300 meters and "hotter" than standard loadings for 1,000 yard Palma Matches using heavy bullets.

One of the most notable match ammunition developments from this period (1958–1962) was known as "White Box" ammunition [so-called because the labels were typed or printed on white boxes, unlike regular commercial ammo]. Different match loads for .30 caliber/.30-06, 7.62mm/.308, and .300 Magnum were developed by the Army Advanced Marksmanship Training Unit (AMTU). The loadings were then produced in quantity by commercial firms on a contract basis. The Army was also looking at improving the .300 H&H Magnum cartridge for long range competition and developed their own oversize capacity magnum round called the .300 AMU. The special Army cartridge emerged at a time when the "belted magnums" were gaining in popularity.

The .30-06 and .308 "White Box" ammunition and the magnum cases were made by Remington and Winchester. The .300 AMU cartridge was eventually dropped when Army shooters began using the 30/338 Magnum round.

Even though some of the White Box ammunition, especially the .30-caliber cartridges, are believed to have reached Vietnam during the early stages of the conflict, the extent of their use remains unconfirmed at present.

As for the Magnum cartridges, in view of the fact that many "unauthorized weapons" were fielded in RVN, the reported combat use of .30-caliber or larger magnum target and sporting rifles "for extra-long-range hunting" is entirely possible. It should be emphasized, however, that the use of such weapons would have been extremely limited at best.

The 7.62mm M118 Special Ball and the M852 Match cartridges currently in use by the military evolved as a direct result of several factors, including the gradual decline in match cartridge quality during the 1970s.

The origins of the 7.62mm contemporary match ammunition are described by Lau as follows:

> In 1980, the Director of Civilian Marksmanship (DCM) and the National Board for the Promotion of Rifle Practice (NBPRP) induced the Army's Armament Research and Development Command (ARRADCOM) and Lake City Army Ammunition Plant to produce a special lot of 7.62mm match ammunition.
>
> The 200,000 round lot of 7.62mm LC 80 SPECIAL MATCH ammunition was made from specially selected components and loaded on the best machines by the most experienced personnel available at the plant. The bullet chosen was the Sierra 168 grain International Hollow Point Boat Tail. Quality control and uniformity was carefully maintained during assembly of the match ammo. The headstamp for these cartridges was "LC 80 SP," and a light cannelure [knurl] was engraved around the case body about 1/2 inch up from the base. Cartridges were packed in M118 boxes that were over-labeled and marked "SPECIAL MATCH CARTRIDGES." The label also read "NOT FOR COMBAT USE" because of the hollow point bullets.
>
> The new ammunition shot well, and competitive rifle shooters found their scores improved during the National Matches in 1980 and 1981. Winning scores were about 15 percent higher than they were in 1979 when the regular M118 cartridge was used last.
>
> Even though the M852 match cartridge makes use of an "open-tip" bullet, this ammunition was employed by U.S. military snipers in the Kuwait Theater of Operations (KTO) during the Persian Gulf War in 1991. Unlike the conventional hollow point bullets intended for hunting purposes the 168 grain Sierra projectile is not considered to be an expanding bullet.
>
> Although 7.62mm M118 ammunition is still available for "special purposes," it is not considered as accurate as the M852 cartridge. The M118 cartridge boxes were over-labeled 7.62mm NATO SPECIAL BALL after the M852 ammunition was introduced. Both M852 and M118 7.62mm cartridges are currently packaged in brown cardboard boxes.

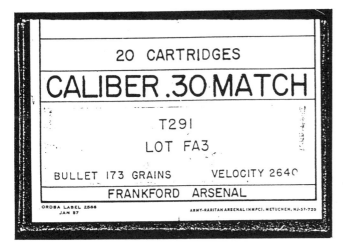

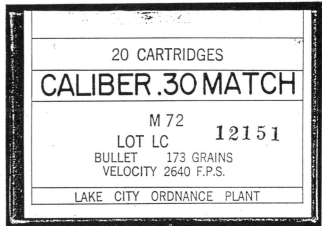

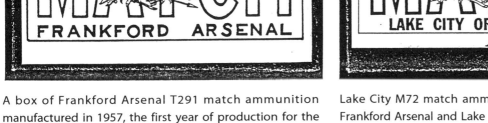

A box of Frankford Arsenal T291 match ammunition manufactured in 1957, the first year of production for the .30-caliber (.30-06) match cartridge. (Lau Collection.)

Lake City M72 match ammunition circa 1962. Although Frankford Arsenal and Lake City both produced .30-caliber match cartridges (T291) beginning in 1957, all M72 ammunition requirements were shifted to Lake City in 1962. (Lau Collection.)

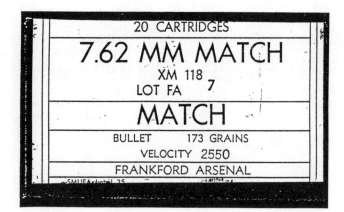

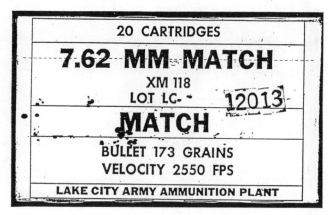

Frankford Arsenal 7.62mm match cartridges produced in 1963, the first year of production for the XM118 National Match round. (Lau Collection.)

Lake City Army Ammunition Plant XM118 7.62mm match ammunition dating from 1963. (Lau Collection.)

1962 NATIONAL RIFLE AND PISTOL MATCHES, CAMP PERRY, OHIO

1964 NATIONAL RIFLE AND PISTOL MATCHES CAMP PERRY, OHIO

Examples of the "Camp Perry" markings found on some of the 20-round match cartridge boxes dating from the 1960s. In this case, the legend appeared on boxes of M72 (1962) and XM118 (1964) Lake City match ammunition. (Lau Collection.

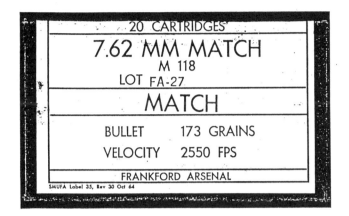

Frankford Arsenal M118 match ammunition circa 1965, the same year the XM118 cartridge was standardized (M118) and also the last year the 7.62mm match round was produced at this facility. (Lau Collection.)

Typical .30-caliber commercial match ammunition made by Winchester-Western during the 1960s. (Lau Collection.)

**20
WESTERN**

**308 WINCHESTER
MATCH**

168 GR. O.P.E. BOATTAIL
HAND LOADED CARTRIDGES

WINCHESTER-WESTERN DIVISION
OLIN MATHIESON CHEMICAL CORPORATION
EAST ALTON, ILLINOIS, U.S.A.

An example of "White Box" match ammunition produced during the late 1950s/early 1960s—in this case, 7.62mm (.308) cartridges made by Winchester-Western. (Lau Collection.)

20 CENTER FIRE CARTRIDGES

CALIBER 7.62mm NATO

168 GRAIN H. P. MATCH

RA-5001

REMINGTON ARMS COMPANY, INCORPORATED

BRIDGEPORT, CONNECTICUT

MADE IN THE UNITED STATES OF AMERICA

Remington manufacture 7.62mm "White Box" match ammunition. (Lau Collection.)

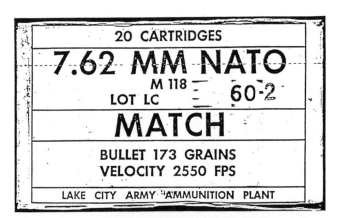

Standard 7.62mm match ammunition produced at the Lake City Army Ammunition Plant in 1977. (Lau Collection.)

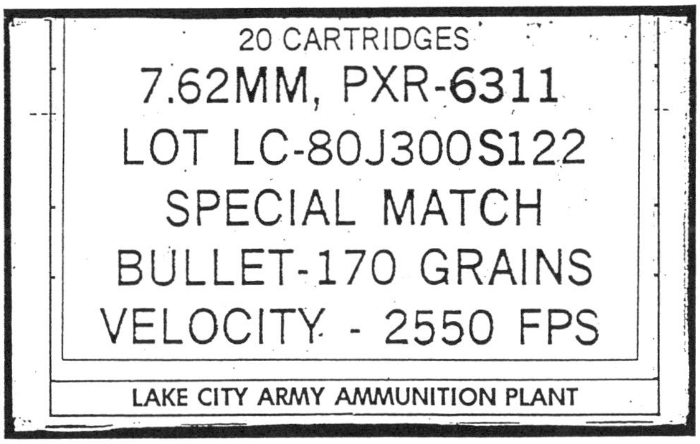

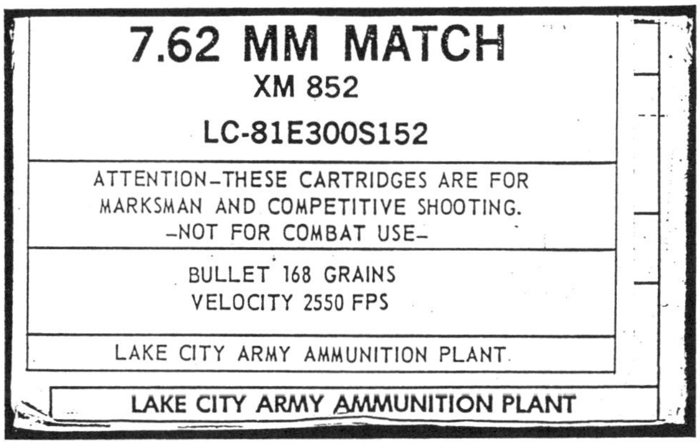

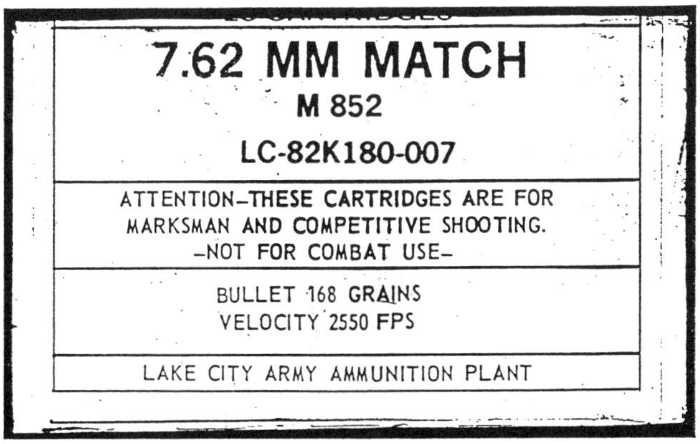

20 CARTRIDGES
7.62MM, PXR-6311
LOT LC-80J300S122
SPECIAL MATCH
BULLET-170 GRAINS
VELOCITY - 2550 FPS

LAKE CITY ARMY AMMUNITION PLANT

7.62 MM MATCH
XM 852

LC-81E300S152

ATTENTION—THESE CARTRIDGES ARE FOR
MARKSMAN AND COMPETITIVE SHOOTING.
—NOT FOR COMBAT USE—

BULLET 168 GRAINS
VELOCITY 2550 FPS

LAKE CITY ARMY AMMUNITION PLANT

LAKE CITY ARMY AMMUNITION PLANT

7.62 MM MATCH
M 852

LC-82K180-007

ATTENTION—THESE CARTRIDGES ARE FOR
MARKSMAN AND COMPETITIVE SHOOTING.
—NOT FOR COMBAT USE—

BULLET 168 GRAINS
VELOCITY 2550 FPS

LAKE CITY ARMY AMMUNITION PLANT

Top: Lake City 7.62mm "LC 80 SPECIAL MATCH" ammunition introduced in 1980. Center: Lake City XM852 7.62mm match cartridges circa 1981. Bottom: Lake City M852 match ammunition (1982). In addition to problems with the MarCor sniper rifle, there was also a gradual decline in the quality and performance of the match cartridges used for sniping. The ammo shown is the result of the measures taken to turn the situation around. This took place at about the same time the Marine Corps made the transition from the Vietnam-era M40 to the contemporary M40A1 sniper rifle. (Lau Collection.)

Lake City 7.62mm M118 Special Ball (1987). (Lau Collection.)

M852 match cartridges (Lake City) manufactured in 1991. (Lau Collection.)

Below: A 1981 ordnance illustration of the "Cartridge, 7.62mm, MATCH, M852" developed for "greater accuracy" following the war in Vietnam. The M852 cartridge was assigned an "XM" number in June 1980; it was standardized in September 1981. Army documents specifically noted: "This cartridge is intended for use in weapons designated as competitive rifles and also for Marksmanship Training. This cartridge is not for combat use." However, despite the use of an open-tip bullet, its construction did not conflict with any treaties or rules of warfare, and the cartridge was eventually cleared for combat use. Note the knurl near the base of the cartridge case. (U.S. Army.)

20 CARTRIDGES
7.62 MM NATO SPECIAL BALL M118
LC-87D 136-025
LAKE CITY ARMY AMMUNITION PLANT

20 CRTG. 7.62 MM
MATCH M852
NOT FOR COMBAT USE
LC-91A185 005

CARTRIDGE, 7.62MM: MATCH, M852

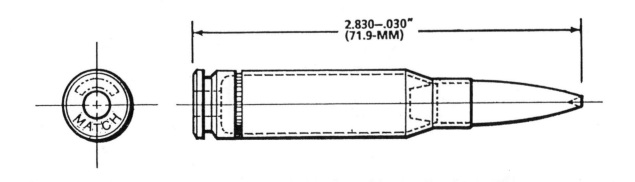

2.830—.030" (71.9-MM)

MATCH

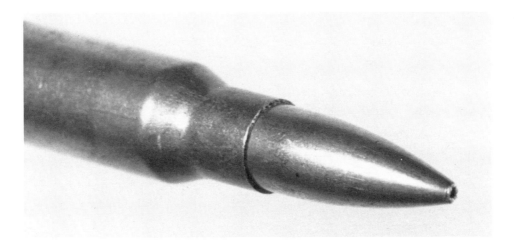

Above: A close-up view of the M852 National Match cartridge open-tip bullet. As the "Special Operations Sniper Training and Employment" manual defines the Sierra bullet, "The M852 bullet is boat-tailed, 168 grains in weight, and has an open-tip. The open-tip is a shallow aperture (about the diameter of the wire in a standard-sized straight pin or paper clip) in the nose of the bullet." At this juncture, the Sierra bullet is still used in the manufacture of the M852 cartridge. (Peter R. Senich.)

Left: A 7.62mm M852 match cartridge manufactured at Lake City Army Ammunition Plant in 1991. According to information contained in "Special Operations Sniper Training and Employment," a publication of the U.S. Army John F. Kennedy Special Warfare Center and School, Fort Bragg, North Carolina: "As of October 1990 the Department of State, Army General Counsel, and the Offices of the Judge Advocate General concluded that the use of open-tip ammunition does not violate the laws-of-war obligation of the United States. This ammunition may be employed in peacetime or in wartime missions of the Army, Navy, and Marine Corps." (Peter R. Senich.)

CHAPTER 21

SNIPER PLATOON ARMORER

Rifle Team Equipment Repairman (MOS 2112) Sgt. William E. Donovan arrived in the Republic of Vietnam on 20 December 1966, where he was assigned to Headquarters Company, Ninth Marine Regiment, Third Marine Division as the Sniper Platoon armorer. At this point, the Ninth Marines were deployed in Quang Nam Province, south and west of Da Nang.

Even though the regiment would move north to Dong Ha by summer, in addition to supporting his own unit in his capacity as a Marine gunsmith, Bill Donovan was also involved with the First Marine Division snipers at Hill 55 south of Da Nang in early 1967. Marine armorers serving in Vietnam, especially the RTE personnel, were often called on to provide support to units other than their own.

In one case, while performing a "service check" on the Winchester rifle Carlos Hathcock was using at the time, Donovan recalled, "The Model 70 was a sporter-barrel type with a five-digit serial number. The barrel was eroded to the extent that the first shot was likely to be the most accurate. From what I understood, however, Hathcock rarely needed more than one round. The Model 70 was probably a Special Services hunting rifle at one time. I had seen others like it back in the States."

It was also during this time that the first shipment of Model 700

Remington sniper rifles arrived (February 1967). According to Donovan, "When we opened the fiberglass cases, each rifle had the free-floating barrel lying against one side of the barrel channel. Packed as they were with the bolt in place, the side pressure had caused the stocks to warp while they were still in the cases. And, if that wasn't insult enough," he added, "the rifles had a combat hold placed on them because the M118 match ammo had not reached us yet."

As then followed, according to Donovan, remedial measures intended to put the rifles in the field as soon as possible included "cleaning out the barrel channels with a wood rasp modified for this purpose" and locating "3 cases" of a contract lot of Canadian-made 7.62mm rifle ammunition that approached "match quality."

It is interesting to note that, in addition to "rectifying the situation" by ordering several pints of a stock sealing agent and glass-bedding kits directly from the manufacturers, in the days that followed, Donovan directed "letters" to Headquarters, U.S. Marine Corps and the Redfield Gun Sight Co. regarding problems with the rifle and the telescopic sight.

Judging from the response by William K. Hayden, assistant head, Marksmanship Branch (Code A03M), Donovan's letters and recommendations were among the first to address the problems with the Remington-Redfield system in Vietnam.

The following article on Sergeant Donovan appeared in *SEA TIGER* in 1967:

> Dong Ha, Vietnam—Sgt. William E. Donovan, armorer for the sniper platoon of the 9th Marine Regiment is a craftsman of precision high-powered rifles and telescopic sights.
>
> His job is keeping those weapons in such condition that in the hands of an expert marksman they will consistently register a kill at ranges up to 1,000 yards.
>
> One of the few Marines listed as a rifle team equipment armorer, Donovan has been in this trade for six of his seven years in the Marine Corps.
>
> Before coming to Vietnam, Donovan was team armorer and a shooter for the Marine Corps Base Rifle Team at Camp Lejeune, North Carolina. As a rifle team member, he acquired tricks of the trade which he now puts to use in combat situations. He personally uses an M14 with a special scope mount.
>
> Donovan has a full-time job insuring that weapons function properly where the targets shoot back.
>
> Of the sniper platoon's 40 rifles, half are M14s and the others are bolt-action Remington M700s mounted with 3X9 power telescopic sights. Both fire match quality 7.62mm ammunition.
>
> Although his job as an armorer keeps him in the workshop most of the time, Donovan likes to test his wares whenever possible. On a patrol near Da Nang last spring, he killed a Viet Cong guerrilla at 700 yards with his specially modified M14.
>
> "I always wanted to be a gunsmith," he said. "To me, the job of keeping the rifle functioning in the field is the most important thing."

Sergeant Donovan returned to the United States following his first tour of duty in Vietnam in January 1968. The Marine gunsmith returned to RVN in late 1968, where he served his second tour with the Third Reconnaissance Battalion (3d MarDiv) in Quang Tri Province.

The actions of Bill Donovan are indicative of the activities and the measures taken by the RTE armorers in support of the Marine Corps sniping program during the war in Vietnam.

Gy.Sgt. William E. Donovan retired from the Marine Corps "on twenty years and seven days" in July 1980.

Rifle Team Equipment Repairman Sgt. William E. Donovan at Hill 55 south of Da Nang in early 1967. The rifle, an accurized M14, is fitted with a 10-power Unertl varmint scope. The M14 mount assembly was fabricated by the Marine armorer following his arrival in Vietnam. The varmint scope makes use of a recoil spring and a standard 1/4-minute click dehorned mount. (The dehorned mount eliminated the large adjustment knobs and graduated thimbles. Although adjustment accuracy was equal to the target type, it was not adjusted as easily. A dehorned mount was intended primarily for use with a varmint scope. The Unertl varmint model was similar to the target scope except that a larger ocular was used and the overall length was somewhat shorter.) The weapon served as Donovan's personal rifle in Vietnam. (William E. Donovan.)

A dovetail telescope base (scope rail) used to mount Bill Donovan's 10-power Unertl to a .50-caliber machine gun at Hill 55 (February/ March 1967). The 7-inch-long, .500-inch-wide steel block was machined to fit the Unertl target-type mounts. The rail was tapered to provide adequate adjustment. The base attached to a steel block configured to fit the dovetail groove on the Browning sight assembly. An enemy kill was registered at 1,865 yards with this rail and the Unertl varmint scope. The range was verified by Seabees using "triangulation," a reliable means of determining the distance between two points. (Peter R. Senich.)

A member of the Ninth Marines Scout-Sniper Platoon is shown with Sergeant Donovan's Unertl-equipped M14 rifle at Hill 55. (William E. Donovan.)

A contemporary M1A mounting a 10-power Unertl Vulture telescopic sight. The M14 mount assembly was made by Sergeant Donovan in Vietnam. Note the Unertl target mount turned to accommodate the veteran Marine gunsmith, a left-handed shooter. (William E. Donovan.)

An overall view of Donovan's M1A rifle (a commercial version of the M14) fitted with the Unertl scope. (William E. Donovan.)

A left-side view of the Vietnam-era M14 telescope mount with a Unertl (Vulture) telescopic sight. The 2-inch objective, 16 1/8-inch-long (1-inch tube) sight makes use of a bright aluminum target rear mount, recoil spring, and Magnum tube clamps. The top of the telescope mount is stamped with Donovan's name, serial number, part identification, the year (1967), and where it was made. (Peter R. Senich.)

A right-side view of the 10-power Unertl scope and the M14 mount made in Vietnam. A piece of 2-inch angle iron (.250-inch thick) was used to fabricate the mount. The raised ridges that engage the alignment grooves on the left side of the M14 receiver were formed by arc welding. The weld beads were hand-filed to their final form. The mounting screw is from an early night vision sight adapter bracket; the retainer clip was made from a soft-drink can. The mount is 6.375 inches long; the scope bases are Unertl. (Peter R. Senich.)

Sergeant Donovan outside his GP tent (living quarters and shop), Dong Ha, 1968. Said Donovan, "The tent was new to begin with: there were 168 patched holes in it when I left." (William E. Donovan.)

A photo of an "improvised hot box" employed by Bill Donovan to help keep the sniper platoon weapons from rusting (Dong Ha, 1968). There are 16 Model 700 sniper rifles shown here: a .50-caliber Browning "used for long-range work" (1,000 to 2,000 yards) and an M14 rifle. Commenting on sniper use of the M14, Donovan related, "We had several match-conditioned M14s zeroed at all times with Starlight Scopes attached for use as required." Judging from the comments of various Marines, match-conditioned M14s fitted with Starlight Scopes saw a fair amount of USMC sniper use in Vietnam. (William E. Donovan.)

An inside view of the Marine armorer's tent. The Ninth Marines sniper about to receive a haircut is holding Donovan's "Jeep gun," an ARVN castoff retrofitted with a barrel from Numrich Arms and a new buttstock made from a salvaged M14 stock. The armorer's workbench can be seen at the left. (William E. Donovan.)

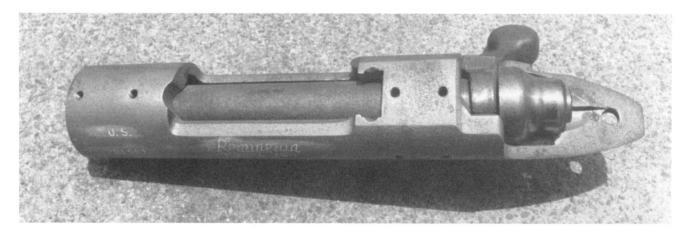

The receiver from a Vietnam-era Remington Model 700 USMC sniper rifle (serial no. 221581) recovered from a Marine bunker destroyed by fire at Gio Linh near the DMZ. According to Donovan, the rifle and one other (serial no. 221453) had been heated enough by the fire to allow the barrels to be unscrewed by hand after they had cooled. (William E. Donovan.)

Another view of Model 700 receiver no. 221581, showing the standard markings employed with this weapon series. As a matter of interest, the barrel from one of the rifles recovered from the bunker later served as "a handle on an action-wrench" fabricated by Donovan in RVN. (William E. Donovan.)

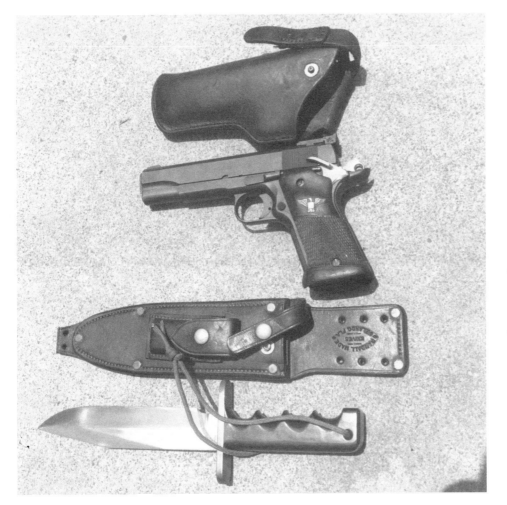

A modified .45-caliber M1911A1 pistol, Berns-Martin Raider Holster, purchased at Evaluators, Ltd. (Quantico, Virginia), and a Randall knife and sheath carried by the Marine armorer during both tours of duty in Vietnam. Commenting on this equipment, Donovan added, "I was never without either item." (William E. Donovan.)

As any American serving in Southeast Asia will bear witness to, there were many things besides the VC and the NVA to watch out for. In this case, one of the "local residents" (a scorpion) was placed next to a pack of cigarettes to indicate its size. (William E. Donovan.)

Browning .50-caliber machine gun being test-fired near the Marine combat base at Dong Ha. As a precautionary measure, "all support weapons" were tested before they were taken into unsecured enemy territory. (William E. Donovan.)

THE KILL FACTOR

As the years pass and the memory of U.S. combat involvement in Southeast Asia begins to fade, the question of sniper kills or, more precisely, the number of kills by a given Army or Marine Corps marksman has taken on greater significance than it did during the war in Vietnam.

At a time when most were simply trying to stay alive and whole, few men knew if an Army or Marine Corps sniper had killed or wounded an inordinate number of the enemy in the line of duty. The sniping proficiency of a given marksman was hardly a matter of common knowledge, and while various contemporary publications would lead their readers to believe otherwise, the quintessential American soldier serving in Southeast Asia had no idea who the top snipers were; nor did he care!

Even though the war in Vietnam was a unique experience, it was the same there as it was in every other conflict that American servicemen have been involved in. That is, no one knew "what the hell was going on" beyond his immediate area of involvement or concern. To suggest otherwise is misleading; it is simply not the way it was. The emphasis on "scoring" came long after the conflict in Southeast Asia was over.

As a part of my ongoing efforts to bring the kill factor of military sniping into perspective, an excerpt dealing with sniper kills from my first book in the sniping in Vietnam series, *The Long-Range War* (Paladin Press 1994), is worth repeating here:

> As a matter of interest, when the number of enemy personnel killed in action (KIA) as a direct result of sniper fire was recorded, while not always the case, it was not supposed to be counted as a "kill" unless the sniper was able to (figuratively speaking) place his foot on the body.
>
> According to a former Army sniper in Vietnam, "I can't speak for the other people, but when it came to keeping track, as I understood it, it wasn't a kill unless I could touch the body. We didn't call them kills; they were simply known as 'step-ons,' for obvious reasons."
>
> Though seldom as uncomplicated as that, despite the honesty and integrity of the vast majority of the Army and Marine Corps snipers serving in Southeast Asia, both the number and the manner in which many sniper kills were recorded, or "logged," in a combat environment remains the subject of controversy to this day. In addition, many people have had some difficulty with the accumulation of kills, or rather, the "keeping score" aspect of it all, regardless of the circumstances. As one veteran Marine Corps sniper perhaps put it best, "We certainly didn't paint little flags on our fuselage every time we scored," or as another Marine summed it up, "I didn't shoot women or children, and I didn't shoot anyone that wasn't out to kill me. If someone has a hard time with that, well, tough shit!"

Few people, if any, have addressed the "kill" situation in Vietnam as well as Carlos N. Hathcock did in Charles Henderson's book *Marine Sniper*. Responding to comments by Gy.Sgt. James D. Wilson (the NCO in charge of the First Marine Division sniper school at that point) reminding Hathcock that he was the "number one sniper," Hathcock stated:

> I never looked at it like this was some sort of shooting match where the man with the most kills wins the gold medal. Hell, Gunny, anybody would be crazy to like to go out and kill folks.
>
> As far as I'm concerned, you can take those numbers and give 'em to somebody who gives a damn about 'em. I like shooting, and I love hunting. But I never did enjoy killing anybody. It's my job. If I don't get those bastards, then they're gonna kill a lot of these kids dressed up like Marines. That's the way I look at it.
>
> Besides Gunny, I got a lot more kills unconfirmed than confirmed, and so does every sniper over here, including you. So what the hell does it mean? Who really has the most? And who gives a shit—this ain't Camp Perry.

Marine sniper Carlos N. Hathcock was credited with 93 confirmed kills in Vietnam.

In the opinion of many veteran snipers, Hathcock's words summarized the matter extremely well. The typical Army and Marine Corps snipers simply did their job, worked at staying alive, and the only thing they really counted were the days until they could return home.

Roger that!

• • •